W9-BFE-614

The Official Guide to the MCAT® Exam

Second Edition

by the staff of the
Medical College Admission Test
Association of American Medical Colleges

How this Guide Is Structured

The Official Guide to the MCAT® Exam has been developed under the direction of the MCAT staff and with the help of many AAMC contributors, and we are pleased to offer this resource to the more than 70,000 examinees who will take the exam this year. To help guide you through this material, we have divided the content into two distinct parts. In brief, these are:

Part I. This section provides extensive information on "everything MCAT." Here you will find a description of the exam's overall format, an explanation of the registration process and test-day procedures, information on examinee and applicant data, an analysis of MCAT performance as part of the admissions process, and a detailed discussion related to your potential decision whether to retake the exam.

Part II. In this segment, we concentrate on the exam itself. Here we provide additional details about the format of each exam section, a complete outline of the content covered, an explanation of the reasoning skills tested, and a review of the different passage types. The bulk of Part II, however, focuses on practice questions and answers—items that have appeared in real MCAT exams—and includes an analysis of correct and incorrect answers, tips to help you fine-tune your approach, identification of each question by content area and cognitive skills tested, and the percentage of examinees who answered that specific question correctly.

The Table of Contents on the following pages outlines these parts in detail.

Table of Contents

Chapter 6: To Retake or Not to Retake: That Is the Question....

Chapter 7: The Strategy Mystique: Debunking the Myths

PART II: PREPARING FOR THE MCAT® EXAM

Chapter 8: Physical Sciences (PS)

Chapter 9: Biological Sciences (BS)

Chapter 10: Verbal Reasoning (VR)

Chapter 11: Writing Sample (WS)

Chapter 12: Practice Effectively

Addendum

Special Insets

Cumulative Frequency Distributions of MCAT Scores for 2010 Medical School Applicants

Mean and Median MCAT Scores for Applicants to the

Likelihood of Admission Based on Combination of

Changes in MCAT Total Multiple-Choice Scores between First and Second Attempts,

Changes in MCAT Physical Sciences Scores between First and Second Attempts,

Changes in MCAT Verbal Reasoning Scores between First and Second Attempts,

Changes in MCAT Writing Sample Scores on the J to T Scale between First and

Changes in MCAT Biological Sciences Scores between First and Second Attempts,

"All glory comes from daring to begin."
Eugene F. Ware

The MCAT exam.

Did you just shudder? If you're like many of your peers, you probably look upon the Medical College Admission Test as an obstacle to overcome—a barrier that lies between you and medical school. The very breadth of the science topics—from acid derivatives to wave characteristics—already has you feeling overwhelmed, and when you consider that you'll also have to contend with a verbal reasoning segment and a writing sample, "near panic" is probably not an overstatement. The publications and courses that promise to give you the tools to beat the test and be on your way are looking pretty good right about now.

We've got good news…and we've got bad news.

First, the bad: The test cannot be beat, or at least not in the way you think. There are no secrets to unravel; no mysteries to reveal. There's simply no getting around the fact that if you don't have the fundamental knowledge tested by the MCAT exam, your scores will expose those shortcomings. All the test-taking strategies in the world won't save you.

The good news, though, is that there's plenty you can do to prepare for the exam and bolster your performance. In fact, we here at the MCAT team sometimes like to say that "you can score worse than you should, but not better." What we mean is that while you can't scheme your way through the test if you haven't mastered the material, you can score less well than you could if you haven't geared up effectively. You need to be adept in the biological and physical sciences, of course, but you also must know what to expect from the verbal reasoning section and learn what the writing sample is all about. Beyond that, you will benefit if you become familiar with the structure of the exam itself, get comfortable with both passage-based and independent questions, experiment with and decide which strategies work best for you, analyze why the correct answers are right and the wrong answers are not, and practice . . . practice . . . practice.

Who better to guide you than the developers and administrators of the exam itself? We are in a unique position to provide you with MCAT passages and questions taken from real MCAT exams, along with thoroughly explained solutions written by the test developers themselves. Beyond that, we include a wide range of additional information—from examinee data to a discussion of MCAT scores and their use in the admissions process.

Welcome to the Official Guide to the MCAT® Exam.

Part I:

Key Questions About the MCAT® Exam

Chapter 1:

Overview of the MCAT® Exam

Questions Answered in this Chapter:

What Is the Role of the Exam?

Does It Test Knowledge or Reasoning Skills?

What Is the Breakdown of the Exam, and Why Is It So Varied?

One of our MCAT staffers overheard a couple of college juniors commiserating with one another about the MCAT exam that loomed ominously in their futures. After about 20 minutes of nonstop talk about various review courses, prep books, practice options, and the sheer arduousness of it all, one student stopped mid-sentence, looked at the other, and asked with a mix of exasperation and fear, "Why do they DO this to us?" The other student shook her head and shrugged in empathy, but we know the answer. It's amazingly simple:

Because the MCAT exam does its job.

I. What Is the Role of the Exam?

The MCAT exam, taken by more than 70,000 students each year, serves as a reliable screening tool for medical school admissions officers who seek to identify which applicants are most likely to succeed in medical school—and beyond—and which are not. In doing so, admissions officers look not only for students whose base knowledge of scientific concepts will serve as a strong foundation in the early years of medical study, but also for those with strong critical reasoning ability and strong written communications skills. And the MCAT exam spots those students well.

So do college grades. But when admissions officers look at MCAT scores in conjunction with undergraduate GPAs—as opposed to grades alone—their ability to predict who will be successful in medical school increases by as much as 50 percent (gauging by first- and second-year medical school grades).* That explains why virtually every medical school in the United States, and many in Canada, require applicants to submit recent MCAT scores.

---

* Those of you who wish to explore the data might want to review the article, "Validity of the Medical College Admission Test for Predicting Medical School Performance", published in *Academic Medicine* and available online at www.aamc.org/mcatguide.

Now that we've added to what undoubtedly is already a high level of anxiety, we'd like to quell your fears: There's more to passing the admissions hurdle than getting high MCAT scores, and a less-than-stellar showing does not mean you cannot be admitted to medical school. Research shows, in fact, that some students with relatively low scores on one or more sections of the test can gain admittance if other factors, such as a high GPA, tip the scales in their favor. (Conversely, students with high MCAT scores and low grades may not find a berth.)* Among the other factors that enter into the admissions decision are the selectivity of your undergraduate institution, letters of recommendation, the interview, a history of community service and/or medically-related work, and personal character traits such as integrity and determination.

> The methods by which MCAT scores are used in conjunction with other selection factors are discussed in Chapter 5, "Your MCAT Score as Part of the Decision-Making Process."

II. Does It Test Knowledge or Reasoning Skills?

We hear the same argument over and over again. Some insist the MCAT exam is a knowledge-based test, designed to assess your mastery of a full range of science topics. Others claim it is really a thinking test, intended to evaluate your problem-solving capacity.

> *"Items should be designed to ascertain not simply the examinee's basic knowledge of science or rote memorization of facts, laws, and definitions, but rather the ability to reason or apply this knowledge to specific situations. The examinee is expected to reason through a problem by applying the background knowledge obtained through introductory-level college coursework."*
>
> **MCAT Item Writer's Guide, AAMC**

Everybody's right. The fact is that the exam tests knowledge and thinking. You can take it right off the pages of the MCAT Item Writer's Guide, the guidelines we provide to the writers who develop the actual passages and related questions. (See box at left.)

Before we move on, we'd like to draw your attention to the word "basic" in the excerpt above. The exam, while indeed requiring that you have a foundation of science upon which to draw (most notably biology, chemistry, and physics), tests nothing more than that ordinarily covered in introductory or entry-level classes.

> **There is no proven benefit to advanced coursework when it comes to MCAT scores.**
>
> While you may find that higher-level science courses better prepare you for medical school in general, there is no evidence that advanced classes lead to higher MCAT scores specifically.

Other areas of the exam, specifically Verbal Reasoning (VR) and the Writing Sample (WS), have no knowledge to test and are therefore clearly a test of one's reasoning and writing skills. These sections are designed to assess your ability to comprehend, evaluate, and synthesize new material; develop concepts; and present ideas in a logical, well-written manner.

What all of this should tell you is that if you haven't mastered the science that's tested on the exam, you won't be able to score well—no matter how well you try to reason your way through a passage. Conversely, rote knowledge alone isn't sufficient, since you've got to apply that understanding to solve the problem. You've got to "know your stuff" and be able to think things through—two traits that every doctor must have.

*See chart, "Likelihood of Admission," on page 39 for more information.

When you look at the format of the exam described below, it's apparent that the purpose of the MCAT exam is to help medical school admissions officers and faculty gauge a student's reasoning skills as well as his or her mastery of basic concepts in biology, general and organic chemistry, and physics. But screening for the two crucial attributes that medical educators have identified as key prerequisites for success—a basic foundation in science and a strong capacity for critical thinking—is just one reason the MCAT exam is structured as it is.

Beyond that, medical school faculty hope to encourage undergraduates with broad educational backgrounds to consider careers in the health professions, and similarly, they want to persuade premed majors to explore a wide variety of courses outside of the natural sciences. That explains why the exam tests for such diverse abilities and knowledge, and why everyone, from English majors to history buffs, has an equal crack at achieving a high score (assuming, of course, they have mastered the entry-level science courses necessary for success on the MCAT exam)*.

Structure of the Exam

We cover the full outline of topics later in this guide, but for now, we'll give you the overview. The MCAT exam is a computer-based test that lasts just over five hours (including optional breaks) and consists of three multiple-choice sections—Physical Sciences, Biological Sciences, and Verbal Reasoning—along with a writing assessment.

EXAM STRUCTURE

Test Section	Number of Passages	Number of Questions	Time
Tutorial (optional)			10 minutes
Non-Disclosure Agreement			10 minutes
Physical Sciences	7	52	70 minutes
Break (optional)			10 minutes
Verbal Reasoning	7	40	60 minutes
Break (optional)			10 minutes
Writing Sample		2	60 minutes
Break (optional)			10 minutes
Biological Sciences	7	52	70 minutes
Void Question			5 minutes
Satisfaction Survey			10 minutes
Total Content Time			4 hours, 25 minutes

Total "Seat" Time	5 hours, 25 minutes

Total time does not include check-in time on arrival at the test center.

*See chart on page 34, which presents the mean and median scores of applicants by undergraduate major.

Here's a closer look at these sections, described in the order you will receive them in the exam:

• Physical Sciences: 70 minutes

The Physical Sciences (PS) section covers general chemistry and physics. A total of 52 questions are presented in two formats —passage-based and independent:

- Most questions are based on *passages*, each about 250 words in length, which describe a situation or problem. All told, there are seven passages, each containing from four to seven questions, for a total of 39 passage-based questions.

- In addition, there are 13 *independent* questions—those not associated with a passage.

How Did We Decide Which Science Topics to Cover?

The decision as to which science topics we cover involved a two-step process:

- We asked medical educators, students, residents, and physicians to rate potential topics on their importance to the study and practice of medicine.

- At the same time, we surveyed faculty members at undergraduate institutions to learn which topics are covered in introductory courses—and to what degree.

The topics that were identified as prerequisite for success in medical school and covered in most undergraduate courses were selected for inclusion in the test.

For this section, you will be tested on your capacity to interpret data presented in graphs and tables, your knowledge of basic physical science concepts and principles, and your ability to solve problems using that knowledge as a foundation.

Please note that each multiple-choice section (PS, VR, and BS) will include some try-out items that do not count toward your score.

• Verbal Reasoning: 60 minutes

The Verbal Reasoning (VR) section evaluates your ability to understand, evaluate, and apply information and arguments presented in writing. This segment consists of seven passages, each about 600 words long, taken from the humanities and social sciences, and from areas of the natural sciences not tested in the science segments of the exam. Each passage-based set consists of five to seven questions, with some designed to test your basic comprehension of the text and others intended to gauge your ability to analyze information, evaluate the validity of an argument, or apply knowledge gained from the passage itself.

No Specific Subject Knowledge Required for VR

It's important to realize that you won't be tested for specific subject knowledge in this segment of the exam. Instead, all the information you'll need is contained within the passage itself.

MCAT® is a program of the
Association of American Medical Colleges

How Much Does the Writing Sample Count?

The short answer: it depends. The weight assigned to your performance in this segment of the exam varies from school to school. That said, there are indeed situations where your performance on the WS can make a difference. For example, some admissions committees will take a close look at your WS score when your VR score is at the lower end of the scale.

• Writing Sample: 60 minutes

The Writing Sample (WS) consists of two 30-minute essays, each addressing specific topics that require a written response. This segment of the exam assesses your skill in developing a central idea; synthesizing concepts and ideas; presenting ideas cohesively and logically; and writing clearly, with the ability to follow accepted rules of grammar, syntax, and punctuation.

• Biological Sciences: 70 minutes

The format of the Biological Sciences (BS) section, which covers biology and organic chemistry, is identical to that of the PS section. It too has seven passages, each containing four to seven questions, for a total of 39, and 13 independent questions. Similarly, this segment tests knowledge of basic biological sciences concepts and the ability to incorporate that knowledge in solving problems.

For an outline of the science content covered; a description of skills assessed; and sample passages, questions, and solutions, please see Part II.

Chapter 2:
MCAT Fundamentals: Leading Up to the Exam

The last thing you want to learn on exam day is that you've somehow overlooked a technical requirement or failed to take advantage of an opportunity because you were unaware of it. That's why long before you walk into a test center, you'll need to have learned about—and followed—the process and procedures associated with the MCAT exam.

Registering for it. Selecting a test location. Scheduling and deadlines. Score release options. Special accommodations requests. Fees and financial assistance. This chapter will address topics such as these—the mechanics of the MCAT exam.

Important:
To be sure that you get the most complete and up-to-date information about these topics, it is crucial that you go to the *MCAT Essentials* at www.aamc.org/mcatguide

I. Who Can Take the Exam...

You're probably more concerned with the fact that you must take the test than with the question of your eligibility to do so. Still, it's important to know that only those students who plan to apply to a health professions school—which include schools of allopathic, osteopathic, podiatric, and veterinary medicine—are ordinarily permitted to take the MCAT exam.

Special Permission Is Required If...

- You are not applying to a health professions school, or

- You are a currently enrolled medical student.

Please see page 24 for more information.

...and How Often?

You may take the exam up to three times in one calendar year. A voided test counts toward the annual limit. There is no lifetime limit.

Your MCAT Scores: A Long "Shelf Life"

Medical schools usually accept scores dating back two or three years. If you've taken the exam previously, we recommend that you check the application policies of each school to which you plan to apply.

II. When Should I Take the Exam?

In most cases, you should take the exam in the calendar year prior to the year in which you plan to enter medical school (so that, for example, if you are applying in 2011 for entrance to medical school in 2012, you should take the exam in 2011). In addition to that, you will want to complete the basic-level science courses the exam covers—biological sciences, physics, and organic and inorganic chemistry—prior to sitting for the exam.

III. How Do I Select an Appropriate Test Date?

2011 MCAT Exam Schedule for the United States and Canada

The MCAT exam is administered multiple times from January through Spetember. While the AAMC selects exam dates to ensure that scores are available to meet most medical school application deadlines in general, you will need to learn of the specific scheduling requirements of the school(s) of your choice to select an appropriate test date. You can obtain this information by referring to the *Medical School Admission Requirements* (MSAR) handbook published by the AAMC at www.aamc.org/mcatguide or by contacting the school(s) directly.

Pictured above to the left is the list of available test sessions for 2011. (In the event that changes have been made since this guide was published, we recommend that you visit the AAMC Web site at www.aamc.org/mcat for the most current MCAT Test Schedules.

IV. Where Can I Find Information About Registration Dates and Deadlines?

Once you've determined which date you prefer, you can find the registration schedule for that particular exam session by reviewing the MCAT Registration Deadline & Score Release Schedule. There you'll learn when the registration period opens (and closes!) as well as the date we expect scores to be released for the test date you selected. As you review the schedule, please be aware that:

- **If you miss the regular deadline, you may be able to register during the late time period (although a late fee will apply).**

- **Early registration is encouraged, as test centers have limited capacity and registrations are processed in the order in which they are received.**

Regular Registration 2011	$235
International Test Site[1, 2]	$70
Late Registration[2]	$60
Date Reschedule[2]	$60
Change of Test Center[2]	$60

Financial Help Available for Qualifying Individuals

The AAMC Fee Assistance Program (FAP) helps individuals with financial limitations by reducing the testing fee from $235 to $85. Please see page 47 for information on this program.

V. What Are the Registration Fees?

There is a registration fee of $235 associated with the MCAT exam, which covers the cost of the test itself as well as distribution of your scores. Beyond that, you will incur additional fees, which are listed in the table at left, for late registration, changes to your registration, and testing at international test sites.

Please be aware that payment must be made by credit card (MasterCard or VISA), payable in U.S. funds.

Note that fees may increase annually; please visit the MCAT web site for current information.

You'll log on to the system, establish an AAMC ID# (if you don't already have one)....

VI. How Do I Register?

All MCAT examinees must register through the online registration system, an electronic process that prompts you to select a test date and research whether seats are available at specific locations. After you have selected your preferred date and site, you will be prompted to reserve the space and submit credit card data.

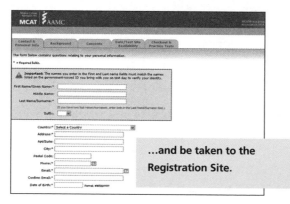

...and be taken to the Registration Site.

---

[1] International sites include all non-U.S. countries, provinces, or territories except Canada, Guam, Puerto Rico, and the U.S. Virgin Islands.

[2] These fees are added to the regular registration fee.

VII. How Do I Select a Test Location?

The MCAT exam is offered at hundreds of locations throughout the United States and the world, with multiple sites available in most major U.S. cities.

You will select a specific test center through the online registration system. It's a relatively simple process in which you select your preferred exam date, state, and country. Select "Find a Seat" to look for an available location, and if the test time appears, select the time to reserve the seat and adavance to the payment screen.

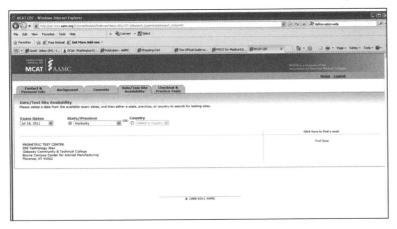

• Test Center or Date Changes

You may change your test date or center—or both—at any time, as long as space is available and you make the change prior to the regular registration deadline associated with your initial test date. If you make a change in both test date and center simultaneously, a single charge will be levied; if you make separate changes, you will be charged individually for each change. Please make your change(s) through our online registration system at www.aamc.org/mcat.

• Cancellations

If you decide not to sit for the exam after you have registered for it, you will be eligible for a partial refund if you cancel prior to the regular registration deadline. (If you received fee assistance from the AAMC, your payment will be refunded in full.) Additional fees for late registration or other changes are not refundable. Please cancel your registration online at www.aamc.org/mcat by the regular registration deadline.

> **Double-check Your Registration!**
>
> Double-check that the details of your registration and contact information are correct two to three weeks prior to your test date.

VIII. What Options Do I Have for Releasing My Scores?

In the next chapter, we'll talk about how we release scores (both to medical schools and to you), but we want to introduce the topic now. That's because you'll be presented with a few options regarding the release of your scores when you register, and the information that follows concerns just that aspect. First, though, we need to distinguish between two types of score release options—primary and secondary:

• Primary Release

When you register, you automatically authorize release of your scores to the AAMC and its affiliated institutions for research purposes. (You'll be required to check "YES" as part of the registration process.) Please understand that we will maintain the confidentiality of your scores and will not report them in any way that identifies you except with your permission.

• Secondary Release

Here's where the scores tie back to you personally. Unless you void your scores (see page 27 for information on this option), you and the American Medical College Application Service* will receive your scores automatically. Beyond that, though, there are three different score release options that may benefit you as you pursue admission to medical school.

> **No Additional Charge**
>
> The three score release options described below are included in the basic registration fee.

• Health Professions Advisor

This release gives the AAMC permission to include your scores and demographic information in a Web-based report to your undergraduate health professions advisor, who may find such data useful when counseling students. In addition, advisors may share your scores with members of their premedical committees or others involved in preparing letters of recommendation; however, they will not share your information with other students or medical schools without your express permission.

• Med-MAR

The Medical Minority Applicant Registry (Med-MAR) is a service created to enhance admission opportunities for U.S. citizens from groups currently under-represented in medicine. If you select this option, you give the AAMC permission to include your scores and biographical information in Med-Mar.

• MCAT Recruiting Service

This release gives the AAMC permission to include your contact and MCAT exam score information in reports produced by the MCAT Recruiting Service. Accredited U.S. and Canadian schools of allopathic medicine, osteopathic medicine, podiatry, and veterinary medicine, along with scholarship programs of the U.S. government (including those of the U.S. military), may request information about examinees and use that information as part of their recruiting efforts.

---

*The American Medical College Application Service (AMCAS) is a centralized application processing service, operated by the AAMC, for applicants to the first-year entering classes at participating U.S. medical schools. For the 2012 entering class, most U.S. medical schools are participating in AMCAS. You can visit www.aamc.org/mcatguide to learn more about this service and see if the schools to which you plan to apply are on the list.

Even Orange Juice Counts!

On occasion, a student will arrive at the test center with an inhaler, or an insulin pump, or even a small container of orange juice—only to learn that he or she should have requested approval for it. So...please be aware...even the most seemingly minor deviation from the standard testing environment is considered accommodated testing and therefore requires pre-approval.

Early Application Encouraged

It is important to know that the MCAT Office of Accommodated Testing Services may require up to 60 days to process your request for accommodations. You should therefore submit your request and related documentation as far in advance of your desired test date as possible.

The AAMC is proud to support the policies of the federal government and will provide accommodations to students whose disabilities—or other conditions—necessitate an adjustment to the test or testing environment, pending review and approval from the MCAT Office of Accommodated Testing Services. (Examples of special accommodations include presentation of test material in large font, extra testing time, a separate testing room, or even approval to bring in a piece of hard candy.)

If you would like to take advantage of this opportunity, you will be required to submit documentation of your disability or condition at the time of registration. The four broad categories of disabilities are:

- Learning Disabilities
- ADD/ADHD
- Psychiatric Disabilities
- Physical Disabilities*

We will notify you in writing if your request has been approved. For complete information on accommodated testing and the associated registration process, please visit www.aamc.org/mcat. If you need additional guidance, you may write to us at accommodations@aamc.org.

X. What Are "Special Permissions"?

As we already mentioned, two circumstances require you to apply for special permission to take the MCAT exam:

- if your purpose is to take the test for any reason other than applying to a health professions school, or
- if you are a currently enrolled medical student

To apply for special permission, e-mail your request to mcat@aamc.org, giving the reason(s) you wish to take the exam. We will review and respond to your request within five business days, if possible.

---

*Applicants with chronic medical conditions (e.g., diabetes, migraines, asthma) or temporarily disabling conditions (such as a broken leg) fall within the Physical Disabilities category.

Chapter 3:

Go for Launch: Test-Day Process and Procedures

Questions Answered in this Chapter:

What Do I Need for Admission to the Test Center?

What Are the Test-Day Regulations and Procedures?

How Does the "Void" Option Work?

"Let us help you. If you have a question about any of the policies and procedures described in the MCAT Essentials or Registration Tips, which are required reading, contact the MCAT Resource Center well in advance of your registration deadline. In most cases we will be able to respond very quickly to your question or solve a problem you are having."

That's the answer we got from our Director of Administration and Reporting when we asked her to come up with the top thing an examinee should do to make sure that test day goes as smoothly as possible—from an administrative standpoint, at least. On one hand, that seems painless enough—just read the MCAT Essentials www.aamc.org/mcatguide, where all the procedures are listed. On the other, it's easy to understand how you might miss some of the procedural components when you're knee-deep in exam study and preparation.

You can reach the MCAT Resource Center at 202-828-0690 or mcat@aamc.org

That's why we've included this chapter—the "nuts-and-bolts" of test day.

I. What Do I Need for Admission to the Test Center?

Protecting the Integrity of the Exam

The AAMC is deeply committed to ensuring the validity of test scores and to providing fair, equal, and secure testing conditions.

Before we talk about admission requirements, we'd like to make clear that we developed these procedures (as well as the other regulations detailed on the following pages) with one basic purpose in mind—to ensure that scores are valid. That said, please know that we will require you to meet the following three conditions to be admitted to the exam:

• **You must report to the test center at least 30 minutes prior to your appointment time.**

This allows adequate time for the test center staff to verify your identity and for you to complete the admissions process and receive your seat assignment.

Please be aware that your photo will be taken for security purposes.

• You must provide a valid form of identification.

Please be prepared to provide personal identification in the form of a current, valid government-issued ID containing your photo, signature, and expiration date (e.g., a driver's license or passport) in which the name matches that of your registration exactly. Please see the MCAT Essentials for more details about identification requirements.

The #1 Problem Area...

...surrounds issues of proper identification. More specifically, the most common error students make is failing to bring an ID that matches their registration exactly.

• You must accept the terms of a nondisclosure agreement.

Via this contract, you agree to not disclose any content of the exam, including passages, questions, or answers.

II. What Are the Test Center Regulations and Procedures?

Among the questions most frequently asked of the MCAT Program Office are those concerning the testing environment. Here's the rundown of test center procedures:

Test Center Concerns

We strive to provide comfortable testing environments and fair, equal, and secure testing conditions. If, after taking the MCAT exam, you believe that test center circumstances interfered with your performance, you may request an investigation by the MCAT Program Office by writing to us at the address below within five calendar days of your test date.

Medical College Admission Test
Attention: Test Center Concerns
AAMC
2450 N Street, N.W.
Washington, D.C. 20037-1127

When writing to us, please include your full name, AAMC ID#, mailing and e-mail addresses, telephone number, date and location of the test, and a detailed description of the problem.

• The center will provide scratch paper, industrial ear covers, and pencils. No other testing aids are allowed. The Test Center Administrator will collect your scratch paper before you leave.

• You may not bring any personal items into the testing room other than your ID. You must store personal belongings, including telephones, pagers, books, handbags, and food in the area that will be assigned to you.

• You must sign in and out on the Signature Log and present identification each time you enter and leave the testing room.

• A digital image of your fingerprint will be taken, and your identification will be rescanned each time you enter the test room.

• The Test Center Administrator will assign you to a seat, which you will maintain for the duration of the exam.

• Access to the examination room will be restricted to test center personnel, examinees, and authorized observers.

- Once the examination begins, you are considered to have tested even if you void or do not complete the test. Please see the information below on voiding the exam.

- The testing clock will begin to count down as soon as the examination is started. The timer is visible on your testing monitor throughout the examination, and time is counted down by section. If you end a section early, you may continue on to the next section, but additional time will not be counted towards any subsequent sections or breaks.

- You may not eat, drink, or smoke in the testing room. The day includes an optional 10-minute break between each section. You may wish to bring snacks for your breaks, since eating facilities may not be located near the test site or may not be equipped to handle large crowds.

- To protect the security of the exam questions, examinees may not study or use cell phones during breaks.

- You may not bring a timer or watch into the test room. A timer is provided on-screen during the exam.

> Dress comfortably, possibly in layers, and be prepared for varying room temperatures, since you may find the testing room colder or warmer than you expected.

III. How Does the "Void" Option Work?

Did you know that the AAMC offers you the chance to void your MCAT exam if you are uncomfortable with your performance? This opportunity occurs at the end of the exam, when you will be asked to select one of the following two options:

❏ I wish to have my MCAT exam scored.

-or-

❏ I wish to VOID my MCAT exam.

Please note that:

> **Does a Voided Test "Count"?**
>
> We will not report your participation in the test if you void the scores, but we will count the attempt toward one of the three permitted each calendar year.

- Voiding your scores on test day means that you will not receive scores.

- Scores cannot be "unvoided" at a later date.

- If you skip the void screen and do not select one of the statements above, the default is to score the test.

- If you begin each section but do not complete one or more of them, your test will not be voided unless you specifically select that option.

- The AAMC will not grant refunds for voided tests.

Chapter 4:
All about MCAT Scores

We've heard conjecture among some students that the worst time to sit for the MCAT exam is July or August. The idea apparently is that the relatively lazy days of summer will provide everyone additional opportunities for study. As a result, these exam takers are more likely to get a higher percentage of the questions right and raise the curve. Best, you figure, to take the test in the fall or spring.

We've also heard the flip side. Some speculate that July and August examinees will skew the curve downward. That's because students who retake the exam tend to do so in the summer, and these are the students who, the theory goes, must have scored disappointingly in the first place. Following that line of thinking, you feel you've identified a lower performing group of examinees against whom to compete. Summer exam, here I come!

Wrong. And wrong.

It's a common but erroneous belief that the exam is graded on a curve. It isn't. In this chapter, we'll discuss the process of "equating"—a method testing experts use in standardized testing to ensure that scores are comparable across forms and test administrations—and the fact that you are measured against a previously established scale (and not against the group of examinees with whom you tested). We'll also address other components of MCAT performance, including a detailed look at examinee data and the manner in which we report scores.

I. How Is the Exam Scored?

The four sections of the exam each result in a separate score (which are reported both individually and in total).

- Each of the three multiple-choice sections—Physical Sciences, Verbal Reasoning, and Biological Sciences—is scored from a low of 1 to a high of 15. Keep in mind that there is no penalty for guessing, as your score will be based on the total number of correct answers. You'll therefore certainly want to pace yourself to allow a little time at the end of each section to answer any questions you skipped.

> Multiple-choice sections:
> **1 to 15**
> (for a total of 3 to 45)

No Curve on Standardized Tests

We opened this chapter with the assertion that there is no curve associated with the MCAT exam. To help us make the point clearer, consider the SAT™ or ACT®—at least one of which most of you have first-hand experience. Like other standardized tests, it did not impact your score if the students with whom you took the test did exceptionally well (or, on the other hand, unusually poorly). Rather, you were measured on a scale that was established previously. The same applies to the MCAT exam. There is no curve.

"Raw-to-Scaled" Conversion Compensates for Variations in Difficulty

Although all test forms measure the same basic skills and contain approximately the same distribution of easy, moderate, and difficult questions, one form may be slightly more difficult or slightly easier than another. Consequently, we convert the raw scores to a scale that considers the difficulty of test questions. This conversion minimizes variability in test scores and provides a more accurate assessment of your abilities, since two examinees of equal ability would be expected to get the same scaled score even though there might be a slight difference in their raw scores.

- The Writing Sample, consisting of two essays, is scored on an alphabetic scale ranging from J to T. Essays are evaluated according to the depth, cohesiveness, and clarity with which the writing tasks are addressed and by the extent to which ideas are developed. (See pages 369 through 390 for examples of essays and the scores associated with them.)

> Writing sample:
> **J to T**

- In addition to the four scores above, you will also receive a score representing the total of your three multiple-choice sections together with your writing sample score. If, for example, you received an 8-10-11 and P, your total score would be reported as 29P. (See sample score report on page 35.)

> Total score:
> **29P**

That's the situation in a nutshell, and for many of you, it's enough. You're probably ready to head right over to the next section, in which we provide comparative data that reveal mean scores, percentile rankings, and the like, so you'll have a benchmark against which to compare your own scores. If you're in this group and/or are already familiar with the concept of equating scores on standardized tests, you might want to skip to the next page where we begin to review exam statistics.

• Equating Scores Across Test Forms

For those of you unfamiliar with equating who want to learn more, we're happy to shed some light on the topic.

Let's look at the SAT™, referred to in the box above, a bit further. Assume for a moment that you scored a 610 in the mathematics section when you took the exam three years ago. A buddy of yours, who took the test one year earlier, also got a 610. (If you're among those who took the ACT®, a parallel scenario can be drawn. Let's say you got a 19 in the mathematics section—the same score your friend got when he took the exam the year before you did.) The test results show that you and your friend are equivalent in math skill. And that's true.

What you may not know, however, is that it's likely the two of you did not get the same number of questions right. His and your numbers of correct answers—or raw scores—may have been different. For example, you may have missed one or more questions than he did. But because

SAT™ is a trademark of the College Board
ACT® is a registered trademark of ACT, Inc.

MCAT® is a program of the
Association of American Medical Colleges

the specific test you took was slightly more difficult than his, the administrators of the SAT and (or ACT) adjusted the scale to compensate for the difference. As such, they ensured that the two scores reported to colleges were comparable in meaning.

• As It Relates to the MCAT Exam

The same holds true for the MCAT exam. There are many different test forms (each with a unique set of questions), and any one of them could end up on your computer come test day. And while each of these forms is just about equivalent in difficulty to the others, it's virtually impossible to construct test forms that are exactly equivalent. We therefore compensate for small disparities using the equating process just mentioned.

II. How Do My Scores Compare with Those Who Apply to Medical School?

You're probably wondering (or will wonder, once you take the exam) how your scores fall in comparison to those who apply to medical school—the group with whom you will compete. Am I in the top quarter....the bottom half....about average? On the following two pages, we provide you with several charts that will help answer that question—charts that display the cumulative distribution and percentile ranks for the total of the three multiple-choice sections as well as each of the four sections scores individually.

In the event that some of you are unfamiliar with charts such as these, let's take a closer look. Imagine your multiple-choice total score is 30, and you're wondering how well you've done compared with other applicants. Turn to the first chart on the next page, which summarizes total scores for those individuals who applied to medical school in 2010. Now find the 30 on the horizontal axis and look directly above it (to the curve that runs from the vertical axis). There you'll see that you're at the 64th percentile compared to 2010 medical school applicants.* Translation? Fully 64 percent of applicants scored worse (or the same) as you did. Put another way, that score would have placed you in the top third of all MCAT examinees who applied to medical school in 2010.

As you review the charts on the following pages, you'll see that some key figures quickly emerge:

- The average total score for all 2010 applicants was 28.3, with about half of them scoring 29 or above and the other half scoring 28 or below. Around 25 percent of applicants received a total score of 31 or higher, and 25 percent received a total score of 24 or less.

- The average score for the Physical Sciences section was 9.4, Verbal Reasoning was 9.1, and Biological Sciences was 9.8.

- The 50th percentile for the Writing Sample—the point at which half score better and half worse—was P. Approximately 25 percent of 2010 applicants received a score of Q or better, and approximately 25 percent received a score of M or worse.

---

*We're getting a little ahead of ourselves, but what you probably really want to know is how likely you are to get accepted to medical school based on specific scores. While there are a multitude of factors that enter into the admissions decision, we provide a chart in the next chapter that gives you some additional insight. See "Likelihood of Admission" (which factors in MCAT scores and undergraduate GPAs combined) on page 39.

Cumulative Frequency Distributions of MCAT Scores for 2010 Medical School Applicants

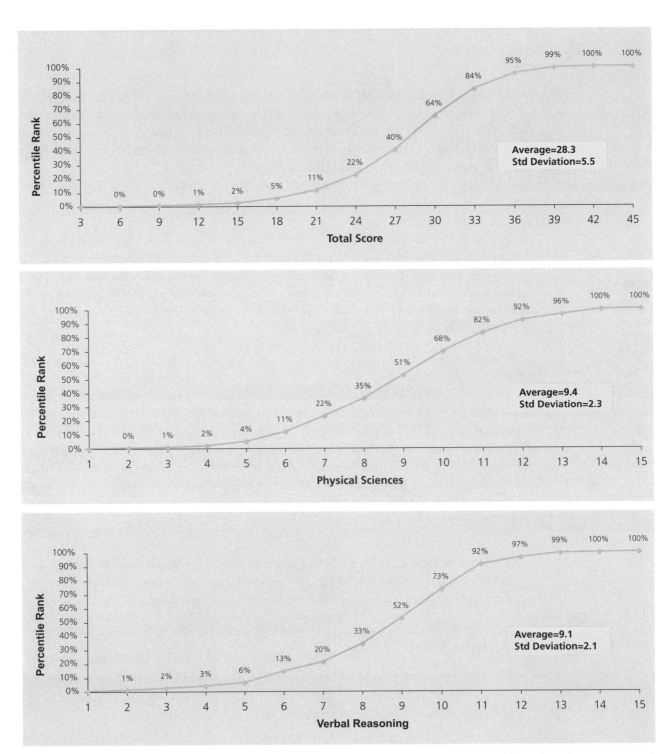

(continued on next page)

Second Edition
The Official Guide to the MCAT® Exam

MCAT® is a program of the
Association of American Medical Colleges

Cumulative Frequency Distributions of MCAT Scores for 2010 Medical School Applicants (continued)

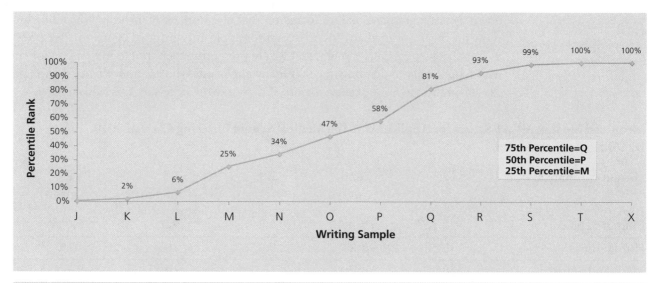

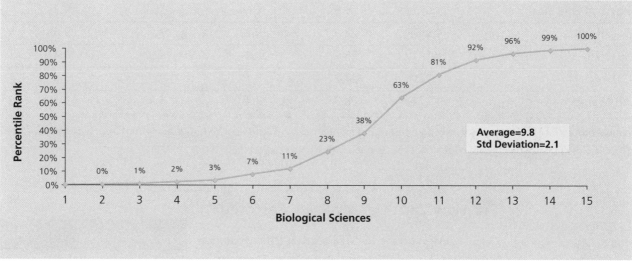

Note: If applicants have taken the MCAT exam more than once, their most recent MCAT scores were used to determine these distributions.

III. How Do Those with Different Undergraduate Majors Do?

Analyzing the data from a different viewpoint, what do the scores look like when they are broken down by undergraduate major? To answer that question, we're including the following chart to show the mean (or median) MCAT scores for applicants grouped by major. Please keep in mind, as you review these data, though, that we are presenting them not to influence your choice of major, but rather to demonstrate that many applicants who are non-science majors perform just as well on the MCAT as science majors, if they take the necessary prerequisite science courses.

Mean and Median MCAT Scores for Applicants to the Medical School Entering Class of 2010 By Undergraduate Major

Undergraduate Major	N	Total (mean)	PS (mean)	BS (mean)	VR (mean)	WS (median)
Biological Sciences	22,327	28.1	9.2	9.9	8.9	P
Humanities	1,950	29.6	9.6	10.0	10.0	Q
Math and Statistics	386	30.5	10.6	10.3	9.7	P
Physical Sciences	4,672	29.8	10.4	10.1	9.3	P
Social Sciences	4,997	28.5	9.3	9.7	9.5	P
Specialized Health Sciences*	1,181	25.7	8.4	8.9	8.4	O
Other	7,229	27.7	9.1	9.6	9.0	P
All Majors	42,742	28.3	9.4	9.8	9.1	P

Note. Source: AAMC Data, 2010; only the most recent score for each examinee who tested more than once was included in the analysis.
*Nursing and physical therapy are examples of specialized health sciences majors.

IV. How Can I Get My Exam Rescored?

The AAMC and the MCAT Program Office maintain a variety of quality-control procedures to ensure the accuracy of scores. If, however, you think a scoring error has occurred, you may request that either your multiple-choice answers or your writing sample, or both, be rescored by hand. You'll receive the results of this rescoring in writing, and the response letter will either confirm that your original scores were correct as reported or inform you of the corrected scores for each test section.

Rescoring Fees	
Multiple-Choice Sections (one fee for PS, VR, and BS combined)	$ 55
Writing Sample	$ 55
Entire Exam	$110

If you wish to have your exam rescored, please write to the MCAT Examinee Services Manager (Attention: Medical College Admisssion Test), AAMC, 2450 N Street, N.W., Washington, DC 20037-1127, no later than 30 days following the score release date. Please include your full name, AAMC ID number, mailing address, e-mail address, telephone number, date of test, sections of

MCAT® is a program of the
Association of American Medical Colleges

the test you wish rescored, explanation as to why you feel rescoring is necessary, and payment for the full fee in the form of a check, money order, or credit card information—MasterCard or VISA 16-digit card number, expiration date, and amount. (You'll also need to provide your signature if you are paying by credit card.) You will receive the results of rescoring about four weeks after we receive your request.

Which Programs Use MCAT Scores?

- American Medical College Application Service (AMCAS)

- American Association of Colleges of Osteopathic Application (AACOMAS)

- American Association of Colleges of Podiatric Medicine Application Service

- Ontario Medical School Application Service and all other Canadian medical schools requiring MCAT scores

- Schools of Public Health Application Service (SOPHAS)

- Texas Medical and Dental Schools Application Service (TMDSAS)

In addition, a number of individual schools and graduate programs use MCAT scores. Many of these schools and programs are listed separately within the THx system.

V. How Do I Check My Scores and Release Them to Medical Schools?

The score release process is handled through the MCAT program's computerized Testing History Report System (THx). This program, located at www.aamc.org/mcatguide, allows you to perform a number of options related to your scores. For example, you may:

• Check your scores.

Just log on to the system. If your scores are available, you'll be prompted to click through to view them.

• Release scores to AMCAS.

If your scores date from April 2003 onward (which is probably your situation), you can skip this step. Your scores will be released automatically. For those of you who have scores dating prior to April 2003, though, this is the option you'll use to make selected scores part of your current AMCAS application and any future AMCAS application you may start. Please be aware that the decision to release scores to AMCAS is a one-time, irrevocable decision.

• Send my scores to non-AMCAS institutions.

You'll use this option to send your MCAT scores to non-AMCAS schools and programs. Scores are submitted electronically on a nightly basis to the recipients you select.

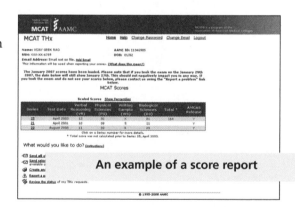

An example of a score report

Remind Me Again....What's AMCAS?

AMCAS, as you might recall from Chapter 2, is the American Medical College Application Service in which most medical schools take part, and the process by which you will manage your application (to participating institutions). Through this system, scores are submitted to each school you've designated.

You can view a list of participating schools at www.aamc.org/mcatguide.

This option will appear if you have at least two sets of MCAT scores, in which one or more are from exams prior to 2003, and the medical school does not require all scores. Through it, you may exclude selected scores from the report if they are from exams prior to April 2003. (You cannot exclude scores from 2003 forward.)

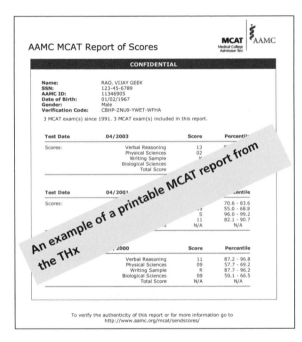

An example of a printable MCAT report from the THx

• Print your own official MCAT score report.

Although the THx supports hundreds of medical schools (both allopathic and osteopathic), schools of veterinary medicine, scholarship programs, and other health professions programs, you may want to send your scores to an organization that is not currently included. If so, the system allows you to select the scores you want to include and print an official report.

• Review the status of your THx requests.

Here you'll have the opportunity to review which scores you've sent to which programs (and when) and check the status of any pending requests.

All Thx options are explained in more detail when you log into the system.

Chapter 5:

Your MCAT Scores as Part of the Decision-Making Process

Before we delve into the variety of factors that medical school admissions officers consider when they decide whom to admit to their programs, we'd like to sing their praises a little bit.

They're very good at what they do.

Indeed, more than 96 percent of applicants accepted to med school complete their programs. (Compare that to the overall rate of other graduate and professional programs, in which only 62 percent of matriculants earn a degree.*) While such an impressive statistic certainly reflects the tenacity with which medical students approach their studies, it also speaks highly to the ability of admissions officers to select students with "the right stuff." Your MCAT score is but one factor—albeit an important one—in helping them determine if you are among that group.

I. How Useful Are MCAT Scores in Predicting Success?

There are as many ways to answer that question as there are ways to calculate it. Perhaps the one that is most important to you is the one that focuses on how much more accurately medical school success can be predicted when one considers undergraduate GPAs and MCAT scores combined as opposed to GPAs alone. As you might recall from the opening chapter, research has shown that the ability to predict medical school grades (first and second year, specifically) increases by as much as 50 percent when MCAT scores are added to undergraduate grades as predictors. If you're interested in learning more about this and other MCAT research, check out our MCAT Research Web page at www.aamc.org/mcatguide.

*Bradburn, E.M., et al. (2006). *Where Are They Now? A Description of 1992-93 Bachelor's Degree Recipients 10 Years Later* (NCES 2007-159). U.S. Department of Education. Washington, DC: National Center for Education Statistics, 5.

II. How Likely (Or Not) Am I to Gain Admission Based on My MCAT Scores and GPA Combined?

Certainly, admissions officers don't view MCAT scores in isolation, but rather in concert with your undergraduate GPA (along with a host of other factors that we discuss in the next segment of this chapter)*. Still, and as you would imagine, the better your grades and the higher your MCAT scores, the more likely you are to be accepted. The chart on the next page, which summarizes data for applicants to medical school from 2008 to 2010, illustrate the point.

- Approximately **90 percent** of applicants with a GPA of 3.80 or higher and a total score between 36 and 38 on the MCAT exam were accepted to medical school. Of those with a GPA between 3.60 and 3.79 and an MCAT total score between 36 and 38, the percent drops to a slightly lower—but still very encouraging—**85 percent**.

- What about the MCAT total score of 30 you've heard will make you an attractive candidate—generally speaking? As you'll see from the chart, **82 percent** of examinees who scored between 30 and 32 and had a GPA of 3.80 or above were accepted to med school.

- Are you looking at a score between 27 and 29? Of those in that range, **67 percent** of those with GPAs of 3.80 and higher were accepted, as were **52 percent** of those with GPAs from 3.60 to 3.79.

- Scored between 24 and 26? Your likelihood of acceptance is still reasonable if you can throw a high GPA into the mix. Looking at the table, we see that **42 percent** of examinees with a total score in that range and a GPA of 3.80 or above were accepted to medical school.

> **The average student accepted to medical school in 2007 had a:**
>
> - **30.8 MCAT Total Score**
> - **P on the Writing Sample**
> - **3.65 Overall GPA**

---

*The MSAR includes a description of the specific selection factors by which individual medical schools evaluate applicants.

Likelihood of Admission Based on Combination of MCAT Total Score and Total Undergraduate GPA

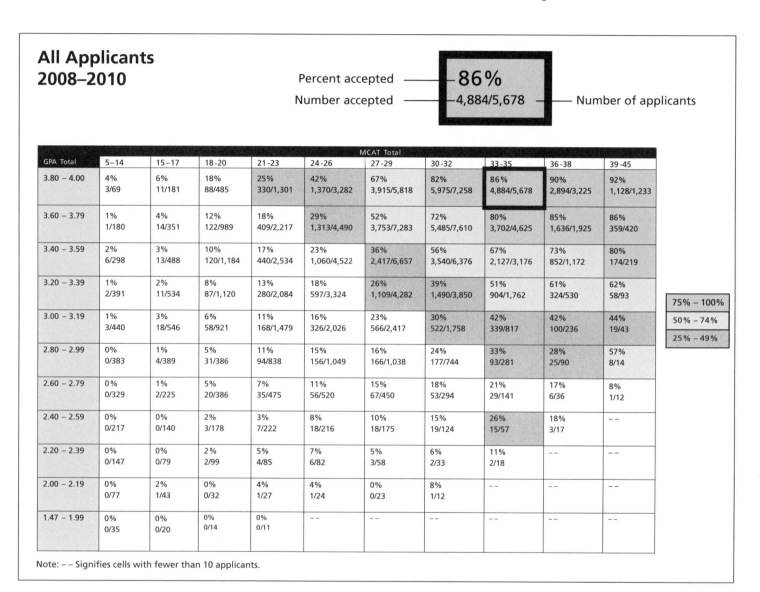

All Applicants
2008–2010

Percent accepted —— **86%**
Number accepted —— **4,884/5,678** —— Number of applicants

GPA Total	5–14	15–17	18–20	21–23	24–26	27–29	30–32	33–35	36–38	39–45
3.80 – 4.00	4% 3/69	6% 11/181	18% 88/485	25% 330/1,301	42% 1,370/3,282	67% 3,915/5,818	82% 5,975/7,258	86% 4,884/5,678	90% 2,894/3,225	92% 1,128/1,233
3.60 – 3.79	1% 1/180	4% 14/351	12% 122/989	18% 409/2,217	29% 1,313/4,490	52% 3,753/7,283	72% 5,485/7,610	80% 3,702/4,625	85% 1,636/1,925	86% 359/420
3.40 – 3.59	2% 6/298	3% 13/488	10% 120/1,184	17% 440/2,534	23% 1,060/4,522	36% 2,417/6,657	56% 3,540/6,376	67% 2,127/3,176	73% 852/1,172	80% 174/219
3.20 – 3.39	1% 2/391	2% 11/534	8% 87/1,120	13% 280/2,084	18% 597/3,324	26% 1,109/4,282	39% 1,490/3,850	51% 904/1,762	61% 324/530	62% 58/93
3.00 – 3.19	1% 3/440	3% 18/546	6% 58/921	11% 168/1,479	16% 326/2,026	23% 566/2,417	30% 522/1,758	42% 339/817	42% 100/236	44% 19/43
2.80 – 2.99	0% 0/383	1% 4/389	5% 31/386	11% 94/838	15% 156/1,049	16% 166/1,038	24% 177/744	33% 93/281	28% 25/90	57% 8/14
2.60 – 2.79	0% 0/329	1% 2/225	5% 20/386	7% 35/475	11% 56/520	15% 67/450	18% 53/294	21% 29/141	17% 6/36	8% 1/12
2.40 – 2.59	0% 0/217	0% 0/140	2% 3/178	3% 7/222	8% 18/216	10% 18/175	15% 19/124	26% 15/57	18% 3/17	– –
2.20 – 2.39	0% 0/147	0% 0/79	2% 2/99	5% 4/85	7% 6/82	5% 3/58	6% 2/33	11% 2/18	– –	– –
2.00 – 2.19	0% 0/77	2% 1/43	0% 0/32	4% 1/27	4% 1/24	0% 0/23	8% 1/12	– –	– –	– –
1.47 – 1.99	0% 0/35	0% 0/20	0% 0/14	0% 0/11	– –	– –	– –	– –	– –	– –

Legend:
- 75% – 100%
- 50% – 74%
- 25% – 49%

Note: – – Signifies cells with fewer than 10 applicants.

PLEASE NOTE!

These data describe acceptance rates for all applicants to medical school from 2008 to 2010. The data may not reflect your particular circumstances. As a result, we recommend that you go to www.aamc.org/mcatguide to see acceptance rates for particular demographic groups.

Note that these results (as well as those reported at www.aamc.org/mcatguide) are presented without regard to any of the other selection factors described on the following pages.

III. What Other Selection Factors Do Admissions Officers Consider?

The value of the MCAT exam is that it provides admissions officers with a standardized measure for all examinees, since differences in undergraduate grading scales and courses can vary significantly from one college to another. Still, as we've just seen in the previous section, MCAT exam scores never stand alone—nor should they—and many other factors (only one of which is your undergraduate GPA) enter into the admission picture.

Here, then, are other factors admissions officers may consider when reviewing a student's application:

- Undergraduate GPA
- Breadth and difficulty of undergraduate coursework
- Selectivity of the degree-granting undergraduate institution
- Medical school interview information
- Letters of evaluation from undergraduate advisors, faculty members, community leaders, research sponsors, and/or employers
- Involvement in extracurricular activities, such as student governance and community service
- Medically related work experience, research, or volunteer service
- "Distance traveled" (the extent to which you've overcome life challanges)
- Contribution to the objective of diversity within the educational environment
- Personal statements on the American Medical College Application Service (AMCAS) and/or institutional application forms

IV. How Do Medical Schools Use MCAT Scores in Conjunction with Other Selection Factors?

"If you've seen one medical school....you've seen one medical school."

That's a cute way of driving home the point that medical schools vary greatly in terms of their goals, purposes, and admissions criteria. You simply can't judge one from another. For just as there's no precise dividing line that separates an "acceptable" score from an "unacceptable" score (as far as entry to medical school, that is), there's no single method by which medical schools consider MCAT scores as part of their decision process. Rather, the degree to which a specific institution weighs scores, as well as nonacademic factors, may be a reflection of that particular school's mission and processes; and therefore what's critical to one may be less significant to another. Ultimately, of course, it's up to you—the applicant—to ascertain which schools value your particular strengths and, conversely, which schools ascribe lesser weight to your weaker areas.*

We turn, then, to Dr. Henry Sondheimer, a senior director here at the AAMC and the former associate dean for admissions at the University of Colorado Medical School. In the article that follows on the next page, he discusses the various ways in which medical schools incorporate MCAT scores into the decision-making process.

---

*You may find the MSAR, published by the AAMC and available for purchase at www.aamc.org/mcatguide, a helpful tool in uncovering which institutions most closely align with your qualifications. If you prefer, you may of course contact schools directly.

How Medical Schools Use MCAT Scores

During my years as the associate dean for admissions at the University of Colorado School of Medicine, I saw many instances in which an applicant accepted by our institution was rejected by a school that he or she thought would be easier to get into—or vice versa. I ascribe this to "fit." Each medical school, and specifically each medical school's admissions committee, places a different emphasis on various facets of a student's academic and personal profile. Perhaps at one school, a record of community service is critical; at another, medical research experience is very significant; and at a third, grades and MCAT scores are the most important.

This contradicts, of course, the commonly held belief that admissions committees select their entering students each year solely on the basis of MCAT scores and grades. While research has shown that these two criteria are indeed strong predictors of success in medical school—and as a result, almost every medical school uses them at some point in its assessment process—there is still a wide range of MCAT scores and GPAs found among accepted applicants. (Conversely, a substantial number of applicants with excellent scores and grades are not accepted.) The AAMC publication, Medical School Admission Requirements (MSAR), includes tables that show the broad range of MCAT scores and grades. In fact, medical schools invest considerable time and energy identifying candidates for admissions who not only have performed competitively in their premedical studies and mastered relevant scientific concepts, but who possess personal experiences, characteristics, and attributes necessary for the future practice of medicine.

All Medical Schools Are Not Alike

That there is such a wide range of scores and grades attests to the different ways in which medical schools balance academic and personal factors in reaching admission decisions. Variations may be based on institutional mission, faculty-approved policies and procedures, school experience, statistical analyses of prior student performance data, and the educational philosophies of the university. Beyond that, though, the mission of one medical school may be quite different from another's. Some schools look for students with a high potential for a research career; some are committed to primary care, whether urban or rural; and still others feel they have a wider mission, including international health. Inevitably, the mission of each medical school will influence the type of applicants that school wishes to matriculate into its entering class.

The Assessment Process: A Thorough Review

Most schools use the MCAT and GPA as one part of mulifaceted, holistic review of each applicant and also consider his or her background, experiences, written essays, and letters of recommendation. The standardized application used by most medical schools (AMCAS) allows this to occur on a level playing field, as each applicant is given an equal opportunity to show his or her strengths, work experiences, community service, college activities, and written work. Specifically, the AMCAS application limits the number of experiences to 15 per applicant, which means you will have to think hard about the particular academic honors, work experiences, research experiences, athletic activities, service work, and travel or other activities you want to list. In the first year of the computerized AMCAS application in 2002, the experience section had no number limit. Some people listed up to 50 different experiences!

> **"Most schools use the MCAT and GPA as one part of a multifaceted, holistic review of each applicant..."**

The Interview Is Key

Every medical school receives far more applicants than its class size. More importantly, every medical school receives far more *qualified* applicants than its class size. In general, each medical school will interview three to five times as many applicants as its class size. The critical thing, therefore, is being offered interviews, as interviews are required of all candidates being considered by every American and Canadian medical school. This is an important distinction of medical schools, as some professional schools (including law schools) do not even interview applicants. Every medical school interviews the applicants it feels will bring strength and diversity to its incoming class prior to making offers of admission. This philosophy among the medical schools reemphasizes the fact that although MCAT scores and GPAs may be important in getting you to be chosen for interviews, ultimately, every medical school is looking at you as an individual. This can be fully evaluated only with in-person interviews.

> **"This philosophy...reemphasizes the fact that although MCAT scores and GPAs may be important in getting you to be chosen for interviews, ultimately, every medical school is looking at you as an individual. This can be fully evaluated only with in-person interviews."**

Many Models in the Admission Process

In summary, medical schools employ many models in their application and admission activities. Each model includes an assessment of academic predictors of success in medical school coupled with an assessment of other indicators of success in the practice of medicine. Certainly the MCAT is one of those predictors of success—at least of academic success. While the emphasis placed on each of these criteria differs from school to school, rest assured that medical school admission committees are serious about their responsibility to select knowledgeable, altruistic, skillful, and dutiful young adults who will become our future physicians. Most medical school admissions officers say that in the final analysis, the interview scores are the largest single factor in acceptance into the majority of medical schools.

Henry Sondheimer, M.D.
Senior Director
Student Affairs and Programs
Association of American Medical Colleges (AAMC)
Former Associate Dean for Admissions
University of Colorado School of Medicine

Now that we have examined the variety of selection factors that figure in the admissions process, you can surely agree that it is important to get familiar with the medical schools that you are considering. *The Medical School Admissions Requirements (MSAR®)* guidebook and web site is the key resource for gathering information about the schools to which you might apply. MSAR's printed guidebook includes abridged profiles of each medical school, while comprehensive listings of U.S. and Canadian medical schools and baccalaureate/M.D. programs appear online. To learn more about MSAR and how to get access to these resources visit www.aamc.org/mcatguide.

You can use *MSAR Online* to view specifics about how a school uses selection factors in admissions decisions. Below is a sample of a school listing. Notice that among the options on the left you will find a section on Selection Factors. Here you can find an overview of each school's unique admission philosophy, as well as coursework requirements, interview format, and data about accepted applicants.

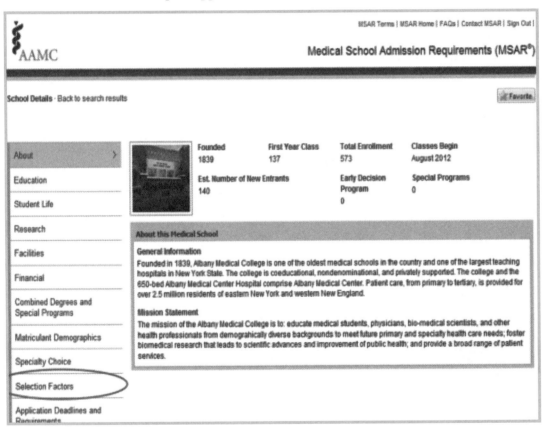

The Selection Factors section offers you some insight into a particular school's admissions model. You will notice differences in community service, research experience, GPA and MCAT scores among the accepted applicants for each school. Taking a closer look at the selection factors will help you to determine your fit with the admissions model for the schools of interest to you. For example, if you have a strong interest in research, looking at the percentage of accepted applicants with research experience can provide some insight into the value that institution places on research as compared to other selection factors.

The fact that there can be such variation in admissions models among schools – even among schools that are equally competitive – is apparent when you look at the entries in the *MSAR Online*. Consider, for example, the discrepancy between the following two medical schools, with the same median MCAT score:

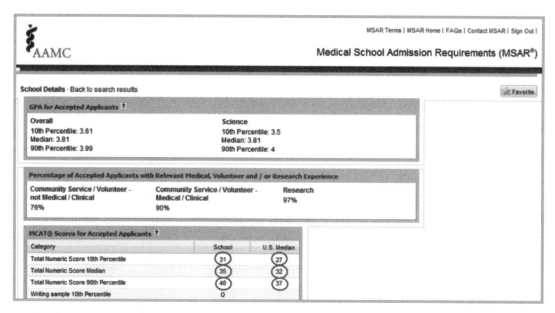

In this first example, the median MCAT "Total Numeric Score" of applicants accepted into this institution was 35, three points higher than the national median. Still, the range for acceptable scores is actually quite broad; with 10 percent of those accepted receiving a total score of 31 or less (and another 10 percent with a total score of 40 or more). At this school, there is a somewhat wide range of MCAT scores among the accepted applicants.

Now we look at the second school. In this case, the median score of accepted students remains 35, three points higher than the national median. In this instance, though, we see that the 10th percentile falls at 32 and the 90th percentile at 39, so that even though the median total scores for the two schools are the same, the range of scores is slightly "tighter."

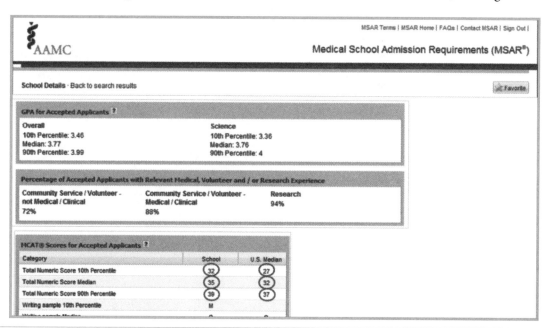

Let's take a look at another school – this time, one where the school median was lower than the national median:

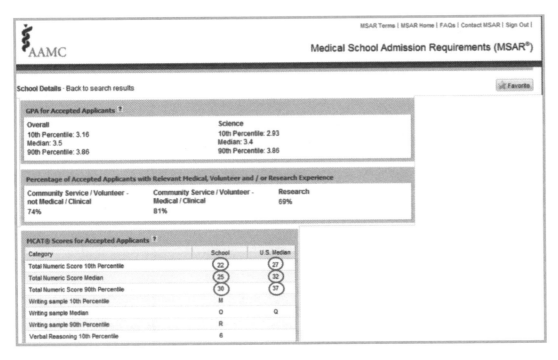

For this school, the median MCAT "Total Numeric Score" of applicants accepted was 25, compared to the national median of 32, with 10 percent of those accepted achieving a score of 22 or lower and 10 percent scoring 30 or higher in the 90th percentile. You can also make similar comparisons based on MCAT section scores.

These are just a few examples of how selection factors vary by school. It's worthwhile to spend time reviewing selection factors so that you can identify medical schools that most closely match to your individual strengths and interests.

MCAT® is a program of the
Association of American Medical Colleges

What Programs Exist to Help Me Overcome Financial or Educational Challenges?

Many of you reading this guide may face special challenges as the MCAT exam and the prospect of medical school approach. Perhaps your finances are limited. Maybe the overall quality of your education wasn't as strong as you'd like. Possibly you're older than the average student and have been out of school for several years. The list can go on and on.

Certainly, you have a hurdle (or hurdles) to jump that many others do not.

At the same time, it is important for you to know that medical schools actively invite those from a wide range of backgrounds to apply to their institutions—no matter their economic status, ethnicity, quality of educational preparation, age, or language of origin. In fact, one of the key goals among medical schools is to increase diversity among the student body, and ultimately, within the physician community at large. As such, there are many programs and resources to help you offset your particular circumstances and better prepare you for admission to medical school. Several of these are described below.

For Financial Assistance

The AAMC's Financial Assistance Program (FAP), available to individuals with financial limitations,* assists MCAT examinees and AMCAS applicants by reducing the costs associated with applying to medical school. In particular, the FAP offers the following benefits** to those who qualify:

• Reduction of the MCAT registration fee.

• Waiver of the application fee for submitting the completed AMCAS application to a designated number of medical schools and a reduced fee for each school beyond the designated free applications.

In addition, most AMCAS-participating medical schools waive their supplemental application fees for applicants who have been granted fee assistance by the AAMC.

Beyond MCAT and AMCAS...Financing Your Medical Education

While your school's financial aid office is the best starting place for assistance with loan applications and information on funding options, the AAMC also offers several resources to help guide you from your premedical years...through medical school...and on to residency. These include:

• descriptions of the types of financial aid for medical students,
• a review of the financial aid application process,
• an analysis of the costs involved with applying to and attending medical school,
• financial calculators, and
• detailed information on debt management.

Please go to www.aamc.org/mcatguide for complete information on financing considerations and a look at the AAMC's educational resource, FIRST for Medical Education.

---

*For the 2011 calendar year, applicants whose total family income is 300 percent or less of the poverty level for their family size are eligible for the program. See www.aamc.org/mcatguide for complete information.

**Subject to change.

For Educational Preparation

• Summer Enrichment Programs

Those of you who need to strengthen your academic preparation in the sciences may wish to explore eligibility requirements for the Summer Medical and Dental Education Program, a free, six-week academic enrichment summer program for college freshmen and sophomores, codirected by the AAMC and the American Dental Education Association. In addition, there are numerous Summer Enrichment Programs around the country; searchable database, located on the AAMC's Web site, will allow you to seek out programs by location, focus, and length.

• Postbaccalaureate Premedical Programs

A number of schools offer postbaccalaureate premedical programs to address the needs of many college graduates for additional science classes (both lectures and labs) as they prepare for the MCAT exam. If you are among this group, you can explore your options via a searchable database found on the AAMC Web site, which identifies each program by length, size, focus, structure, cost, admission requirements, and more.

Other Resources

Sometimes just figuring out where to turn for information can be a challenge in itself! The following can help answer many of your questions:

• AspiringDocs.org Web Site

The AAMC has developed AspiringDocs.org to connect you to key resources for preparing for and applying to medical school. This Web site includes information and advice from experts, inspiring stories from medical students and doctors who have realized their dreams, and an online community in which you can share your views with other students and ask questions of medical school experts.

• Career Fairs

Many career fairs are available that will allow you to discuss individual medical schools, enrichment programs, financial aid, and more. Many of these are listed in our Resources Section at the back of this guide, in addition to links provided at www.aamc.org/mcatguide.

For more information on these and other programs, please visit www.aamc.org/mcatguide.

Chapter 6:

To Retake or Not to Retake: That Is the Question….

Questions Answered in this Chapter:

Are My Scores Competitive?

Could I Do Better?

To What Degree Do Retakers Improve or Impair Their Scores?

How Does the Rest of My Application Look?

Am I Willing to Delay Entry into Medical School?

Talk about your life-changing decisions!

OK, granted. Your decision whether or not to retake the MCAT exam isn't exactly on par with the one Hamlet pondered in his famous soliloquy. Either way, you'll live, but your decision could have important consequences. What if your scores were "marginal," and you're afraid you're as likely to make things worse as you are to improve them? Or what if your scores are adequate for many schools, but not the specific institution you've had your heart set on since sophomore year…what then?

In most cases, we can't give you definitive answers—either to these specific questions or to others like them. What we can do, though, is provide you with insights and data to help you arrive at the answers yourself.

How Many Times Did Students Take the Exam in 2010*?

85%
took the exam once

14%
took the exam twice

< 1%
took the exam three times

*Based on the number of administrations of students who took their first exam in 2010

I. Are My Scores Competitive?

As you've just seen from the previous chapter, scores that help move you to the top of the heap at one medical school barely get you into the running at another. So, really, the question you need to ask yourself is fourfold:

Remember…

Scoring below the mean doesn't imply you're "out" any more than scoring above it guarantees an acceptance. Still, the more you deviate from the mean, the better or worse your chances.

1. **Are my scores competitive for the school I want to attend?** Let's say that you have dreamt of the day you'd join the entering class of a particular medical school. A glance at the MSAR, or inquiry made directly to the admissions office, tells you that your scores are several points below the median for that institution, and the rest of your application—while decent—is not exceptional. You fear you just won't make the cut. You then have to decide whether to retest (and run the risk of decreasing your scores) or to apply to other medical schools where you may be a more competitive candidate.

2. **Are my scores competitive for a school I'd be willing to attend?** The next thing you need to ask yourself, then, is whether your scores are in line with a medical school you'd be willing to attend. Here again, a search through the MSAR will tell you at which institutions—if any—your scores make you a viable applicant.

3. **Are my scores competitive at all?** The worst has happened, and your scores don't seem to be in the ballpark at all. The good news is that your decision is easy: You've little to lose by retaking the exam.

4. **Are my scores borderline?** Sometimes your course of action is more clear. You take a look at the MSAR and see that your score places you below the 10th percentile for the school you hope (or are willing) to attend. It's a pretty safe bet that, barring any unusual circumstances elsewhere in your application that make you an appealing candidate, you'll want to retake the exam. On the other hand, if your score is well above the median for that particular school (and the rest of your application is strong, too)…well, you're probably in excellent shape. *It's that grey area that causes students the most anguish.* For example, what if you're slightly below the median for the school you have your sights on (and can lay claim to only decent, but not outstanding, grades)? Should you…or shouldn't you? If you're in this group, you especially will need to think about the questions that follow.

How Do Med Schools Use Multiple Scores?

You'll also want to consider how the medical schools to which you want to apply use multiple or "repeat" scores.

Keep in mind that unless you void your scores at the end of an exam, scores for all your testing dates will be sent to med schools. Some of them will take the average; others will consider how much of an improvement you've made; still others may take the most current.

II. Could I Do Better?

You have to ask yourself if you could do better. Perhaps you discovered that your coursework (or study) didn't cover some topics as thoroughly as you needed, and you'd like the opportunity to go back and review those areas more carefully. Possibly you found your practice sessions inadequate and feel you could do better with another couple of "run-throughs." Or maybe you were just ill the day of the test.

Sometimes….you just know.

III. To What Degree Do Retakers Improve or Impair Their Scores?

More often, though, you don't "just know," and you need cold, hard data to help you judge how likely you are to increase your score, stay the same, or—and this of course is the risk—actually do worse.

As you might expect, the data show that retest increases are more likely for those examinees who initially score at the lower end of the scale. (Obviously, the lower one's initial score, the greater the potential on the upside—and the less on the down.) Conversely, the higher your score, the more likely you are to do worse on the second attempt. You'll therefore be better able to judge the cost-benefit ratio of a retest if you know where the "break-even point" lies.

The chart below shows you that very thing. Although it is fairly self-explanatory, we'll draw out a few data points to illustrate the findings. Let's consider, for example, examinees who scored from 24 to 26 initially. Looking at the 24-26 score row, we see that of the 6,164 retakers who fell into this range, 11 percent stayed the same, 14 percent increased by one point, 14 percent increased by two points, and so on. Looking at it from the other side, we see that 9 percent decreased by one point, 6 percent decreased by two points, and so forth. Looking further across, we can see that in this particular range, there was greater score change on the upside than on the down. (To

Changes in MCAT Total Multiple-Choice Scores between First and Second Attempts, as a Function of Scores on the First Attempt (Results reported in percentages)*

Initial Total Score Range	N	Total Multiple-Choice Score Change											
		-4 or less	-3	-2	-1	0	1	2	3	4	5	6	7 or more
5-14	1256	5	4	5	6	9	9	10	11	12	8	8	14
15-17	1695	5	4	6	8	9	11	11	11	9	8	7	11
18-20	3148	5	3	5	8	11	11	12	12	11	9	6	8
21-23	4951	5	4	6	8	11	12	13	12	10	8	5	6
24-26	6164	4	3	6	9	11	14	14	13	11	7	4	4
27-29	4500	4	4	6	10	12	14	14	12	10	7	4	3
30-32	1500	3	4	6	10	13	15	13	13	10	7	4	3
33-35	382	6	3	8	11	15	16	15	9	8	5	3	1
36-38	50	6	4	14	20	12	0	20	12	4	2	4	2
39-45	5	0	20	20	20	20	20	0	0	0	0	0	0

* Based on students who took their first MCAT exam and tested at least twice in a given year. Data from the 2008, 2009, and 2010 testing years.

help you quickly discern where the greatest score changes occurred, be they increases or decreases, we've highlighted those entries with percentages of 10 percent or more.)

As you review the chart on the preceding page in an effort to gauge how likely you are to improve your overall score, you're also apt to wonder to what degree examinees increase or decrease their scores in any one particular exam section. We therefore have broken down the data even further in the charts that follow, examining the change in scores in each of the four sections (again based on initial scores).

You'll probably notice, quite quickly, that the shaded entries—those with percentages of at least 10 percent—skew to the right in the lower-scoring rows, and to the left in the rows with the higher initial scores. That illustrates the point we made earlier: that examinees with lower initial scores tend to gain more when they retest, and test takers with higher initial scores tend to gain less (or decrease more) the second time around.

Here, then, are the charts for all four sections of the exam—PS, VR, WS, and BS—broken down by initial score:

Changes in MCAT Physical Sciences Scores between First and Second Attempts, as a Function of Scores on the First Attempt (Results reported in percentages)*

| Physical Sciences Score Change | | | | | | | | | | | | | |
Initial PS Score	N	-4 or less	-3	-2	-1	0	1	2	3	4	5	6	7 or more
1	7					71	0	0	0	0	14	0	14
2	57				0	11	30	26	18	9	4	4	0
3	372			0	5	20	13	26	22	10	4	0	0
4	575		0	1	8	14	27	27	16	6	1	0	0
5	1734	0	1	4	7	23	31	24	8	2	1	0	0
6	3745	0	2	3	11	25	31	16	8	3	1	0	0
7	5555	0	1	4	15	28	23	16	8	4	1	0	0
8	4471	0	1	5	19	22	22	17	10	3	1	0	0
9	3178	0	2	10	18	23	22	16	7	1	1	0	
10	2055	1	5	12	18	23	22	14	3	3	0		
11	1157	3	6	13	21	25	20	7	6	0			
12	515	2	10	15	26	25	10	12	0				
13	129	2	9	22	27	17	23	0					
14	96	7	19	24	18	26	6						
15	5	20	40	0	40	0							

* Based on students who took their first MCAT exam and tested at least twice in a given year. Data from the 2008, 2009, and 2010 testing years.

MCAT® is a program of the
Association of American Medical Colleges

Changes in MCAT Verbal Reasoning Scores between First and Second Attempts, as a Function of Scores on the First Attempt (Results reported in percentages)*

Initial VR Score	N	Verbal Reasoning Score Change											
		-4 or less	-3	-2	-1	0	1	2	3	4	5	6	7 or more
1	142					13	13	14	22	13	20	1	5
2	373				9	11	11	22	15	18	8	5	2
3	505			4	9	9	20	16	22	11	7	2	1
4	1276		2	4	6	15	13	24	15	11	6	2	0
5	1643	1	3	4	9	11	24	18	15	9	4	1	0
6	3851	1	2	5	8	20	17	20	16	8	3	0	0
7	3395	1	2	5	13	15	22	20	14	6	1	0	0
8	4361	2	2	9	11	20	24	21	9	1	0	0	0
9	3739	2	5	8	16	25	26	16	2	1	0	0	
10	2842	3	4	11	22	29	23	6	3	0	0		
11	1259	2	6	15	30	33	9	4	1	0			
12	184	3	4	27	42	12	9	1	2				
13	67	8	15	49	19	8	2	0					
14	10	20	30	20	10	10	10						
15	4	25	25	25	25	0							

* Based on students who took their first MCAT exam and tested at least twice in a given year. Data from the 2008, 2009, and 2010 testing years.

Changes in MCAT Writing Sample Scores on the J to T Scale between First and Second Attempts, as a Function of Scores on the First Attempt (Results reported in percentages)*

Initial WS Score	N	Writing Sample Score Change											
		-4 or less	-3	-2	-1	0	1	2	3	4	5	6	7 or more
J	150					29	25	22	17	3	1	2	1
K	718				6	21	26	32	6	5	2	3	0
L	1711			1	9	22	44	10	7	3	3	0	0
M	5402		0	3	10	40	13	15	8	10	1	0	0
N	2191	0	1	5	29	15	19	12	16	3	1	0	
O	3205	0	3	22	13	20	14	23	5	1	0		
P	2387	2	15	11	18	15	30	8	2	0			
Q	4726	8	7	15	14	38	15	3	0				
R	2110	5	8	11	36	29	13	1					
S	911	3	3	22	35	32	6						
T	103	2	8	17	40	34							

* Based on students who took their first MCAT exam and tested at least twice in a given year. Data from the 2008, 2009, and 2010 testing years.

Changes in MCAT Biological Sciences Scores between First and Second Attempts, as a Function of Scores on the First Attempt (Results reported in percentages)*

Initial BS Score	N	Biological Sciences Score Change											
		-4 or less	-3	-2	-1	0	1	2	3	4	5	6	7 or more
1	131					17	7	15	25	10	15	8	4
2	113				11	5	18	15	17	20	10	3	3
3	391			8	3	15	16	15	22	11	9	1	0
4	846		3	4	8	15	16	24	12	14	4	1	0
5	953	2	1	5	12	12	22	15	19	9	3	1	0
6	2430	1	3	6	7	20	15	26	15	7	1	0	0
7	2083	2	3	4	14	13	29	21	13	2	1	0	0
8	4923	1	2	8	10	26	24	21	6	1	0	0	0
9	4620	1	3	5	19	26	30	12	4	1	0	0	
10	4523	1	2	10	20	35	20	9	2	1	0		
11	1794	1	4	11	29	29	17	5	3	1			
12	664	1	6	23	27	24	9	7	2				
13	130	1	17	24	26	11	15	6					
14	40	8	23	33	18	15	5						
15	10	20	20	10	20	30							

* Based on students who took their first MCAT exam and tested at least twice in a given year. Data from the 2008, 2009, and 2010 testing years.

MCAT® is a program of the
Association of American Medical Colleges

IV. How Does the Rest of My Application Look?

What Does My Advisor Suggest?

As you deliberate, make sure you ask your pre-health advisor for guidance. He or she will have recommendations that help make your decision easier.

For more information about how your pre-health advisor can help, see page 398.

As you mull over whether to retake the exam, you also need to factor in other aspects of your application. For instance, your grades are another way to demonstrate your proficiency in those areas tested by the MCAT exam. Is your GPA, and particularly your track record in the sciences, strong?

Beyond that, are there any especially impressive facets to your application? Consider the other selection factors we touched upon in the previous chapters. Do you have exceptionally striking letters of recommendation, perhaps, or a remarkable tale of hardships to overcome? (Remember that "Distance Traveled" concept that some admissions officers consider.) What about a year's stint volunteering in a medical clinic in an underserved community? Factors such as these may help tilt the scales in your favor.

V. Am I Willing to Delay Entry into Medical School?

There's another alternative altogether. Are you willing to delay your entry into medical school by one year? If so, you can take the time to study more thoroughly.

Or you might be interested in enrolling in a postbaccalaureate program to strengthen your weak areas and better position yourself for another attempt at the MCAT exam in a year or so. If you'd like to explore this last option, you should know that the AAMC offers a searchable database—*available at no charge*—that provides information on numerous postbaccalaureate programs, including duration, size, purpose, structure, cost, and admission requirements. Go to www.aamc.org/mcatguide to learn more.

Chapter 7:

The Strategy Mystique: Debunking the Myths

Questions Answered in this Chapter:

What Are Some Shortcomings of MCAT Test-Taking Strategies?

So...What Should I Do When It Comes to Test Preparation?

When we embarked on this guide, we conducted focus groups with students just like you—ones who were preparing for the MCAT exam—to determine what topics would be most valuable to them. We kept everything they said in mind and included, for example, material on registration procedures, scoring and the score release process, the admissions decision, examinee data, considerations on retaking the exam, lots (and lots) of sample questions, and thoroughly explained solutions.

What hung us up, though, was the request that we include the "true" strategies. Students seemed to believe that MCAT staffers, who have the inside track, would certainly know which test-taking approach would give them an edge, and all we needed to do was let them in on it. If only it were that easy….

I. What Are Some Shortcomings of MCAT Test-Taking Strategies?

After reading the various strategies advocated in MCAT exam prep guides and/or batted around among students, we can understand why you'd want to hear from the "ultimate authority." There seems to be something lacking in many of the current strategies for one of several reasons:

• They're common sense.

First, there's an entire barrage of so-called strategies out there that are little more than common sense. (You've probably already come across them.) We'd venture a guess that you didn't get this far in your academic career without honing your basic test-taking skills, and you don't need a publication to tell you to "get a good night's sleep the night before," or "focus on the task at hand," or "use a process of elimination to narrow your choice." The best thing we can say about suggestions such as these is that they do no harm.

What's a "Distractor"?

It's a fancy term for a simple concept: the wrong answer. In the solutions section of this book, we provide you with not only an explanation of the right answer, but a short explanation of the distracters (with some tips on identifying them).

Be Careful....

...to practice only with strategies that can be implemented in the actual exam! We recommend that you apply your strategies to an official MCAT Practice Test, which emulates the operational exam precisely. (See Chapter 12 for more information).

"Extreme terms, such as unique, always, never, and every, should be avoided in distractors. They signal to test-takers that a response is probably wrong."

MCAT Item Writer's Guide,
AAMC

On the other hand, some "strategies" are harmful. One book suggested you return to the difficult questions you may have skipped if—if!—you have time. In actuality, you should always come back to unanswered questions since there is no penalty for guessing. At worst, you have a 25-percent chance of getting it right, and if you're able to eliminate even one possibility, your odds are 1 in 3. (Remember, though, that you can return to unanswered questions within a section during the time allocated to that particular section only.)

• They're not as useful as they seem.

Then we see strategies that seem to hold some merit. As just one example, there's "advice" floating around to be alert for absolutes such as "all of the above" or "none of the above" in answer choices. The theory here is that answers containing absolutes—all, none, never, always—are less likely to be correct, and, all things being equal, you might do well to eliminate them as possibilities. The catch? If you've heard of this strategy, you can be sure we have also—and that we've instructed our test writers to avoid creating distractors that employ it. (See box at left.) Consequently, even though this bit of advice sounds logical, it's likely to be of little value.

• They sound good, but who knows?

We'll admit it. Not all strategies are useless (or worse). There are indeed a number of test-taking tactics, many of which you'll come across in guidebooks or commercial prep courses, that may actually work very well for you. The problem with these strategies, though, is that no research or statistics exist that prove their advantage. That's why you'll sometimes come across two strategies in direct conflict with each other:

- Consider the often suggested strategy to highlight key words or phrases. Sounds good, you think, until you come across another book that tells you not to waste time with this approach. Which is right?

- Or reflect on the strategy that recommends you take questions in order, rather than skip around. (This strategy suggests that if you come across a difficult question that stumps you, take your best guess and move on, rather than return to it later.) The other side, as we've already noted, suggests you pass over the difficult questions and come back to answer them at the end of each section. Which is right?

So...Which Strategies Are "Right"?

We don't know. We haven't seen evidence one way or the other. The only way to learn which strategies are "right" is to test them out, making sure your practice sessions most closely replicate the actual exam.

- Or think of the strategy that suggests you approach the passages by reading the first line of each paragraph first. Another advises you to read the passage in its entirety right from the start. Yet another tells you to read the first and last paragraphs initially, and only then return to read the whole passage. Which is right?

The bottom line is that there is no "best" strategy, since an approach that is useful for one individual may be totally ineffective for another. We want to emphasize, however, that we are not discounting strategies such as the ones just addressed above. Indeed, there are dozens of recommendations put out by guidebooks and prep courses that could be helpful. So, with that in mind, we advise you experiment with various tactics. See which—if any—impact your score.

It's all part of effective preparation, which we discuss next.

So...What Should I Do When It Comes to Test Preparation?

As much as you probably would like to hear otherwise, there are no real mysteries when it comes to test preparation.

The entire process is analogous to the process of losing weight. For no matter how you approach it—making a go of it on your own, joining a formal weight-loss program with regular meetings, signing up with a pre-packaged food plan, following a structured diet—it all works out to the same basic thing: You have to reduce the number of calories you take in or increase the number of calories you burn off. (Ideally, both.) Still, when a person who's dropped some pounds tells people who ask about it that he "ate less and exercised more," he's often met with disappointment. These people want to know some secret, some mystery, some "magic button." Eat less and exercise more? That's no help.

The same goes for MCAT test preparation. Although there are a number of ways to tackle it—signing up for commercial prep courses, poring over various review guides, studying your class notes and rereading your textbooks—at the core everyone needs to (a) master the content, (b) become familiar with the test, and (c) practice effectively.

Let's take a closer look:

What College Courses Should I Take Before Tackling the Exam?
You should complete coursework in: • General Biology • Inorganic Chemistry • Organic Chemistry • General Physics For additional guidance, please see your pre-health advisor.

a. Master the content.

Stoichiometry to electrostatics...amines to hydrocarbons...circulatory system to digestive. Obviously, you've got to know what material the exam covers—and master it. In the following chapters, we give you a detailed outline of the topics to help you get started.

b. Become familiar with the test.

Just as we try to get "into your head" via the exam, it will be helpful for you to get into OURS. To a large extent, that includes understanding what cognitive skills we are testing for and learning to recognize various passage types. Beyond that, though, you should get familiar with the passage-based testing format, prepare with "real" items (i.e., passages and questions that have appeared on previously administered MCAT exams), and gain insights as to why specific answers are correct...why wrong ones are incorrect...and what pitfalls sometimes trip up examinees. The chapters that follow will provide you with all this information.

c. Practice effectively.

In real estate, it's "location...location...location."
In the MCAT world, it's "practice... practice...
practice."

Finally, in chapter 12 at the end of this guide, we
tell you how to make your practice sessions as productive as possible. We explain how official
AAMC practice tests can be used to emulate "real-world" testing conditions, reduce stress on
test day (at least to some extent!), and help you focus on your weaker areas.

Free AAMC Practice Test for All

In addition to the practice tests you may
purchase from the AAMC, we offer one at no
charge at all. Learn how to get your free
practice test at www.aamc.org/mcatguide.

*At this point, we "shift gears" as we focus the remainder of the guide on the three tasks
described above.*

*In fact, you might note a shift in tone and language in much of the material, as well. That's
because we thought it best that at this point we have our test developers—the actual people
who write the exam passages and questions!—provide most of the information that follows.
From a detailed look at the content and skills assessed to a thorough explanation of solutions
to question samples, the test developers will, we hope, provide you with insights and understanding to help you bolster your performance.*

Part II:

Preparing for the MCAT® Exam

The Four Exam Segments

Physical Sciences
Biological Sciences
Verbal Reasoning
Writing Sample

MCAT Sciences Sections:
General Concepts/Techniques Required

The next two chapters focus on the sciences sections—that of Physical and Biological Sciences. Before you delve into these next chapters, though, we want you to know that you will be expected to analyze and manipulate scientific data throughout the Physical and Biological Sciences sections. The following list contains several concepts, skills, and techniques that may be required when answering the questions in the science sections of the MCAT exam.

1. The ability to interpret and analyze data found in figures, graphs, and tables, including recognizing and interpreting linear, semilog, and log-log scales; calculating slopes

2. The ability to recognize meaningful experimental results, including a general understanding of the following: random versus systematic errors; arithmetic mean; standard deviation; the effect of propagation of error; concepts of statistical association and correlation

3. A general understanding of significant digits and the use of reasonable numerical estimates in performing measurements and calculations

4. The ability to use metric units, including conversion of units within the metric system; conversions between metric and English units (conversion factors will be provided when needed); dimensional analysis (using units to balance equations)

5. The ability to perform arithmetic calculations involving the following: probability; proportion; ratio; percentage; square-root estimations

6. A general understanding (Algebra II-level) of exponentials and logarithms (natural and base ten); scientific notation; solving simultaneous equations

7. A general understanding of the following trigonometry concepts: definitions of basic (sine, cosine, tangent) and inverse (sin^{-1}, cos^{-1}, tan^{-1}) functions; sin and cos values of 0°, 90°, and 180°; relationships between the lengths of sides of right triangles containing angles of 30°, 45°, and 60°

8. A general understanding of vector addition and subtraction; right-hand rule (knowledge of dot and cross products is not required)

An understanding of calculus is not required.

The periodic table will be available to you during the actual exam. It is also included on page 398 for your reference.

MCAT® is a program of the
Association of American Medical Colleges

Chapter 8:

Physical Sciences (PS)

Included in this Chapter:

Overall Section Format

Types of Passages

The PS Content Outline

Cognitive Skills Assessed

Introduction to Practice Sets for Physical Sciences

Practice Sets of Sample Passages, Questions, and Solutions

The material that follows captures our "must-do" preparation tasks for the Physical Sciences section. We first explain the four different types of passages; next we provide you with a detailed outline of the content; we then describe the cognitive skills assessed; and finally we segue into the review section—which includes dozens and dozens of pages of MCAT passages and questions from *real* MCAT exams, and a comprehensive explanation of the answers (and even "tips" to help you get to them).

PS Section Recap

- Covers general chemistry and physics

- 52 questions

  - Seven passages with four to seven questions each, for a total of 39 passage-based questions

  - Thirteen independent questions

- 70 minutes

I. Overall Section Format

The MCAT Physical Sciences section is composed of 52 multiple-choice questions—either passage-based or discrete*—that test your reasoning in general chemistry and physics. The scientific competencies you will be expected to demonstrate are drawn from basic principles and concepts in these two disciplines and are taught at the introductory level at the vast majority of undergraduate institutions. As we've mentioned elsewhere in this guide, advanced coursework in chemistry and physics is not needed for the test.

II. Types of Passages

As we just mentioned, the majority of the questions in the two science sections are tied to passages. We thought it might be helpful, therefore, to give you a brief overview of each of the four different passage types you will come across as you work through the exam.

Passage Type Identified in Sample Questions

The sample passages in this chapter will be identified by type. See page 66 for a description of each type.

---

*Discrete questions are not tied to passages but rather are independent. Of the 52 total questions, 39 are passage-based and 13 are discrete.

A. Information Presentation

Information is presented in a textbook or journal article format. The information assumes appropriate background knowledge but also contains new information or new ways of using information. The questions test your understanding and evaluation of the given information and your ability to use the information in various ways.

B. Problem Solving

A situation is presented that describes an event or phenomenon in one of the science content areas. The questions require you to determine the probable causes of the situation described and to select an effective method for solving the problem.

C. Research Study

The passage describes all or a part of the rationale, methods, and results of a particular research project. The questions test your understanding of the project.

D. Persuasive Argument

Information presented is designed to persuade the reader that a particular perspective, methodology, piece of evidence, or product is correct. The passage may also present an opposing point of view.

Now on to the outline.

III. The PS Content Outline

The questions in the Physical Sciences section will test your background knowledge of the topics listed in the outline below. You are expected to be able to apply your background knowledge of these topic areas and their subdivisions to situations or problems you may not have previously encountered. Each major topic area is shown in boldface, uppercase font, followed by a brief description of the subject matter.

> ### Content Area Identified in Practice Questions
>
> In the practice questions that follow later in this guide, we identify the specific content area(s) each one tests.

MCAT® is a program of the
Association of American Medical Colleges

GENERAL CHEMISTRY

ELECTRONIC STRUCTURE AND PERIODIC TABLE

Questions May Overlap

As you review the outline, please keep in mind that a test question may fall under more than one topic area.

Electronic structure is the key link between quantum theories and the chemical and physical properties of elements and compounds. This link is also critical to understanding the dynamics and complexities of chemical reactions. In addition, the order and location of elements in the periodic table are directly related to electronic structure. You will need to understand these relationships and apply them to the general periodic trends.

A. Electronic Structure

1. Orbital structure of hydrogen atom, principal quantum number n, number of electrons per orbital
2. Ground state, excited states
3. Absorption and emission spectra
4. Quantum numbers l, m, s, and number of electrons per orbital
5. Common names and geometric shapes for orbitals s, p, d
6. Conventional notation for electronic structure
7. Bohr atom
8. Effective nuclear charge

B. The Periodic Table: Classification of Elements into Groups by Electronic Structure; Physical and Chemical Properties of Elements

1. Alkali metals
2. Alkaline earth metals
3. Halogens
4. Noble gases
5. Transition metals
6. Representative elements
7. Metals and nonmetals
8. Oxygen group

C. The Periodic Table: Variations of Chemical Properties with Group and Row

1. Electronic structure
   a. representative elements
   b. noble gases
   c. transition metals
2. Valence electrons
3. First and second ionization energies
   a. definition
   b. prediction from electronic structure for elements in different groups or rows

4. Electron affinity
   a. definition
   b. variations with group and row
5. Electronegativity
   a. definition
   b. comparative values for some representative elements and important groups
6. Electron shells and the sizes of atoms

BONDING

Most physical and chemical properties of substances can be related to bond formation and characteristics. Covalent and ionic bonds are an extension of the electronic structures of the elements involved. Questions may range from the clarification or explanation of a molecule's structure and reactivity to the hypothetical evaluation of compounds and their relative polarity or ionic character.

A. The Ionic Bond (Electrostatic Forces Between Ions)

1. Electrostatic energy $\propto q_1q_2/r$
2. Electrostatic energy $\propto$ lattice energy
3. Electrostatic force $\propto q_1q_2/r^2$

B. The Covalent Bond

1. Sigma and pi bonds
   a. hybrid orbitals (sp^3, sp^2, sp, and respective geometries)
   b. valence shell electron-pair repulsion (VSEPR) theory, predictions of shapes of molecules (e.g., NH_3, H_2O, CO_2)
2. Lewis electron dot formulas
   a. resonance structures
   b. formal charge
   c. Lewis acids and bases
3. Partial ionic character
   a. role of electronegativity in determining charge distribution
   b. dipole moment

In addition to undergoing reactions, substances are dynamic in phase and change with conditions into gas, liquid, or solid forms. The gas phase was well studied by a number of early scientists who identified several relations that can be expressed as the ideal gas law. Later, the kinetic theory of gases provided a firmer theoretical basis for the properties of gases. Intermolecular forces are a major factor in determining the individual phase characteristics of substances. The equilibrium or relationship between phases is often represented in a phase diagram. You will need to understand these concepts to answer questions about phases and phase equilibria.

A. Gas Phase

1. Absolute temperature, K
2. Pressure, simple mercury barometer
3. Molar volume at 0°C and 1 atm = 22.4 L/mol
4. Ideal gas
   a. definition
   b. ideal gas law ($PV = nRT$)
      i. Boyle's law
      ii. Charles's law
      iii. Avogadro's law
5. Kinetic theory of gases
6. Deviation of real-gas behavior from ideal gas law
   a. qualitative
   b. quantitative (van der Waals equation)
7. Partial pressure, mole fraction
8. Dalton's law relating partial pressure to composition

B. Intermolecular Forces

1. Hydrogen bonding
2. Dipole interactions
3. London dispersion forces

C. Phase Equilibria

1. Phase changes, phase diagrams
2. Freezing point, melting point, boiling point, condensation point
3. Molality
4. Colligative properties
   a. vapor pressure lowering (Raoult's law)
   b. boiling point elevation ($\Delta T_b = K_b m$)
   c. freezing point depression ($\Delta T_f = K_f m$)
   d. osmotic pressure
5. Colloids
6. Henry's law

STOICHIOMETRY

An important skill in chemistry is the ability to understand and balance chemical equations. This skill requires understanding the mole concept, chemical formulas, and oxidation numbers. You should be able to apply the concepts below to experimental situations and be able to reason about the relationships between elements and compounds in chemical reactions.

1. Molecular weight
2. Empirical formula versus molecular formula
3. Metric units commonly used in the context of chemistry
4. Description of composition by percent mass
5. Mole concept, Avogadro's number
6. Definition of density
7. Oxidation number
   a. common oxidizing and reducing agents
   b. disproportionation reactions
   c. redox titration
8. Description of reactions by chemical equations
   a. conventions for writing chemical equations
   b. balancing equations including redox equations
   c. limiting reactants
   d. theoretical yields

THERMODYNAMICS AND THERMOCHEMISTRY

Thermodynamics and thermochemistry are the links between chemical bonding and energy. Although they can be explained in terms of bond energies, the thermodynamics of a reaction are most evident in the heat evolved or absorbed during a reaction. In addition, the concept of thermodynamics is useful in explaining why a reaction occurs or does not occur under specific conditions. Questions in the test will require you to understand and apply these concepts.

A. Energy Changes in Chemical Reactions: Thermochemistry

1. Thermodynamic system, state function
2. Endothermic and exothermic reactions
   a. enthalpy H, standard heats of reaction and formation
   b. Hess's law of heat summation
3. Bond dissociation energy as related to heats of formation
4. Measurement of heat changes (calorimetry), heat capacity, specific heat capacity (specific heat capacity of water = 4.184 J/g·K)
5. Entropy as a measure of "disorder," relative entropy for gas, liquid, and crystal states
6. Free energy G
7. Spontaneous reactions and $\Delta G°$

B. Thermodynamics

1. Zeroth law (concept of temperature)
2. First law ($\Delta E = q + w$, conservation of energy)
3. Equivalence of mechanical, chemical, electrical, and thermal energy units
4. Second law (concept of entropy)
5. Temperature scales, conversions
6. Heat transfer (conduction, convection, radiation)
7. Heat of fusion, heat of vaporization
8. *PV* diagram (work done = area under or enclosed by curve)

RATE PROCESSES IN CHEMICAL REACTIONS: KINETICS AND EQUILIBRIUM

Reactions occur at a wide variety of rates and to various degrees of completion. Reaction equilibrium and rate concepts help chemists understand how to optimize conditions for the reactions that are wanted and to limit conditions for reactions that are not. In addition, there may be situations in which a reaction is either kinetically or thermodynamically controlled, requiring a full understanding of both concepts. In a biological setting, enzymes are the catalysts that maintain control of the chemical pathways needed for life. You should be able to apply your understanding of these concepts to the questions in this topic area.

1. Reaction rates
2. Rate law, dependence of reaction rate on concentrations of reactants
   a. rate constant
   b. reaction order
3. Rate-determining step
4. Dependence of reaction rate on temperature
   a. activation energy
      i. activated complex or transition state
      ii. interpretation of energy profiles showing energies of reactants and products, activation energy, ΔH for the reaction
   b. Arrhenius equation
5. Kinetic control versus thermodynamic control of a reaction
6. Catalysts, enzyme catalysis
7. Equilibrium in reversible chemical reactions
   a. law of mass action
   b. the equilibrium constant
   c. application of Le Châtelier's principle
8. Relationship of the equilibrium constant and $\Delta G°$

SOLUTION CHEMISTRY

Most chemical reactions necessary for life occur in aqueous solutions. You should be familiar with ions in solution, solubility, and precipitation reactions.

A. Ions in Solution

1. Anion, cation (common names, formulas, and charges for familiar ions; e.g., NH_4^+, ammonium; PO_4^{3-}, phosphate; SO_4^{2-}, sulfate)
2. Hydration, the hydronium ion

B. Solubility

1. Units of concentration (e.g., molarity)
2. Solubility product constant, the equilibrium expression
3. Common-ion effect, its use in laboratory separations
4. Complex ion formation
5. Complex ions and solubility
6. Solubility and pH

ACIDS AND BASES

Acids and bases, both weak and strong, are major factors in many reactions. The concepts below are important for understanding many of the complex processes and equilibria needed to sustain life.

A. Acid–Base Equilibria

1. Brønsted–Lowry definition of acids and bases
2. Ionization of water
    a. K_w, its approximate value ($K_w = [H_3O^+][OH^-] = 10^{-14}$ at 25°C)
    b. pH definition, pH of pure water
3. Conjugate acids and bases
4. Strong acids and bases (common examples; e.g., nitric, sulfuric)
5. Weak acids and bases (common examples; e.g., acetic, benzoic)
    a. dissociation of weak acids and bases with or without added salt
    b. hydrolysis of salts of weak acids or bases
    c. calculation of pH of solutions of weak acids or bases
6. Equilibrium constants K_a and K_b (pK_a and pK_b)
7. Buffers
    a. definition, concepts (common buffer systems)
    b. influence on titration curves

B. Titration

1. Indicators
2. Neutralization
3. Interpretation of titration curves

Electrochemistry combines aspects of ionic solution chemistry, thermodynamics, and phase equilibria to explain how electric current is produced in a galvanic cell or used in an electrolytic cell. You should be prepared to employ the following concepts in the analysis of galvanic and electrolytic cells.

1. Electrolytic cell
   a. electrolysis
   b. anode, cathode
   c. electrolytes
   d. Faraday's law relating amount of elements deposited (or gas liberated) at an electrode to current
   e. electron flow, oxidation and reduction at the electrodes
2. Galvanic (voltaic) cell
   a. half-reactions
   b. reduction potentials, cell potential
   c. direction of electron flow

PHYSICS

TRANSLATIONAL MOTION

The concepts of distance, speed, velocity, and acceleration describe the location and motion of an object at a point in time. Questions in this topic area require you to interpret relationships among these variables and apply these relationships to problems.

1. Dimensions (length or distance, time)
2. Vectors, components
3. Vector addition
4. Speed, velocity (average and instantaneous)
5. Acceleration
6. Freely falling bodies

Different forces act on objects to cause motion. Newton's second and third laws and the law of gravitation describe the movement of objects under the influence of force. The motions that occur can be circular or linear and with or without acceleration. Questions in this topic area of the test require you to interpret the ways objects move when acted upon by forces.

1. Center of mass
2. Newton's first law (inertia)
3. Newton's second law ($F = ma$)
4. Newton's third law (forces equal and opposite)
5. Concept of a field
6. Law of gravitation ($F = -Gm_1m_2/r^2$)
7. Uniform circular motion
8. Centripetal force ($F = -mv^2/r$)
9. Weight
10. Friction (static and kinetic)
11. Motion on an inclined plane
12. Analysis of pulley systems
13. Force

EQUILIBRIUM AND MOMENTUM

Equilibrium occurs when a body is at rest or moves with a constant velocity. Forces, torques, Newton's first law, and inertia describe translational and rotational equilibria. Questions about equilibrium call upon your understanding of the way forces act on an object.

Momentum is a vector property that describes the motion of a system. The momentum of a system of particles can be used to describe the motion of the system by itself or when it is involved in elastic or inelastic collisions with other systems. Questions about momentum require you to interpret the motions of interacting bodies.

A. Equilibrium

1. Concept of force, units
2. Translational equilibrium ($\sum F_i = 0$)
3. Rotational equilibrium ($\sum \tau_i = 0$)
4. Analysis of forces acting on an object
5. Newton's first law (inertia)
6. Torques, lever arms
7. Weightlessness

B. Momentum

1. Momentum = mv
2. Impulse = Ft
3. Conservation of linear momentum
4. Elastic collisions
5. Inelastic collisions

MCAT® is a program of the
Association of American Medical Colleges

WORK AND ENERGY

Work and energy describe how objects interact with their environment and with other objects. The concepts of conservation of energy, work, and power describe the forms of energy and the transformations that occur among these forms. Questions about work and energy require you to apply your knowledge of these concepts to experimental situations.

A. Work

1. Derived units, sign conventions
2. Path independence of work done in gravitational field
3. Mechanical advantage
4. Work–energy theorem
5. Power

B. Energy

1. Kinetic energy (KE = $mv^2/2$, units)
2. Potential energy
   a. gravitational, local (PE = mgh)
   b. spring (PE = $kx^2/2$)
   c. gravitational, general (PE = $-GmM/r$)
3. Conservation of energy
4. Conservative forces
5. Power, units

WAVES AND PERIODIC MOTION

Wave characteristics and periodic motion describe the motion of systems that vibrate. Concepts used to describe this motion include transverse and longitudinal waves, superposition of waves, resonance, Hooke's law, and simple harmonic motion. Questions in this topic area involve the interpretation of wave characteristics and the analysis of systems exhibiting periodic motion.

A. Periodic Motion

1. Amplitude, period, frequency
2. Phase
3. Hooke's law ($F = -kx$)
4. Simple harmonic motion, displacement as a sinusoidal function of time
5. Motion of a pendulum
6. General periodic motion (velocity, amplitude)

B. Wave Characteristics

1. Transverse and longitudinal waves
2. Wavelength, frequency, wave speed
3. Amplitude and intensity
4. Superposition of waves, interference, wave addition
5. Resonance
6. Standing waves (nodes, antinodes)
7. Beat frequencies
8. Refraction and general nature of diffraction

SOUND

Sound waves are longitudinal waves that can travel only in a material medium. The concepts of speed, resonance, and the Doppler effect describe the behavior of sound waves in different media. To answer questions in this topic area, you should understand wave behavior as it specifically applies to sound waves.

1. Production of sound
2. Relative speed of sound in solids, liquids, and gases
3. Intensity of sound (decibel units, log scale)
4. Attenuation
5. Doppler effect (moving sound source or observer, reflection of sound from a moving object)
6. Pitch
7. Resonance in pipes and strings
8. Harmonics
9. Ultrasound

FLUIDS AND SOLIDS

This topic area deals with the physical properties of fluids at rest and the way in which fluids move. Archimedes' principle and Bernoulli's equation describe fluid statics and dynamics, respectively. Analysis of instrumentation and experiments involving fluids are important applications of these concepts. Questions about fluids require you to understand and apply these concepts.

Solids that are subjected to forces can undergo stress and/or strain. Questions about solids require you to analyze the elastic properties of solids and interpret the reactions of solids to stress and strain.

A. Fluids

1. Density, specific gravity
2. Archimedes' principle (buoyancy)
3. Hydrostatic pressure
   a. Pascal's law
   b. pressure versus depth ($P = \rho g h$)

MCAT® is a program of the
Association of American Medical Colleges

4. Poiseuille flow (viscocity)
5. Continuity equation (Av = constant)
6. Concept of turbulence at high velocities
7. Surface tension
8. Bernoulli's equation

B. Solids

1. Density
2. Elastic properties (elementary properties)
3. Elastic limit
4. Thermal expansion coefficient
5. Shear
6. Compression

ELECTROSTATICS AND ELECTROMAGNETISM

When electrically charged objects interact, their behavior can be described in terms of charge, electric force, electric field, and potential difference. Questions on electrostatics require you to interpret the electrostatic properties of a particular situation.

The motions of charged particles are affected by magnetic fields. The characteristics of the magnetic field determine the specifics of this movement. Electromagnetic waves are generated by accelerating electric charges and do not need a medium for propagation. The spectrum of electromagnetic waves includes a wide range of waves, including light and X-rays. Questions on electromagnetism require you to interpret the ways that magnetic fields act upon charged particles.

A. Electrostatics

1. Charges, conductors, charge conservation
2. Insulators
3. Coulomb's law ($F = kq_1q_2/r^2$, sign conventions)
4. Electric field
   a. field lines
   b. field due to charge distribution
5. Potential difference, absolute potential at point in space
6. Equipotential lines
7. Electric dipole
   a. definition of dipole
   b. behavior in electric field
   c. potential due to dipole
8. Electrostatic induction
9. Gauss's law

B. Magnetism

1. Definition of the magnetic field **B**
2. Existence and direction of force on charge moving in magnetic field

C. Electromagnetic Radiation (Light)

1. Properties of electromagnetic radiation (general properties only)
   a. radiation velocity equals constant c in vacuo
   b. radiation consists of oscillating electric and magnetic fields that are mutually perpendicular to each other and to the propagation direction
2. Classification of electromagnetic spectrum (radio, infrared, UV, X-rays, etc.)

ELECTRONIC CIRCUIT ELEMENTS

To understand the workings of electric circuits, you must analyze the current through and the voltage across electric circuit elements wired in a variety of configurations. When batteries or other power supplies are wired to resistors and capacitors in parallel or series, the application of Ohm's law interprets how the current and voltage vary. Questions in this topic area require you to understand the motion of current through various circuits.

A. Circuit Elements

1. Current ($I = \Delta Q / \Delta t$, sign conventions, units)
2. Battery, electromotive force, voltage
3. Terminal potential, internal resistance of battery
4. Resistance
   a. Ohm's law ($I = V/R$)
   b. resistors in series
   c. resistors in parallel
   d. resistivity ($\rho = RA/L$)
5. Capacitance
   a. concept of parallel-plate capacitor
   b. energy of charged capacitor
   c. capacitors in series
   d. capacitors in parallel
   e. dielectrics
6. Discharge of a capacitor through a resistor
7. Conductivity theory

B. Circuits

1. Power in circuits ($P = VI$, $P = I^2R$)

Second Edition
The Official Guide to the MCAT® Exam

MCAT® is a program of the
Association of American Medical Colleges

C. Alternating Currents and Reactive Circuits

1. Root-mean-square current
2. Root-mean-square voltage

LIGHT AND GEOMETRICAL OPTICS

Optical devices can be used to modify the appearance of light. The concepts of reflection and refraction describe the behavior of light as it encounters these devices. The nature of light and the way it behaves when traveling through different media are also important in understanding the behavior of light. To answer questions in this topic area, you will need to understand the interaction of light with mirrors and lenses in various media.

A. Light (Electromagnetic Radiation)

1. Concept of interference, Young's double-slit experiment
2. Thin films, diffraction grating, single-slit diffraction
3. Other diffraction phenomena, X-ray diffraction
4. Polarization of light
5. Doppler effect (moving light source or observer)
6. Visual spectrum, color
   a. energy
   b. lasers

B. Geometrical Optics

1. Reflection from plane surface (angle of incidence equals angle of reflection)
2. Refraction, refractive index n, Snell's law ($n_1\sin\theta_1 = n_2\sin\theta_2$)
3. Dispersion (change of index of refraction with wavelength)
4. Conditions for total internal reflection
5. Spherical mirrors
   a. mirror curvature, radius, focal length
   b. use of formula $(1/p) + (1/q) = 1/f$ with sign conventions
   c. real and virtual images
6. Thin lenses
   a. converging and diverging lenses, focal length
   b. use of formula $(1/p) + (1/q) = 1/f$ with sign conventions
   c. real and virtual images
   d. lens strength, diopters
   e. lens aberration
7. Combination of lenses
8. Ray tracing
9. Optical instruments

The internal structure of the atom can be described as a nucleus orbited by electrons in different energy levels. The components of the nucleus and the transitions of electrons between energy levels are important aspects of the physical description of the atom. Questions in this topic area require you to understand the characteristics of these atomic components.

A. Atomic Structure and Spectra

1. Emission spectrum of hydrogen (Bohr model)
2. Atomic energy levels
   a. quantized energy levels for electrons
   b. calculation of energy emitted or absorbed when an electron changes energy levels

B. Atomic Nucleus

1. Atomic number, atomic weight
2. Neutrons, protons, isotopes
3. Nuclear forces
4. Radioactive decay (α, β, γ, half-life, stability, exponential decay, semilog plots)
5. General nature of fission
6. General nature of fusion
7. Mass deficit, energy liberated, binding energy

IV. Cognitive Skills Assessed

Because the Physical and Biological Sciences sections are designed to test both your background knowledge in the sciences and your ability to reason scientifically, it is useful for you to have a general sense of the cognitive skills you will be asked to demonstrate. The questions in these sections require you to apply skills from one or more of the following primary cognitive categories*:

The Biological Sciences section assesses the same cognitive skills as does the Physical Sciences section.

A. **Identification of Main Ideas**
B. **Identification of Components in a Situation and Relationships Among Them**
C. **Seeking Clarification**
D. **Hypothesis Testing**
E. **Evaluation Processes**
F. **Flexibility and Adaptability in Scientific Reasoning**
G. **Reasoning Using Quantitative Data**

Cognitive Skill Identified in Practice Questions

In addition to content area, each practice question (that follows later in this chapter) will name the cognitive skill(s) it tests.

Questions from the first three categories—*Identification of Main Ideas, Identification of Components in a Situation and Relationships Among Them,* and *Seeking Clarification*—generally focus on relatively simple identifications and applications of basic concepts regarding the presented information and relevant background knowledge. The remaining four categories—*Hypothesis Testing, Evaluation Processes, Flexibility and Adaptability in Scientific Reasoning,* and *Reasoning Using Quantitative Data*—involve more in-depth analyses of scientific concepts and often require combining background knowledge with the presented information to arrive at an answer.

Many of the following descriptions of the cognitive categories refer to information presented in a science passage; the same descriptions also apply to information that is presented in the text of a question itself. On the actual MCAT exam, any reference to "the passage" in a question indicates that you would either (a) find information in the accompanying passage that would help you answer the question or (b) base your answer on a general understanding of the information or perspective that is presented in the passage.

*Although each question receives a single cognitive classification, an individual question may sometimes call on you to use more than one cognitive skill.

A. Identification of Main Ideas

Questions in this category refer to the main idea of a passage or other major points that are explicitly or implicitly made in the passage. These questions ask for the simple identification or interpretation of material rather than in-depth analysis or evaluation. Questions often require you to demonstrate understanding of the material by identifying any of the following:

- The general purpose of a research study
- Key differences among viewpoints
- Major points or arguments
- A major problem not specifically mentioned in the passage
- Alternate ways of representing material from the passage

B. Identification of Components of a Situation and Relationships Among Them

Questions in this category refer to specific pieces of information that are important for understanding the passage. The questions test your ability to identify these components or variables and to determine basic relationships among them and may require you to incorporate pertinent background knowledge. The components and variables typical of this category include the following:

- Hypotheses
- Assumptions
- Relevant issues
- Conclusions
- Supporting evidence
- Rationales
- Experimental variables

C. Seeking Clarification

Questions in this category ask for a closer definition of material in the passage or for background information that clarifies a particular scientific concept. You may be asked to provide additional information that is relevant to concepts presented in the passage or to concepts presented within the question itself. Questions typical of this category include those that require you to do the following:

- Identify relevant background information
- Translate presented information into a more understandable or useful form
- Identify appropriate clarifying information

MCAT® is a program of the
Association of American Medical Colleges

D. Hypothesis Testing

Questions in this category test, relate, or extend the hypotheses or assumptions presented in the passage or require the development of new hypotheses. These questions tend to focus on assumptions from the passage, rather than pre-drawn conclusions, and may ask you to do the following:

- Predict a result on the basis of background knowledge and specific facts about a situation
- Form a hypothesis to explain a particular scientific phenomenon
- Identify plausible alternative hypotheses or solutions
- Design an experiment to test a hypothesis according to appropriate criteria (e.g., data-collection procedures, control of variables, relevance to the hypothesis)
- Determine the likely cause of a particular event or result
- Combine steps in a research design in an appropriate sequence to test a hypothesis

E. Evaluation Processes

Questions in this category evaluate scientific data, procedures, conclusions, evidence, or perspectives. You are often required to make some sort of judgment based on generally accepted scientific criteria. These questions may or may not require the use of background knowledge. Questions in this category include those that ask you to do the following:

- Judge whether a conclusion follows necessarily from a given set of premises
- Appraise the rationale for a procedure or generalization
- Judge whether a conclusion is justified by the evidence
- Judge the credibility of given information or evidence
- Determine whether a product, argument, or perspective is acceptable on the basis of specific given criteria (e.g., whether it fulfills task requirements, fully resolves all relevant aspects of a problem, fits available data)

F. Flexibility and Adaptability in Scientific Reasoning

Questions in this category require the extension of concepts presented or implied in the passage and often ask you to apply the given information or your background knowledge to unfamiliar situations. Typical questions in this category ask you to do the following:

- Use given information to solve a problem
- Arrive at a conclusion based on the evidence
- Determine the implications of results for real-world situations
- Develop a general theory or model based on the given information
- Determine how a conclusion can be modified to be consistent with additional information
- Recognize methods, results, or evidence that would challenge or invalidate a hypothesis, model, or theory

G. Reasoning Using Quantitative Data

Questions in this category involve the interpretation of a graph, table, or figure or the manipulation of data found therein. Typical questions include those that require you to do the following:

- Understand basic principles and methods used in the presentation of data
- Explain, describe, identify, or compare components of graphs, charts, figures, diagrams, and tables
- Identify background knowledge relevant to an interpretation of graphs, charts, figures, diagrams, and tables
- Select the most appropriate format for representing data or other information
- Discern trends in data
- Identify relationships inherent in data

Now that we have discussed the format of the PS section, the types of passages it includes, and the content and cognitive skills it tests, we have asked the authors of the exam to select and describe for you some passages and questions from real MCAT exams.

We now move on to practice passages and questions, all of which have appeared on real MCAT exams and were chosen to represent a variety of the content areas and cognitive skills we have just described in this chapter. The format of this section is summarized below.

1. First, we will provide you with "**passage sets**." Each set includes a passage and questions related to it.

2. We next analyze each passage-based question by providing:

   > **Hint:** As you work your way through the material that follows, take note if the questions you miss tend to fall into one particular type of cognitive classification.

   • a detailed explanation of the correct answer along with any thought processes and/or specific content knowledge necessary to answer correctly.

   • explanations as to why the distractors are incorrect.

   • the relevant cognitive classification and the appropriate content classification (or classifications) corresponding to the content outline included earlier in this chapter.

   • the difficulty level of each question, which we have labeled as easy, medium, or hard, as judged by the percentage of examinees who answered it correctly on an actual MCAT administration. (See box at right.)

Difficulty level: % of examinees choosing the correct answer*	
Easy	71–90
Medium	41–70
Hard	20–40

   *In this guide, figures have been rounded to the nearest 5%. Please note, as well, that the mix of questions by difficulty level in this guide does not represent the mix on the actual exam.

3. Toward the end of this section, we also include several discrete questions so you can become familiar with this format of testing, as well. (Just as with the passage-based questions, we explain the correct answer, analyze the distractors, identify the cognitive and content classifications, and provide the difficulty level.)

4. Finally, we provide "tip boxes"—for both passage-based and discrete questions—to offer you insights about reading the passages, broad approaches to answering certain styles of questions, specific phrases that suggest an approach to a question, and general points relating to the content covered on the exam.

We have diagrammed a sample question on the following page, in which we pull out the points above, for further clarification.

1. If the CO_2 partial pressure above the carbonated water is 4 atm in the closed can, this pressure, in kilopascals, is equal to which of the following?

A. 40.53 kPa
B. 304.0 kPa
C. 405.3 kPa
D. 3040 kPa

Points out where this question falls within the Content Outline

Identifies the cognitive classification

Content Classification: Phases and Phase Equilibria/Gas Phase

Cognitive Classification: Flexibility and Adaptability in Scientific Reasoning

This question requires you to solve a problem using the given information and your background knowledge. The information given is the partial pressure in atmospheres (atm), and the background knowledge required is the atm-to-kPa unit conversion factor. Since 1 atm is equal to 101.325 kPa, 4 atm is equal to 405.3 kPa.

 Incorrect understanding of the relationships between different pressure units and/or being off by a factor of 10 will lead to the wrong answers in this question.

Key: C

The value is correct.

Analyzes the correct answer… and explains why the wrong ones are wrong.

Distractors

Tells of a common oversight or error students might make

A   Thinking that 1 atm is equal to 10.1325 kPa will lead to this answer.

B   Not only is 1 atm equal to 101.325 kPa, but it is also equal to 760 mmHg. Thinking that 1 atm is equal to 76 kPa will lead to this answer.

D   Not only is 1 atm equal to 101.325 kPa, but it is also equal to 760 mmHg. Thinking that 1 atm is equal to 760 kPa will lead to this answer.

Difficulty Level: Medium (55%)

Describes the difficulty level by disclosing the approximate percentage of examinees who answered correctly

Sample Question and Solution

General Chemistry

Passage Set I

General Chemistry

(Passage Format: Persuasive Argument)

Carbonated water is water with CO_2 gas dissolved in it under pressure.

Two students offer their points of view on why fizzing occurs when a closed can of carbonated water equilibrated to 3°C in a refrigerator is taken out and immediately opened in a room at 25°C.

Student 1

In the closed can, an equilibrium exists between the CO_2 that is dissolved in the carbonated water and the CO_2 in the space above the carbonated water. Opening the can causes the CO_2 partial pressure above the carbonated water to decrease, disturbing this equilibrium. Therefore, some of the dissolved gas bubbles out of the carbonated water as the system tries to reattain equilibrium.

Student 2

When the can is opened, the temperature of the carbonated water increases as a result of a drop in the CO_2 partial pressure above the carbonated water. Because CO_2 is a gas, its solubility in water decreases as the temperature increases. Therefore, some of the dissolved CO_2 bubbles out of the carbonated water.

MCAT® is a program of the
Association of American Medical Colleges

1. If the CO_2 partial pressure above the carbonated water is 4 atm in the closed can, this pressure, in kilopascals, is equal to which of the following?

    A. 40.53 kPa
    B. 304.0 kPa
    C. 405.3 kPa
    D. 3040 kPa

2. Which of the following would be best concluded about the relationship between the solubility of a gas (S_{gas}) and the partial pressure of the gas (P_{gas}) above the solution from Student 1's point of view, and about the sign of the heat of solution (ΔH_{soln}) of CO_2 in water from Student 2's point of view?

    A. $S_{gas} \propto P_{gas}$; $-\Delta H_{soln}$
    B. $S_{gas} \propto 1/P_{gas}$; $-\Delta H_{soln}$
    C. $S_{gas} \propto P_{gas}$; $+\Delta H_{soln}$
    D. $S_{gas} \propto 1/P_{gas}$; $+\Delta H_{soln}$

3. Which, if either, of the species H_3O^+ and HCO_3^- would be present in carbonated water?

    A. H_3O^+ only
    B. HCO_3^- only
    C. Both H_3O^+ and HCO_3^-
    D. Neither H_3O^+ nor HCO_3^-

4. A panel of scientists accepts that the equilibrium in the closed can described by Student 1 does exist and also that the CO_2 partial pressure above the carbonated water does decrease upon opening the can. Which of the following objections, if any, will the panel have in regard to the rest of Student 1's point of view?

    A. The decrease in the CO_2 partial pressure above the carbonated water does not disturb the equilibrium.
    B. When a chemical system at equilibrium is disturbed, it does not try to reattain equilibrium.
    C. The disturbance of the equilibrium by the decrease in the CO_2 partial pressure above the carbonated water causes more CO_2 to dissolve in the carbonated water, and, therefore, bubbles form.
    D. The panel will have no objection.

Solutions for this passage begin on next page.

1. If the CO_2 partial pressure above the carbonated water is 4 atm in the closed can, this pressure, in kilopascals, is equal to which of the following?

    A. 40.53 kPa
    B. 304.0 kPa
    C. 405.3 kPa
    D. 3040 kPa

Content Classification: Phases and Phase Equilibria/Gas Phase

Cognitive Classification: Flexibility and Adaptability in Scientific Reasoning

This question requires you to solve a problem using the given information and your background knowledge. The information given is the partial pressure in atmospheres (atm), and the background knowledge required is the atm-to-kPa unit conversion factor. Since 1 atm is equal to 101.325 kPa, 4 atm is equal to 405.3 kPa.

 Incorrect understanding of the relationships between different pressure units and/or being off by a factor of 10 will lead to the wrong answers to this question.

Key: C

The value is correct.

Distractors

A   Thinking that 1 atm is equal to 10.1325 kPa will lead to this answer.

B   Not only is 1 atm equal to 101.325 kPa, but it is also equal to 760 mmHg. Thinking that 1 atm is equal to 76 kPa will lead to this answer.

D   Not only is 1 atm equal to 101.325 kPa, but it is also equal to 760 mmHg. Thinking that 1 atm is equal to 760 kPa will lead to this answer.

Difficulty Level: Medium (55%)

2. Which of the following would be best concluded about the relationship between the solubility of a gas (S_{gas}) and the partial pressure of the gas (P_{gas}) above the solution from Student 1's point of view, and about the sign of the heat of solution (ΔH_{soln}) of CO_2 in water from Student 2's point of view?

A. $S_{gas} \propto P_{gas}$; $-\Delta H_{soln}$
B. $S_{gas} \propto 1/P_{gas}$; $-\Delta H_{soln}$
C. $S_{gas} \propto P_{gas}$; $+\Delta H_{soln}$
D. $S_{gas} \propto 1/P_{gas}$; $+\Delta H_{soln}$

Content Classifications: Phases and Phase Equilibria/Gas Phase; Thermodynamics and Thermochemistry/Energy Changes in Chemical Reactions: Thermochemistry

Cognitive Classification: Identification of Components of a Situation and Relationships Among Them

This question requires you to identify conclusions from the two points of view. Student 1 says that the equilibrium is disturbed by the decrease in the CO_2 partial pressure above the carbonated water and that, therefore, some of the dissolved CO_2 bubbles out of the carbonated water. It would be best concluded from this view that as P_{gas} decreases, S_{gas} decreases, and thus S_{gas} is directly proportional to P_{gas}. Student 2 says that the solubility of CO_2 in water decreases as the temperature increases. It would be best concluded from this statement that the process of dissolving CO_2 in water is exothermic ($\Delta H_{soln} < 0$).

 The topic of Henry's law is acceptable background knowledge. However, based on the passage information itself, it can be easily concluded that S_{gas} is directly proportional to P_{gas}, which eliminates B and D as the key.

Key: A

S_{gas} is directly proportional to P_{gas}, and the sign of ΔH_{soln} is negative. Thus, both conclusions are correct.

Distractors

B S_{gas} is inversely proportional to P_{gas}, and the sign of ΔH_{soln} is negative. Thus, only one conclusion is correct.

C S_{gas} is directly proportional to P_{gas}, and the sign of ΔH_{soln} is positive. Thus, only one conclusion is correct.

D S_{gas} is inversely proportional to P_{gas}, and the sign of ΔH_{soln} is positive. Thus, both conclusions are incorrect.

Difficulty Level: Hard (35%)

3.   Which, if either, of the species H_3O^+ and HCO_3^- would be present in carbonated water?

   A. H_3O^+ only
   B. HCO_3^- only
   C.   Both H_3O^+ and HCO_3^-
   D.   Neither H_3O^+ nor HCO_3^-

Content Classification: Acids and Bases/Acid–Base Equilibria

Cognitive Classification: Hypothesis Testing

This question requires you to predict a result on the basis of background knowledge. The background knowledge needed to answer this question is that in carbonated water, a small fraction of the dissolved CO_2 reacts with water to form the weak acid H_2CO_3, which dissociates in water to produce H_3O^+ and HCO_3^-.

To eliminate **B** and **D** as the key, simply recall that pure water also contains some H_3O^+ as a result of autoionization.

Key: C

Both species are said to be present.

Distractors

A   Only H_3O^+ is said to be present.

B   Only HCO_3^- is said to be present.

D   Neither species is said to be present.

Difficulty Level: Medium (65%)

4.   A panel of scientists accepts that the equilibrium in the closed can described by Student 1 does exist and also that the CO_2 partial pressure above the carbonated water does decrease upon opening the can. Which of the following objections, if any, will the panel have in regard to the rest of Student 1's point of view?

 A. The decrease in the CO_2 partial pressure above the carbonated water does not disturb the equilibrium.
 B. When a chemical system at equilibrium is disturbed, it does not try to reattain equilibrium.
 C. The disturbance of the equilibrium by the decrease in the CO_2 partial pressure above the carbonated water causes more CO_2 to dissolve in the carbonated water, and, therefore, bubbles form.
 D. The panel will have no objection.

Content Classification: Rate Processes in Chemical Reactions: Kinetics and Equilibrium/Equilibrium in Reversible Chemical Reactions

Cognitive Classification: Flexibility and Adaptability in Scientific Reasoning

This question requires you to recognize evidence that would challenge a model. According to Le Châtelier's principle, when a chemical system at equilibrium is disturbed, it tries to reattain equilibrium by undergoing a net reaction that reduces the effect of the disturbance.

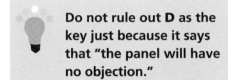

Do not rule out **D** as the key just because it says that "the panel will have no objection."

Key: D

No objection will be raised by the panel because Student 1's point of view is consistent with Le Châtelier's principle.

Distractors

A Since CO_2 in the space above the carbonated water is part of the equilibrium, the decrease in the CO_2 partial pressure above the carbonated water does disturb the equilibrium.

B When a chemical system at equilibrium is disturbed, it tries to reattain equilibrium.

C If the equilibrium is disturbed by the decrease in the CO_2 partial pressure above the carbonated water, the effect of the disturbance is reduced by some of the dissolved CO_2 bubbling out of the carbonated water and not by the dissolution of more CO_2 in the carbonated water.

Difficulty Level: Medium (60%)

General Chemistry
Passage Set II

General Chemistry

(Passage Format: Information Presentation)

Suspended solid particles in water can be removed by adding $Al_2(SO_4)_3$ and $Ca(OH)_2$, which leads to the formation of a gelatinous precipitate of $Al(OH)_3$. As this precipitate settles by gravity, it traps and removes the suspended solid particles. $Al(OH)_3$ is much more soluble in an acidic or a basic solution than in water.

$Ca(OH)_2$ (slaked lime) is also used in conjunction with Na_2CO_3 (soda ash) in the lime–soda process for water softening. In this process, the ions that are responsible for making water hard, such as Mg^{2+}, Ca^{2+}, and Fe^{2+}, are removed as $Mg(OH)_2$, $CaCO_3$, and $Fe(OH)_2$, respectively.

Table 1 gives the K_{sp} values at 25°C of the compounds mentioned herein.

Table 1 K_{sp} Values at 25°C

Compound	K_{sp}
$Ca(OH)_2$	6.5×10^{-6}
$CaCO_3$	3.3×10^{-9}
$Mg(OH)_2$	6.3×10^{-10}
$Fe(OH)_2$	4.1×10^{-15}
$Al(OH)_3$	3.0×10^{-34}

The energy required to separate 1 mole of an ionic compound in the solid state into gaseous component ions is equal in magnitude but opposite in sign to the compound's lattice energy, and is important in determining the heat of solution (ΔH_{soln}) of the compound in water. When two ionic compounds have a common anion but have different cations of the same charge, the compound with the cation that is larger in size has the smaller magnitude of lattice energy. Among Ca^{2+}, Mg^{2+}, and Fe^{2+}, Ca^{2+} has the largest and Fe^{2+} has the smallest ionic radius.

MCAT® is a program of the
Association of American Medical Colleges

5. Which hydroxide listed in Table 1 is neither an alkaline earth metal hydroxide nor a transition metal hydroxide?

   A. $Ca(OH)_2$
   B. $Mg(OH)_2$
   C. $Fe(OH)_2$
   D. $Al(OH)_3$

6. Based on the passage, the molar solubility (S) of $CaCO_3$ at 25°C would be closest to which of the following?

   A. 5.5×10^{-5} M
   B. 6.5×10^{-9} M
   C. 1.5×10^{-9} M
   D. 1.0×10^{-17} M

7. Mg and Al are both period 3 elements. How do Mg^{2+} and Al^{3+} compare in terms of their ionic radius and charge density? Mg^{2+} has a:

   A. larger ionic radius and a higher charge density than does Al^{3+}.
   B. larger ionic radius and a lower charge density than does Al^{3+}.
   C. smaller ionic radius and a higher charge density than does Al^{3+}.
   D. smaller ionic radius and a lower charge density than does Al^{3+}.

8. On the basis of the passage, can any conclusion be drawn about how the K_{sp} at 25°C varies with the magnitude of lattice energy among $Ca(OH)_2$, $Mg(OH)_2$, and $Fe(OH)_2$?

   A. No; the information in the passage is insufficient to determine which one of the three compounds has the greatest and which one has the smallest magnitude of lattice energy.
   B. Yes; the greater the magnitude of lattice energy, the smaller the K_{sp}.
   C. Yes; the greater the magnitude of lattice energy, the larger the K_{sp}.
   D. Yes; as the magnitude of lattice energy becomes greater, the K_{sp} does not exhibit a trend.

9. Based on the passage, the ranking of saturated aqueous solutions of $Ca(OH)_2$, $Mg(OH)_2$, and $Fe(OH)_2$ at 25°C in order of decreasing pH would be:

   A. $Fe(OH)_2 > Ca(OH)_2 > Mg(OH)_2$.
   B. $Fe(OH)_2 > Mg(OH)_2 > Ca(OH)_2$.
   C. $Ca(OH)_2 > Mg(OH)_2 > Fe(OH)_2$.
   D. $Ca(OH)_2 > Fe(OH)_2 > Mg(OH)_2$.

Solutions for this passage begin on next page.

5.   Which hydroxide listed in Table 1 is neither an alkaline earth metal hydroxide nor a transition metal hydroxide?

   A. $Ca(OH)_2$
   B. $Mg(OH)_2$
   C. $Fe(OH)_2$
   D. $Al(OH)_3$

Content Classification: Electronic Structure and Periodic Table/The Periodic Table: Classification of Elements into Groups by Electronic Structure; Physical and Chemical Properties of Elements

Cognitive Classification: Reasoning Using Quantitative Data

This question requires you to identify the components of the periodic table. The metals in group 2 of the periodic table are designated as alkaline earth metals, and the metals that are in groups 3–12 in the main body of the periodic table are designated as transition metals.

Key: D

Al is neither an alkaline earth metal nor a transition metal.

Distractors

A   Ca is an alkaline earth metal.

B   Mg is an alkaline earth metal.

C   Fe is a transition metal.

Difficulty Level: Easy (85%)

6.   Based on the passage, the molar solubility (S) of $CaCO_3$ at 25°C would be closest to which of the following?

   A. 5.5×10^{-5} M
   B. 6.5×10^{-9} M
   C. 1.5×10^{-9} M
   D. 1.0×10^{-17} M

Content Classification: Solution Chemistry/Solubility

Cognitive Classification: Reasoning Using Quantitative Data

This question requires you to identify the relationships inherent in data. The K_{sp} of $CaCO_3$ at 25°C is related to the S of $CaCO_3$ at 25°C. For an ionic compound whose formula unit contains one cation unit and one anion unit of an equal and opposite charge, S is equal to the square root of K_{sp}.

 Recall that the square root of 10^x is $10^{x/2}$ and the square of 10^x is 10^{2x}.

Key: A

The value is closest to the square root of K_{sp}.

Distractors

B   The value is closest to K_{sp} multiplied by 2.

C   The value is closest to K_{sp} divided by 2.

D   The value is closest to the square of K_{sp}.

Difficulty Level: Hard (35%)

7. Mg and Al are both period 3 elements. How do Mg^{2+} and Al^{3+} compare in terms of their ionic radius and charge density? Mg^{2+} has a:

  A. larger ionic radius and a higher charge density than does Al^{3+}.
  B. larger ionic radius and a lower charge density than does Al^{3+}.
  C. smaller ionic radius and a higher charge density than does Al^{3+}.
  D. smaller ionic radius and a lower charge density than does Al^{3+}.

Content Classification: Electronic Structure and Periodic Table/The Periodic Table: Variations of Chemical Properties with Group and Row

Cognitive Classification: Seeking Clarification

This question requires you to identify relevant background information, which consists of periodic trends in atomic radius. Going from left to right across a period, atomic radius generally decreases. Both Mg and Al are in period 3, and Mg has a larger atomic radius than Al. Mg loses two electrons per atom in forming Mg^{2+}, and Al loses three electrons per atom in forming Al^{3+}. Thus, Mg^{2+} has a larger ionic radius than Al^{3+}. Because Mg^{2+} has a larger ionic radius and a lower ionic charge than Al^{3+}, it has a lower charge density than Al^{3+}.

Key: B

Mg^{2+} has a larger ionic radius and a lower charge density than does Al^{3+}.

Distractors

A The comparison is correct in terms of ionic radius but incorrect in terms of charge density.

C The comparison is incorrect in terms of ionic radius and charge density.

D The comparison is correct in terms of charge density but incorrect in terms of ionic radius.

Difficulty Level: Medium (65%)

MCAT® is a program of the
Association of American Medical Colleges

8. On the basis of the passage, can any conclusion be drawn about how the K_{sp} at 25°C varies with the magnitude of lattice energy among $Ca(OH)_2$, $Mg(OH)_2$, and $Fe(OH)_2$?

    A. No; the information in the passage is insufficient to determine which one of the three compounds has the greatest and which one has the smallest magnitude of lattice energy.
    B. Yes; the greater the magnitude of lattice energy, the smaller the K_{sp}.
    C. Yes; the greater the magnitude of lattice energy, the larger the K_{sp}.
    D. Yes; as the magnitude of lattice energy becomes greater, the K_{sp} does not exhibit a trend.

Content Classifications: Solution Chemistry/Solubility; Bonding/The Ionic Bond

Cognitive Classification: Evaluation Processes

This question requires you to judge whether a conclusion follows necessarily from given premises. The passage gives information to determine that among the compounds under consideration, $Ca(OH)_2$ has the smallest and $Fe(OH)_2$ has the greatest magnitude of lattice energy. According to Table 1, among these three compounds, $Ca(OH)_2$ has the largest and $Fe(OH)_2$ has the smallest K_{sp}.

Key: B

It can be concluded that the greater the magnitude of lattice energy, the smaller the K_{sp} (10^{-15} is smaller than 10^{-6}).

Distractors

A   The information in the passage is sufficient to determine which one of the three compounds has the greatest and which one has the smallest magnitude of lattice energy.

C   Thinking that 10^{-6} is smaller than 10^{-15} will lead to this answer.

D   As the magnitude of lattice energy becomes greater, the K_{sp} does exhibit a trend.

Difficulty Level: Medium (65%)

9. Based on the passage, the ranking of saturated aqueous solutions of $Ca(OH)_2$, $Mg(OH)_2$, and $Fe(OH)_2$ at 25°C in order of decreasing pH would be:

A. $Fe(OH)_2 > Ca(OH)_2 > Mg(OH)_2$.
B. $Fe(OH)_2 > Mg(OH)_2 > Ca(OH)_2$.
C. $Ca(OH)_2 > Mg(OH)_2 > Fe(OH)_2$.
D. $Ca(OH)_2 > Fe(OH)_2 > Mg(OH)_2$.

Content Classifications: Solution Chemistry/Solubility; Acids and Bases/Acid–Base Equilibria

Cognitive Classification: Flexibility and Adaptability in Scientific Reasoning

The question requires you to develop a general theory based on given information. All three compounds mentioned have the same general formula: $M(OH)_2$. Because the molar solubility, S, for each is related to the K_{sp} values as $K_{sp} = 4S^3$, we can make direct comparisons without computation. As K_{sp} values increase, S increases, [OH-] of a saturated solution increases, and so does the pH (of a saturated solution). Look at the K_{sp} values to make the necessary comparisons. From Table 1, we find ranking for K_{sp} is $Ca(OH)_2 > Mg(OH)_2 > Fe(OH)_2$, and this is also the ranking by pH for saturated solutions of each.

 According to Table 1, the K_{sp} at 25°C of $Mg(OH)_2$ is smaller than that of $Ca(OH)_2$ and larger than that of $Fe(OH)_2$. This is a good indicator that in the key, $Mg(OH)_2$ would be placed in the middle.

Key: C

The ranking is in order of decreasing pH.

Distractors

A   The placement of all three compounds is incorrect.

B   The ranking is in order of increasing pH.

D   The placement of $Mg(OH)_2$ and $Fe(OH)_2$ is incorrect.

Difficulty Level: Medium (60%)

General Chemistry

Passage Set III

General Chemistry

A student prepared acetylsalicylic acid (molecular formula $C_9H_8O_4$, molar mass 180 g/mol) from salicylic acid (molecular formula $C_7H_6O_3$, molar mass 138 g/mol) and acetic anhydride (molecular formula $C_4H_6O_3$, molar mass 102 g/mol) according to Reaction 1, which was catalyzed by H_3PO_4 (85% w/w aqueous H_3PO_4).

$$C_7H_6O_3 + C_4H_6O_3 \rightarrow C_9H_8O_4 + C_2H_4O_2$$

Reaction 1

The other product of the reaction was acetic acid (molecular formula $C_2H_4O_2$, molar mass 60.0 g/mol). The student started the reaction with 3.0 g of salicylic acid and 6.5 g of acetic anhydride, and ended up isolating 2.0 g of pure acetylsalicylic acid from the reaction.

The student then determined the percent yield of acetylsalicylic acid in the reaction.

10. Which of the following compounds discussed in the passage has the lowest mass percent of carbon?

   A. Salicylic acid
   B. Acetic anhydride
   C. Acetylsalicylic acid
   D. Acetic acid

11. The molar mass of H_3PO_4 is closest to the molar mass of which of the other compounds discussed in the passage?

   A. Salicylic acid
   B. Acetic anhydride
   C. Acetylsalicylic acid
   D. Acetic acid

12. Based on the passage, the limiting reactant in the reaction was:

   A. salicylic acid, because the amount of it used in the reaction was stoichiometrically smaller.
   B. acetic anhydride, because the amount of it used in the reaction was stoichiometrically greater.
   C. salicylic acid, because the amount of it used in the reaction was stoichiometrically greater.
   D. acetic anhydride, because the amount of it used in the reaction was stoichiometrically smaller.

13. Which of the following compounds discussed in the passage has an empirical formula different from its molecular formula?

   A. Salicylic acid
   B. Acetic anhydride
   C. Acetylsalicylic acid
   D. Acetic acid

Solutions for this passage begin on next page.

10. Which of the following compounds discussed in the passage has the lowest mass percent of carbon?

    A. Salicylic acid
    B. Acetic anhydride
    C. Acetylsalicylic acid
    D. Acetic acid

Content Classification:
Stoichiometry/Description of
Composition by Percent Mass

Cognitive Classification: Identification of
Components of a Situation and Relationships Among Them

This question requires you to identify
relevant issues. The passage provides the
molecular formula and molar mass of
each of the four compounds under
consideration. The mass percent of carbon
in each compound is calculated as follows:

 It is not necessary to calculate exact mass percents to answer this question. For example, using 140 g/mol for the molar mass of salicylic acid instead of 138 g/mol makes the calculation easy and gives an answer of 60.0%, which is sufficient to eliminate **A** as the key. One can easily estimate the carbon mass percent in acetylsalicylic acid as >50% in a similar manner (108 is more than half of 180). It can be determined that acetic anhydride has a lower carbon mass percent than salicylic acid by simply comparing their molecular formulas, which differ only in the carbon's subscript.

$$\frac{\text{carbon's subscript in the molecular formula} \times 12.0\ \text{g} \times 100\%}{\text{mass of 1 mole of compound (g)}}$$

Key: D

The mass percent of carbon in acetic acid is $\dfrac{2 \times 12.0\ \text{g} \times 100\%}{60.0\ \text{g}}$ or 40.0%.

Distractors

A   The mass percent of carbon in salicylic acid is 60.9%.

B   The mass percent of carbon in acetic anhydride is 47.1%.

C   The mass percent of carbon in acetylsalicylic acid is 60.0%.

Difficulty Level: Medium (70%)

MCAT® is a program of the
Association of American Medical Colleges

11. The molar mass of H_3PO_4 is closest to the molar mass of which of the other compounds discussed in the passage?

    A. Salicylic acid
    B. Acetic anhydride
    C. Acetylsalicylic acid
    D. Acetic acid

Content Classification: Stoichiometry/Molecular Weight

Cognitive Classification: Reasoning Using Quantitative Data

This question requires you to identify relationships inherent in data. The molar mass of H_3PO_4 is 98.0 g/mol, which is closest to the molar mass of acetic anhydride, 102 g/mol.

 Although this question is easy, you need to be careful because the information needed to answer it is not presented in an organized manner such as a table.

Key: B

Acetic anhydride's molar mass is 4 units higher than the molar mass of H_3PO_4.

Distractors

A   Salicylic acid's molar mass is 40 units higher than the molar mass of H_3PO_4.

C   Acetylsalicylic acid's molar mass is 82 units higher than the molar mass of H_3PO_4.

D   Acetic acid's molar mass is 38 units lower than the molar mass of H_3PO_4.

Difficulty Level: Easy (90%)

12. Based on the passage, the limiting reactant in the reaction was:

    A. salicylic acid, because the amount of it used in the reaction was stoichiometrically smaller.
    B. acetic anhydride, because the amount of it used in the reaction was stoichiometrically greater.
    C. salicylic acid, because the amount of it used in the reaction was stoichiometrically greater.
    D. acetic anhydride, because the amount of it used in the reaction was stoichiometrically smaller.

Content Classification: Stoichiometry/Description of Reactions by Chemical Equations

Cognitive Classification: Seeking Clarification

This question requires you to translate presented information into a more useful form. Stoichiometrically, a 1:1 ratio of the numbers of moles of the reactants is required in Reaction 1. The student used 3.0 g of salicylic acid and about 6.5 g of acetic anhydride in the reaction. Dividing each reactant's mass used by its molar mass gives the number of moles used. The molar mass of acetic anhydride (102 g/mol) is lower than that of salicylic acid (138 g/mol). Thus, the number of moles of acetic anhydride used in the reaction exceeded the number of moles of salicylic acid used. The limiting reactant is the one whose amount used in the reaction is stoichiometrically smaller.

 Exact calculations are not needed to answer this question. Simply recognize that the number obtained by dividing 3 by 138 is smaller than the number obtained by dividing 6.5 by 102.

Key: A

The amount of salicylic acid used in the reaction was stoichiometrically smaller, making it the limiting reactant.

Distractors

B   Thinking that the limiting reactant is the one whose amount used in the reaction is stoichiometrically greater will lead to this answer.

C   Thinking that the amount of salicylic acid used in the reaction was stoichiometrically greater and also that the limiting reactant is the one whose amount used in the reaction is stoichiometrically greater will lead to this answer.

D   Thinking that the amount of acetic anhydride used in the reaction was stoichiometrically smaller will lead to this answer.

Difficulty Level: Medium (70%)

13. Which of the following compounds discussed in the passage has an empirical formula different from its molecular formula?

    A. Salicylic acid
    B. Acetic anhydride
    C. Acetylsalicylic acid
    D. Acetic acid

Content Classification: Stoichiometry/Empirical Formula versus Molecular Formula

Cognitive Classification: Reasoning Using Quantitative Data

This question requires you to identify relationships inherent in data. The molecular formula of a compound shows the actual numbers of atoms of the constituent elements present in one molecule of the compound. The empirical formula of a compound shows the simplest whole-number ratio of the numbers of atoms of the constituent elements present in one molecule of the compound.

Key: D

The empirical formula of acetic acid is CH_2O and is thus different from its molecular formula, $C_2H_4O_2$.

 An empirical formula is most often derived from the molecular formula by dividing it in half. Occasionally it is divided by three, and rarely by four or more. The rigorous method for finding an empirical formula requires finding the greatest common denominator (GCD) for the subscripts.

Distractors

A Salicylic acid's empirical formula is the same as its molecular formula.

B Acetic anhydride's empirical formula is the same as its molecular formula.

C Acetylsalicylic acid's empirical formula is the same as its molecular formula.

Difficulty Level: Easy (80%)

General Chemistry

Passage Set IV

General Chemistry

The steps in the mechanism of an overall reaction are called *elementary reactions*, and they must add up to the overall reaction. For each reactant in an elementary reaction, the coefficient represents the number of particles involved. The molecularity of an elementary reaction is defined by the total number of particles on the reactant side. Most elementary reactions are either unimolecular or bimolecular because the probability of three particles colliding simultaneously with sufficient energy and correct orientation is very low. The rate law for an elementary reaction is expressed mathematically as a rate constant (specific to the reaction) multiplied by the concentrations of each reactant raised to powers equal to their stoichiometric coefficients.

Applying these concepts, the elementary reaction $2A + B \rightarrow 2C$ is termolecular and has the rate law

$$\text{rate} = k_{\text{elementary reaction}}[A]^2[B]$$

The elementary reaction that determines the rate of the overall reaction is called the *rate-determining* elementary reaction. When the rate-determining elementary reaction is the first step in the mechanism, none of its reactants is an intermediate. Thus, its rate law, as is, is identical to the rate law of the overall reaction, with its rate constant (k_1) equal to the rate constant of the overall reaction (k).

For the overall reaction $P + Q \rightarrow R + S$, the proposed mechanism consists of the two sequential elementary reactions shown:

$$2P \rightarrow T + R$$
Elementary reaction 1 (rate-determining)

$$T + Q \rightarrow P + S$$
Elementary reaction 2

(Note: The discussion in the passage applies to balanced elementary reactions.)

14. Based on the passage, in terms of their molecularities, elementary reactions 1 and 2 would be described as:

   A. unimolecular and bimolecular, respectively.
   B. bimolecular and unimolecular, respectively.
   C. both unimolecular.
   D. both bimolecular.

15. In elementary reaction 2, if T is replaced with $NO_3(g)$, Q is replaced with $CO(g)$, P is replaced with $NO_2(g)$, and S is replaced with $CO_2(g)$, the oxidation number of nitrogen will change from:

   A. +6 to +4.
   B. +4 to +6.
   C. +3 to +2.
   D. +2 to +3.

16. The proposed mechanism consisting of elementary reactions 1 and 2 would NOT be invalidated if it is found experimentally that with all else remaining constant, doubling the initial concentration of:

   A. Q doubles the initial rate of the overall reaction.
   B. P doubles the initial rate of the overall reaction.
   C. Q has no effect on the initial rate of the overall reaction.
   D. P has no effect on the initial rate of the overall reaction.

17. In the proposed mechanism, how do elementary reactions 1 and 2 compare in terms of speed and activation energy? Compared to elementary reaction 2, elementary reaction 1 is:

   A. faster and has a lower activation energy.
   B. slower and has a higher activation energy.
   C. faster and has a higher activation energy.
   D. slower and has a lower activation energy.

18. An overall reaction and its experimental rate law are shown.

   $(CH_3)_3CBr(aq) + H_2O(l) \rightarrow (CH_3)_3COH(aq) + H^+(aq) + Br^-(aq)$

   rate $= k[(CH_3)_3CBr]$

   Given that the rate-determining elementary reaction is the first step in the mechanism, this elementary reaction most likely involves which of the following events?

   A. Formation of an ionic bond
   B. Breaking of an ionic bond
   C. Formation of a covalent bond
   D. Breaking of a covalent bond

19. The overall reaction $NO_2(g) + CO(g) \rightarrow NO(g) + CO_2(g)$ has the experimental rate law

   rate $= k[NO_2]^2$

   Consider the mechanism shown for this overall reaction.

   (1) $2NO_2(g) \rightarrow N_2(g) + 2O_2(g)$ (rate-determining)

   (2) $O_2(g) + 2CO(g) \rightarrow 2CO_2(g)$

   (3) $N_2(g) + O_2(g) \rightarrow 2NO(g)$

   Based on the passage, which of the following *weakens* the credibility of this mechanism?

   A. The three elementary reactions in the mechanism do not add up to the overall reaction.
   B. The power of [NO_2] in the experimental rate law of the overall reaction is different from that in the rate law of the rate-determining elementary reaction, which is the first step in the mechanism.
   C. The mechanism involves a termolecular elementary reaction.
   D. The mechanism involves three elementary reactions.

Solutions for this passage begin on next page.

14. Based on the passage, in terms of their molecularities, elementary reactions 1 and 2 would be described as:

    A. unimolecular and bimolecular, respectively.
    B. bimolecular and unimolecular, respectively.
    C. both unimolecular.
    D. both bimolecular.

Content Classification: Rate Processes in Chemical Reactions: Kinetics and Equilibrium/Rate Law, Dependence of Reaction Rate on Concentrations of Reactants

Cognitive Classification: Identification of Main Ideas

This question requires you to identify a major point in the passage. According to the passage, the molecularity of an elementary reaction is defined by the total number of particles on the reactant side.

Key: D

Elementary reaction 1 has only one reactant, and the number of its particles is 2. There are two reactants in elementary reaction 2, and the number of particles of each reactant is 1. Thus, the total number of particles on the reactant side in elementary reaction 2 is 2. Thus, both reactions would be described as bimolecular.

Distractors

A   Elementary reaction 2 is described correctly, but elementary reaction 1 is not.

B   Elementary reaction 1 is described correctly, but elementary reaction 2 is not.

C   Neither elementary reaction 1 nor elementary reaction 2 is described correctly.

Difficulty Level: Medium (60%)

15. In elementary reaction 2, if T is replaced with $NO_3(g)$, Q is replaced with $CO(g)$, P is replaced with $NO_2(g)$, and S is replaced with $CO_2(g)$, the oxidation number of nitrogen will change from:

   A. +6 to +4.
   B. +4 to +6.
   C. +3 to +2.
   D. +2 to +3.

Content Classification: Stoichiometry/Oxidation Number

Cognitive Classification: Flexibility and Adaptability in Scientific Reasoning

This question requires you to solve a problem using the given information and your background knowledge. The given information is essentially the elementary reaction

$$NO_3(g) + CO(g) \rightarrow NO_2(g) + CO_2(g).$$

The background knowledge needed is that the oxidation number of nitrogen in NO_3 (nitrogen trioxide) and in NO_2 (nitrogen dioxide) is +6 and +4, respectively.

 In an oxide with a formula of the type XO_n, the oxidation number of X is not equal to $+n$ but is equal to $+2n$ because the oxidation number of oxygen is –2. When a reaction is shown with a forward arrow ($\rightarrow$), the forward direction is the one that matters.

Key: A

This is the change in the oxidation number of nitrogen in the elementary reaction considered.

Distractors

B   This is the change in the oxidation number of nitrogen in the reverse of the elementary reaction considered.

C   This is the change in the number of oxygen atoms attached to the nitrogen atom in the elementary reaction considered.

D   This is the change in the number of oxygen atoms attached to the nitrogen atom in the reverse of the elementary reaction considered.

Difficulty Level: Easy (85%)

16. The proposed mechanism consisting of elementary reactions 1 and 2 would NOT be invalidated if it is found experimentally that with all else remaining constant, doubling the initial concentration of:

    A. Q doubles the initial rate of the overall reaction.
    B. P doubles the initial rate of the overall reaction.
    C. Q has no effect on the initial rate of the overall reaction.
    D. P has no effect on the initial rate of the overall reaction.

Content Classification: Rate Processes in Chemical Reactions: Kinetics and Equilibrium/Rate Law, Dependence of Reaction Rate on Concentrations of Reactants

Cognitive Classification: Flexibility and Adaptability in Scientific Reasoning

This question requires you to recognize evidence that would invalidate a hypothesis. The first step in the proposed mechanism is the rate-determining elementary reaction. Its rate law is

$$rate = k_1[P]^2$$

Thus, for the proposed mechanism to be consistent with the experimental rate law of the overall reaction, the latter must be shown to be

$$rate = k[P]^2$$

with k_1 equal to k. This rate law means that the overall reaction is second order in P and zero order in Q.

Key: C

If doubling the initial concentration of Q has no effect on the initial rate of the overall reaction, it means the overall reaction is zero order in Q. This experimental finding would not invalidate the proposed mechanism.

Distractors

A   If doubling the initial concentration of Q doubles the initial rate of the overall reaction, it means the overall reaction is first order in Q. This experimental finding would invalidate the proposed mechanism.

B   If doubling the initial concentration of P doubles the initial rate of the overall reaction, it means the overall reaction is first order in P. This experimental finding would invalidate the proposed mechanism.

D   If doubling the initial concentration of P has no effect on the initial rate of the overall reaction, it means the overall reaction is zero order in P. This experimental finding would invalidate the proposed mechanism.

Difficulty Level: Medium (55%)

MCAT® is a program of the
Association of American Medical Colleges

17. In the proposed mechanism, how do elementary reactions 1 and 2 compare in terms of speed and activation energy? Compared to elementary reaction 2, elementary reaction 1 is:

    A. faster and has a lower activation energy.
    B. slower and has a higher activation energy.
    C. faster and has a higher activation energy.
    D. slower and has a lower activation energy.

Content Classification: Rate Processes in Chemical Reactions: Kinetics and Equilibrium/Dependence of Reaction Rate on Temperature

Cognitive Classification: Hypothesis Testing

This question requires you to identify alternative hypotheses. As the elementary reaction that determines the rate of the overall reaction, elementary reaction 1 is slower than elementary reaction 2. According to the Arrhenius equation, the higher the activation energy of a reaction, the slower the reaction. Elementary reaction 1 has a higher activation energy than elementary reaction 2.

Key: B

Elementary reaction 1 is slower than elementary reaction 2, and the activation energy of elementary reaction 1 is higher than that of elementary reaction 2.

Distractors

A   The comparison is incorrect in both the speed and activation energy.

C   Although the comparison is correct in activation energy, it is incorrect in speed.

D   Although the comparison is correct in speed, it is incorrect in activation energy.

Difficulty Level: Easy (80%)

18. An overall reaction and its experimental rate law are shown.

$$(CH_3)_3CBr(aq) + H_2O(l) \rightarrow (CH_3)_3COH(aq) + H^+(aq) + Br^-(aq)$$
$$\text{rate} = k[(CH_3)_3CBr]$$

Given that the rate-determining elementary reaction is the first step in the mechanism, this elementary reaction most likely involves which of the following events?

A. Formation of an ionic bond
B. Breaking of an ionic bond
C. Formation of a covalent bond
D. Breaking of a covalent bond

Content Classifications: Rate Processes in Chemical Reactions: Kinetics and Equilibrium/Rate Law, Dependence of Reaction Rate on Concentrations of Reactants; Bonding/The Covalent Bond

Cognitive Classification: Hypothesis Testing

This question requires you to predict a result on the basis of background knowledge and specific facts about a situation. Because the rate-determining elementary reaction is the first step in the mechanism, its rate law must be

$$\text{rate} = k_1[(CH_3)_3CBr]$$

with k_1 equal to k. Thus, this elementary reaction is unimolecular with $(CH_3)_3CBr$, a covalent compound, as the only reactant. The product of the overall reaction is $(CH_3)_3COH$, indicating that the covalent C–Br bond in $(CH_3)_3CBr$ must break.

 You may recognize the overall reaction as an example of S$_N$1 reactions, which are covered under organic chemistry. Recall that a carbocation is formed in the first step in the mechanism of an S$_N$1 reaction.

Key: D

A covalent bond breaks in the rate-determining elementary reaction.

Distractors

A   The rate-determining elementary reaction does not involve formation of an ionic bond.

B   The rate-determining elementary reaction does not involve breaking of an ionic bond.

C   The rate-determining elementary reaction does not involve formation of a covalent bond.

Difficulty Level: Medium (65%)

19. The overall reaction $NO_2(g) + CO(g) \rightarrow NO(g) + CO_2(g)$ has the experimental rate law

$$rate = k[NO_2]^2$$

Consider the mechanism shown for this overall reaction.

(1) $2NO_2(g) \rightarrow N_2(g) + 2O_2(g)$ (rate-determining)

(2) $O_2(g) + 2CO(g) \rightarrow 2CO_2(g)$

(3) $N_2(g) + O_2(g) \rightarrow 2NO(g)$

Based on the passage, which of the following *weakens* the credibility of this mechanism?

A. The three elementary reactions in the mechanism do not add up to the overall reaction.
B. The power of $[NO_2]$ in the experimental rate law of the overall reaction is different from that in the rate law of the rate-determining elementary reaction, which is the first step in the mechanism.
C. The mechanism involves a termolecular elementary reaction.
D. The mechanism involves three elementary reactions.

Content Classification: Rate Processes in Chemical Reactions: Kinetics and Equilibrium/Rate Law, Dependence of Reaction Rate on Concentrations of Reactants

Cognitive Classification: Evaluation Processes

This question requires you to judge the credibility of information. According to the passage, most elementary reactions are either unimolecular or bimolecular because the probability of three particles colliding simultaneously with sufficient energy and correct orientation is very low.

Key: C

The second step of the mechanism is a termolecular elementary reaction and thus weakens the credibility of the mechanism.

Distractors

A In agreement with the passage, the three elementary reactions in the mechanism do add up to the overall reaction (when each reactant and product has a coefficient of 2, it is canceled throughout).

B In agreement with the passage, the power of $[NO_2]$ is the same in the experimental rate law of the overall reaction and in the rate law of the rate-determining elementary reaction, which is the first step in the mechanism.

D The passage contains no information that would lead one to think that the presence of three elementary reactions in this mechanism weakens its credibility.

Difficulty Level: Hard (30%)

General Chemistry

Passage Set V

General Chemistry

A student was given a flask containing 25.0 mL of an aqueous solution of propanoic acid (CH_3CH_2COOH, pK_a at 25°C = 4.87) of unknown concentration. The student was asked to determine the concentration of this solution by titrating it against a standard 0.10 M aqueous NaOH solution that was placed in a burette. A solution of phenolphthalein indicator was also provided to the student. Phenolphthalein undergoes a colorless-to-pink color change over the pH range 8.20–10.0. The student added 2 drops of the phenolphthalein solution to the propanoic acid solution and titrated it against the NaOH solution. The experimental temperature was 25°C. The student noted that 40.0 mL of the NaOH solution was needed to reach the equivalence point.

MCAT® is a program of the
Association of American Medical Colleges

20. The student determined the concentration of the propanoic acid solution to be closest to:

    A. 0.05 M.
    B. 0.10 M.
    C. 0.15 M.
    D. 0.25 M.

21. Upon the addition of 20.0 mL of the NaOH solution to the flask, which of the following was most likely true of the flask solution?

    A. Its pH was less than 7.00.
    B. Its color was pink.
    C. In it, $[CH_3CH_2COOH]$ was much lower than $[CH_3CH_2COO^-]$.
    D. In it, $[CH_3CH_2COOH]$ was much higher than $[CH_3CH_2COO^-]$.

22. At the equivalence point, the number of Na^+ ions in the flask solution was closest to which of the following?

    A. 1.00×10^{20}
    B. 1.00×10^{21}
    C. 1.00×10^{22}
    D. 1.00×10^{23}

23. The pH of the titrant was equal to which of the following?

    A. 10.00
    B. 11.00
    C. 13.00
    D. 14.00

Solutions for this passage begin on next page.

20. The student determined the concentration of the propanoic acid solution to be closest to:

   A. 0.05 M.
   B. 0.10 M.
   C. 0.15 M.
   D. 0.25 M.

Content Classification: Acids and Bases/Titration

Cognitive Classification: Reasoning Using Quantitative Data

This question requires you to identify relationships inherent in data. The volume of the propanoic acid solution was 25.0 mL. The student noted that to reach the equivalence point, 40.0 mL of the 0.10 M NaOH solution was required. The student must have determined the concentration of the propanoic acid solution to be

$$40.0 \text{ mL} \times 0.10 \text{ M}/25.0 \text{ mL} = 0.16 \text{ M}$$

Key: C

This value is closest to 0.16 M.

 The volume of 0.10 M NaOH needed to reach the equivalence point was larger than the volume of the propanoic acid solution, which means that the propanoic acid solution had to be more concentrated than the NaOH solution. Thus, A and B can be quickly ruled out as the key.

Distractors

A   This value is closest to 0.04 M, which is 4.00 times smaller.

B   This value is closest to 0.08 M, which is 2.00 times smaller.

D   This value is closest to 0.24 M, which is 1.50 times larger.

Difficulty Level: Medium (65%)

21. Upon the addition of 20.0 mL of the NaOH solution to the flask, which of the following was most likely true of the flask solution?

    A. Its pH was less than 7.00.
    B. Its color was pink.
    C. In it, $[CH_3CH_2COOH]$ was much lower than $[CH_3CH_2COO^-]$.
    D. In it, $[CH_3CH_2COOH]$ was much higher than $[CH_3CH_2COO^-]$.

Content Classification: Acids and Bases/Acid–Base Equilibria

Cognitive Classification: Hypothesis Testing

This question requires you to predict a result on the basis of background knowledge and specific facts about a situation. Based on the passage, the addition of 20.0 mL of the NaOH solution to the flask corresponded to the half-equivalence point, or the midpoint of the buffer region. At this point, 50% of the propanoic acid was neutralized, and the pH of the flask solution was equal to the pKa of propanoic acid.

 Do not let the parallelism of C and D lead you to assume that one of them must be the key. The equality between [CH₃CH₂COOH] and [CH₃CH₂COO⁻] at the half-equivalence point is based on reasonable assumptions.

Key: A

The pH of the flask solution was 4.87 and thus less than 7.00.

Distractors

B   Based on the passage, at pH 4.87, the colorless acidic form of phenolphthalein existed. Thus, the flask solution was colorless.

C   Because 50% of the propanoic acid was neutralized at this point, $[CH_3CH_2COOH]$ was equal to $[CH_3CH_2COO^-]$.

D   Because 50% of the propanoic acid was neutralized at this point, $[CH_3CH_2COOH]$ was equal to $[CH_3CH_2COO^-]$.

Difficulty Level: Medium (50%)

22. At the equivalence point, the number of Na⁺ ions in the flask solution was closest to which of the following?

  A. 1.00×10^{20}
  B. 1.00×10^{21}
  C. 1.00×10^{22}
  D. 1.00×10^{23}

Content Classification: Stoichiometry/Mole Concept, Avogadro's Number

Cognitive Classification: Flexibility and Adaptability in Scientific Reasoning

This question requires you to use the given information and your background knowledge to solve a problem. The addition of 40.0 mL of the standard 0.10 M NaOH solution to the flask corresponded to the equivalence point. Thus, the number of moles of Na⁺ added at this point was equal to

$$40.0 \text{ mL} \times 0.10 \text{ mol}/(1.00 \times 10^{3}) \text{ mL} = 4.00 \times 10^{-3} \text{ mol}$$

Thus, the number of Na⁺ ions added at this point was equal to

$$4.00 \times 10^{-3} \text{ mol} \times 6.02 \times 10^{23} \text{ ions/mol} = 2.41 \times 10^{21} \text{ ions}$$

where 6.02×10^{23} is Avogadro's number.

Key: B

This value is 2.41 times lower and thus closest to 2.41×10^{21}.

Distractors

A   This value is 24.1 times smaller.

C   This value is about 4 times larger.

D   This value is about 40 times larger.

Difficulty Level: Hard (35%)

23.   The pH of the titrant was equal to which of the following?

    A. 10.00
    B. 11.00
    C. 13.00
    D. 14.00

Content Classification: Acids and Bases/Acid–Base Equilibria

Cognitive Classification: Reasoning Using Quantitative Data

This question requires you to identify relationships inherent in data. The concentration of the titrant, the standard aqueous solution of NaOH, was 0.10 M. Thus, $[OH^-]$ of the titrant was 0.10 M and the pOH of the titrant was $-\log [OH^-]$, or $-\log (1.0 \times 10^{-1})$. The pH of the titrant was $14.00 - pOH$.

 Recall that $\log (1 \times 10^x)$ is equal to $\log 1 + \log 10^x$; $\log 1$ is equal to 0; and $\log 10^x$ is equal to x.

Key: C

Because $-\log (1.0 \times 10^{-1})$ is equal to 1.00, the pH of the titrant was $14.00 - 1.00$, or 13.00.

Distractors

A   This would be the pH of a 1.0×10^{-4} M aqueous NaOH solution.

B   This would be the pH of a 1.0×10^{-3} M aqueous NaOH solution.

D   This would be the pH of a 1.0 M aqueous NaOH solution.

Difficulty Level: Medium (45%)

General Chemistry
Discrete Questions

General Chemistry

24. Which of the following best describes a galvanic (voltaic) cell in terms of the sign of ΔG of the cell reaction it uses and whether it generates or consumes electrical energy? A galvanic cell uses a cell reaction with a:

    A. negative ΔG and generates electrical energy.
    B. negative ΔG and consumes electrical energy.
    C. positive ΔG and generates electrical energy.
    D. positive ΔG and consumes electrical energy.

25. An ideal gas sample has a certain volume at 350 K and 1 atm. The volume of the same sample at STP will be closest to the volume at 350 K and 1 atm multiplied by:

    A. 350/273.
    B. 350/298.
    C. 298/350.
    D. 273/350.

26. Among the halogens F_2, Cl_2, Br_2, and I_2, an increase in which of the following types of intermolecular forces causes an increase in boiling point going down the group?

    A. Dipole–dipole forces
    B. Ion–dipole forces
    C. Ion–induced dipole forces
    D. London dispersion forces

27. Given the half-reactions

    $Ag^+(aq) + e^- \rightarrow Ag(s)$ $E°$ at 25°C = +0.80 V

    $Cu(s) \rightarrow Cu^{2+}(aq) + 2e^-$ $E°$ at 25°C = −0.34 V

    what is the $E°_{cell}$ at 25°C for the overall reaction $Cu(s) + 2Ag^+(aq) \rightarrow Cu^{2+}(aq) + 2Ag(s)$?

    A. −1.94 V
    B. +0.46 V
    C. +1.14 V
    D. +1.26 V

28. *Molality* is defined as the number of moles of solute per kilogram of solvent. In dilute aqueous solutions of electrolytes, the greater the number of particles produced by the electrolyte per kilogram of water, the lower the freezing point of the solution. The freezing points of dilute aqueous solutions of equal molality of the two electrolytes in which of the following pairs would be most different from each other?

    A. K_2SO_4 and CoI_2
    B. $AgClO_4$ and $Ni(NO_3)_2$
    C. $LiBr$ and $Al_2(SO_4)_3$
    D. $MgCl_2$ and $ZnSO_4$

Solutions for these discrete questions begin on next page.

24. Which of the following best describes a galvanic (voltaic) cell in terms of the sign of ΔG of the cell reaction it uses and whether it generates or consumes electrical energy? A galvanic cell uses a cell reaction with a:

A. negative ΔG and generates electrical energy.
B. negative ΔG and consumes electrical energy.
C. positive ΔG and generates electrical energy.
D. positive ΔG and consumes electrical energy.

Content Classifications: Electrochemistry/Galvanic (Voltaic) Cell; Thermodynamics and Thermochemistry/Energy Changes in Chemical Reactions: Thermochemistry

Cognitive Classification: Seeking Clarification

This question requires you to identify relevant background information. A galvanic cell uses a spontaneous cell reaction, which has a negative ΔG. The free energy released in the cell reaction is converted into electrical energy.

Key: A

The description is correct in both criteria.

Distractors

B   The description is correct in only one criterion. The cell reaction does have a negative ΔG. However, the cell generates, not consumes, electrical energy.

C   The description is correct in only one criterion. The cell does generate electrical energy. However, the cell reaction has a negative, not positive, ΔG.

D   The description is incorrect in both criteria.

Difficulty Level: Easy (80%)

25. An ideal gas sample has a certain volume at 350 K and 1 atm. The volume of the same sample at STP will be closest to the volume at 350 K and 1 atm multiplied by:

A. 350/273.
B. 350/298.
C. 298/350.
D. 273/350.

Content Classification: Phases and Phase Equilibria/Gas Phase

Cognitive Classification: Flexibility and Adaptability in Scientific Reasoning

This question requires you to solve a problem using the given information and your background knowledge. The standard temperature is 0°C, or 273.15 K, and the standard pressure is 1 atm. According to Charles's law, at constant pressure, the volume of a fixed amount of an ideal gas is directly proportional to its absolute temperature.

 It is true that data such as physical properties of substances and thermodynamic data are often reported at 25°C. However, 25°C is not the standard temperature.

Key: D

The volume of the sample at STP will be closest to the volume at 350 K and 1 atm multiplied by 273/350.

Distractors

A   This answer is obtained by thinking that at constant pressure the volume of a fixed amount of an ideal gas is inversely proportional to its absolute temperature.

B   This answer is obtained by thinking that at constant pressure the volume of a fixed amount of an ideal gas is inversely proportional to its absolute temperature and that the standard temperature is 25°C, or 298.15 K.

C   This answer is obtained by thinking that the standard temperature is 25°C, or 298.15 K.

Difficulty Level: Hard (40%)

26. Among the halogens F_2, Cl_2, Br_2, and I_2, an increase in which of the following types of intermolecular forces causes an increase in boiling point going down the group?

   A. Dipole–dipole forces
   B. Ion–dipole forces
   C. Ion–induced dipole forces
   D. London dispersion forces

Content Classifications: Phases and Phase Equilibria/Intermolecular Forces; Bonding/The Covalent Bond

Cognitive Classification: Identification of Components of a Situation and Relationships Among Them

This question requires you to identify rationales. All of the halogens considered consist of homonuclear diatomic molecules that are similarly shaped and contain nonpolar covalent single bonds. Among these halogens, the molecular size increases; hence, the molecular polarizability (the ease with which the molecule's electron cloud can be distorted) increases going down the group.

Key: D

Among the halogens considered, the boiling point increases going down the group because of an increase in London dispersion forces, which are caused by momentary electron cloud distortions.

Distractors

A   Polar molecules interact with other polar molecules via dipole–dipole forces.

B   Ions interact with polar molecules via ion–dipole forces.

C   Ions interact with nonpolar molecules via ion–induced dipole forces.

Difficulty Level: Medium (55%)

MCAT® is a program of the
Association of American Medical Colleges

27. Given the half-reactions

$$Ag^+(aq) + e^- \rightarrow Ag(s) \quad E° \text{ at } 25°C = +0.80 \text{ V}$$

$$Cu(s) \rightarrow Cu^{2+}(aq) + 2e^- \quad E° \text{ at } 25°C = -0.34 \text{ V}$$

what is the $E°_{cell}$ at 25°C for the overall reaction $Cu(s) + 2Ag^+(aq) \rightarrow Cu^{2+}(aq) + 2Ag(s)$?

A. −1.94 V
B. +0.46 V
C. +1.14 V
D. +1.26 V

Content Classification: Electrochemistry/Galvanic (Voltaic) Cell

Cognitive Classification: Flexibility and Adaptability in Scientific Reasoning

This question requires you to solve a problem using the given information and your background knowledge. In the top half-reaction, $Ag^+(aq)$ undergoes reduction to $Ag(s)$. In the bottom half-reaction, $Cu(s)$ undergoes oxidation to $Cu^{2+}(aq)$. In the overall reaction, $Cu(s)$ undergoes oxidation to $Cu^{2+}(aq)$, and $Ag^+(aq)$ undergoes reduction to $Ag(s)$. Therefore, simply adding the $E°$ values of the two half-reactions gives the $E°_{cell}$ value of the overall reaction.

 Changing the balancing coefficients in a half-reaction has no effect on its $E°$ value. Reversing the sign of the $E°$ value of a half-reaction is necessary only when the opposite of this half-reaction occurs in the overall reaction.

Key: B

$E°_{cell} = +0.80 \text{ V} + (-0.34 \text{ V}) = +0.46 \text{ V}$

Distractors

A Doubling the $E°$ value of the top half-reaction and reversing its sign will lead to this answer.

C Reversing the sign of the $E°$ value of the bottom half-reaction will lead to this answer.

D Doubling the $E°$ value of the top half-reaction will lead to this answer.

Difficulty Level: Medium (55%)

28. *Molality* is defined as the number of moles of solute per kilogram of solvent. In dilute aqueous solutions of electrolytes, the greater the number of particles produced by the electrolyte per kilogram of water, the lower the freezing point of the solution. The freezing points of dilute aqueous solutions of equal molality of the two electrolytes in which of the following pairs would be most different from each other?

A. K_2SO_4 and CoI_2
B. $AgClO_4$ and $Ni(NO_3)_2$
C. $LiBr$ and $Al_2(SO_4)_3$
D. $MgCl_2$ and $ZnSO_4$

Content Classification: Phases and Phase Equilibria/Phase Equilibria

Cognitive Classification: Identification of Main Ideas

This question requires you to identify major points. For each electrolyte pair, you need to determine the difference between the total number of cations and anions in the formula unit of one electrolyte and the total number of cations and anions in the formula unit of the other electrolyte. The electrolyte pair for which this difference is the highest is the correct answer.

Key: C

There are two ions in $LiBr$ and five ions in $Al_2(SO_4)_3$ $(5 - 2 = 3)$.

Distractors

A   There are three ions in K_2SO_4 and three ions in CoI_2 $(3 - 3 = 0)$.

B   There are two ions in $AgClO_4$ and three ions in $Ni(NO_3)_2$ $(3 - 2 = 1)$.

D   There are three ions in $MgCl_2$ and two ions in $ZnSO_4$ $(3 - 2 = 1)$.

Difficulty Level: Easy (80%)

MCAT® is a program of the
Association of American Medical Colleges

Physics

Passage Set I

Global warming of the atmosphere and the oceans due to natural causes and by human processes has disruptive consequences for all living creatures. Sea level will rise and inundate low-lying coastal areas. Regions suitable for growing specific crops will shift in latitude. Weather patterns will become more erratic and storms more severe. These changes can influence health through heat waves, floods, droughts, and increases in disease-causing insect populations. Mosquito-borne diseases such as malaria, dengue fever, and encephalitis will increase as floods create new areas of stagnant water. Cholera will spread when potable water supplies become polluted.

The average surface temperature of Earth (land, oceans, and lower atmosphere) is approximately 15°C. An energy balance is maintained between the incident radiation from the Sun—mainly in the visible region—and infrared radiation that is sent back into space from the warm Earth surface. A long-term shift upward of the average temperature will cause a shift in the ecological balance of life on Earth.

One mechanism causing atmospheric warming is the *greenhouse effect*. Certain gases—such as CO_2 generated in the burning of fossil fuels for energy and CH_4 produced by industry and agriculture—absorb infrared radiation from Earth, causing heating of the atmosphere. As the atmosphere becomes warmer, it transfers heat to the oceans. Higher temperature causes seawater to expand in volume. A warmer atmosphere accelerates the melting of land-supported glaciers, which also increases the volume of seawater. Radiation detectors in satellites monitor the temperature of the oceans; balloon-borne thermometers monitor the temperature of the atmosphere at various altitudes.

1. Which of the following best explains why a warmer atmosphere will have a higher humidity?

   A. More heat is available for evaporation from the oceans.
   B. The air is less dense, leaving room for evaporated molecules.
   C. The air has less pressure over the oceans, allowing easier evaporation.
   D. Higher-temperature air causes stronger winds to evaporate ocean water.

2. The oceans and the atmosphere exchange heat mainly by conduction. What microscopic process is responsible for this exchange?

   A. Electronic transitions in atoms
   B. Elastic molecular collisions
   C. Atomic ionization
   D. Molecular dissociation

3. Global atmospheric circulation is driven by the differences in air temperature at different latitudes. Equatorial regions are heated more by the incident sunlight than are polar regions because:

   A. Earth rotates.
   B. the atmosphere absorbs more sunlight in the equatorial regions.
   C. the amounts of greenhouse gases in the polar regions are less than at the equator.
   D. sunlight is incident on Earth at smaller angles to the horizontal in the polar regions.

4. What is the effect on the sea level when icebergs melt in the ocean?

   A. Sea level rises because of the increase of liquid from the melted ice.
   B. Sea level lowers because of the lower salinity of the freshwater added to the sea.
   C. Sea level remains approximately the same because a floating iceberg displaces its weight of water.
   D. Sea level rises because the local temperature of the water is lowered.

5. Greenhouse gases absorb infrared radiation in what kind of process?

   A. Atomic transitions
   B. Molecular vibrational and rotational transitions
   C. Molecular dissociation
   D. Phase transitions

Solutions for this passage begin on next page.

1. Which of the following best explains why a warmer atmosphere will have a higher humidity?

    A. More heat is available for evaporation from the oceans.
    B. The air is less dense, leaving room for evaporated molecules.
    C. The air has less pressure over the oceans, allowing easier evaporation.
    D. Higher-temperature air causes stronger winds to evaporate ocean water.

Content Classifications: Fluids and Solids/Fluids; Phases and Phase Equilibria/Phase Equilibria

Cognitive Classification: Identification of Components of a Situation and Relationships Among Them

This question requires you to identify supporting evidence. You are expected to understand the concept of partial pressure and that the partial pressure of a liquid increases as its temperature increases. Increasing the temperatures of the air and the ocean allows more evaporated water in the air.

Key: A

More heat is available for evaporation from the oceans.

Distractors

B   There is no reason to assume that lower density *leaves room for evaporated molecules*. The number of molecules per unit volume of a gas is dependent on temperature.

C   The average atmospheric pressure is the same over land and water.

D   There is no direct correlation between air temperature and wind velocity. Wind tends to be driven by temperature *differences*.

Difficulty Level: Medium (70%)

2. The oceans and the atmosphere exchange heat mainly by conduction. What microscopic process is responsible for this exchange?

    A. Electronic transitions in atoms
    B. Elastic molecular collisions
    C. Atomic ionization
    D. Molecular dissociation

Content Classifications: Work and Energy/Conservation of Energy; Thermodynamics and Thermochemistry/Thermodynamics

Cognitive Classification: Seeking Clarification

This question requires you to identify relevant background information. The temperature of a material is a measure of the average kinetic energy of the atoms that comprise the material. For materials at the temperatures of oceans and atmospheres, the average kinetic energies are of the order of 0.02 eV and very small compared to the energies associated with transitions of electrons in atoms and the energies associated with dissociation of atoms and molecules.

Remember that the question specifically asks about "conduction." Infrared radiative transfer is excluded.

Key: B

Elastic molecular collisions are responsible for the exchange.

Distractors

A   Electronic transitions have energies of the order of eV, much higher than thermal energies at room temperature.

C   Atomic ionization requires energies of the order of many eV, much higher than thermal energies at room temperature.

D   Dissociation of the molecular constituents of oceans and the atmosphere requires energies of the order of eV, much higher than thermal energies at room temperature.

Difficulty Level: Medium (70%)

3. Global atmospheric circulation is driven by the differences in air temperature at different latitudes. Equatorial regions are heated more by the incident sunlight than are polar regions because:

A. Earth rotates.
B. the atmosphere absorbs more sunlight in the equatorial regions.
C. the amounts of greenhouse gases in the polar regions are less than at the equator.
D. sunlight is incident on Earth at smaller angles to the horizontal in the polar regions.

Content Classification: Light and Geometric Optics/Electromagnetic Radiation

Cognitive Classification: Evaluation Processes

This question requires you to judge whether a conclusion follows from the given reasons. The local temperature of the surface of Earth is dependent on a balance between solar energy in and radiation and convection out. Solar energy onto the surface depends on the elevation angle of the Sun relative to the surface. This angle is much smaller in polar regions than at the equator, resulting in dramatically lower heating rates in polar regions.

Key: D

Equatorial regions are heated more because sunlight is incident on Earth at smaller angles to the horizontal in polar regions.

Distractors

A   Earth's rotation averages out the daily variation in solar heating. It is not responsible for the latitudinal variation in solar energy input.

B   The atmosphere absorbs very little solar radiation. The vast majority of the absorption occurs on Earth's surface.

C   The global circulation keeps the composition of the atmosphere homogeneous.

Difficulty Level: Easy (75%)

4. What is the effect on the sea level when icebergs melt in the ocean?

    A. Sea level rises because of the increase of liquid from the melted ice.
    B. Sea level lowers because of the lower salinity of the freshwater added to the sea.
    C. Sea level remains approximately the same because a floating iceberg displaces its weight of water.
    D. Sea level rises because the local temperature of the water is lowered.

Content Classification: Fluids and Solids/Buoyancy

Cognitive Classification: Seeking Clarification

This question requires you to identify relevant background information. The density of liquid water (1.00 g/cc) is very close to the density of ice (0.92 g/cc). When 1 g of ice floats in water it displaces the volume of 1 g of liquid water, and a small portion of the ice lies above the surface of the liquid. As the ice melts, the top of the ice falls closer and closer to the surface of the water. The thermal expansion of water is small compared to the change in volume associated with melting.

Key: C

Sea level remains approximately the same because a floating iceberg displaces its weight of water.

Distractors

A   The melted ice replaces the volume of the water it displaced. Sea level is essentially unchanged.

B   Regardless of the salinity, the ice displaces its own weight in seawater. In addition, the effect of salinity on density is less significant than the effect of temperature.

D   Apart from the temperature interval 0°C to 4°C, water expands (slightly) with increasing temperature. Sea level will fall only slightly if the temperature is lowered.

Difficulty Level: Hard (40%)

5. Greenhouse gases absorb infrared radiation in what kind of process?

    A. Atomic transitions
    B. Molecular vibrational and rotational transitions
    C. Molecular dissociation
    D. Phase transitions

Content Classification: Atomic and Nuclear Structure/Atomic Structure and Spectra

Cognitive Classification: Identification of Main Ideas

This question requires you to identify major points. The energy levels associated with vibrational and rotational motion of molecules are very closely spaced. Vibrational states are separated by energies of the order of 0.2 eV, which corresponds to the infrared region of the electromagnetic spectrum. For rotational transitions, typical energy differences are of the order of 0.001 eV. The large number of possible rotational states leads to broad bands of infrared wavelengths that can be absorbed by greenhouse gas molecules.

Key: B

Greenhouse gases absorb infrared radiation by means of molecular vibrational and rotational transitions.

Distractors

A   Ground-state atoms require energies of several eV to change electron energy levels. These energies are much higher than those carried by infrared radiation.

C   The dissociation energy of greenhouse gas molecules is much higher than the energies of infrared radiation. Furthermore, if greenhouse gases were to dissociate, they would cease functioning as greenhouse gases.

D   Phase transitions are not associated with absorption of electromagnetic radiation.

Difficulty Level: Medium (60%)

Physics
Passage Set II

Guns and cannons from the 1700s and 1800s all operate on a similar principle: gases from the burned gunpowder accelerate the bullet or cannonball from rest by adiabatic expansion (that is, $Q = 0$ in the first law of thermodynamics). Consider the following simplified rifle (Figure 1) with a barrel length $\ell \approx 80$ cm that uses a form of gunpowder (called *black powder*) with an energy yield of 3.0 J/mg.

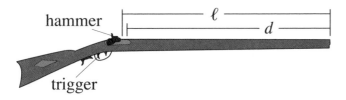

Figure 1 Black powder rifle

This rifle is loaded by pouring 60 grains (4.0 g) of the black powder down the muzzle, using a 30 grain (1.5-cm³) measuring spoon. Next, a tiny cloth patch of negligible mass is wrapped around the *bullet*, a 16-g lead ball that fits snugly into the muzzle of the 1.5-cm² barrel. The bullet is then pushed down the barrel a distance d, where it is firmly pressed against the powder. Pulling the trigger lets the hammer snap forward, igniting the black powder and firing the bullet with a speed of ~300 m/s.

The fired bullet lodges in a suspended 1.584 kg wooden block, causing the block to behave as a pendulum of length L, and pushing a slider back a distance r along a horizontally mounted meterstick. This arrangement is known as a *ballistic pendulum* (Figure 2).

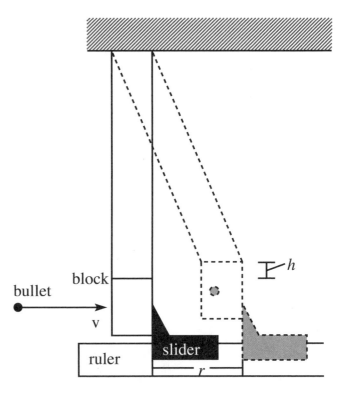

Figure 2 Ballistic pendulum

(Note: Assume that the black powder completely burns prior to any movement of the bullet and that the entire energy yield of the black powder goes into the internal energy of the gases and smoke produced, giving them an average temperature of T_b immediately before the bullet begins moving. Under a constant acceleration a, an object's position x and speed v as a function of time t are

$$x = x_0 + v_0 t + \frac{at^2}{2}$$

and

$$v = v_0 + at$$

Use $g = 10$ m/s².)

6. Based on the passage, the percentage of the energy released from the black powder that goes into the motion of the bullet is closest to which of the following?

   A. 8%
   B. 15%
   C. 30%
   D. 60%

7. If the oscillation frequency of the bullet and block together is f, the frequency of oscillation for the block alone would be closest to which of the following?

   A. $0.99f$
   B. $1.00f$
   C. $1.01f$
   D. $1.10f$

8. Immediately after colliding with the block in Figure 2, the speed of the bullet in the passage is closest to:

   A. 0.03 m/s.
   B. 0.37 m/s.
   C. 3.0 m/s.
   D. 37 m/s.

9. Compared to the ballistic pendulum in the passage, if the ballistic pendulum were to have a length of $2L$ instead of L, the maximum height h of the block would be:

   A. the same.
   B. half as much.
   C. one-fourth as much.
   D. twice as much.

10. If the absolute sound intensity from firing the bullet is 2.0 W/m² at a distance of 2 m from the rifle, what will be the absolute sound intensity at a distance of 100 m from the rifle?

    A. 2.0×10^{-4} W/m²
    B. 8.0×10^{-4} W/m²
    C. 4.0×10^{-2} W/m²
    D. 2.8×10^{-1} W/m²

11. The density of the black powder used in the passage is closest to which of the following?

    A. 0.75 g/cm³
    B. 1.33 g/cm³
    C. 1.83 g/cm³
    D. 2.67 g/cm³

_____

Solutions for this passage begin on next page.

6.   Based on the passage, the percentage of the energy released from the black powder that goes into the motion of the bullet is closest to which of the following?

A.   8%
B.   15%
C.   30%
D.   60%

Content Classification: Work and Energy/Kinetic and Potential Energy

Cognitive Classification: Seeking Clarification

This question requires you to translate presented information into more functionally useful forms. In comparing the bullet's kinetic energy to the available chemical energy that is released when the black powder is burned, the important information is that 4.0 g of black powder is burned (releasing 3.0 J/mg), and the 16 g bullet leaves the barrel at 300 m/s. This means that a total of 12 kJ (4000 mg × 3.0 J/mg) is released, while the bullet carries 720 J (0.016 kg × [300 m/s]^2/2) of kinetic energy. Thus, the ratio of the bullet's kinetic energy to the released chemical energy is 720/12,000, or 6/100, which is 6%.

You must be careful when converting units and constructing ratios.

Key: A

The value of 8% is closest to the exact value of 6%.

Distractors

B   Forgetting the factor of 1/2 in the kinetic energy will lead to this answer.

C   This answer can result from forgetting the power of 2 in the kinetic energy and inverting the energy ratio.

D   Thinking that 16 g = 0.16 kg or missing a factor of 10 in the chemical potential energy can lead to this answer.

Difficulty Level: Hard (20%)

7. If the oscillation frequency of the bullet and block together is *f*, the frequency of oscillation for the block alone would be closest to which of the following?

    A. $0.99f$
    B. $1.00f$
    C. $1.01f$
    D. $1.10f$

Content Classification: Waves and Periodic Motion/Motion of a Pendulum

Cognitive Classification: Identification of Components of a Situation and Relationships Among Them

This question requires you to identify the relevant issues in the behavior of a pendulum. Because the frequency of oscillation of a pendulum depends only on the pendulum's length and the acceleration of gravity, changing the bob's mass has no effect on the pendulum's frequency.

 You need to know what variables depend on other variables and the kind of dependence that exists between them.

Key: B

A pendulum's frequency does *not* change with the bob's mass.

Distractors

A Thinking that decreasing the bob's mass by 1% will also decrease the pendulum frequency by 1% leads to this answer.

C Thinking that decreasing the bob's mass by 1% will increase the pendulum frequency by 1% leads to this answer.

D This answer results from thinking that decreasing the bob's mass by 1% will increase the pendulum frequency by a factor of $\sqrt{0.01}$, or 0.1 (10%).

Difficulty Level: Medium (45%)

8. Immediately after colliding with the block in Figure 2, the speed of the bullet in the passage is closest to:

   A. 0.03 m/s.
   B. 0.37 m/s.
   C. 3.0 m/s.
   D. 37 m/s.

Content Classification: Equilibrium and Momentum/Conservation of Linear Momentum

Cognitive Classification: Flexibility and Adaptability in Scientific Reasoning

This question requires you to solve a conservation of momentum problem using the given information and your background knowledge. Because the bullet and block move together after the collision, the total mass in motion after the collision is 100 times the bullet's mass; thus, the speed of the bullet (and block) after collision is 1/100 of the bullet's speed before collision.

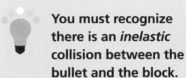 You must recognize there is an *inelastic* collision between the bullet and the block.

Key: C

The value of 3.0 m/s is 1/100 of the bullet's pre-collision speed.

Distractors

A Making an error by a factor of 100 will lead to this answer.

B This answer will result from conserving energy instead of momentum and making an error by a factor of 100.

D Conserving energy instead of momentum will lead to this answer.

Difficulty Level: Medium (55%)

9.   Compared to the ballistic pendulum in the passage, if the ballistic pendulum were to have a length of *2L* instead of *L*, the maximum height *h* of the block would be:

   A. the same.
   B. half as much.
   C. one-fourth as much.
   D. twice as much.

Content Classification: Work and Energy/Conservation of Energy

Cognitive Classification: Hypothesis Testing

This question asks you to predict the result of a hypothetical change, testing your understanding of the conditions that bring a pendulum to a stop at either end of its motion. When a pendulum is in motion, it stops momentarily when all of the kinetic energy at the bottom of the pendulum's swing has been converted to gravitational potential energy (*mgh*).

 Remember that conservation of energy concepts can provide a much simpler analysis of some aspects of pendulum motion than force concepts can.

Key: A

Because the kinetic energy at the bottom of the pendulum's motion depends only on the speed of the block after collision, the height *h* will be the same regardless of the pendulum's length. Thus, the maximum height *h* will be the same for both the length *L* pendulum and the length *2L* pendulum.

Distractors

B   Thinking that the maximum height is inversely proportional to the pendulum's length will lead to this answer.

C   Thinking that the maximum height is inversely proportional to the square of the pendulum's length will lead to this answer.

D   Thinking that the maximum height is directly proportional to the pendulum's length will lead to this answer.

Difficulty Level: Hard (35%)

10. If the absolute sound intensity from firing the bullet is 2.0 W/m² at a distance of 2 m from the rifle, what will be the absolute sound intensity at a distance of 100 m from the rifle?

    A. 2.0×10^{-4} W/m²
    B. 8.0×10^{-4} W/m²
    C. 4.0×10^{-2} W/m²
    D. 2.8×10^{-1} W/m²

Content Classification: Sound/Intensity of Sound

Cognitive Classification: Hypothesis Testing

This question tests your knowledge of how the intensity of a spherical wave falls off with distance from the source by requiring you to predict the result of this hypothetical change. The information given is the absolute (sound power per unit area) intensity at a distance $r = 2$ m from the source. You can assume the sound travels out in a spherical shell with an area $4\pi r^2$ and calculate the source power from this ($P = 4\pi r^2 [I_2] = 32\pi$ W) and then calculate the new absolute intensity I_{100}.

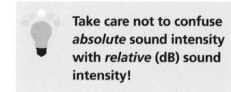
Take care not to confuse *absolute* **sound intensity with** *relative* **(dB) sound intensity!**

Key: B

Another way to solve this problem is to recognize the inverse square relationship between intensity and distance and go directly to the equation

$$I_{100} = I_2 \times [(2\text{ m})^2/(100\text{ m})^2] = 8 \times 10^{-4}\text{ W/m}^2$$

Distractors

A   Forgetting about the 2 m distance inherent in I_2 will lead to this answer.

C   Multiplying I_2 by $(2/100)$ instead of $(2/100)^2$ will lead to this answer.

D   Multiplying I_2 by $\sqrt{2/100}$ instead of $(2/100)^2$ will lead to this answer.

Difficulty Level: Hard (30%)

MCAT® is a program of the
Association of American Medical Colleges

11. The density of the black powder used in the passage is closest to which of the following?

    A. 0.75 g/cm³

    B. 1.33 g/cm³

    C. 1.83 g/cm³

    D. 2.67 g/cm³

Content Classification: Fluids and Solids/Density

Cognitive Classification: Identification of Components of a Situation and Relationships Among Them

This question requires you to identify the relevant values from the given information. The rifle-loading information mentions that 60 grains of black powder masses 4.0 g, and the 30 grain measuring spoon used to measure powder has a volume of 1.5 cm³. From this, you can see that 2 measuring spoons of black powder would be used to load the rifle, corresponding to 4.0 g of black powder having a volume of 3.0 cm³. Thus, the density is (4/3) g/cm³.

To solve this problem, you need to know how *density* is defined. This will lead you to look for the appropriate mass and volume information needed to find the answer.

Key: B

The answer is 1.33 g/cm³.

Distractors

A   Inverting the mass and volume will lead to this answer.

C   Making mathematical errors that yield a value between the values of **B** and **D** will lead to this answer.

D   Using 1.5 cm³ instead of 3.0 cm³ will lead to this answer.

Difficulty Level: Medium (45%)

Physics
Passage Set III

A model rocket of initial mass M sits on a launch pad. At time $t = 0$, the solid propellant rocket motor ignites, sending smoke and hot gases downward through the nozzle in the tail of the rocket, and the rocket ascends vertically through the atmosphere. Figure 1 shows the thrust of the rocket motor as a function of time during the burn phase.

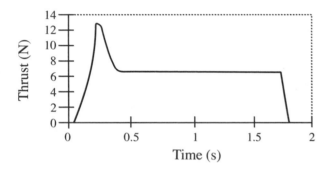

Figure 1 Thrust vs time curve of the rocket motor

After a time T, the rocket propellant stops burning. The rocket has a velocity v_1 and is at an altitude of h. The total amount of rocket propellant burned is equal to m_1. In a vacuum, this rocket is able to attain an altitude of H_0; but, because of air friction, the rocket achieves only an altitude of $H < H_0$. Shortly after the rocket begins to fall back to Earth, the rocket deploys a parachute and thereafter falls at a constant velocity.

(Note: Let $M = 100$ g, $T = 1.72$ s, $m_1 = 16$ g, $H = 300$ m, $h = 75$ m, $v_1 = 81$ m/s, and $g = 9.8$ m/s^2.)

MCAT® is a program of the
Association of American Medical Colleges

12. Which of the following best describes the energy conversion processes that occur during the flight of the rocket?

   A. Heat to kinetic energy
   B. Kinetic energy to gravitational potential energy and back to kinetic energy
   C. Chemical energy to kinetic energy and gravitational potential energy and then to heat
   D. Chemical energy to heat energy to gravitational potential energy

13. The rocket motor's average thrust during the burn phase is closest to which of the following?

   A. 4.0 N
   B. 6.2 N
   C. 9.5 N
   D. 13 N

14. Doubling the total impulse of the rocket motor would double which of the following quantities?

   A. The maximum energy produced by the motor
   B. The burn time of the rocket motor
   C. The maximum altitude of the rocket
   D. The momentum imparted to the rocket

15. Which of the following is closest to the acceleration of the falling rocket after the parachute is deployed?

   A. Zero
   B. -9.8 m/s^2
   C. $+9.8$ m/s^2
   D. -84 g $\times$ 9.8 m/s^2

16. Which of the following physics principles best explains why the model rocket accelerates upward?

   A. The force of gravity weakens as the rocket rises.
   B. For every action there is an equal and opposite reaction.
   C. The thermal energy of the burning propellant is conserved.
   D. An object continues in uniform motion until acted on by an external force.

17. Based on Figure 1, the burn rate of the propellant as a function of time is best described as:

   A. a constant rate until the propellant is exhausted.
   B. a variable but steadily increasing rate until the propellant is exhausted.
   C. a steadily decreasing rate until the propellant is exhausted.
   D. an initially fast rate, then a constant rate until the propellant is exhausted.

Solutions for this passage begin on next page.

12. Which of the following best describes the energy conversion processes that occur during the flight of the rocket?

    A. Heat to kinetic energy
    B. Kinetic energy to gravitational potential energy and back to kinetic energy
    C. Chemical energy to kinetic energy and gravitational potential energy and then to heat
    D. Chemical energy to heat energy to gravitational potential energy

Content Classification: Work and Energy/Conservation of Energy

Cognitive Classification: Seeking Clarification

This question asks you to add the appropriate clarifying information on the conversion of one kind of energy to another during the model rocket's flight. The rocket engine contains a mixture that is chemically burned to produce the thrust that simultaneously gives the rocket speed (kinetic energy) and height (gravitational potential energy), which are eventually dissipated into the atmosphere. This dissipation heats the air molecules (by a tiny amount).

 For answering questions that ask about energy conversion processes, it is best to take an overall viewpoint (from the beginning of the action to the end).

Key: C

This process is best described as converting from chemical energy to kinetic energy and gravitational potential energy and then to heat.

Distractors

A   This answer reverses the heat and kinetic energy while ignoring the chemical and gravitational energies present.

B   This answer ignores the chemical energy and heat present.

D   This answer ignores the heat dissipated into the atmosphere.

Difficulty Level: Hard (35%)

13. The rocket motor's average thrust during the burn phase is closest to which of the following?

   A. 4.0 N
   B. 6.2 N
   C. 9.5 N
   D. 13 N

Content Classification: Force, Motion, and Gravitation/Force

Cognitive Classification: Reasoning Using Quantitative Data

This question asks you to identify the basic components of the graph in Figure 1. The graph itself shows the engine thrust has a rapid rise to a peak at about 13 N, then quickly drops back to a plateau just above 6 N within the first 0.4 s, where it remains constant until it rapidly drops off to zero again at the 1.7-s mark. Because the thrust is on the plateau for over 76% (1.3/1.7 = 0.764) of the total burn time, the average thrust should also be near this value. To account for the peak in the curve before the plateau, the average should be a little *above* the plateau value.

 Estimating the average value over an interval in a graph like this is a skill also used when estimating the area bounded by a curve, such as when determining the work done by a force on a *Force vs Distance* graph, the impulse delivered by a force to an object on a *Force vs Time* graph, or the work done by a gas during a cycle on a *PV (Pressure vs Volume)* graph.

Key: B

This value is closest to the plateau value while still above it.

Distractors

A   Misreading the vertical scale of Figure 1 can lead to this answer.

C   This answer tries to average the peak value (13 N) with the plateau value (6 N) while ignoring the relative time interval spent at each point.

D   This answer focuses only on the peak value (13 N).

Difficulty Level: Medium (70%)

14. Doubling the total impulse of the rocket motor would double which of the following quantities?

    A. The maximum energy produced by the motor
    B. The burn time of the rocket motor
    C. The maximum altitude of the rocket
    D. The momentum imparted to the rocket

Content Classification: Equilibrium and Momentum/Impulse

Cognitive Classification: Identification of Main Ideas

This question requires you to identify which quantity best corresponds to the *impulse* that the rocket engine delivers. The impulse is defined as the product of the force **F** applied to an object and the time interval Δt over which it is applied.

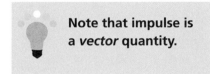

Note that impulse is a *vector* quantity.

Key: D

The impulse acting on an object is directly related to the change in the object's momentum through the relation $\mathbf{F}\Delta t = \Delta(m\mathbf{v})$.

Distractors

A   Thinking that impulse directly relates to energy will lead to this answer.

B   Although impulse is related to Δt, this statement can be true only if **F** is also constant in time—but Figure 1 clearly opposes this notion.

C   The maximum altitude of the rocket depends on both the energy imparted to it and the air friction losses. While air friction is proportional to v (and therefore to Δmv), the energy imparted to the rocket is not directly related to impulse, rendering this answer incorrect.

Difficulty Level: Medium (70%)

MCAT® is a program of the
Association of American Medical Colleges

15. Which of the following is closest to the acceleration of the falling rocket after the parachute is deployed?

    A. Zero
    B. -9.8 m/s^2
    C. $+9.8 \text{ m/s}^2$
    D. $-84 \text{ g} \times 9.8 \text{ m/s}^2$

Content Classification: Translational Motion/Acceleration

Cognitive Classification: Seeking Clarification

This question requires you to identify relevant background knowledge. You are told that after the parachute is deployed, the model rocket returns to the ground at a constant velocity.

Key: A

An object that moves at a constant velocity does so only because the net force on it is zero; thus, the acceleration is also zero.

 Remember that the idea "a constant velocity implies a zero force" works both as a full vector concept and as a component concept. For instance, consider an object sliding on an inclined plane: in the direction perpendicular to the plane, the speed of the object is constant (actually, zero), so the net force *perpendicular to the plane* is zero—no matter what is happening parallel to the plane.

Distractors

B   Thinking that the sign of gravitational acceleration should be "−" because "−" means "downward" can lead to this answer.

C   This answer results from thinking that the sign of gravitational acceleration is irrelevant or that the rocket is moving in the same direction as gravity, which means that the "+" sign is correct.

D   This is an expression for the weight of the model rocket with a "−" sign included because gravity points downward; this is not an acceleration.

Difficulty Level: Medium (65%)

16. Which of the following physics principles best explains why the model rocket accelerates upward?

    A. The force of gravity weakens as the rocket rises.
    B. For every action there is an equal and opposite reaction.
    C. The thermal energy of the burning propellant is conserved.
    D. An object continues in uniform motion until acted on by an external force.

Content Classification: Force, Motion, and Gravitation/Newton's Third Law

Cognitive Classification: Evaluation Processes

This question requires you to judge which of the rationales listed best explains why the rocket accelerates upward. The passage states that the hot gases and smoke from the rocket propellant are ejected downward from the tail of the rocket; thus, the mass of these gases and smoke are expelled downward with a velocity v. Because the gases and smoke carry away a downward momentum, the rocket is given an equal and opposite upward momentum (because momentum must be conserved within the combination of rocket and burned fuel).

 You must be aware of the differences between external and internal forces and how to interpret them with basic physics principles.

Key: B

This explanation, a restatement of Newton's third law, fits best with the way the rocket engine functions when the force that pushes the gases downward has a reaction force lifting the rocket upward.

Distractors

A   Although gravity does weaken with increasing altitude above Earth's surface, it changes only minimally ($< 0.01\%$) over an altitude of $H \approx 300$ m; so this choice is not the best explanation.

C   Although the thermal energy of the burning propellant is mainly conserved by the gases and smoke produced, it does not convert directly into the rocket's kinetic energy, and so this choice is not the best explanation.

D   This explanation is a restatement of Newton's first law; however, the expulsion of hot gases from the rocket's engine is considered an *internal*, not an external, force. Thus, Newton's first law is not relevant to this question.

Difficulty Level: Medium (65%)

17.   Based on Figure 1, the burn rate of the propellant as a function of time is best described as:

   A.   a constant rate until the propellant is exhausted.
   B.   a variable but steadily increasing rate until the propellant is exhausted.
   C.   a steadily decreasing rate until the propellant is exhausted.
   D.   an initially fast rate, then a constant rate until the propellant is exhausted.

Content Classification: Force, Motion, and Gravitation/Force

Cognitive Classification: Reasoning Using Quantitative Data

This question requires you to interpret the components of the graph in Figure 1 and then identify the background knowledge relevant to that interpretation. Because the force exerted by the rocket engine is proportional to the rate at which the propellant is being burned and ejected, the force values interpreted from the graph can be used to evaluate the burn rate throughout the time period of Figure 1. The burn rate initially increases rapidly (for the first 0.3 s or so), then drops down to a constant level from about the 0.5-s mark until about the 1.7-s mark, then drops off rapidly to zero, where it can be assumed the propellant is all gone.

Interpreting graphs is a skill that is important to practice, especially if you are not very familiar with it.

Key: D

The best description among the choices is "an initially fast rate, then a constant rate until the propellant is exhausted."

Distractors

A   This answer ignores the initial 0.3-s of the propellant burn.

B   This answer misinterprets the flat portion of the graph.

C   This answer ignores the initial 0.3-s of the propellant burn and misinterprets the remainder of the graph.

Difficulty Level: Easy (75%)

Physics
Passage Set IV

Gallium arsenide (GaAs) is a semiconductor of great interest to scientists in the microelectronics industry. GaAs crystals for electronic devices can be grown by depositing a few atomic layers at a time. The crystals are grown in a high vacuum chamber into which Ga and As_2 gases are introduced. Above a particular partial pressure of As_2 gas, the rate of growth of the crystals is determined strictly by the rate that Ga atoms arrive at the surface where the crystals are being deposited.

To form the best devices, the crystals should form a film that is atomically smooth. Ideally, no atoms should be deposited on an upper layer until the layer below is complete. In practice, the surface becomes rougher as more layers of material are added.

The smoothness of the surface is measured by the process of *reflection high energy electron diffraction* (RHEED), a process that takes advantage of the fact that electrons behave like waves, with wavelengths inversely proportional to their momenta. A beam of electrons is bounced off the surface, and the reflection pattern is studied. When the surface is smooth, most of the electrons are reflected specularly, as light would be from a perfect mirror. A rough surface diffuses the reflected beam, reducing the intensity of reflection that is detected. A surface is smoothest when a monolayer has just been completed, and it is roughest about halfway through the completion of a monolayer. Figure 1 shows a graph of RHEED intensity versus time while GaAs film is being deposited.

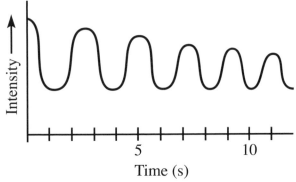

Figure 1 RHEED intensity vs time

Second Edition
The Official Guide to the MCAT® Exam

MCAT® is a program of the
Association of American Medical Colleges

18. According to Figure 1, what is the approximate amount of time required for the addition of one monolayer of material?

    A. 0.5 s
    B. 1 s
    C. 2 s
    D. 4 s

19. Which of the following observations in a RHEED process illustrates the wavelike properties of electrons?

    A. Interference patterns arise from electrons reflected off different parts of the surface.
    B. A small number of electrons are transmitted through the film.
    C. The incident electron-beam energy is equal to the reflected electron-beam energy.
    D. The momentum of incident electrons is equal to the momentum of reflected electrons.

20. If the current associated with the incident electron beam is 1.0×10^{-5} A, how many electrons are striking the surface each second? (Note: The charge of an electron is 1.6×10^{-19} C, and the energy of an electron in this case is 2.0×10^{-15} J.)

    A. 6.3×10^{13}
    B. 2.0×10^{10}
    C. 5.0×10^{9}
    D. 1.3×10^{4}

21. Electrons incident on a rough surface, making an angle of 45° with respect to the normal to the reflecting surface, will be reflected:

    A. at 90° to the normal only.
    B. at 45° to the normal only.
    C. parallel to the normal only.
    D. at a variety of angles.

Solutions for this passage begin on next page.

18. According to Figure 1, what is the approximate amount of time required for the addition of one monolayer of material?

    A. 0.5 s
    B. 1 s
    C. 2 s
    D. 4 s

Content Classification: Waves and Periodic Motion/Periodic Motion

Cognitive Classification: Reasoning Using Quantitative Data

This question requires you to explain, describe, identify, or compare components of graphs, charts, figures, diagrams, and tables. The passage says that the surface is roughest halfway through the completion of a monolayer and smoothest when the monolayer is completed. You must read the data in Figure 1 of the passage and determine that the period of the oscillation is about 2.2 s.

Key: C

The time required is approximately 2 s.

Distractors

A   The time for the intensity to fall is about one-half of a second.

B   This is about the time for half of a cycle.

D   The time of the second minimum on the graph is about 4 s.

Difficulty Level: Medium (70%)

MCAT® is a program of the
Association of American Medical Colleges

19. Which of the following observations in a RHEED process illustrates the wavelike properties of electrons?

    A. Interference patterns arise from electrons reflected off different parts of the surface.
    B. A small number of electrons are transmitted through the film.
    C. The incident electron-beam energy is equal to the reflected electron-beam energy.
    D. The momentum of incident electrons is equal to the momentum of reflected electrons.

Content Classification: Waves and Periodic Motion/Wave Characteristics

Cognitive Classification: Identification of Main Ideas

This question requires you to identify major points of the passage. When the surface is smooth, electrons reflect in much the same way that light reflects from a perfect mirror. When a monolayer is partially completed, the electron beam is scattered in different directions.

Key: A

Interference patterns arise from electrons reflected off different parts of the surface.

Distractors

B   Electrons transmitted through the film lower the overall amount of reflection but do not contribute to the pattern of maxima and minima in the reflected intensity.

C   The energies of the incident and reflected electron beams are not related to the wavelike properties of the electrons.

D   Conservation of momentum does not explain the wavelike properties of the electrons.

Difficulty Level: Medium (55%)

20. If the current associated with the incident electron beam is 1.0×10^{-5} A, how many electrons are striking the surface each second? (Note: The charge of an electron is 1.6×10^{-19} C, and the energy of an electron in this case is 2.0×10^{-15} J.)

    A. 6.3×10^{13}
    B. 2.0×10^{10}
    C. 5.0×10^{9}
    D. 1.3×10^{4}

Content Classification: Electronic Circuit Elements/Current

Cognitive Classification: Flexibility and Adaptability in Scientific Reasoning

You are required to use the given information to solve a problem. Current is equal to charge (Coulombs) per unit time (seconds). You are given the charge per electron and the total current. The number of electrons per second is equal to the current (1.0×10^{-5} C/s) divided by the charge per electron (1.6×10^{-19} C/electron).

Check the units of an answer (electrons/second in this problem) to confirm that the result is reasonable.

Key: A

About 6.3×10^{13} electrons strike the surface each second.

Distractors

B   This value is the result of dividing the energy by the current and dropping a minus sign in the exponent.

C   This value results from dividing the current by the energy.

D   This value is obtained by dividing the energy by the charge of an electron.

Difficulty Level: Hard (35%)

21. Electrons incident on a rough surface, making an angle of 45° with respect to the normal to the reflecting surface, will be reflected:

    A. at 90° to the normal only.
    B. at 45° to the normal only.
    C. parallel to the normal only.
    D. at a variety of angles.

Content Classification: Light and Geometric Optics/Geometric Optics

Cognitive Classification: Identification of Main Ideas

This question requires you to identify a main idea in the passage. The passage discusses reflection of electrons from smooth and rough surfaces and compares the behavior of the electrons to that of light. Rough surfaces reduce the intensities of reflected electrons and of reflected light by scattering the incident beams in multiple directions.

Key: D

Electrons will be reflected at a variety of angles.

Distractors

A   If you add the 45° angle of incidence to a 45° angle of reflection, you obtain 90°.

B   This is the behavior of electrons reflecting from a smooth surface, not a rough one.

C   If you think the reflected beam will come out of the surface, you may arrive at this answer.

Difficulty Level: Medium (55%)

Physics
Discrete Questions

Physics

22. In which of the following media—solids, liquids, gases, and vacuum—can sound waves be transmitted?

    A. Gases and vacuum only
    B. Liquids and solids only
    C. Liquids, solids, and gases only
    D. Liquids and gases only

23. Which of the following is an example of α decay?

    A. $^{214}\text{Pb} \rightarrow \,^{214}\text{Bi}$
    B. $^{222}\text{Rn} \rightarrow \,^{218}\text{Po}$
    C. $^{210}\text{At} \rightarrow \,^{210}\text{Po}$
    D. $^{252}\text{Cf} \rightarrow \,^{132}\text{Sn}$

24. In an ac circuit, capacitors and inductors have frequency-dependent *reactances*

$$X_C = \frac{1}{2\pi f C} \quad \text{and} \quad X_L = 2\pi f L$$

which are similar to resistance and are also measured in ohms. In these expressions, f is frequency, C is capacitance, and L is inductance. Which of the following graphs best plots X_C and X_L against frequency?

A.
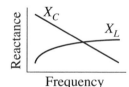

B.
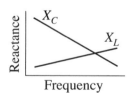

C.
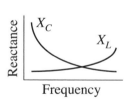

D.
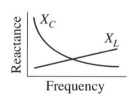

25. A rock is dropped from a cliff that is 100 m above ground level. How long does it take the rock to reach the ground? (Note: Use $g = 10$ m/s².)

    A. 4.5 s
    B. 10 s
    C. 14 s
    D. 20 s

26. An image of the Sun formed by a convex lens of focal length f appears at what distance from the lens?

    A. f in front of the lens
    B. f behind the lens
    C. $2f$ in front of the lens
    D. $2f$ behind the lens

27. Suppose electrons are moving at a constant velocity away from a source of microwaves. The electrons will interact with microwaves having a frequency that:

    A. increases with time.
    B. decreases with time.
    C. is higher than the frequency of the waves emitted by the source.
    D. is lower than the frequency of the waves emitted by the source.

28. Starting from a resting position, a certain toy catapult applies a constant force of 3.0 N to a projectile with a mass of 0.06 kg. How long will it take for the projectile to move 1.0 m?

    A. 0.02 s
    B. 0.04 s
    C. 0.20 s
    D. 0.40 s

Solutions for these discrete questions begin on next page.

22.   In which of the following media—solids, liquids, gases, and vacuum—can sound waves be transmitted?

    A. Gases and vacuum only
    B. Liquids and solids only
    C. Liquids, solids, and gases only
    D. Liquids and gases only

Content Classification: Phases and Phase Equilibria/Gas Phase

Cognitive Classification: Identification of Main Ideas

This question requires you to identify a major property of sound waves. For sound waves to propagate, there must be a physical medium consisting of atoms that can interact with each other. Recalling one example of each kind of medium is sufficient to determine the correct answer.

While many test questions you encounter will have sound waves in air, sound waves can also be carried in solids and liquids as well.

Key: C

Sound wave transmission is stopped only by a vacuum, so this is the best answer.

Distractors

A   Thinking that sound waves require big spaces to propagate will lead to this answer.

B   Thinking that sound waves require the molecules of the medium to be in continuous contact with one another to propagate will lead to this answer.

D   Thinking that sound waves require some kind of fluid to propagate will lead to this answer.

Difficulty Level: Easy (85%)

23. Which of the following is an example of α decay?

    A. $^{214}Pb \rightarrow {}^{214}Bi$

    B. $^{222}Rn \rightarrow {}^{218}Po$

    C. $^{210}At \rightarrow {}^{210}Po$

    D. $^{252}Cf \rightarrow {}^{132}Sn$

Content Classification: Atomic and Nuclear Structure/Radioactive Decay

Cognitive Classification: Identification of Main Ideas

This question requires you to identify the key differences that distinguish α decays from other kinds of decays. An α decay features the emission of an α particle (which contains 2 protons and 2 neutrons) from the nucleus of the decaying atom. Thus, the daughter atom's atomic number and atomic weight are 2 less and 4 less, respectively, than those of the mother atom.

Remember that γ decays do not change either A or Z, and you have unlimited use of the periodic table of the elements.

Key: B

Polonium's atomic number is 84, which is 2 less than radon's 86, and the atomic mass drops by 4.

Distractors

A   This product results from a β⁻ decay.

C   This product results from a β⁺ decay.

D   This product results from spontaneous fission.

Difficulty Level: Easy (85%)

24. In an ac circuit, capacitors and inductors have frequency-dependent *reactances*

$$X_C = \frac{1}{2\pi fC} \quad \text{and} \quad X_L = 2\pi fL$$

which are similar to resistance and are also measured in ohms. In these expressions, f is frequency, C is capacitance, and L is inductance. Which of the following graphs best plots X_C and X_L against frequency?

A. 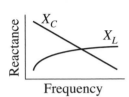　　　B. 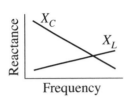　　　C. 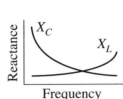　　　D.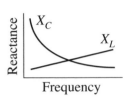

Content Classification: Electric Circuit Elements/Alternating Current Circuits

Cognitive Classification: Reasoning Using Quantitative Data

This question requires you to identify the appropriate graphs for X_L and X_C. The equation for X_L is linearly proportional to the frequency f with a positive slope, while X_C is inversely proportional to the frequency f.

Key: D

This graph shows the correct proportionalities for X_L and X_C.

Distractors

A　In this graph, X_L is proportional to the square root of f, while X_C is linearly proportional to the frequency f and has a negative slope.

B　In this graph, X_L is linearly proportional to f with a positive slope, but X_C is linearly proportional to f and has a negative slope.

C　In this graph, X_C is inversely proportional to the frequency f, but X_L is proportional to the square (or some higher power) of f.

Difficulty Level: Hard (30%)

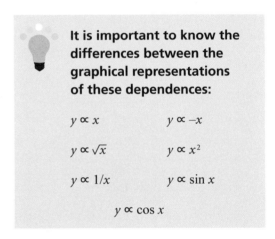

It is important to know the differences between the graphical representations of these dependences:

$y \propto x$　　　$y \propto -x$

$y \propto \sqrt{x}$　　　$y \propto x^2$

$y \propto 1/x$　　　$y \propto \sin x$

$y \propto \cos x$

MCAT® is a program of the
Association of American Medical Colleges

25. A rock is dropped from a cliff that is 100 m above ground level. How long does it take the rock to reach the ground? (Note: Use $g = 10$ m/s².)

A. 4.5 s

B. 10 s

C. 14 s

D. 20 s

Content Classification: Translational Motion/Freely Falling Bodies

Cognitive Classification: Flexibility and Adaptability in Scientific Reasoning

This question requires you to use the given information to solve a problem of the total fall time for the rock. You are told the rock falls from a 100-m height to the ground under the influence of a 10-m/s² acceleration. Since the rock starts at rest (*dropped*), evaluating the distance equation is relatively simple:

Be aware of the little words and phrases that indicate specific physical conditions, such as "dropped" ($v_0 = 0$, $a = g$), "from rest" ($v_0 = 0$), "uniform speed" (v_0 = constant), "accelerate uniformly" (a = constant), or "uniform B-field" (B is constant in both magnitude and direction).

$$d = v_0 t + \frac{1}{2} a t^2$$

$$\therefore \quad t = \sqrt{\frac{2d}{a}} = \sqrt{\frac{2(100 \text{ m})}{(10 \text{ m/s}^2)}} \approx 4.5 \text{ s}$$

Key: A

This is closest to the exact answer of $\sqrt{20}$ s.

Distractors

B This answer results from forgetting the square root and a factor of 2.

C This answer results from forgetting a factor of 10.

D This answer results from forgetting the square root.

Difficulty Level: Easy (75%)

26. An image of the Sun formed by a convex lens of focal length *f* appears at what distance from the lens?

    A. *f* in front of the lens
    B. *f* behind the lens
    C. 2*f* in front of the lens
    D. 2*f* behind the lens

Content Classification: Light and Geometrical Optics/Geometrical Optics

Cognitive Classification: Seeking Clarification

This question asks you for appropriate clarifying information about the location of the image of the Sun produced by this lens. Because the Sun is millions of times farther away from the lens than its focal length, the object distance can be considered to be infinite, and so the image distance will be very nearly equal to the focal length of the lens and will appear after the sunlight passes through the lens.

Key: B

This (real) image is on the side opposite to the Sun and at a distance *f*.

Remember, the focal length of a convex (positive) lens is the distance at which parallel rays entering the lens intersect after being refracted by the lens material. In a convex lens, this always occurs on the side of the lens opposite to the object emitting light.

Distractors

A Confusing *convex* and *concave* lenses leads to this answer.

C This answer results both from confusing *convex* and *concave* lenses and from misunderstanding the concept of focal length.

D Misunderstanding the concept of focal length leads to this answer.

Difficulty Level: Medium (45%)

27. Suppose electrons are moving at a constant velocity away from a source of microwaves. The electrons will interact with microwaves having a frequency that:

   A. increases with time.
   B. decreases with time.
   C. is higher than the frequency of the waves emitted by the source.
   D. is lower than the frequency of the waves emitted by the source.

Content Classification: Electricity and Electromagnetism/Electromagnetic Spectrum

Cognitive Classification: Hypothesis Testing

This question requires you to use your background knowledge and the specific facts given to predict the resulting wave frequency that would be seen by an observer traveling with the electrons. The microwave frequency that the electrons experience is understood through the application of the Doppler effect: when the observer approaches a source, wavelengths are shortened and frequencies increase; when the observer recedes from a source, wavelengths are lengthened and frequencies decrease. Furthermore, the frequency change is proportional to the observer's velocity; however, as long as the observer's velocity is a constant, the frequency change is also a constant.

 The properties of the Doppler effect are basically the same for all kinds of waves.

Key: D

The electrons are receding from the microwave source at a constant velocity.

Distractors

A   This answer results from mistakenly assuming that the detected frequency increases with increasing distance from the source.

B   This answer results from mistakenly assuming that the detected frequency decreases with increasing distance from the source.

C   Misinterpreting the relationship between the frequency change and the electrons' velocity leads to this answer.

Difficulty Level: Medium (50%)

28. Starting from a resting position, a certain toy catapult applies a constant force of 3.0 N to a projectile with a mass of 0.06 kg. How long will it take for the projectile to move 1.0 m?

 A. 0.02 s
 B. 0.04 s
 C. 0.20 s
 D. 0.40 s

Content Classification: Translational Motion/Acceleration

Cognitive Classification: Flexibility and Adaptability in Scientific Reasoning

This question requires you to use the given information to solve for the time required to move a projectile 1.0 m from rest. Because you are told that the force is a constant 3.0 N and that it acts on the projectile's mass of 0.06 kg, solving for the time can be done in three steps: (1) find the speed at the end of the 1.0 m; (2) convert the force information to the acceleration of the projectile; and (3) use the definition of *average acceleration*.

 You may encounter questions that involve both force and translational motion. When given the force that produces motion, however, it is not possible to complete any related translational motion calculation without also having the object's mass.

Step 1 uses the work–energy theorem

$$W = \Delta KE$$

$$Fd = \left(\frac{1}{2}mv^2 - 0\right)$$

$$\therefore \quad v = \sqrt{\frac{2Fd}{m}} = \sqrt{\frac{2(3.0\ \text{N})(1.0\ \text{m})}{(0.06\ \text{kg})}} = 10\ \text{m/s}$$

Step 2 applies Newton's second law

$$F = ma$$

$$\therefore \quad a = \frac{F}{m} = \frac{(3.0\ \text{N})}{(0.06\ \text{kg})} = 50\ \text{m/s}^2$$

Step 3 uses average acceleration to find t

$$\bar{a} = \frac{\Delta v}{t}$$

$$\therefore \quad t = \frac{(10\ \text{m/s} - 0\ \text{m/s})}{(50\ \text{m/s}^2)} = \frac{1}{5}\ \text{s} = 0.20\ \text{s}$$

MCAT® is a program of the
Association of American Medical Colleges

Key: C

This value results from the correct calculation.

Distractors

A   Making an error by a factor of 10 in the acceleration can lead to this answer.

B   This answer results from forgetting to calculate the square root.

D   Making an error by a factor of 10 in the acceleration and forgetting to calculate the square root can lead to this answer.

Difficulty Level: Medium (55%)

MCAT
Medical College
Admission Test

AAMC

Chapter 9:

Biological Sciences (BS)

I. Overall Section Format

The format of the MCAT Biological Sciences section is similar to that of the Physical Sciences section. There are 52 multiple-choice questions—39 are passage-based and 13 are independent—that test reasoning in biology and organic chemistry. Concepts included in the BS section, just like those in the PS section, are considered basic and are taught at the introductory level at the vast majority of undergraduate institutions. Advanced coursework is not required for the test.

BS Section Recap

- Covers biology and organic chemistry

- 52 questions

  - Seven passages with four to seven questions each, for a total of 39 passage-based questions

  - Thirteen independent questions

- 70 minutes

II. Types of Passages and Cognitive Skills Assessed

The four different passage formats in the BS section are the same as those in the PS section. As a reminder, these formats are information presentation, problem solving, research study, and persuasive argument. If you'd like to review these before beginning the BS practice section, please see page 66.

The cognitive skills tested in the BS section are identical to those in the PS section, as well. Please see pages 81 through 84 in the previous chapter for explanations and examples.

We follow with the content outline for the BS section.

Passage Type Identified in Sample Questions

Just as with the PS section, each BS sample in this chapter will be identified by type.

Cognitive Skill Identified in Sample Questions

Each sample BS question will identify the cognitive skill(s) it tests, such as "Seeking Clarification."

BIOLOGY

MOLECULAR BIOLOGY: ENZYMES AND METABOLISM

Molecular biology is concerned with the biochemical reactions and other processes that occur within living cells, including cellular metabolism and its regulation by enzymes. Questions in this topic area require you to understand enzyme structure and function and how different metabolites are processed within the cell.

A. Enzyme Structure and Function

1. Function of enzymes in catalyzing biological reactions
2. Reduction of activation energy
3. Substrates and enzyme specificity

B. Control of Enzyme Activity

1. Feedback inhibition
2. Competitive inhibition
3. Noncompetitive inhibition

C. Basic Metabolism

1. Glycolysis (anaerobic and aerobic, substrates and products)
2. Krebs cycle (substrates and products, general features of the pathway)
3. Electron transport chain and oxidative phosphorylation (substrates and products, general features of the pathway)
4. Metabolism of fats and proteins

MOLECULAR BIOLOGY: DNA AND PROTEIN SYNTHESIS

DNA contains the instructions necessary for the development and maintenance of living organisms. The processing of this genetic information to produce proteins is an important component of molecular biology. Questions in this topic area require you to understand nucleic acid structure and its functions in protein synthesis and the transmission of genetic information to future generations of cells.

DNA Structure and Function

A. DNA Structure and Function

1. Double-helix structure
2. DNA composition (purine and pyrimidine bases, deoxyribose, phosphate)
3. Base-pairing specificity, concept of complementarity
4. Function in transmission of genetic information

B. DNA Replication

1. Mechanism of replication (separation of strands, specific coupling of free nucleic acids, DNA polymerase, primer required)
2. Semiconservative nature of replication

C. Repair of DNA

1. Repair during replication
2. Repair of mutations

D. Recombinant DNA Techniques

1. Restriction enzymes
2. Hybridization
3. Gene cloning
4. PCR

Protein Synthesis

A. Genetic Code

1. Typical information flow (DNA → RNA → protein)
2. Codon–anticodon relationship, degenerate code
3. Missense and nonsense codons
4. Initiation and termination codons (function, codon sequences)

B. Transcription

1. mRNA composition and structure (RNA nucleotides, 5′ cap, poly-A tail)
2. tRNA and rRNA composition and structure (e.g., RNA nucleotides)
3. Mechanism of transcription (RNA polymerase, promoters, primer not required)

C. Translation

1. Roles of mRNA, tRNA, and rRNA; RNA base-pairing specificity
2. Role and structure of ribosomes

Chromosome organization plays an important role in gene expression within eukaryotic cells. To answer questions in this topic area, you will need to understand eukaryotic chromosome structure and the regulation of gene expression in eukaryotes.

A. Eukaryotic Chromosome Organization

1. Chromosomal proteins
2. Telomeres, centromeres

B. Control of Gene Expression in Eukaryotes

1. Transcription regulation
2. DNA binding proteins, transcription factors
3. Cancer as a failure of normal cellular controls, oncogenes, tumor suppressor genes
4. Posttranscriptional control, basic concept of splicing (introns, exons)

MICROBIOLOGY

Viruses, bacteria, and fungi represent a vast and integral part of life on Earth. They are essential to Earth's ecology and to the lives of many organisms yet often are sources of disease and death. Questions in this topic area require you to understand the general structures and life cycles of these groups of microbes.

A. Fungi

1. General characteristics
2. General aspects of life cycle

B. Virus Structure

1. General structural characteristics (nucleic acid and protein, enveloped and nonenveloped)
2. Lack of organelles and nucleus
3. Structural aspects of typical bacteriophage
4. Genomic content (RNA or DNA)
5. Size relative to bacteria and eukaryotic cells

C. Viral Life Cycle

1. Self-replicating biological units that must reproduce within specific host cell
2. Generalized phage and animal virus life cycles
    a. attachment to host cell, penetration of cell membrane or cell wall, entry of viral material
    b. use of host synthetic mechanisms to replicate viral components
    c. self-assembly and release of new viral particles
3. Retrovirus life cycle, integration into host DNA, reverse transcriptase
4. Transduction, transfer of genetic material by viruses

D. Prokaryotic Cell: Bacteria Structure

1. Lack of nuclear membrane and mitotic apparatus
2. Lack of typical eukaryotic organelles
3. Major classifications: bacilli (rod-shaped), spirilli (spiral-shaped), cocci (spherical); eubacteria, archaebacteria
4. Presence of cell wall
5. Flagellar propulsion

E. Prokaryotic Cell: Growth and Physiology

1. Reproduction by fission
2. High degree of genetic adaptability, acquisition of antibiotic resistance
3. Exponential growth
4. Existence of anaerobic and aerobic variants

F. Prokaryotic Cell: Genetics

1. Existence of plasmids, extragenomic DNA, transfer by conjugation
2. Transformation (incorporation into bacterial genome of DNA fragments from external medium)
3. Regulation of gene expression, coupling of transcription and translation

GENERALIZED EUKARYOTIC CELL

The cell is the basic unit from which all complex organisms are formed, and organelles within the cell carry out many life processes. To answer questions in this topic area, you will need to understand the general structure and functions of the eukaryotic cell and its components, including the plasma membrane, major organelles, and cytoskeleton. An understanding of eukaryotic cell processes, such as the movement of materials across membranes, signaling pathways, and the mitotic cell cycle, is also required.

A. Nucleus and Other Defining Characteristics

1. Defining characteristics (membrane-bound nucleus, presence of organelles, mitotic division)
2. Nucleus (compartmentalization, storage of genetic information)
3. Nucleolus (location, function)
4. Nuclear envelope, nuclear pores

B. Membrane-bound Organelles

1. Mitochondria
   a. site of ATP production
   b. self-replication; have own DNA and ribosomes
   c. inner and outer membrane
2. Lysosomes (vesicles containing hydrolytic enzymes)

3. Endoplasmic reticulum
   a. rough (RER) and smooth (SER)
   b. RER (site of ribosomes)
   c. role in membrane biosynthesis: SER (lipids), RER (transmembrane proteins)
   d. RER (role in biosynthesis of transmembrane and secreted proteins that are cotranslationally targeted to RER by signal sequence)
4. Golgi apparatus (general structure; role in packaging, secretion, and modification of glycoprotein carbohydrates)

C. Plasma Membrane

1. General function in cell containment
2. Protein and lipid components, fluid mosaic model
3. Osmosis
4. Passive and active transport
5. Membrane channels
6. Sodium–potassium pump
7. Membrane receptors, cell signaling pathways, second messengers
8. Membrane potential
9. Exocytosis and endocytosis
10. Cell–cell communication (general concepts of cellular adhesion)
    a. gap junctions
    b. tight junctions
    c. desmosomes

D. Cytoskeleton

1. General function in cell support and movement
2. Microfilaments (composition; role in cleavage and contractility)
3. Microtubules (composition; role in support and transport)
4. Intermediate filaments (role in support)
5. Composition and function of eukaryotic cilia and flagella
6. Centrioles, microtubule organizing centers

E. Cell Cycle and Mitosis

1. Interphase and mitosis (prophase, metaphase, anaphase, telophase)
2. Mitotic structures and processes
   a. centrioles, asters, spindles
   b. chromatids, centromeres, kinetochores
   c. nuclear membrane breakdown and reorganization
   d. mechanisms of chromosome movement
3. Phases of cell cycle (G_0, G_1, S, G_2, M)
4. Growth arrest

F. Apoptosis (Programmed Cell Death)

SPECIALIZED EUKARYOTIC CELLS AND TISSUES

Many eukaryotic cells become highly specialized to perform specific functions within the body. Questions in this topic area require you to understand the structure and function of the specialized cells that comprise the four basic tissue types.

A. Nerve Cell/Neural

1. Cell body (site of nucleus and organelles)
2. Axon (structure, function)
3. Dendrites (structure, function)
4. Myelin sheath, Schwann cells, oligodendrocytes, insulation of axon
5. Nodes of Ranvier (role in propagation of nerve impulse along axon)
6. Synapse (site of impulse propagation between cells)
7. Synaptic activity
   a. transmitter molecules
   b. synaptic knobs
   c. fatigue
   d. propagation between cells without resistance loss
8. Resting potential (electrochemical gradient)
9. Action potential
   a. threshold, all-or-none
   b. sodium–potassium pump
10. Excitatory and inhibitory nerve fibers (summation, frequency of firing)

B. Muscle Cell/Contractile

1. Abundant mitochondria in red muscle cells (ATP source)
2. Organization of contractile elements (actin and myosin filaments, cross bridges, sliding filament model)
3. Calcium regulation of contraction, sarcoplasmic reticulum
4. Sarcomeres ("I" and "A" bands, "M" and "Z" lines, "H" zone—general structure only)
5. Presence of troponin and tropomyosin

C. Other Specialized Cell Types

1. Epithelial cells (cell types, simple epithelium, stratified epithelium)
2. Endothelial cells
3. Connective tissue cells (major tissues and cell types, fiber types, loose versus dense, extracellular matrix)

The nervous and endocrine systems work together to regulate and coordinate activities of the whole organism. This is accomplished by exerting precise control over processes at the cellular and molecular levels. Questions require an understanding of the major structures and molecules involved in these regulatory systems and the general mechanisms by which both systems work. You will also need to understand how the systems detect and process sensory signals from the external and internal environments.

A. Endocrine System: Hormones

1. Function of endocrine system (specific chemical control at cell, tissue, and organ levels)
2. Definitions of endocrine gland, hormone
3. Major endocrine glands (names, locations, products)
4. Major types of hormones

B. Endocrine System: Mechanisms of Hormone Action

1. Cellular mechanisms of hormone action
2. Transport of hormones (bloodstream)
3. Specificity of hormones (target tissue)
4. Integration with nervous system (feedback control)

C. Nervous System: Structure and Function

1. Major functions
   a. high-level control and integration of body systems
   b. response to external influences
   c. sensory input
   d. integrative and cognitive abilities
2. Organization of vertebrate nervous system
3. Sensor and effector neurons
4. Sympathetic and parasympathetic nervous systems (functions, antagonistic control)
5. Reflexes
   a. feedback loop, reflex arc, effects on flexor and extensor muscles
   b. roles of spinal cord, brain
   c. efferent control

D. Nervous System: Sensory Reception and Processing

1. Skin, proprioceptive and somatic sensors
2. Olfaction, taste
3. Hearing
   a. ear structure
   b. mechanism of hearing
4. Vision
   a. light receptors
   b. eye structure
   c. visual image processing

The transport of gases, nutrients, and waste products toward and away from body tissues, and the protective activities of the immune system are among the vital functions performed by the circulatory, lymphatic, and immune systems. You should understand the structure and functions of these systems and the general mechanisms by which they carry out their functions.

A. Circulatory System

1. Functions (circulation of oxygen, nutrients, hormones, ions, and fluids; removal of metabolic waste)
2. Role in thermoregulation
3. Four-chambered heart (structure, function)
4. Systolic and diastolic pressure
5. Pulmonary and systemic circulation
6. Arterial and venous systems (arteries, arterioles, venules, veins)
   a. structural and functional differences
   b. pressure and flow characteristics
7. Capillary beds
   a. mechanisms of gas and solute exchange
   b. mechanism of heat exchange
8. Composition of blood
   a. plasma, chemicals, blood cells
   b. erythrocyte production and destruction (spleen, bone marrow)
   c. regulation of plasma volume
   d. coagulation, clotting mechanisms, role of liver in production of clotting factors
9. Oxygen and carbon dioxide transport by blood
   a. hemoglobin, hematocrit
   b. oxygen content
   c. oxygen affinity
10. Details of oxygen transport: biochemical characteristics of hemoglobin
    a. modification of oxygen affinity

B. Lymphatic System

1. Major functions
   a. equalization of fluid distribution
   b. transport of proteins and large glycerides
   c. return of materials to the blood
2. Composition of lymph (similarity to blood plasma; substances transported)
3. Source of lymph (diffusion from capillaries by differential pressure)
4. Lymph nodes (activation of lymphocytes)

C. Immune System: Innate and Adaptive Systems

1. Cells and their basic functions
   a. macrophages, neutrophils, mast cells, natural killer cells, dendritic cells
   b. T lymphocytes
   c. B lymphocytes, plasma cells
2. Tissues
   a. bone marrow
   b. spleen
   c. thymus
   d. lymph nodes
3. Basic aspects of innate immunity and inflammatory response
4. Concepts of antigen and antibody
5. Structure of antibody molecule
6. Mechanism of stimulation by antigen; antigen presentation

DIGESTIVE AND EXCRETORY SYSTEMS

The digestive system regulates the intake, processing, and absorption of nutrients. The excretory system processes and eliminates waste material from the body. Questions in this topic area require an understanding of the major structures of both systems, the order in which materials are processed, and the general mechanisms by which these processes occur.

A. Digestive System

1. Ingestion
   a. saliva as lubrication and source of enzymes
   b. epiglottal action
   c. pharynx (function in swallowing)
   d. esophagus (transport function)
2. Stomach
   a. storage and churning of food
   b. low pH, gastric juice, protection by mucus against self-destruction
   c. production of digestive enzymes, site of digestion
   d. structure (gross)
3. Liver
   a. production of bile
   b. roles in nutrient metabolism, vitamin storage
   c. roles in blood glucose regulation, detoxification
   d. structure (gross)
4. Bile
   a. storage in gallbladder
   b. function
5. Pancreas
   a. production of enzymes, bicarbonate
   b. transport of enzymes to small intestine
   c. structure (gross)

MCAT® is a program of the
Association of American Medical Colleges

6. Small intestine
    a. absorption of food molecules and water
    b. function and structure of villi
    c. production of enzymes, site of digestion
    d. neutralization of stomach acid
    e. structure (anatomic subdivisions)
7. Large intestine
    a. absorption of water
    b. bacterial flora
    c. structure (gross)
8. Rectum (storage and elimination of waste, feces)
9. Muscular control
    a. sphincter muscle
    b. peristalsis

B. Excretory System

1. Roles in homeostasis
    a. blood pressure
    b. osmoregulation
    c. acid–base balance
    d. removal of soluble nitrogenous waste
2. Kidney structure
    a. cortex
    b. medulla
3. Nephron structure
    a. glomerulus
    b. Bowman's capsule
    c. proximal tubule
    d. loop of Henle
    e. distal tubule
    f. collecting duct
4. Formation of urine
    a. glomerular filtration
    b. secretion and reabsorption of solutes
    c. concentration of urine
    d. countercurrent multiplier mechanism (basic function)
5. Storage and elimination (ureter, bladder, urethra)

The muscle and skeletal systems are concerned with the movement and support of the vertebrate body. They owe their structure and organization to the specialized contractile and connective tissues described under the topic area of specialized eukaryotic cells. Questions under the topic area of muscle and skeletal systems require an understanding of the various types of muscles, their control by the nervous system, and how these muscles are associated with the bones, ligaments, and tendons of the skeletal system.

A. Muscle System

1. Functions
    a. support, mobility
    b. peripheral circulatory assistance
    c. thermoregulation (shivering reflex)
2. Structural characteristics of skeletal, smooth, and cardiac muscle; striated versus nonstriated
3. Nervous control
    a. motor neurons
    b. neuromuscular junctions, motor end plates
    c. voluntary and involuntary muscles
    d. sympathetic and parasympathetic innervation

B. Skeletal System

1. Functions
    a. structural rigidity and support
    b. calcium storage
    c. physical protection
2. Skeletal structure
    a. specialization of bone types; structures
    b. joint structures
    c. endoskeleton versus exoskeleton
3. Cartilage (structure, function)
4. Ligaments, tendons
5. Bone structure
    a. calcium–protein matrix
    b. bone growth (osteoblasts, osteoclasts)

RESPIRATORY SYSTEM

The respiratory system functions in the exchange of gases between the body and the outside environment. You will need to understand the structure and function of the respiratory system.

A. Respiratory System

1. General structure and function
    a. gas exchange, thermoregulation
    b. protection against disease, particulate matter
2. Breathing mechanisms
    a. diaphragm, rib cage, differential pressure
    b. resiliency and surface tension effects

SKIN SYSTEM

The skin is the largest organ in the human body and has important roles in homeostasis. Questions in this topic area require an understanding of the basic structure and functions of the skin.

A. Skin System

1. Functions in homeostasis and osmoregulation
2. Functions in thermoregulation
    a. hair, erectile musculature
    b. fat layer for insulation
    c. sweat glands, location in dermis
    d. vasoconstriction and vasodilation in surface capillaries
3. Physical protection
    a. nails, calluses, hair
    b. protection against abrasion, disease organisms
4. Structure
    a. layer differentiation, cell types, tissue types (epithelial, connective)
    b. relative impermeability to water

REPRODUCTIVE SYSTEM AND DEVELOPMENT

This topic area covers the formation and development of vertebrate organisms. Questions require an understanding of the processes of gametogenesis, sexual reproduction (including the cells and organs involved), and embryogenesis.

A. Reproductive System

1. Male and female reproductive structures and their functions
    a. gonads
    b. genitalia
    c. differences between male and female structures
2. Gametogenesis by meiosis

3. Ovum and sperm
    a. differences in formation
    b. differences in morphology
    c. relative contribution to next generation
4. Reproductive sequence (fertilization, implantation, development, birth)

B. Embryogenesis

1. Stages of early development (order and general features of each)
    a. fertilization
    b. cleavage
    c. blastula formation
    d. gastrulation
        i. first cell movements
        ii. formation of primary germ layers (endoderm, mesoderm, ectoderm)
    e. neurulation
2. Major structures arising out of primary germ layers

C. Developmental Mechanisms

1. Cell specialization
    a. determination
    b. differentiation
    c. tissue types
2. Cell communication in development
3. Gene regulation in development
4. Programmed cell death

GENETICS

Much of the current understanding of heredity stems from the concepts of Mendelian genetics and the process of meiosis. For this topic area, you will need to have an understanding of Mendelian concepts, different modes of inheritance, the process of meiosis, and various types of mutations that lead to genetic variability.

A. Mendelian Concepts

1. Phenotype and genotype (definitions, probability calculations, pedigree analysis)
2. Gene
3. Locus
4. Allele (single, multiple)
5. Homozygosity and heterozygosity
6. Wild type
7. Recessiveness
8. Complete dominance
9. Codominance
10. Incomplete dominance, leakage, penetrance, expressivity
11. Gene pool

B. Meiosis and Genetic Variability

1. Significance of meiosis
2. Important differences between meiosis and mitosis
3. Segregation of genes
   a. independent assortment
   b. linkage
   c. recombination
   d. single crossovers
   e. double crossovers
4. Sex-linked characteristics
   a. very few genes on Y chromosome
   b. sex determination
   c. cytoplasmic inheritance, mitochondrial inheritance
5. Mutation
   a. general concept of mutation
   b. types of mutations (random, translation error, transcription error, base substitution, insertion, deletion, frameshift)
   c. chromosomal rearrangements (inversion, translocation)
   d. advantageous versus deleterious mutation
   e. inborn errors of metabolism
   f. relationship of mutagens to carcinogens

C. Analytic Methods

1. Hardy–Weinberg principle
2. Testcross (backcross; concepts of parental, F1, and F2 generations)

EVOLUTION

Genetic variability has led to the evolution of a diverse set of species through natural selection. Questions require a general understanding of the processes involved in natural selection and speciation, and the features that distinguish chordates from other organisms.

A. Evolution

1. Natural selection
   a. fitness concept
   b. selection by differential reproduction
   c. concepts of natural and group selection
   d. evolutionary success as increase in percent representation in the gene pool of the next generation

2. Speciation
   a. definition of species
   b. polymorphism
   c. adaptation and specialization
   d. concepts of ecological niche, competition
   e. concept of population growth through competition
   f. inbreeding
   g. outbreeding
   h. bottlenecks, genetic drift
   i. divergent, parallel, and convergent evolution
   j. symbiotic relationships
      i. parasitism
      ii. commensalism
      iii. mutualism
3. Relationship between ontogeny and phylogeny
4. Evolutionary time as measured by gradual random changes in genome
5. Origin of life

B. Comparative Anatomy

1. Chordate features
   a. notochord
   b. pharangeal pouches, brachial arches
   c. dorsal nerve cord
2. Vertebrate phylogeny (vertebrate classes and relations to each other)

ORGANIC CHEMISTRY

THE COVALENT BOND

The structures, bond descriptions, and bond strengths of organic compounds are important when determining their reactions and chemistry. You should be familiar with common nomenclature, methods for evaluating stereochemistry, hybrid orbitals, bond strengths, and resonance.

A. Sigma and Pi Bonds

1. Hybrid orbitals (sp^3, sp^2, sp, and their respective geometries)
2. Valence shell electron-pair repulsion (VSEPR) theory, predictions of shapes of molecules (e.g., NH_3, H_2O, CO_2)
3. Structural formulas
4. Delocalized electrons and resonance in ions and molecules

B. Multiple Bonding

1. Its effect on bond length and bond energies
2. Rigidity in molecular structure

C. Stereochemistry of Covalently Bonded Molecules

1. Isomers
   a. constitutional isomers
   b. stereoisomers (e.g., diastereomers, enantiomers, cis and trans isomers)
   c. conformational isomers
2. Polarization of light, specific rotation
3. Absolute and relative configuration
   a. conventions for writing R and S forms
   b. conventions for writing E and Z forms
4. Racemic mixtures, separation of enantiomers

MOLECULAR STRUCTURE AND SPECTRA

The identification of organic compounds is of prime interest when determining the products of a particular reaction. You should understand the major spectroscopic techniques employed to determine the structures of the major groups of organic compounds as well as understand the features of the compounds that affect their spectra. You should be familiar with proton nuclear magnetic resonance (^{1}H NMR) spectroscopy, infrared (IR) spectroscopy, ultraviolet (UV) spectroscopy, and mass spectrometry.

A. Absorption Spectroscopy

1. Infrared region
   a. intramolecular vibrations and rotations
   b. recognizing common characteristic group absorptions, fingerprint region
2. Visible region
   a. absorption in visible region yielding complementary color
   b. effect of structural changes on absorption
4. Ultraviolet region
   a. π-electron and nonbonding electron transitions
   b. conjugated systems

B. Mass Spectrometry

1. Mass-to-charge ratio (m/z)
2. Molecular ion peak

C. ^{1}H NMR Spectroscopy

1. Protons in a magnetic field, equivalent protons
2. Spin–spin splitting

SEPARATIONS AND PURIFICATIONS

Although reactions and properties of organic compounds make up a major portion of organic chemistry, another important area is the separation and purification of these compounds. You should be familiar with the methods used in these processes as well as with the features of the different organic compounds that make the separation and purification possible.

A. Extraction (Distribution of Solute Between Two Immiscible Solvents)

B. Distillation

C. Chromatography (Basic Principles Involved in Separation Process)

1. Gas–liquid chromatography
2. Paper chromatography
3. Thin-layer chromatography

D. Recrystallization (Solvent Choice from Solubility Data)

HYDROCARBONS

The chemistry of alkanes is a major part of organic chemistry. Concepts such as combustion, stability of free radicals, and ring strain are included in this topic area. You will need to understand these concepts to answer questions on hydrocarbons.

A. Alkanes

1. Description
   a. nomenclature
   b. physical properties
2. Important reactions
   a. combustion
   b. substitution reactions with halogens, etc.
3. General principles
   a. stability of free radicals, chain reaction mechanism, inhibition
   b. ring strain in cyclic compounds
   c. bicyclic molecules

OXYGEN-CONTAINING COMPOUNDS

The principal reactions of oxygen-containing compounds are critical to the interpretation of many reactions in organic chemistry. The fundamental principles and mechanisms of these reactions offer a good guide to the understanding of organic reactions. The concepts of nucleophiles, electrophiles, organic acids and bases, acidic protons, oxidations, reductions, and physical properties of various oxygen-containing compounds are outlined below. In addition, you should understand the major reactions involving condensations, rearrangements, and dimerizations, as well as the steric and electronic effects of substituents.

A. Alcohols

1. Description
   a. nomenclature
   b. physical properties
2. Important reactions
   a. substitution reactions (S_N1 or S_N2, depending on alcohol and derived alkyl halide)
   b. oxidation
   c. pinacol rearrangement in polyhydroxyalcohols, synthetic uses
   d. protection of alcohols
   e. reactions with $SOCl_2$ and PBr_3
   f. preparation of mesylates and tosylates
   g. esterification
   h. inorganic esters
3. General principles
   a. hydrogen bonding
   b. acidity of alcohols compared to other classes of oxygen-containing compounds
   c. effect of chain branching on physical properties

B. Aldehydes and Ketones

1. Description
   a. nomenclature
   b. physical properties
2. Important reactions
   a. nucleophilic addition reactions at C=O bond
      i. acetal, hemiacetal
      ii. imine, enamine
   b. reactions at adjacent positions
      i. haloform reactions
      ii. aldol condensation
      iii. oxidation
   c. 1,3-dicarbonyl compounds, internal hydrogen bonding
   d. keto–enol tautomerism
   e. organometallic reagents
   f. Wolff–Kishner reaction
   g. Grignard reagents
3. General principles
   a. effect of substituents on reactivity of C=O; steric hindrance
   b. acidity of α hydrogens; carbanions
   c. α,β–unsaturated carbonyl compounds, their resonance structures

C. Carboxylic Acids

1. Description
   a. nomenclature
   b. physical properties and solubility
2. Important reactions
   a. carboxyl group reactions
      i. nucleophilic attack
      ii. reduction
      iii. decarboxylation
      iv. esterification
   b. reactions at α position
      i. halogenation
      ii. substitution reactions
3. General principles
   a. hydrogen bonding
   b. dimerization
   c. acidity of the carboxyl group
   d. inductive effect of substituents
   e. resonance stability of carboxylate anion

D. Acid Derivatives (Acid Chlorides, Anhydrides, Amides, Esters)

1. Description
   a. nomenclature
   b. physical properties
2. Important reactions
   a. preparation of acid derivatives
   b. nucleophilic substitution
   c. Hofmann rearrangement
   d. transesterification
   e. hydrolysis of fats and glycerides (saponification)
   f. hydrolysis of amides
3. General principles
   a. relative reactivity of acid derivatives
   b. steric effects
   c. electronic effects
   d. Strain (e.g., β-lactams)

E. Keto Acids and Esters

1. Description
   a. nomenclature
2. Important reactions
   a. decarboxylation
   b. acetoacetic ester synthesis

MCAT® is a program of the
Association of American Medical Colleges

3. General principles
    a. acidity of α hydrogens in β–keto esters
    b. keto–enol tautomerism

AMINES

Nitrogen-containing compounds often have unique properties due to their basicity and electronic effects. The stabilization of adjacent carbocations and the solubility properties of the ammonium salts are vital to a wide area of biological and organic reactions. Major reactions of amide formation and alkylations are also important. Questions about amines require you to understand these concepts.

1. Description
    a. nomenclature
    b. stereochemistry, physical properties
2. Important reactions
    a. amide formation
    b. reaction with nitrous acid
    c. alkylation
    d. Hofmann elimination
3. General principles
    a. basicity
    b. stabilization of adjacent carbocations
    c. effect of substituents on basicity of aromatic amines

BIOLOGICAL MOLECULES

You should be familiar with the general types of molecules that are biologically significant and the respective reactions of these molecules. Emphasis will be placed on the descriptions and reactions of the molecules listed below.

A. Carbohydrates

1. Description
    a. nomenclature, classification, common names
    b. absolute configurations
    c. cyclic structure and conformations of hexoses
    d. epimers and anomers
2. Hydrolysis of the glycoside linkage
3. Reactions of monosaccharides

B. Amino Acids and Proteins

1. Description
    a   absolute configuration(s)
    b. amino acids classified as dipolar ions
    c. classification
        i.   acidic or basic
        ii. hydrophobic or hydrophilic
2. Important reactions
    a. peptide linkage
    b. hydrolysis
4. General principles
    a. 1° structure of proteins
    b. 2° structure of proteins

C. Lipids

1. Description, structure
    a. steroids
    b. terpenes
    c. triacyl glycerols
    d. free fatty acids

D. Phosphorus Compounds

1. Description
    a. structure of phosphoric acids (anhydrides, esters)
2. Important reactions
    a. Wittig reaction

The BS sample passages, questions, and solutions begin on the next page.

Biology

Passage Set I

Biology

Glucocerebrosides are a type of glycolipid found in the plasma membrane of red blood cells (RBCs). Normally, worn-out RBCs are engulfed and destroyed by macrophages in the spleen, where catabolism of the glucocerebrosides is initiated by *acid beta-glucocerebrosidase*, a lysosomal enzyme abbreviated as "GBA." The human *GBA* gene is located on chromosome 1 and produces a 2571-nucleotide mRNA, which is translated into a 536-amino acid protein.

Many mutations in *GBA* have been characterized that render the GBA enzyme either partially or completely nonfunctional. Although individuals who have only one mutant *GBA* allele are healthy, those that carry two mutant *GBA* alleles develop Gaucher disease. The ability of macrophages to catabolize glucocerebrosides is compromised in people who have Gaucher disease, causing the macrophages to store undigested glucocerebrosides within their lysosomes. These enlarged macrophages collect in tissues such as the spleen, liver, and bone marrow, causing malfunctions of those tissues. The spleens of people who have Gaucher disease often become enlarged and overactive, and their bones become weak and sometimes painful. Blood cell production is also compromised.

MCAT® is a program of the
Association of American Medical Colleges

1. Based on the passage, which of the following best describes Gaucher disease? Gaucher disease is:

   A. a heritable lysosomal storage disorder.
   B. a nonheritable lipid metabolism disorder.
   C. caused by the inappropriate synthesis of glucocerebrosides.
   D. characterized by increased numbers of circulating RBCs.

2. Which of the following best traces the cellular location of GBA immediately after its release from the ribosome to its arrival at its functional location?

   A. Rough endoplasmic reticulum → Golgi apparatus → plasma membrane
   B. Rough endoplasmic reticulum → Golgi apparatus → lysosome
   C. Cytosol → plasma membrane
   D. Cytosol → lysosome

3. Of an overactive spleen and a compromised ability to produce blood cells, which, if either, would be likely to contribute to anemia, a condition common in individuals who have Gaucher disease?

   A. An overactive spleen only
   B. A compromised ability to produce blood cells only
   C. Both an overactive spleen and a compromised ability to produce blood cells
   D. Neither an overactive spleen nor a compromised ability to produce blood cells

4. Based on the passage, what can be determined about the inheritance pattern of Gaucher disease in humans?

   A. Only that it is dominant
   B. Only that it is recessive
   C. Only that it is autosomal
   D. That it is autosomal recessive

5. In all, how many nucleotides of the GBA mRNA are NOT translated into an amino acid in the GBA protein?

   A. 3
   B. 963
   C. 1,608
   D. 2,035

6. Which of the following treatment strategies would be LEAST likely to alleviate the symptoms of Gaucher disease in a person who carries two completely non-functional alleles of GBA?

   A. Stimulating the development of the person's own macrophages
   B. Targeting wild-type copies of the GBA enzyme to the person's macrophages
   C. Taking bone marrow from a person who does not have Gaucher disease and transplanting it into the person who does
   D. Chemically reducing glucocerebroside synthesis in the person

7. One common GBA mutation results in the replacement of a single amino acid in the enzyme: the asparagine at position 370 is replaced with serine. Otherwise, the sequence of the mutant enzyme is identical to that of the wild-type enzyme. Which of the following mutations is most likely to have generated this mutant allele?

   A. A nonsense mutation most likely resulting from a single base pair substitution in the DNA
   B. A nonsense mutation most likely resulting from the deletion of a single base pair in the DNA
   C. A missense mutation most likely resulting from a single base pair substitution in the DNA
   D. A missense mutation most likely resulting from the deletion of a single base pair in the DNA

Solutions for this passage begin on next page.

1. Based on the passage, which of the following best describes Gaucher disease? Gaucher disease is:

   A. a heritable lysosomal storage disorder.
   B. a nonheritable lipid metabolism disorder.
   C. caused by the inappropriate synthesis of glucocerebrosides.
   D. characterized by increased numbers of circulating RBCs.

Content Classification: Generalized Eukaryotic Cell/Membrane-Bound Organelle

Cognitive Classification: Identification of Main Ideas

This question requires you to identify the statement that most accurately describes Gaucher disease. The passage indicates that Gaucher disease is caused by mutations in the *GBA* gene, which encodes a lysosomal enzyme that catabolizes glucocerebrosides. The uncatabolized glucocerebrosides accumulate and are stored in macrophagic lysosomes, leading to the symptoms of the disease.

 Confusing the meanings of *metabolism*, *catabolism*, and *anabolism* could lead to the incorrect answer choice of **C**. Metabolism is the sum of an organism's chemical processes and includes both degradative (catabolic) and synthetic (anabolic) pathways.

Key: A

Gaucher disease is correctly described as a heritable lysosomal storage disorder.

Distractors

B   Although Gaucher disease can correctly be described as a lipid metabolism disorder, it is caused by mutations in a specific gene, implying the disease is heritable.

C   Gaucher disease affects the catabolism (breaking down) of glucocerebrosides, not their synthesis.

D   Gaucher disease causes the spleen to be overactive and blood cell production to be compromised. Both of these conditions would lead to *decreased*, not increased, numbers of circulating RBCs.

Difficulty Level: Easy (85%)

2. Which of the following best traces the cellular location of GBA immediately after its release from the ribosome to its arrival at its functional location?

    A. Rough endoplasmic reticulum → Golgi apparatus → plasma membrane
    B. Rough endoplasmic reticulum → Golgi apparatus → lysosome
    C. Cytosol → plasma membrane
    D. Cytosol → lysosome

Content Classification: Generalized Eukaryotic Cell/Membrane-Bound Organelles

Cognitive Classification: Seeking Clarification

This question requires you to identify relevant background information about protein trafficking in eukaryotic cells. Similar to secreted and integral plasma membrane proteins, lysosomal proteins are synthesized on the rough endoplasmic reticulum and travel to the Golgi apparatus, where they are sorted according to the protein's ultimate destination, in this case, the lysosome.

Key: B

The cellular location of GBA is correctly traced from the rough endoplasmic reticulum, to the Golgi apparatus, to its functional location, the lysosome.

Distractors

A   The functional location of GBA is incorrectly identified as the plasma membrane.

C   The site of GBA synthesis is incorrectly identified as the cytosol, and the functional location of GBA is incorrectly identified as the plasma membrane.

D   The site of GBA synthesis is incorrectly identified as the cytosol.

Difficulty Level: Medium (65%)

3. Of an overactive spleen and a compromised ability to produce blood cells, which, if either, would be likely to contribute to anemia, a condition common in individuals who have Gaucher disease?

    A. An overactive spleen only
    B. A compromised ability to produce blood cells only
    C. Both an overactive spleen and a compromised ability to produce blood cells
    D. Neither an overactive spleen nor a compromised ability to produce blood cells

Content Classification: Circulatory, Lymphatic, and Immune Systems/Circulatory System

Cognitive Classification: Hypothesis Testing

This question requires you to determine the likely cause or causes of anemia in individuals who have Gaucher disease. Anemia is an inability to deliver normal levels of oxygen to the body's cells. It has many causes, including a lack of iron, hemoglobin, or RBCs. An overactive spleen would contribute to anemia by destroying a greater-than-normal number of RBCs, thus reducing the total number of circulating RBCs. Similarly, a compromised ability to produce blood cells would lead to a decrease in the total number of circulating RBCs.

Key: C

This choice correctly identifies both an overactive spleen and an inability to produce blood cells as likely contributors to anemia.

Distractors

A   This choice fails to identify a compromised ability to produce blood cells as a likely contributor to anemia.

B   This choice fails to identify an overactive spleen as a likely contributor to anemia.

D   This choice fails to identify both an overactive spleen and a compromised ability to produce blood cells as likely contributors to anemia.

Difficulty Level: Medium (55%)

Neither the passage nor the question describes anemia. However, many people can make an association between anemia and low levels of iron in the body. Even if this is all you remember about anemia, you can still reason through the question.

Consider how low levels of iron might relate to each of the options presented in the question. Iron plays a critical role in the ability of hemoglobin to carry oxygen. Hemoglobin is produced by RBCs. Therefore, it is reasonable to assume that either low levels of hemoglobin or low levels of RBCs are likely to have an effect similar to the effect of low levels of iron on the body. Thus, a compromised ability to produce blood cells would be likely to contribute to anemia.

A major function of the spleen is to destroy worn-out RBCs. An overactive spleen would be likely to destroy excess RBCs, lowering the total amount of RBCs in the blood, which would also be likely to contribute to anemia.

In general, when presented with a term or question of which you are uncertain, break it down into smaller parts and assess how what you do know relates to each part. It is often useful to look back in the passage or in the question itself for additional background information that can help you reason out the most logical answer.

MCAT® is a program of the
Association of American Medical Colleges

4. Based on the passage, what can be determined about the inheritance pattern of Gaucher disease in humans?

    A. Only that it is dominant
    B. Only that it is recessive
    C. Only that it is autosomal
    D. That it is autosomal recessive

Content Classification: Genetics/Mendelian Concepts

Cognitive Classification: Flexibility and Adaptability in Scientific Reasoning

This question requires you to extend concepts presented in the passage in order to assess which conclusion or conclusions about the inheritance pattern of Gaucher disease are supported by the passage. The passage states that *GBA*, the gene that causes Gaucher disease, is located on chromosome 1; therefore, it can be concluded that the inheritance pattern of Gaucher disease is autosomal. The passage also states that individuals who have only one wild-type allele of *GBA* are healthy, but that individuals who carry two mutant alleles of *GBA* have Gaucher disease. An inheritance pattern in which only those individuals who are homozygous for mutant alleles display the disease phenotype and heterozygotes display a healthy phenotype leads to the conclusion that the disease phenotype is inherited in a recessive pattern.

The information needed to answer this question is found in two different parts of the passage. Failure to locate either piece of information would lead to an incomplete conclusion about the inheritance pattern of *GBA*.

Key: D

The inheritance pattern of Gaucher disease is correctly identified as autosomal recessive.

Distractors

A The inheritance pattern of Gaucher disease is incorrectly identified as dominant.

B Although the inheritance pattern of Gaucher disease is correctly identified as recessive, this choice fails to identify that the inheritance pattern of Gaucher disease is also autosomal.

C Although the inheritance pattern of Gaucher disease is correctly identified as autosomal, this choice fails to identify that the inheritance pattern of Gaucher disease is also recessive.

Difficulty Level: Medium (50%)

5. In all, how many nucleotides of the *GBA* mRNA are NOT translated into amino acids in the GBA protein?

    A. 3
    B. 963
    C. 1608
    D. 2035

Content Classification: DNA and Protein Synthesis/Protein Synthesis

Cognitive Classification: Flexibility and Adaptability in Scientific Reasoning

This question requires you to use the information given in the passage and background knowledge of the genetic code to compute the number of nucleotides of the *GBA* mRNA that are NOT translated into an amino acids. The passage states that the *GBA* mRNA is 2571 nucleotides long and that the *GBA* protein contains 536 amino acids. Knowing that each amino acid codon consists of 3 nucleotides, you can calculate the number of nucleotides in the *GBA* mRNA that code for amino acids by multiplying 536 by 3. Subtracting this number from the total number of nucleotides in the *GBA* mRNA gives the number of nucleotides that are NOT translated into an amino acid.

 The use of all capital letters in "NOT" signifies that you are looking for an exception. In this case, the exception is in the question itself: you are to calculate the number of nucleotides in the *GBA* mRNA that do NOT code for an amino acid. Failure to notice this "NOT" could lead you to calculate the number of nucleotides in the *GBA* mRNA that *do* code for an amino acid in the GBA protein, which is presented as a distractor.

Key: B

Using the described method, the number of nucleotides in the *GBA* mRNA that do NOT code for an amino acid is calculated to be 963. That is,

$$2571 \text{ total nucleotides} - (3 \text{ nucleotides/amino acid} \times 536 \text{ amino acids}) =$$
$$(2571 - 1608) \text{ nucleotides} = 963 \text{ nucleotides}$$

 When asked to do a calculation, keep track of the units. Double-check that you are adding or subtracting numbers with like units and that when you are multiplying or dividing, the units cancel out in a way that gives you an answer with the units you need. In this question, the 3 nucleotides/amino acid conversion factor is critical to convert the number of amino acids (which you are given) to the corresponding number of nucleotides (the units you need).

Distractors

A   Three is the number of nucleotides in a single codon. This answer could be reached by assuming the *GBA* mRNA contains only nucleotides that code for amino acids and a single stop codon. Following this logic, the three nucleotides would be for the stop codon. However, mRNA contains 5' and 3' untranslated regions in addition to the nucleotides in the coding region. This is supported by the passage, which states that the *GBA* mRNA is 2571 nucleotides, a number that is significantly greater than the 1608 nucleotides that code for amino acids.

C   The number of nucleotides in the *GBA* mRNA that *code* for amino acids is 1608. This number is reached using the following calculation:

3 nucleotides/amino acid × 536 amino acids = 1608 nucleotides

This calculation neglects to subtract the number of nucleotides that code for amino acids from the total number of nucleotides in the *GBA* mRNA.

D   The number of 2035 nucleotides can be reached by failing to multiply the number of amino acids in *GBA* by the 3 nucleotides/amino acid conversion factor:

2571 total nucleotides − 536 amino acids = 2035

This calculation could be eliminated as incorrect by noticing that it subtracts unlike units: amino acids are being subtracted from nucleotides.

Difficulty Level: Easy (80%)

6. Which of the following treatment strategies would be LEAST likely to alleviate the symptoms of Gaucher disease in a person who carries two completely nonfunctional alleles of *GBA*?

A. Stimulating the development of the person's own macrophages
B. Targeting wild-type copies of the GBA enzyme to the person's macrophages
C. Taking bone marrow from a person who does not have Gaucher disease and transplanting it into the person who does
D. Chemically reducing glucocerebroside synthesis in the person

---

Content Classification: Circulatory, Lymphatic, and Immune Systems/Circulatory System

Cognitive Classification: Evaluation Processes

This question requires you to determine whether a procedure fulfills a task requirement by evaluating whether certain treatments would be likely to alleviate the symptoms of Gaucher disease. You are asked to choose the treatment that is LEAST likely to do so. It can be inferred from the passage that the main cause of symptoms in Gaucher disease is the accumulation of glucocerebrosides within macrophagic lysosomes. Treatments that reduce the accumulation of glucocerebrosides are therefore likely to alleviate the symptoms of the disease. One general strategy is to reduce the amount of glucocerebrosides produced by the person who has Gaucher disease; a second strategy is to increase the degradation of glucocerebrosides by providing functional GBA enzyme to the person who has Gaucher disease.

Key: A

Since the person being considered carries only completely nonfunctional alleles of *GBA*, stimulating the development of the person's own macrophages would not provide functional GBA enzyme. Any GBA these macrophages produce would be nonfunctional and would not help reduce the amount of glucocerebrosides. Additional macrophages are also unlikely to slow the synthesis of glucocerebrosides. Therefore, this treatment is unlikely to alleviate the symptoms of Gaucher disease.

Distractors

B   Providing wild-type copies of the GBA enzyme to the person's macrophages would allow the macrophages to successfully catabolize glucocerebrosides and would thus alleviate the symptoms of the disease.

C   Transplanting bone marrow from a healthy person into a person who has Gaucher disease would allow the person with Gaucher disease to produce macrophages capable of synthesizing functional GBA enzyme. In turn, this would allow the person to catabolize glucocerebrosides, alleviating the symptoms of the disease.

D   Chemically reducing the synthesis of glucocerebrosides would decrease the amount of glucocerebrosides available to accumulate and would thus alleviate the symptoms of the disease.

Difficulty Level: Medium (60%)

7. One common *GBA* mutation results in the replacement of a single amino acid in the enzyme: the asparagine at position 370 is replaced with serine. Otherwise, the sequence of the mutant enzyme is identical to that of the wild-type enzyme. Which of the following mutations is most likely to have generated this mutant allele?

    A. A nonsense mutation most likely resulting from a single base-pair substitution in the DNA
    B. A nonsense mutation most likely resulting from the deletion of a single base pair in the DNA
    C. A missense mutation most likely resulting from a single base-pair substitution in the DNA
    D. A missense mutation most likely resulting from the deletion of a single base pair in the DNA

Content Classifications: Genetics/Meiosis and Genetic Variability; DNA and Protein Synthesis/Genetic Code

Cognitive Classification: Flexibility and Adaptability in Scientific Reasoning

This question requires you to apply the given information and your background knowledge to develop a hypothesis about the type of mutation that would have produced the mutant *GBA* allele that is described in the question. You are told that a single amino acid was replaced with another single amino acid. This mutation occurred at amino acid 370 of a 536–amino acid protein and was the only change in the protein sequence. This best describes a missense mutation, a mutation that alters a codon so that it codes for a different amino acid. Because only one amino acid in this particular protein is changed, the missense mutation should be the result of a change in the genetic sequence that affects only one codon.

 One way to keep nonsense and missense mutations straight is to remember that a nonsense mutation makes "no sense" in that it codes for *no* amino acid. On the other hand, a missense mutation codes for an amino acid with a *mis*taken identity relative to the amino acid that is in the wild-type protein.

Key: C

The mutation is correctly identified as a missense mutation and is associated with a single base-pair substitution, a change in the DNA sequence that would affect only one codon.

Distractors

A   Although a base-pair substitution would affect only one codon, a nonsense mutation is a mutation in which a codon that codes for an amino acid is replaced with a stop codon—not with a codon for another amino acid—and results in a truncated protein.

B   The mutation is incorrectly identified as a nonsense mutation and is incorrectly associated with the deletion of a single base pair in the DNA, a change in the DNA sequence that would shift the reading frame of the gene, potentially changing the sequence of all the amino acids encoded by the remainder of the gene. Although frameshift mutations often change the length of the protein by changing the placement of the stop codon, they are not equivalent to non-sense mutations.

D   The mutation is correctly identified as a missense mutation but is incorrectly associated with the deletion of a single base pair in the DNA, a change in the DNA sequence that would shift the reading frame of the gene, potentially changing the sequence of all the amino acids encoded by the remainder of the gene.

Difficulty Level: Easy (75%)

Biology
Passage Set II

Biology

In many animals, including mice and humans, the liver quickly regenerates to its original size after a partial hepatectomy in which two-thirds of this organ is removed. Hepatocyte proliferation in response to this surgery is significantly reduced in mice with inadequate platelet activity or number.

Platelets carry 95% of blood serotonin, which is made by endocrine cells that line the gastrointestinal tract. Researchers experimentally tested the hypothesis that platelet serotonin is responsible for platelets' positive effect on hepatocyte proliferation. The number of hepatocytes expressing Ki67 protein was used as a measure of liver regeneration because Ki67 is detected exclusively in the nuclei of proliferating cells.

Experiment 1

Wild-type mice were treated with an anti-platelet antibody that destroys 90% of their circulating platelets; a subset of these mice was also injected with a serotonin *agonist*, which mimics serotonin's actions on its receptors (Figure 1).

Figure 1 Effects of platelet depletion and serotonin agonist on hepatocyte proliferation

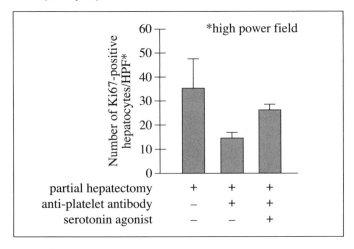

Experiment 2

Wild-type mice were treated with *antagonists* of the serotonin receptors 5 HT2A and 5 HT2B, receptors that are expressed on hepatocytes and other cell types (Figure 2).

Figure 2 Effects of serotonin receptor antagonists on hepatocyte proliferation

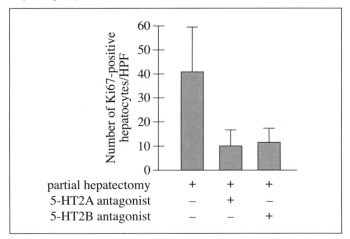

Experiment 3

This experiment used $TPH1^{-/-}$ mice, which lack the gastrointestinal cell enzyme TPH1 necessary to make circulating serotonin; some of the $TPH1^{-/-}$ mice were injected with a serotonin biosynthetic precursor that could be converted into serotonin and then imported into platelets (Figure 3).

Figure 3 Effects of $TPH1^{-/-}$ genotype and serotonin precursor on hepatocyte proliferation

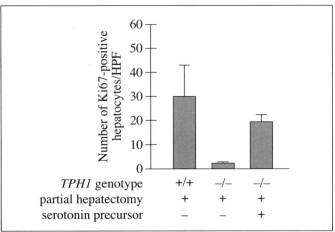

Adapted from M. Lesurtel et al., Platelet-derived serotonin mediates liver regeneration, *Science*. © 2006 by American Association for the Advancement of Science.

8. Individuals requiring a liver transplant often have reduced platelet counts. Given the experimental results presented in the passage, an appropriate treatment for these individuals after they have received a portion of a donor's liver would most likely be intravenous injections of:

   A. 5 HT2A and 5 HT2B antagonists.
   B. an anti-platelet antibody.
   C. an anti-TPH1 antibody.
   D. a serotonin agonist.

9. With respect to serotonin's actions in liver regeneration as presented in the passage, serotonin can be functionally classified as:

   A. an enzyme.
   B. a hormone.
   C. a clotting factor.
   D. a neurotransmitter.

10. The serotonin precursor discussed in the passage associates directly with the enzyme TPH1. Given this, the data presented best support the conclusion that in the serotonin biosynthetic pathway, this serotonin precursor is:

    A. the substrate of the TPH1-catalyzed reaction.
    B. the product of the TPH1-catalyzed reaction.
    C. a coenzyme of the TPH1-catalyzed reaction.
    D. an inhibitor of the TPH1-catalyzed reaction.

11. The liver synthesizes factors that act cooperatively with platelets to facilitate which of the following physiological processes?

    A. Cholesterol synthesis
    B. Glucose metabolism
    C. Blood clotting
    D. Fat digestion

12. Based on the passage, platelets are LEAST likely to contain:

    A. transmembrane serotonin transporters.
    B. ribosomes.
    C. serotonin.
    D. Ki67.

_____

Solutions for this passage begin on next page.

8. Individuals requiring a liver transplant often have reduced platelet counts. Given the experimental results presented in the passage, an appropriate treatment for these individuals after they have received a portion of a donor's liver would most likely be intravenous injections of:

    A. 5-HT2A and 5 HT2B antagonists.
    B. an anti-platelet antibody.
    C. an anti-TPH1 antibody.
    D. a serotonin agonist.

Content Classification: Digestive and Excretory Systems/Digestive System

Cognitive Classification: Flexibility and Adaptability in Scientific Reasoning

This question requires you to determine the implications of results for real-world situations. Proliferation of hepatocytes would be necessary to regenerate a full-sized liver from some transplanted liver tissue. Therefore, to answer this question you need to identify which treatment presented as an answer choice would stimulate liver cell (hepatocyte) proliferation in individuals who have received transplanted liver tissue. In these individuals, a reduced level of platelets (the primary carriers of serotonin in the blood) would result in reduced blood serotonin levels. In the experiments presented in the passage figures, the number of Ki67-positive cells was directly proportional to the rate of hepatocyte proliferation because only dividing cells express this protein. Because the experiments presented in the passage were done using mice, you need to assume that the treatments will have the same effects in humans and in mice.

Key: D

Figure 1 shows that a serotonin agonist, which mimics the actions of serotonin, stimulated hepatocyte proliferation in mice that have had a hepatectomy (part of the liver removed) and have been depleted of most of their circulating platelets by an anti-platelet antibody. This answer is correct because this treatment would stimulate hepatocyte proliferation.

Distractors

A   Figure 2 shows that blocking the action of the serotonin receptors 5 HT2A and 5 HT2B by using antagonists of these receptors inhibited the hepatocyte proliferation that occurs after a hepatectomy when these antagonists are absent. This answer is incorrect because this treatment would inhibit hepatocyte proliferation.

B   Figure 1 shows that an anti-platelet antibody alone inhibited hepatocyte proliferation in hepatectomized mice most likely because reducing the platelet number by using this antibody reduced the blood serotonin level. This answer is incorrect because this treatment would inhibit hepatocyte proliferation.

C   Figure 3 shows that hepatocytes proliferated poorly after a hepatectomy if these cells have a mutation that prevents the production of the serotonin biosynthetic enzyme TPH1. From this it can be assumed that an antibody against TPH1 would either inhibit hepatocyte proliferation (if it were a neutralizing antibody) or have no effect on hepatocyte proliferation (if the antibody could not enter the cells).

Difficulty Level: Easy (85%)

9. With respect to serotonin's actions in liver regeneration as presented in the passage, serotonin can be functionally classified as:

   A. an enzyme.
   B. a hormone.
   C. a clotting factor.
   D. a neurotransmitter.

Content Classification: Nervous and Endocrine System/Endocrine System: Hormones

Cognitive Classification: Seeking Clarification

This question requires you to use your background knowledge to translate the presented information into a more useful form. To do this, you need to know the characteristics of a circulating hormone. Circulating hormones are chemical messengers that are secreted by endocrine tissues and are transported by the bloodstream, instead of by ducts, to the target tissues where they alter cellular activity.

 A common error would be to assume that because serotonin is a neurotransmitter in neuronal tissues that it is also acting as a neurotransmitter in liver regeneration.

Key: B

Serotonin is synthesized by endocrine gastrointestinal tract cells and carried by platelets in the bloodstream to serotonin's target tissue, the liver. Consequently, serotonin is acting as a hormone.

Distractors

A   The passage does not present evidence that serotonin has the catalytic activity of an enzyme.

C   Serotonin is carried in the blood by platelets, which have a role in blood clotting, but the passage does not address the role of serotonin, if any, in blood clotting or how this role would affect liver regeneration.

D   Although, in neuronal tissue, serotonin acts as a neurotransmitter (a chemical messenger that acts on postsynaptic neurons after being released by presynaptic axons in response to an action potential), in the system described in the passage, serotonin is being synthesized by and acting on nonneuronal tissue.

Difficulty Level: Easy (80%)

10. The serotonin precursor discussed in the passage associates directly with the enzyme TPH1. Given this, the data presented best support the conclusion that in the serotonin biosynthetic pathway, this serotonin precursor is:

    A. the substrate of the TPH1-catalyzed reaction.
    B. the product of the TPH1-catalyzed reaction.
    C. a coenzyme of the TPH1-catalyzed reaction.
    D. an inhibitor of the TPH1-catalyzed reaction.

Content Classification: Enzymes and Metabolism/Enzyme Structure and Function

Cognitive Classification: Identification of Components of a Situation and the Relationships Among Them

This question requires you to identify supporting evidence. Specifically, you need to identify which conclusion is most compatible with the data in Figure 3. Figure 3 shows that the serotonin precursor largely compensated for the lack of the serotonin biosynthetic enzyme TPH1 in hepatectomized mice by increasing hepatocyte proliferation. This means that the serotonin precursor must fit downstream of the step catalyzed by TPH1 in the serotonin biosynthetic pathway. All of the possible answers are factors that could interact directly with TPH1 and therefore fulfill the requirement set by the question that the factor presented as an option associates directly with this enzyme.

Key: B

Of the options given, the product of the TPH1-catalyzed reaction is the only answer that is downstream of the TPH1-catalyzed step.

Distractors

A   The substrate is upstream of the TPH1-catalyzed reaction.

C   A coenzyme facilitates but cannot replace an enzyme's activity. Therefore, a TPH1 coenzyme should have no effect on serotonin-stimulated hepatocyte proliferation if TPH1 is absent.

D   A TPH1 inhibitor should have no effect if TPH1 is absent. In addition, even if TPH1 were present, the TPH1 inhibitor would decrease serotonin synthesis and thus decrease, not increase, hepatocyte proliferation. This is not consistent with the data in Figure 3 that show that the serotonin precursor stimulated proliferation of hepatocytes lacking TPH1.

Difficulty Level: Medium (45%)

11. The liver synthesizes factors that act cooperatively with platelets to facilitate which of the following physiological processes?

    A. Cholesterol synthesis
    B. Glucose metabolism
    C. Blood clotting
    D. Fat digestion

Content Classification: Circulatory, Lymphatic, and Immune System/Circulatory System

Cognitive Classification: Seeking Clarification

This question requires you to identify relevant background knowledge. Specifically, you need to know that platelets and the liver have cooperative roles in blood clotting.

Key C:

Platelets form a plug at the site where a blood vessel has been damaged. Blood clotting factors that have been synthesized in the liver in an inactive form then participate in a cascade that leads to a blood clot.

Distractors

A   Synthesis of cholesterol is an important function of the liver. Platelets may also synthesize cholesterol, but the liver and platelets are not acting together in this process.

B   The liver plays an important role in energy homeostasis by storing glucose in the form of glycogen under conditions of glucose excess and by breaking down glycogen and releasing glucose into the bloodstream under conditions of glucose limitation. The liver also synthesizes glucose from non-carbohydrate molecules. Glucose and insulin imbalances can affect the activation of platelets during coagulation, but the liver and platelets are not acting together in energy homeostasis.

D   The liver synthesizes bile that emulsifies fat and facilitates its digestion in the small intestine. Platelets do not have an obvious role in this process.

Difficulty Level: Easy (75%)

12. Based on the passage, platelets are LEAST likely to contain:

   A. transmembrane serotonin transporters.
   B. ribosomes.
   C. serotonin.
   D. Ki67.

Content Classification: Circulatory, Lymphatic, and Immune System/Circulatory System

Cognitive Classification: Hypothesis Testing

This question requires you to predict a result on the basis of specific facts about a situation. Specifically, you need to know that platelets do not have nuclei, and you need to note that the question is asking for what is "LEAST likely" to be true.

 For questions that ask for what is "LEAST likely," determine which answer choices are very likely to be true and remember that any option that is very likely to be true is not the key.

Key: D

Platelets are cell fragments without nuclei and therefore would not be expected to contain a protein like Ki67 that is detected exclusively in the nuclei of proliferating whole cells. Because this option presents a situation that is unlikely to be true, it is the correct answer to the question.

Distractors

A   The passage states that platelets are carrying serotonin that has been synthesized outside the platelets; therefore, there must be a mechanism for transporting serotonin into platelets. Serotonin would be transported into platelets by transmembrane transporters. Because this option presents a situation that is very likely to be true, it is not the correct answer to the question.

B   Platelets are formed from large cells called *megakaryocytes*. Platelets consist of plasma membrane–encased megakaryocyte cytoplasm, which contains ribosomes. Because this option presents a situation that is very likely to be true, it is not the correct answer to the question.

C   A major point of the passage is that platelets carry serotonin. Because this option presents a situation that is true, it is not the correct answer to the question.

Difficulty Level: Medium (65%)

MCAT® is a program of the
Association of American Medical Colleges

Biology

Passage Set III

Biology

Obesity is a risk factor for type 2 diabetes. One link between obesity and the reduced insulin sensitivity of skeletal muscle found in people with type 2 diabetes is a high concentration of circulating fatty acids (FAs). These FAs are taken up by skeletal muscle, which converts them into triglycerides (TGs) as follows:

$$\text{glycerol-3-phosphate} + \text{activated FA} \rightarrow \rightarrow \rightarrow$$

$$\text{1,2-diacylglycerol} + \text{activated FA} \xrightarrow{\text{DGAT}} \text{TG}$$

(Note: DGAT catalyzes the final step in TG synthesis.)

Because a strong positive correlation exists between the level of intramuscular triglycerides (IMTGs) and insulin resistance, it was originally hypothesized that IMTGs are the FA-derived products directly responsible for activating the proinflammatory stress pathways that reduce insulin sensitivity in skeletal muscle.

Exercise improves insulin sensitivity in skeletal muscle by increasing the oxidative breakdown of FAs, thus reducing the intramuscular pool of FAs available for IMTG synthesis. Even though exercising improves insulin sensitivity, a seemingly contradictory observation was made in that the concentration of IMTGs *increases* after exercise. The following study was designed to try to explain this observation.

Eight nonobese human subjects each participated in two 2-day experimental trials. The only difference between the trials was whether the subjects exercised or remained sedentary on Day 1. In addition to receiving controlled meals, each subject was given an overnight intravenous infusion of lipids to elevate the concentration of circulating FAs. After the infusion was stopped on Day 2, the following factors were measured: IMTG, diacylglycerol, and DGAT concentrations, and inflammatory response indicators. It was observed that the subjects' DGAT concentration increased with exercise.

Adapted from S. Schenk and J. Horowitz, Acute exercise increases triglyceride synthesis in skeletal muscle and prevents fatty acid–induced insulin resistance, *Journal of Clinical Investigation.* © 2007 by American Society for Clinical Investigation.

13. Based on the passage, which of the following conditions is most likely to exist in a person who is obese and does not exercise?

    A. Activation of skeletal muscle proinflammatory stress pathways
    B. Low skeletal muscle concentrations of IMTGs
    C. Increased skeletal muscle insulin sensitivity
    D. Low concentrations of circulating FAs

14. Relative to the subjects' levels of diacylglycerol and inflammatory response indicators in the sedentary trials, how would the levels of these variables most likely change during the trials in which the subjects exercised?

    A. The level of each variable would increase.
    B. The level of each variable would decrease.
    C. The level of diacylglycerol would increase, and the level of inflammatory response indicators would decrease.
    D. The level of diacylglycerol would decrease, and the level of inflammatory response indicators would increase.

15. Based on the passage, in which of the following pairs of variables relating to IMTG synthesis, insulin sensitivity, and exercise would the variables in the pair be most likely to demonstrate an inverse relationship?

    A. Intramuscular DGAT concentration and IMTG synthesis
    B. Circulating FAs and IMTG concentrations
    C. Insulin sensitivity and intramuscular diacylglycerol concentration
    D. Insulin sensitivity and exercise

16. In designing the study presented in the passage, the researchers used the alternative hypothesis that intramuscular diacylglycerol, rather than IMTG, activates the proinflammatory stress pathways that reduce insulin sensitivity. Are the results of the study consistent or inconsistent with this hypothesis?

    A. Inconsistent, because the only way to decrease diacylglycerol synthesis in exercising skeletal muscle is to increase the oxidative breakdown of FAs

    B. Inconsistent, because the increased intramuscular levels of DGAT caused by exercise would increase the level of intramuscular diacylglycerol as well as increase the level of IMTG
    C. Consistent, because exercise, an activity that increases insulin sensitivity, creates conditions that decrease intramuscular diacylglycerol levels while simultaneously increasing IMTG levels
    D. Consistent, because the increased intramuscular levels of DGAT caused by exercise would increase the level of intramuscular diacylglycerol as well as increase the level of IMTG

17. Skeletal muscle can be distinguished from other muscle types in that skeletal muscle is the only type of muscle that:

    A. uses a sliding-filament mechanism of contraction.
    B. is innervated by the somatic nervous system.
    C. contracts when there is a cytosolic influx of Ca^{2+}.
    D. contains gap junctions between individual cells.

18. The most likely reason the subjects in the research study received an overnight infusion of lipids was to:

    A. provide extra energy for the subjects when they exercised.
    B. mimic the conditions that tend to increase insulin sensitivity in people who are obese.
    C. cause a decrease in DGAT activity.
    D. mimic the conditions that tend to increase insulin resistance in people who are obese.

Solutions for this passage begin on next page.

13. Based on the passage, which of the following conditions is most likely to exist in a person who is obese and does not exercise?

    A. Activation of skeletal muscle proinflammatory stress pathways
    B. Low skeletal muscle concentrations of IMTGs
    C. Increased skeletal muscle insulin sensitivity
    D. Low concentrations of circulating FAs

Content Classification: Muscle and Skeletal Systems/Muscle System

Cognitive Classification: Identification of Main Ideas

This question requires you to identify a main point made in the passage regarding the connection between obesity and the conditions that cause type 2 diabetes.

Key: A

The passage states that people who are obese have a high concentration of circulating FAs that are converted into TGs in skeletal muscle and that FA-derived products are responsible for activating proinflammatory stress pathways in skeletal muscle. Therefore, it follows that a person who is obese is likely to activate proinflammatory stress pathways in skeletal muscle. Exercise can decrease this inflammation, but the question specifies that the person does not exercise.

Distractors

B   The passage indicates that the high concentration of circulating FAs in people who are obese leads to a significant amount of TG synthesis in skeletal muscle, which would lead to *high*, not low, levels of IMTGs. Even though exercise further increases IMTG levels, the high concentration of circulating FAs in people who are obese would cause these people to have a high baseline level of IMTGs.

C   The passage outlines how the high concentration of circulating FAs in people who are obese leads to the activation of proinflammatory stress pathways in skeletal muscle that cause *reduced*, not increased, insulin sensitivity. Exercise can increase insulin sensitivity, but the question specifies that the person does not exercise.

D   The passage directly states that people who are obese have a *high*, not low, concentration of circulating FAs.

Difficulty Level: Medium (70%)

14. Relative to the subjects' levels of diacylglycerol and inflammatory response indicators in the sedentary trials, how would the levels of these variables most likely change during the trials in which the subjects exercised?

    A. The level of each variable would increase.
    B. The level of each variable would decrease.
    C. The level of diacylglycerol would increase, and the level of inflammatory response indicators would decrease.
    D. The level of diacylglycerol would decrease, and the level of inflammatory response indicators would increase.

Content Classification: Enzymes and Metabolism/Basic Metabolism

Cognitive Classification: Hypothesis Testing

This question requires you to predict how the subjects' levels of diacylglycerol and inflammatory response indicators would be affected by exercise. Exercise increases the oxidative breakdown of FAs, thus reducing the available pool of FAs from which diacylglycerol is synthesized. This would tend to decrease the intramuscular concentration of diacylglycerol. In addition, the passage states that the subjects' DGAT concentration increased following exercise. DGAT is an enzyme that converts diacylglycerol into TG. With more DGAT present, more diacylglycerol would be converted into TG, which also lowers diacylglycerol levels. The passage also indicates that proinflammatory stress pathways are responsible for decreased insulin sensitivity in people who are obese and that exercise improves insulin sensitivity in skeletal muscle. Therefore, it follows that exercise is likely to reduce the activation of these pathways, leading to a reduction in inflammatory response indicators.

Key: B

This choice correctly indicates that the subjects' levels of diacylglycerol and inflammatory response indicators would both decrease following exercise.

Distractors

A   This choice incorrectly indicates that the subjects' levels of diacylglycerol and inflammatory response indicators would both increase following exercise.

C   This choice incorrectly indicates that the subjects' diacylglycerol levels would increase following exercise.

D   This choice incorrectly indicates that the subject's level of inflammatory response indicators would increase following exercise.

Difficulty Level: Hard (30%)

15. Based on the passage, in which of the following pairs of variables relating to IMTG synthesis, insulin sensitivity, and exercise would the variables in the pair be most likely to demonstrate an inverse relationship?

   A. Intramuscular DGAT concentration and IMTG synthesis
   B. Circulating FAs and IMTG concentrations
   C. Insulin sensitivity and intramuscular diacylglycerol concentration
   D. Insulin sensitivity and exercise

Content Classification: Nervous and Endocrine Systems/Endocrine System (Hormones)

Cognitive Classification: Identification of Components in a Situation and Relationships Among Them

This question requires you to identify the set of variables from the passage that would demonstrate an inverse relationship. An inverse relationship is one in which one of the variables increases as the other variable decreases.

Key: C

The passage states that exercise increases insulin sensitivity, and the results from the study indicate that the subjects' concentration of DGAT also increases with exercise. Because diacylglycerol is a substrate of DGAT, its concentration should decrease as the concentration of DGAT increases. Therefore, as insulin sensitivity increases with exercise, the level of diacylglycerol should decrease. This is an inverse relationship.

 If necessary, this question can be answered by a process of elimination. In three of the four choices, the variables clearly demonstrate a positive correlation, leaving only answer choice C. You can then use the passage to verify that the variables in C are likely to demonstrate an inverse relationship.

Distractors

A   The passage directly states that the intramuscular DGAT and IMTG concentrations both increase with exercise. Therefore, these variables would show a positive correlation with each other.

B   The passage states that circulating FAs are taken up by skeletal muscle which uses the FAs to synthesize TGs. Thus, as the concentration of circulating FAs increases, the concentration of IMTGs should also increase. Therefore, these variables would show a positive correlation with each other.

D   The passage directly states that exercise causes an increase in insulin sensitivity. Therefore, these variables would show a positive correlation with each other.

Difficulty Level: Medium (50%)

16. In designing the study presented in the passage, the researchers used the alternative hypothesis that intramuscular diacylglycerol, rather than IMTG, activates the proinflammatory stress pathways that reduce insulin sensitivity. Are the results of the study consistent or inconsistent with this hypothesis?

    A. Inconsistent, because the only way to decrease diacylglycerol synthesis in exercising skeletal muscle is to increase the oxidative breakdown of FAs

    B. Inconsistent, because the increased intramuscular levels of DGAT caused by exercise would increase the level of intramuscular diacylglycerol as well as increase the level of IMTG

    C. Consistent, because exercise, an activity that increases insulin sensitivity, creates conditions that decrease intramuscular diacylglycerol levels while simultaneously increasing IMTG levels

    D. Consistent, because the increased intramuscular levels of DGAT caused by exercise would increase the level of intramuscular diacylglycerol as well as increase the level of IMTG

Content Classification: Muscle and Skeletal Systems/Muscle System

Cognitive Classification: Evaluation Processes

This question requires you to judge whether the results of the study described in the passage are consistent with the hypothesis that intramuscular diacylglycerol, rather than IMTG, activates the proinflammatory pathways that reduce insulin sensitivity. The observation that exercise increases the concentration of IMTG, while simultaneously increasing insulin sensitivity, contradicts the original hypothesis that IMTG directly activates the proinflammatory stress pathways that cause reduced insulin sensitivity in skeletal muscles. However, this observation could be explained if one of the *substrates* used to synthesize IMTG activates these proinflammatory stress pathways. Increasing the synthesis of IMTG would both increase the concentration of IMTG and decrease the concentration of the substrates used to synthesize it, thus reducing the concentration of the molecules putatively responsible for activating the proinflammatory stress pathways that cause a reduction in insulin sensitivity.

Key: C

The study showed that the concentration of DGAT increased in the subjects following exercise. DGAT is the enzyme that synthesizes TGs from diacylglycerol and activated FAs. An increase in DGAT would tend to increase the concentration of its product (TG) and decrease the concentration of its substrates (diacylglycerol and activated FA). This is consistent with the researchers' hypothesis.

Distractors

A   Although increasing the oxidative breakdown of FAs would decrease the available pool of FAs for diacylglycerol synthesis and would thus likely reduce the concentration of diacylglycerol, this concentration can also be reduced by increasing the synthesis of TG. In addition, this choice incorrectly asserts that the results of the study are inconsistent with the researchers' hypothesis.

B   This choice incorrectly asserts that the results of the study are inconsistent with the researchers' hypothesis. In addition, the results of the study indicate that the concentration of diacylglycerol is likely to *decrease,* not increase, as stated in this answer choice.

D   The results of the study indicate that the concentration of diacylglycerol is likely to *decrease,* not increase, as stated in this answer choice.

Difficulty Level: Medium (50%)

17. Skeletal muscle can be distinguished from other muscle types in that skeletal muscle is the only type of muscle that:

    A. uses a sliding-filament mechanism of contraction.
    B. is innervated by the somatic nervous system.
    C. contracts when there is a cytosolic influx of Ca^{2+}.
    D. contains gap junctions between individual cells.

Content Classifications: Specialized Eukaryotic Cells and Tissues/Muscle Cell (Contractile); Muscle and Skeletal Systems/Muscle System; Nervous and Endocrine Systems/Nervous System (Structure and Function)

Cognitive Classification: Seeking Clarification

This question requires you to identify relevant background information about skeletal muscle. Specifically, you are to identify a characteristic of skeletal muscle that distinguishes it from smooth and cardiac muscle.

Key: B

Skeletal muscle is the only type of muscle that is innervated by the somatic nervous system. Smooth and cardiac muscle are innervated by the autonomic nervous system.

 Choice D may be an appealing answer because it focuses on a characteristic that distinguishes skeletal muscle from other muscle types. In this situation, take a moment to assess whether the characteristic is attributed to the correct muscle type.

Distractors

A   All three muscle types use the sliding-filament mechanism of contraction, so this characteristic does not distinguish skeletal muscle from smooth or cardiac muscle.

C   A cytosolic influx of Ca^{2+} causes contraction of all three muscle types, so this characteristic does not distinguish skeletal muscle from smooth or cardiac muscle.

D   Skeletal muscle is the only type of muscle that *does not* contain gap junctions between individual cells, so this characteristic does distinguish skeletal muscle from smooth and cardiac muscle. However, this choice is incorrect because it indicates that skeletal muscle *does* contain gap junctions between individual cells, which it does not.

Difficulty Level: Medium (65%)

18. The most likely reason the subjects in the research study received an overnight infusion of lipids was to:

    A. provide extra energy for the subjects when they exercised.
    B. mimic the conditions that tend to increase insulin sensitivity in people who are obese.
    C. cause a decrease in DGAT activity.
    D. mimic the conditions that tend to increase insulin resistance in people who are obese.

Content Classification: Nervous and Endocrine Systems/Endocrine System (Hormones)

Cognitive Classification: Evaluation Processes

This question requires you to determine the researchers' rationale for administering an overnight infusion of lipids to the subjects in the research study.

Key: D

The purpose of the study was to examine the link between high concentrations of circulating FAs and the increased insulin resistance (reduced insulin sensitivity) in people who are obese. However, the subjects of the study were not obese and, therefore, not as likely to have high concentrations of circulating FAs. Thus, the researchers artificially recreated this condition in the subjects by administering an overnight infusion of lipids.

 Remember that *increasing* insulin *resistance* is the same as *reducing* insulin *sensitivity*.

Distractors

A   The subjects either remained sedentary or exercised on Day 1, which was before they received the overnight infusion of lipids. Therefore, these lipids were not available as a source of energy for the exercise session.

B   High concentrations of circulating FAs are linked with *reduced*, not increased, insulin sensitivity in people who are obese. Therefore, intravenous administration of FAs, which would raise the concentration of circulating FAs, would not mimic conditions that increase insulin sensitivity.

C   Administration of intravenous lipids would increase the concentration of circulating FAs that can be taken up by skeletal muscle. This increases the pool of available substrates for DGAT and would be likely to *increase* its activity, rather than decrease it.

Difficulty Level: Easy (85%)

Biology
Passage Set IV

Biology

Macroautophagy is a stress-activated cellular process in which organelles and long-lived proteins are degraded. During macroautophagy, the degradation substrates become encased in vesicles called *autophagosomes* that fuse with lysosomes.

In theory, macroautophagy could have opposing effects on cancer progression. Macroautophagy could enhance cancer cell survival by supplying macromolecules to starved cells inside a tumor. In contrast, macroautophagy could kill cancer cells because it sometimes leads to a nonapoptotic form of programmed cell death. Macroautophagy could either promote or inhibit tumor progression by removing damaged mitochondria, which generate mutagenic free radicals.

One copy of the gene encoding the macroautophagy protein *beclin 1* is often deleted in human breast cancer cells. The following data elucidate the role of *beclin 1* in tumor formation.

Experiment 1

Expression constructs containing either the human wild-type *beclin 1* allele or a mutant variant with a nonsense mutation were introduced into human breast cancer cells, and the autophagosomes in the resulting cell lines were counted (Figure 1).

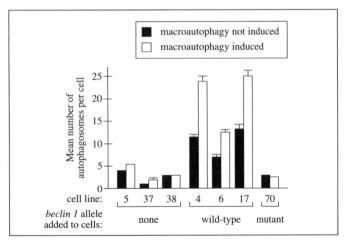

Figure 1 Beclin 1's effect on autophagosome number

Experiment 2

The frequency with which the cell lines from Experiment 1 formed tumors after being injected into mice was determined (Figure 2).

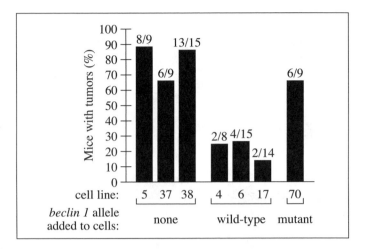

Figure 2 Beclin 1's effect on tumor development

Researchers also observed that spontaneous tumors developed in 14% of mice homozygous for the wild-type *beclin 1* allele and in 59% of mice with one wild-type and one inactivated *beclin 1* allele.

Adapted from X. Liang et al., Induction of autophagy and inhibition of tumorigenesis by beclin 1, *Nature*. © 1999 by Macmillan Magazines Ltd.; Z. Yue et al., Beclin 1, an autophagy gene essential for early embryonic development, is a haploinsufficient tumor suppressor, *Proceedings of the National Academy of Sciences of the USA*. © 2003 by National Academy of Sciences.

19. Do the data presented in the passage more strongly support the conclusion that the *beclin 1* gene is a proto-oncogene or a tumor suppressor gene?

   A. Proto-oncogene, because increased expression of the wild-type *beclin 1* gene product resulted in more tumors
   B. Proto-oncogene, because increased expression of the wild-type *beclin 1* gene product resulted in fewer tumors
   C. Tumor suppressor gene, because increased expression of the wild-type *beclin 1* gene product resulted in more tumors
   D. Tumor suppressor gene, because increased expression of the wild-type *beclin 1* gene product resulted in fewer tumors

20. Based on the passage, therapeutic treatments that inhibit macroautophagy in cancer cells could inadvertently promote tumor progression by:

   A. starving cancer cells for macromolecules.
   B. inducing macroautophagic programmed cell death.
   C. supplying macromolecules to the unvascularized regions of the tumor.
   D. increasing the rate at which mutations that enhance cell division are generated.

21. Which of the following graphs best depicts the expected degradation rates of long-lived proteins in cell lines 17, 38, and 70 presented in Experiment 1 when grown under conditions that induce macroautophagy?

A.
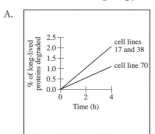

B.
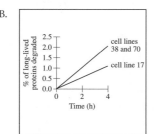

C.
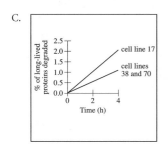

D.
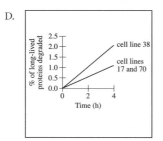

22. Consider the proteins encoded by the expression constructs described in Experiment 1. Relative to the primary sequence of human wild-type *beclin 1* protein, the primary sequence of the protein encoded by the mutant variant of the *beclin 1* gene is:

   A. longer.
   B. shorter.
   C. the same length but differs at a single amino acid residue.
   D. the same length but differs at three sequential amino acid residues.

23. Based on the passage, what is the relative number of autophagosomes expected in cells from *beclin 1*$^{+/+}$ mice, *beclin 1*$^{+/-}$ mice, and *beclin 1*$^{-/-}$ mice when macroautophagy is induced in these cells? (Note: The symbols "+" and "−" denote wild-type and inactivated *beclin 1* alleles, respectively.) The autophagosome number is:

   A. *beclin 1*$^{+/+}$ cells > in *beclin 1*$^{+/-}$ cells > in *beclin 1*$^{-/-}$ cells.
   B. *beclin 1*$^{+/+}$ cells = in *beclin 1*$^{+/-}$ cells > in *beclin 1*$^{-/-}$ cells.
   C. *beclin 1*$^{+/+}$ cells = in *beclin 1*$^{+/-}$ cells = in *beclin 1*$^{-/-}$ cells.
   D. *beclin 1*$^{+/+}$ cells < in *beclin 1*$^{+/-}$ cells < in *beclin 1*$^{-/-}$ cells.

24. Based on the passage, macroautophagy decreases the intracellular levels of mutagenic free radicals that are generated by:

   A. glycolysis.
   B. transcription.
   C. the electron transport chain.
   D. protein degradation in lysosomes.

25. Relative to the pH of the cytosol or of the nucleoplasm, the optimal pH of the enzymes that degrade organelles and long-lived proteins during macroautophagy is most likely:

   A. less than the pH of the cytosol.
   B. greater than the pH of the cytosol.
   C. the same as the pH of the cytosol.
   D. greater than the pH of the nucleoplasm.

Solutions for this passage begin on next page.

19. Do the data presented in the passage more strongly support the conclusion that the *beclin 1* gene is a proto-oncogene or a tumor suppressor gene?

    A. Proto-oncogene, because increased expression of the wild-type *beclin 1* gene product resulted in more tumors

    B. Proto-oncogene, because increased expression of the wild-type *beclin 1* gene product resulted in fewer tumors

    C. Tumor suppressor gene, because increased expression of the wild-type *beclin 1* gene product resulted in more tumors

    D. Tumor suppressor gene, because increased expression of the wild-type *beclin 1* gene product resulted in tumors

---

Content Classification: Eukaryotes/Control of Gene Expression in Eukaryotes

Cognitive Classification: Reasoning Using Quantitative Data

This question requires you to identify relationships inherent in data and to identify background information relevant to an interpretation. Specifically, you need to determine whether the *beclin 1* gene is a proto-oncogene or a tumor suppressor gene, using the data presented in the passage and your background knowledge of types of cancer-related genes. Proto-oncogenes are genes that increase tumorigenesis, or tumor formation, when their expression is inappropriately elevated. Tumor suppressor genes are genes whose expression helps to block tumorigenesis.

Key: D

Figure 2 shows that adding the wild-type *beclin 1* allele to breast cancer cells reduced the frequency at which these cells formed tumors when injected into mice. In addition, the passage states that tumors formed much more readily in mice carrying only one copy of the wild-type *beclin 1* allele (heterozygotes) than tumors formed in mice carrying two copies of the wild-type *beclin 1* allele (homozygotes). Both these results show that increased *beclin 1* expression suppresses tumorigenesis and therefore that *beclin 1* is a tumor suppressor gene.

 A common error would be to choose an answer with either the correct conclusion ("tumor suppressor gene") or the correct supportive statement ("because increased expression of the wild-type *beclin 1* gene product resulted in fewer tumors") but to not confirm that the supportive statement is consistent with the conclusion.

Distractors

A   The conclusion that *beclin 1* is a proto-oncogene is incorrect. The supportive statement is also incorrect; increased expression of *beclin 1* resulted in fewer, not more, tumors.

B   The conclusion that *beclin 1* is a proto-oncogene is incorrect. Increased expression of *beclin 1* did result in fewer tumors, but this explanation does not support the conclusion that *beclin 1* is a proto-oncogene.

C   The conclusion that *beclin 1* is a tumor suppressor gene is correct. However, the supportive statement given was not the experimental observation, and this statement, if it were correct, would support the conclusion that *beclin 1* is a proto-oncogene, not a tumor suppressor gene.

Difficulty Level: Easy (85%)

20. Based on the passage, therapeutic treatments that inhibit macroautophagy in cancer cells could inadvertently promote tumor progression by:

A. starving cancer cells for macromolecules.
B. inducing macroautophagic programmed cell death.
C. supplying macromolecules to the unvascularized regions of the tumor.
D. increasing the rate at which mutations that enhance cell division are generated.

Content Classification: Eukaryotes/Control of Gene Expression in Eukaryotes

Cognitive Classification: Flexibility and Adaptability in Scientific Reasoning

This question requires you to relate the information in the passage and your background knowledge to a real-world situation (cancer treatment). You should know that mutations that facilitate the uncontrolled cell division associated with cancer accumulate in cancer cells during tumor progression.

Key: D

The passage states that macroautophagy removes damaged mitochondria that would generate free radicals that cause mutations. These mutations may either be so deleterious that they kill the cell or may contribute to cancer progression if they do not kill the cell. Therefore, inhibiting macroautophagy may allow mutation-inducing mitochondria to persist and contribute to tumor progression.

This question is difficult because it requires that you predict the effect of *inhibiting* a process (macroautophagy), rather than predict the effect of the process itself. You then must predict how inhibiting this process will affect a second process (tumor progression). Try evaluating each answer first for whether it would result from inhibiting macroautophagy and then for whether it would promote tumor progression.

Distractors

A Starving cancer cells for macromolecules would inhibit, rather than promote, the survival and proliferation of these cells.

B Inhibiting macroautophagy would not induce a form of programmed cell death that is dependent on acroautophagy. In addition, inducing programmed cell death in cancer cells would inhibit, not promote, tumor progression.

C Macroautophagy supplies macromolecules to starving cells such as those that are not in direct contact with the circulatory system. Inhibiting macroautophagy would starve these cancer cells and thus reduce, not promote, their survival and proliferation.

Difficulty Level: Hard (30%)

21. Which of the following graphs best depicts the expected degradation rates of long-lived proteins in cell lines 17, 38, and 70 presented in Experiment 1 when grown under conditions that induce macroautophagy?

A.
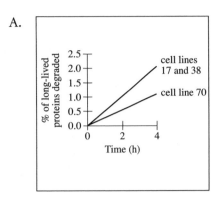

B.
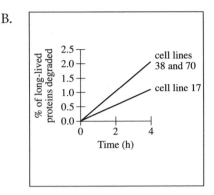

C.
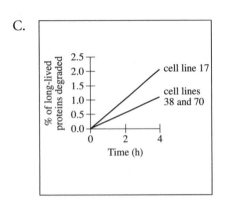

D.
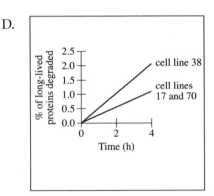

Content Classification: Generalized Eukaryotic Cell/Membrane-Bound Organelles

Cognitive Classification: Reasoning Using Quantitative Data

This question requires you to identify relationships inherent in the data in the graphs presented in the passage and to use this understanding to predict a result also presented in graph form in the answer choices. You need to draw a correlation between the *beclin 1* allele introduced into a cell line (if one was introduced) and autophagosome formation in those cells. Figure 1 shows that cell line 17, which contains the wild-type exogenous *beclin 1* allele, had an increased number of autophagosomes when macroautophagy was induced. In contrast, cell line 38, which does not contain any exogenous *beclin 1* allele, and cell line 70, which contains a mutant exogenous *beclin 1* allele, had far fewer autophagosomes when macroautophagy was induced. Long-lived proteins are degraded in autophagosomes, and therefore cells with more autophagosomes will degrade long-lived proteins at a faster rate than will cells with fewer autophagosomes.

A common error would be to miss the connection between macroautophagy and long-lived protein degradation because you did not read the passage carefully or in its entirety. Answering this question requires you to combine information in the first paragraph with information in Figure 1.

MCAT® is a program of the
Association of American Medical Colleges

Key: C

The line representing the rate of long-lived protein degradation in cell line 17 should have the steepest slope because the rate of this degradation will be greatest in this cell line. The line representing the rate of long-lived protein degradation in cell lines 38 and 70, which had an equally low number of autophagosomes when macroautophagy was induced, should be less steep.

 On the basis of your understanding of the relative number of autophagosomes in each cell line, try predicting the long-lived protein degradation rate in each cell line and then looking for the graph that best fits your prediction.

Distractors

A   This graph incorrectly shows cell line 38 as having the same faster rate of long-lived protein degradation as cell line 17 instead of the same slower rate as cell line 70.

B   This graph incorrectly shows cell lines 38 and 70 as having a faster rate of long-lived protein degradation than cell line 17.

D   This graph incorrectly shows cell line 38 as having a faster rate of long-lived protein degradation than cell lines 17 and 70, instead of a rate that is slower than that of cell line 17 and equal to that of cell line 70.

Difficulty Level: Easy (85%)

22. Consider the proteins encoded by the expression constructs described in Experiment 1. Relative to the primary sequence of human wild-type *beclin 1* protein, the primary sequence of the protein encoded by the mutant variant of the *beclin 1* gene is:

A. longer.
B. shorter.
C. the same length but differs at a single amino acid residue.
D. the same length but differs at three sequential amino acid residues.

Content Classification: DNA and Protein Synthesis/Protein Synthesis

Cognitive Classification: Hypothesis Testing

This question requires you to predict a result on the basis of background knowledge and specific facts about a situation. In this case, you need to understand how a nonsense mutation affects the length of a protein. You should know that a nonsense mutation causes translation of an mRNA to stop prematurely, thus resulting in the synthesis of a truncated protein.

Key: B

The primary sequence of a truncated protein would be shorter than that of the wild-type protein.

Passages will often contain simple facts that will be used later in the questions to test your background knowledge. In this case, you were told in the passage that the mutant *beclin 1* allele contained a nonsense mutation. Try to note facts like this while reading the passage because these facts may be required to answer a question.

Distractors

A   This answer incorrectly states that the primary sequence of a truncated protein would be longer, not shorter, than the wild-type protein.

C   This answer describes the effect of a single missense mutation, not of a nonsense mutation.

D   This answer does not describe the effect of a nonsense mutation but instead describes the effect of either a triple missense mutation or a frameshift mutation that remarkably does not change the length of the protein.

Difficulty Level: Medium (50%)

23. Based on the passage, what is the relative number of autophagosomes expected in cells from *beclin 1*$^{+/+}$ mice, *beclin 1*$^{+/-}$ mice, and *beclin 1*$^{-/-}$ mice when macroautophagy is induced in these cells? (Note: The symbols "+" and "−" denote wild-type and inactivated *beclin 1* alleles, respectively.) The autophagosome number is:

A. *beclin 1*$^{+/+}$ cells > in *beclin 1*$^{+/-}$ cells > in *beclin 1*$^{-/-}$ cells.
B. *beclin 1*$^{+/+}$ cells = in *beclin 1*$^{+/-}$ cells > in *beclin 1*$^{-/-}$ cells.
C. *beclin 1*$^{+/+}$ cells = in *beclin 1*$^{+/-}$ cells = in *beclin 1*$^{-/-}$ cells.
D. *beclin 1*$^{+/+}$ cells < in *beclin 1*$^{+/-}$ cells < in *beclin 1*$^{-/-}$ cells.

Content Classification: Genetics/Mendelian Concepts

Cognitive Classification: Hypothesis Testing

 A common error would be to not read the passage in its entirety. To answer this question, you need to assimilate information from many different parts of the passage.

This question requires you to predict a result on the basis of specific facts about a situation. Figure 1 shows that the presence of an exogenous copy of the wild-type *beclin 1* allele in cells increases the number of autophagosomes in those cells. Figure 2 shows that the presence of the exogenous wild-type *beclin 1* allele in cells decreases the likelihood that those cells will form tumors, strongly suggesting a direct correlation between the number of autophagosomes and the ability to suppress tumor formation. The passage goes on to say that mice with two copies of the wild-type *beclin 1* allele are less likely to develop tumors than mice with only one copy. Because the *beclin 1* genotype is associated with the rate of tumor formation, and the rate of tumor formation is associated with autophagosome number, the relationship between the *beclin 1* genotype and autophagosome number can be predicted. Combining all of the presented data, it can be assumed that there is a direct correlation between the number of wild-type *beclin 1* alleles that a mouse carries and the number of autophagosomes that will form in the cells of those mice when macroautophagy is induced.

Key: A

Given the expected direct relationship between the number of wild-type *beclin 1* alleles and the number of autophagosomes in these cells under inducing conditions, the cells of mice with two copies of the wild-type *beclin 1* allele should have more autophagosomes than the cells of mice with only one copy of the wild-type *beclin 1* allele, and the cells of mice with only one copy of the wild-type *beclin 1* allele should have more autophagosomes than the cells of mice with no copies of the wild-type *beclin 1* allele.

 Despite not being told the incidence of tumor formation in postnatal *beclin 1*$^{-/-}$ mice (which was not measured because these mice die during embryogenesis), you should be able to use the data presented to identify the relationships among the number of wild-type *beclin 1* alleles, autophagosome number, and tumor formation. You should then be able to make a reasonable prediction of what the researchers saw when they counted autophagosomes in the embryonic cells of mice with the three different *beclin 1* genotypes.

Distractors on next page

Distractors

B   Assuming that the difference in cancer susceptibility between *beclin 1*$^{+/+}$ mice and *beclin 1*$^{+/-}$ mice is due to the difference in autophagosome number under inducing conditions, the number of autophagosomes in the cells of these mice should not be equal.

C   This answer incorrectly implies that there is no relationship between the number of wild-type *beclin 1* alleles that a mouse carries and the autophagosome number in the cells of those mice under inducing conditions.

D   This answer incorrectly describes an inverse, instead of a direct, relationship between the number of wild-type *beclin 1* alleles that cells carry and the number of autophagosomes in those cells under inducing conditions.

Difficulty Level: Medium (70%)

MCAT® is a program of the
Association of American Medical Colleges

24. Based on the passage, macroautophagy decreases the intracellular levels of mutagenic free radicals that are generated by:

   A. glycolysis.
   B. transcription.
   C. the electron transport chain.
   D. protein degradation in lysosomes.

Content Classification: Enzymes and Metabolism/Basic Metabolism

Cognitive Classification: Identification of Main Ideas

This question requires you to identify a point that was implicitly made in the passage. The passage states that macroautophagy degrades mitochondria, which generate mutagenic free radicals. Therefore, you need to recognize which processes that take place in the mitochondria would generate these free radicals.

Key: C

The electron transport chain is in the mitochondria, and faulty electron transfer in this chain results in the formation of highly reactive free radicals and their precursors.

Distractors

A   Glycolysis takes place in the cytoplasm, not in the mitochondria.

B   Transcription of genes in the mitochondrial genome does take place in the mitochondria, but transcription is much less likely than the electron transport chain to generate free radicals.

D   The passage states that mutagenic free radicals are being generated by mitochondria, not by lysosomes, which are located outside the mitochondria.

Difficulty Level: Easy (75%)

25. Relative to the pH of the cytosol or of the nucleoplasm, the optimal pH of the enzymes that degrade organelles and long-lived proteins during macroautophagy is most likely:

A. less than the pH of the cytosol.
B. greater than the pH of the cytosol.
C. the same as the pH of the cytosol.
D. greater than the pH of the nucleoplasm.

Content Classification: Generalized Eukaryotic Cell/Membrane-Bound Organelles

Cognitive Classification: Seeking Clarification

This question requires that you use background information relevant to the passage. The passage states that autophagosomes containing organelles and long-lived proteins fuse with lysosomes—acidic, membrane-bound organelles that contain degradative enzymes with optimal activity at acidic pH. You should assume that these hybrid fusion vesicles have a pH that is similar to the pH of lysosomes because lysosomal enzymes are presumably responsible for degrading the contents of the autophagosomes.

 You do not need to have specific background knowledge of the pH of the nucleoplasm to be able to eliminate D. Your general knowledge of the nucleus should lead you to conclude that it is very unlikely that the nucleus has an acidic pH.

Key: A

The acidic pH of the lysosomes is less than the near-neutral pH of the cytosol.

Distractors

B   This answer incorrectly states that the pH of the lysosomes is greater than, not less than, that of the cytosol.

C   This answer incorrectly states that the pH of the lysosomes is equal to, not less than, that of the cytosol.

D   The pH of the nucleoplasm is similar to the pH of the cytosol, which is greater than, not less than, that of the lysosomes.

Difficulty Level: Easy (85%)

Biology
Passage Set V

Biology

In vertebrate heme catabolism, heme is cleaved by heme oxygenase to yield Fe^{2+}, CO, and the blue-green molecule biliverdin, which in humans is reduced by biliverdin reductase to the yellow molecule bilirubin. Most of the bilirubin is transported to the liver where it is converted to bilirubin diglucuronide and excreted in bile. Biliverdin and bilirubin each are potent antioxidants.

Most birds produce very little biliverdin reductase and primarily excrete biliverdin. Some birds use biliverdin to provide blue-green coloring to their eggshells, the value of which is not immediately apparent because eggs with blue-green shells are not well camouflaged. One hypothesis is that the blue-green color intensity of the eggshell may serve to signal male birds both to the condition of the laying female and to the quality of the eggs, thus influencing the amount of time the males invest caring for the resulting brood. Pied flycatchers lay eggs with blue-green shells and consistently exhibit biparental care. It was observed that healthier female pied flycatchers lay eggs with more intensely colored shells. The blue-green color intensity also shows a positive correlation with the level of maternal antibodies (IgY) deposited in the eggs and with the survival rate of the fledglings. Maternal antibodies provide the first form of humoral immunity for newly hatched chicks.

Adapted from J. Morales, J. Sanz, and J. Moreno, Egg colour reflects the amount of yolk maternal antibodies and fledging success in a songbird, *Biology Letters*. © 2006 by Royal Society Publishing.

26. Do the observations presented in the passage indicate that the blue-green color intensity of pied flycatcher eggshells functions as a signal of egg quality to pied flycatcher males?

    A. Yes, because higher amounts of maternal antibodies are found in eggs with more intensely colored shells

    B. Yes, because the blue-green color intensity of the eggshells correlates with fledgling survival rates

    C. No, because male pied flycatchers help care for their broods regardless of the color intensity of the eggshells

    D. No, because the observations do not address whether male pied flycatchers' parenting behavior changes in response to eggshell color intensity

27. In humans, which of the following is LEAST likely to lead to jaundice, a yellowing of the skin caused by high levels of circulating bilirubin?

    A. Absence of the gallbladder
    B. Liver disease
    C. Obstruction of the common bile duct
    D. Excess lysis of erythrocytes

28. In the reduction of biliverdin to bilirubin, the role of biliverdin reductase is to:

    A. decrease the Gibbs free energy of biliverdin.
    B. increase the Gibbs free energy of bilirubin.
    C. decrease the activation energy of the chemical reaction.
    D. increase the activation energy of the chemical reaction.

29. Assuming the hypothesis presented in the passage is correct, which of the following conditions is most likely to be true in order for the blue-green color intensity of eggshells to have evolved by natural selection?

    A. No natural predators that feed on eggs with blue-green shells exist.
    B. Only species of birds that exhibit biparental care of their fledglings produce eggs with blue-green shells.
    C. The fitness advantage of increased paternal involvement in fledgling care outweighs any disadvantage caused by the lack of camouflaged eggs.

    D. The high levels of bilirubin in eggs with blue-green shells increase the fitness of the fledglings by providing the developing embryos with high levels of antioxidants.

30. Which of the following best describes the function of bile in the human digestive system?

    A. It increases duodenal pH and breaks covalent bonds within fat molecules.
    B. It increases duodenal pH and disrupts intermolecular interactions among fat molecules.
    C. It decreases duodenal pH and breaks covalent bonds within fat molecules.
    D. It decreases duodenal pH and disrupts intermolecular interactions among fat molecules.

31. Assume that a bird species exists that lays eggs with blue-green shells and exhibits biparental care. Further assume that a positive correlation exists between this species' fledgling survival rate and the blue-green color intensity of the eggshells, but not between eggshell color intensity and the level of egg IgY. Is it possible that eggshell color intensity serves as a signal of the female birds' health and of egg quality to the males of this species?

    A. No; healthy females would deposit high levels of IgY into their eggs.
    B. No; without high levels of IgY, the fledglings would not be able to fight infections.
    C. No; higher levels of antioxidants are deposited into more intensely colored blue-green eggshells.
    D. Yes; the color intensity of the eggshells could indicate fitness factors other than IgY levels to the males of this species.

32. Like birds, human mothers also provide the first humoral immunity to their young. In humans, IgG antibodies cross the placenta to the developing fetus in utero. These maternal antibodies are produced by cells that are derived from which of the following types of immune cells?

    A. T lymphocytes
    B. B lymphocytes
    C. Natural killer cells
    D. Macrophages

Solutions for this passage begin on next page.

26. Do the observations presented in the passage indicate that the blue-green color intensity of pied flycatcher eggshells functions as a signal of egg quality to pied flycatcher males?

    A. Yes, because higher amounts of maternal antibodies are found in eggs with more intensely colored shells
    B. Yes, because the blue-green color intensity of the eggshells correlates with fledgling survival rates
    C. No, because male pied flycatchers help care for their broods regardless of the color intensity of the eggshells
    D. No, because the observations do not address whether male pied flycatchers' parenting behavior changes in response to eggshell color intensity

Content Classification: Evolution/Evolution

Cognitive Classification: Evaluation Processes

This question requires you to judge whether the observations presented in the passage indicate that the hypothesis relating eggshell color intensity to male pied flycatchers' parenting behavior is valid. The key to concluding that the blue-green color intensity of pied flycatcher eggshells functions as a signal of egg quality to pied flycatcher males would be a measurable observation that links the color intensity of the eggshells to the amount and/or quality of care that male pied flycatchers invest in their young.

Key: D

Even though the observations in the passage link the blue-green color intensity of eggshells with overall egg quality and with fledgling survival rates, none of the observations addresses whether male pied flycatchers' parenting behavior changes in response to eggshell color intensity.

Distractors

A   This choice indicates that the data from the passage support the hypothesis. However, even though high amounts of maternal antibodies may indicate that the fledgling in a particular egg has a higher chance of survival and may therefore be a better time investment for male pied flycatchers, by itself this observation does not demonstrate that male pied flycatchers' parenting behavior has been influenced.

B   This choice indicates that the data from the passage support the hypothesis. However, even though fledgling survival rates correlate with eggshell color intensity, indicating that eggshell color intensity *could* serve as a signal to overall egg quality, by itself this observation does not indicate that this influences male pied flycatchers' parenting behavior.

C   This choice indicates that the data from the passage *do not* support the hypothesis. However, even though it is true that male pied flycatchers generally help care for their broods regardless of eggshell color intensity, the *amount and quality* of care they provide to their young could vary on the basis of eggshell color intensity. Therefore, this observation does not necessarily invalidate the hypothesis.

Difficulty Level: Medium (45%)

MCAT® is a program of the
Association of American Medical Colleges

27. In humans, which of the following is LEAST likely to lead to *jaundice*, a yellowing of the skin caused by high levels of circulating bilirubin?

    A. Absence of the gallbladder
    B. Liver disease
    C. Obstruction of the common bile duct
    D. Excess lysis of erythrocytes

Content Classification: Digestive and Excretory Systems/Digestion

Cognitive Classification: Flexibility and Adaptability in Scientific Reasoning

This question requires you to apply your knowledge of digestive system processes and anatomy to the information presented in the passage to determine which answer choice is LEAST likely to result in jaundice. Because jaundice is caused by excess circulating bilirubin, it is likely to be caused by those processes that release an excess of bilirubin into the bloodstream and by those that prevent the body from effectively disposing of bilirubin.

Key: A

The gallbladder is a storage compartment located off the duct that transfers bile from the liver to the small intestine. The passage indicates that bilirubin is excreted from the body in bile. Although the absence of the gallbladder eliminates a storage compartment for bile, it does not affect the body's ability to excrete bile. Therefore, it is the least likely of the choices to cause bilirubin to back up into the bloodstream and cause an increase in the level of circulating bilirubin. Nor does the absence of a gallbladder cause additional bilirubin to be generated.

In many questions that use "LEAST," "NOT," or "EXCEPT," three of the four answer choices will fulfill a specific requirement presented in the question, and you must choose the one answer that *does not* meet this requirement. A common error is to mistakenly choose one of the answer choices that *does* meet the requirement presented in the question.

Distractors

B   The liver is responsible for converting bilirubin to bilirubin diglucuronide and excreting it in bile. Liver disease is likely to disrupt this process and cause a backup of bilirubin in the bloodstream, creating an excess of circulating bilirubin.

C   Obstruction of the common bile duct would cause bile to back up in the liver, which would subsequently cause bilirubin to back up into the bloodstream, creating an excess of circulating bilirubin.

D   Excess lysis of erythrocytes would release excess heme from hemoglobin. This excess heme would be converted into bilirubin, resulting in excess bilirubin in the bloodstream.

Difficulty Level: Medium (45%)

Even though this question can be answered on the basis of the information presented in the passage and the expected background knowledge, this is a case in which common knowledge or your own experiences may reinforce your answer choice. Surgery to remove the gallbladder is fairly common, and most people do not have to follow fat-restricted diets after recovering from it. This implies that bile production and delivery to the small intestine are functioning in these people, and it is unlikely that the removal of the gallbladder is causing bile to back up into the liver (or bilirubin to back up into the bloodstream). In general, if you are uncertain about a particular answer choice, it may help to evaluate whether the choice in question is consistent with your own life experiences.

28. In the reduction of biliverdin to bilirubin, the role of biliverdin reductase is to:

    A. decrease the Gibbs free energy of biliverdin.
    B. increase the Gibbs free energy of bilirubin.
    C. decrease the activation energy of the chemical reaction.
    D. increase the activation energy of the chemical reaction.

Content Classification: Enzymes and Metabolism/Enzyme Structure and Function

Cognitive Classification: Seeking Clarification

This question requires you to identify appropriate clarifying information about the function of enzymes in catalyzing chemical reactions. Although the passage does not directly state that biliverdin reductase is an enzyme, this can be inferred by its stated function of reducing biliverdin to bilirubin and by the suffix -*ase* in *reductase*. In a chemical reaction, the activation energy is the energy required to break the chemical

 Mistakenly thinking that enzymes alter the net free energy change of a chemical reaction (ΔG) would lead you into concluding that enzymes can change $G_{reactants}$ and $G_{products}$.

bonds in the reactants so that the chemical bonds of the products can form. Chemical reactions require a minimum energy input equivalent to the activation energy in order to proceed. Enzymes employ a variety of mechanisms to reduce the activation energy so that chemical reactions are more likely to occur. These mechanisms include distorting and destabilizing the bonds of the reactants and providing specific microenvironments that are more conducive to the reaction. However, enzymes do not change the inherent Gibbs free energy values (G = energy available to do work) of the reactants and the products. Nor do they alter the net free energy change of a chemical reaction (ΔG = $G_{products} - G_{reactants}$).

Key: C

The role of biliverdin reductase is correctly identified as decreasing the activation energy of the reaction.

Distractors

A   The role of biliverdin reductase is incorrectly identified as decreasing the Gibbs free energy of the reactant, biliverdin.

B   The role of biliverdin reductase is incorrectly identified as increasing the Gibbs free energy of the product, bilirubin.

D   The role of biliverdin reductase is incorrectly identified as *increasing*, not decreasing, the activation energy of the reaction.

Difficulty Level: Easy (85%)

29. Assuming the hypothesis presented in the passage is correct, which of the following conditions is most likely to be true in order for the blue-green color intensity of eggshells to have evolved by natural selection?

    A. No natural predators that feed on eggs with blue-green shells exist.

    B. Only species of birds that exhibit biparental care of their fledglings produce eggs with blue-green shells.

    C. The fitness advantage of increased paternal involvement in fledgling care outweighs any disadvantage caused by the lack of camouflaged eggs.

    D. The high levels of bilirubin in eggs with blue-green shells increase the fitness of the fledglings by providing the developing embryos with high levels of antioxidants.

Content Classification: Evolution/Evolution

Cognitive Classification: Hypothesis Testing

This question requires you to apply background knowledge of natural selection to identify the condition that would validate the hypothesis presented in the passage. Natural selection is based on the premise that certain heritable phenotypes contribute more to the reproductive success of an organism than do other phenotypes. How these different phenotypes interact with an individual organism's environment determines the individual's reproductive success. The contribution an individual makes to the gene pool of the next generation, relative to the contributions of other individuals in the population, is that individual's fitness. The fitness of an individual relies on the sum of all its phenotypes; a phenotype that increases the longevity of an individual, potentially increasing the amount of time that individual has to reproduce, would be outweighed by a phenotype that renders the individual sterile and unable to reproduce at all.

When two answer choices seem reasonable, read each choice very carefully to see if there is a misstatement in one of them. In the case of choice **D**, the passage directly states that biliverdin, not bilirubin, is the antioxidant molecule that is found in eggshells.

Key: C

Assuming the hypothesis presented in the passage is correct, the phenotype of blue-green eggshells has at least two different possible effects on the fitness of pied flycatchers. The lack of camouflaged eggs is potentially detrimental to fitness if the bright colors allow predators to more easily locate and feed on the eggs. However, increased paternal care of the fledglings potentially increases their fitness if the increase in paternal care leads to an increase in the fledgling survival rate. When the increase in fitness due to increased paternal care is greater than the decrease in fitness caused by a lack of camouflaged eggs, natural selection can act to select for the phenotype of blue-green eggshells. This answer choice most closely meets the basic prerequisites for natural selection to occur by implying that having blue-green eggshells provides a net fitness advantage.

Distractors

A   It is unlikely that there are no natural predators that feed on blue-green eggs. Even if this statement were true, it is not a prerequisite condition for natural selection. As long as the blue-green color intensity of the eggshell provides a net fitness advantage, this trait can be selected for by natural selection.

B   It is unlikely that only species of birds that exhibit biparental care of their fledglings produce eggs with blue-green shells. Even if this statement were true, it is not a prerequisite condition for natural selection. As long as the blue-green color intensity of the eggshell provides a net fitness advantage, this trait can be selected for by natural selection.

D   Although providing high levels of antioxidants to developing embryos may give a survival advantage to fledglings, it may or may not relate to the fitness advantage provided by increased paternal care of the fledglings. In this case, the more general statement in choice **C** is better because it would apply to more potential causes of the increased fitness. In addition, this answer choice contains an incorrect statement in that *biliverdin*, not *bilirubin*, gives the eggshells their blue-green color.

Difficulty Level: Medium (65%)

30. Which of the following best describes the function of bile in the human digestive system?

  A. It increases duodenal pH and breaks covalent bonds within fat molecules.
  B. It increases duodenal pH and disrupts intermolecular interactions among fat molecules.
  C. It decreases duodenal pH and breaks covalent bonds within fat molecules.
  D. It decreases duodenal pH and disrupts intermolecular interactions among fat molecules.

Content Classification: Digestive and Excretory Systems/Digestive System

Cognitive Classification: Seeking Clarification

This question requires you to identify relevant background information regarding the function of bile. Bile is an aqueous alkaline fluid produced in the liver and secreted into the duodenum where it acts as an emulsifier of lipids. It breaks large globules of fat into smaller globules, increasing the surface area available for the action of pancreatic lipase. Bile does not contain any enzymes; therefore, it interferes with reactions between individual fat molecules only—it does not break any covalent bonds within fat molecules. One component of bile is NaHCO₃, which helps increase the pH of the contents of the duodenal lumen.

Assuming that bile contains digestive enzymes just because it is involved in fat digestion could lead to the wrong answer choice. Bile acts as an emulsifier only; it is unable to break covalent bonds within fat molecules. Lipase-containing secretions from the pancreas are responsible for breaking these covalent bonds.

Key: B

The function of bile is correctly recognized as both increasing the pH of the duodenum and disrupting intermolecular interactions among fat molecules.

Distractors

A This choice correctly recognizes that bile increases duodenal pH but incorrectly states that it breaks covalent bonds within fat molecules.

C This choice incorrectly states that bile both decreases duodenal pH and breaks covalent bonds within fat molecules.

D This choice correctly recognizes that bile disrupts intermolecular interactions among fat molecules but incorrectly states that it decreases duodenal pH.

Even if you do not know that the NaHCO₃ content of bile makes it alkaline, you can still use your background knowledge to make a reasonable guess. Knowing that (1) the chyme coming from the stomach is extremely acidic, (2) the pH of the chyme must be increased so that pancreatic enzymes can function, and (3) bile is being added directly to the contents of the duodenal lumen, it is most reasonable to assume that bile is itself alkaline, so that its presence increases the pH of the duodenal lumen, helping create an environment conducive to the function of pancreatic enzymes.

Difficulty Level: Medium (50%)

31. Assume that a bird species exists that lays eggs with blue-green shells and exhibits biparental care. Further assume that a positive correlation exists between this species' fledgling survival rate and the blue-green color intensity of the eggshells, but not between eggshell color intensity and the level of egg IgY. Is it possible that eggshell color intensity serves as a signal of the female birds' health and of egg quality to the males of this species?

    A. No; healthy females would deposit high levels of IgY into their eggs.
    B. No; without high levels of IgY, the fledglings would not be able to fight infections.
    C. No; higher levels of antioxidants are deposited into more intensely colored blue-green eggshells.
    D. Yes; the color intensity of the eggshells could indicate fitness factors other than IgY levels to the males of this species.

Content Classification: Evolution/Evolution

Cognitive Classification: Evaluation Processes

This question requires you to judge whether a conclusion follows necessarily from the given premises. It is stated in the question that there is a positive correlation between this species' fledgling survival rate and the blue-green color intensity of the eggshells. Although IgY antibodies provide humoral immunity for newly hatched chicks and, thus, high levels of IgY are likely to be beneficial to fledgling survival, you must realize that the blue-green color intensity of the eggshells could directly correlate with any one of a number of factors to indicate the overall quality of the egg to males of this species.

Key: D

Because there is a positive correlation between the species' fledgling survival rate and the blue-green color intensity of the eggshells, it is reasonable to assume that the blue-green color intensity could serve as a signal of female health and egg quality to the males of this species. Even though there is no correlation between eggshell color intensity and IgY levels, the color intensity of the eggshells could indicate other fitness factors to the males of this species.

 In questions that pair a "yes"–"no" option with a supportive statement, be sure that the statement actually supports the given "yes"–"no" option. The statement given in choice C would better support an answer of "yes" than "no." This makes **C** a poor answer choice.

Distractors

A   This choice incorrectly indicates that because the blue-green color intensity does not relate to IgY levels, it is not possible that eggshell color intensity serves as a signal of the female birds' health and of egg quality to the males of this species. In addition, it is possible that these eggs *do* have high levels of IgY. The observation that there is no correlation between the eggshell color intensity and the amount of IgY does not actually allow you to draw conclusions about the amount of IgY in the egg. There could be consistently high levels, consistently low levels, or random levels of IgY in the egg.

B   This choice incorrectly indicates that it is not possible that eggshell color intensity serves as a signal of the female birds' health and of egg quality to the males of this species. The observation that there is no correlation between the eggshell color intensity and the amount of IgY does not actually allow you to draw conclusions about the amount of IgY in the egg. There could be consistently high levels, consistently low levels, or random levels of IgY in the egg. Even if the eggs do have low levels of IgY, it has not been determined how detrimental this condition would be to fledgling survival.

C   The blue-green color intensity of eggshells does correlate with the amount of the antioxidant biliverdin in the shell, and antioxidants may help increase the fitness of the embryo within the egg. However, this answer choice incorrectly indicates that it is not possible that eggshell color intensity serves as a signal of the female birds' health and of egg quality to the males of this species.

Difficulty Level: Easy (75%)

32. Like birds, human mothers also provide the first humoral immunity to their young. In humans, IgG antibodies cross the placenta to the developing fetus in utero. These maternal antibodies are produced by cells that are derived from which of the following types of immune cells?

A. T lymphocytes
B. B lymphocytes
C. Natural killer cells
D. Macrophages

Content Classification: Circulatory, Lymphatic, and Immune Systems/Immune System

Cognitive Classification: Seeking Clarification

This question requires you to identify relevant background information about immune system cell types. When B lymphocytes are stimulated by antigen, they either differentiate into memory cells or into plasma cells, which produce secreted antibodies such as IgG. Antibodies recognize extracellular antigens such as bacteria and free viruses. The other types of immune cells do not produce secreted antibodies.

Key: B

This choice correctly identifies that antibodies are produced by cells that are derived from B lymphocytes.

Distractors

A   While T lymphocytes do produce highly specific antigen receptors, these receptors are distinct from antibodies and remain embedded in the cellular membrane. T lymphocytes are responsible for cell-mediated immunity and are activated by foreign antigens in association with major histocompatibility complex molecules, which are presented to T lymphocytes by antigen-presenting cells. T cells also stimulate humoral immunity.

C   Natural killer cells are innate immune system cells that lyse and destroy virus-infected host cells and cancer cells. They do not produce antibodies.

D   Macrophages are phagocytic immune cells that engulf and destroy bacteria, viruses, and other foreign material in addition to engulfing and destroying abnormal "self" cells. They secrete chemicals that help mediate the inflammatory response and act as antigen-presenting cells, but they do not produce antibodies.

Difficulty Level: Easy (80%)

Biology
Discrete Questions

Biology

Biology Discrete (Questions 33–41)

33. The host cell is LEAST likely to contribute which of the following enzymes or enzymatic complexes to the retroviral life cycle?
    A. Ribosomes
    B. DNA-dependent RNA polymerase
    C. RNA-dependent DNA polymerase
    D. DNA-dependent DNA polymerase

34. Which of the following would NOT change within a sarcomere during skeletal muscle contraction?
    A. The length of the thick filaments
    B. The overlap between the thick and the thin filaments
    C. The position of troponin–tropomyosin complexes on the thin filaments
    D. The positions at which the globular heads of the thick filaments bind to the thin filaments

35. During the respiratory cycle, contraction of the diaphragm causes:
    A. exhalation.
    B. elevation of the ribs.
    C. the intrapleural pressure to increase.
    D. the intra-alveolar pressure to decrease.

36. The layer of adipose tissue that insulates and cushions the human body is located directly between the:
    A. skin sublayer of keratinized dead cells and the rest of the epidermis.
    B. skin sublayer of keratinized dead cells and the rest of the dermis.
    C. dermis and underlying muscle or bone.
    D. epidermis and the dermis.

37. Constriction of the afferent arteriole that supplies blood directly to the glomerulus of a nephron would most immediately affect the volume of renal filtrate in which of the following tubular components of that nephron?
    A. Loop of Henle
    B. Proximal tubule
    C. Collecting tubule
    D. Bowman's capsule

38. Assume that a certain trait is determined by a single gene that has only two alleles and that the phenotype produced by the dominant allele is completely dominant. Given that 9% of a particular population in Hardy–Weinberg equilibrium displays the recessive phenotype, what percentage of this population would both display the dominant phenotype and be capable of producing a child who displays the recessive phenotype? (Note: Assume no new mutations in the gene occur.)
    A. 21%
    B. 42%
    C. 49%
    D. 91%

39. Of postpubescent human male and female reproductive organs, in which, if either, do the germ cells regularly undergo mitosis to produce daughter cells that go on to become gametes?
    A. In male reproductive organs only
    B. In female reproductive organs only
    C. In both male and female reproductive organs
    D. In neither male nor female reproductive organs

40. Osteoblasts and osteoclasts were noted to be extensively remodeling a certain tissue in a patient's arm. To which tissue type does this remodeled tissue most likely belong, and from which of the primary germ layers was the tissue most likely derived?
    A. Epithelial tissue derived from the ectoderm
    B. Connective tissue derived from the endoderm
    C. Endothelial tissue derived from the mesoderm
    D. Connective tissue derived from the mesoderm

MCAT® is a program of the
Association of American Medical Colleges

41. The affinity that hemoglobin has for oxygen is affected by many factors, including the partial pressure of oxygen in the blood (P_{O_2}), the partial pressure of carbon dioxide in the blood (P_{CO_2}), and temperature. Which of the following best describes what happens to these parameters in the blood as blood flows through highly metabolically active tissue and how hemoglobin's affinity for oxygen would most likely be affected under these conditions?

A. P_{O_2}, P_{CO_2}, and temperature would all increase, causing hemoglobin's affinity for oxygen to decrease.

B. P_{O_2} would decrease, and P_{CO_2} and temperature would increase, causing hemoglobin's affinity for oxygen to increase.

C. P_{O_2} would decrease, and P_{CO_2} and temperature would increase, causing hemoglobin's affinity for oxygen to decrease.

D. P_{O_2} would increase, and P_{CO_2} and temperature would decrease, causing hemoglobin's affinity for oxygen to increase.

Solutions for this passage begin on next page.

33. The host cell is LEAST likely to contribute which of the following enzymes or enzymatic complexes to the retroviral life cycle?

    A. Ribosomes
    B. DNA-dependent RNA polymerase
    C. RNA-dependent DNA polymerase
    D. DNA-dependent DNA polymerase

Content Classification: Microbiology/Viral Life Cycle

Cognitive Classification: Hypothesis Testing

This question requires you to predict a result on the basis of background knowledge. You need to consider which enzymes or enzymatic complexes are contributed by the host cell at each step of the retroviral life cycle. The retroviral genome is a single-stranded, positive-sense RNA that is converted by retroviral reverse transcriptase into a double-stranded DNA version after the viral particle enters the host cell. This DNA version integrates into the host cell chromosome, creating a *provirus*. The provirus is replicated and transcribed as part of the host cell chromosome. To answer this question, you need to realize that "RNA-dependent" and "DNA-dependent" refer to the type of nucleic acid that is serving as the template for the polymerase.

 Note that this question is asking for what is "LEAST likely," and therefore the answers that are very likely to be true are not the key. This question can be answered either by eliminating the three answer choices that describe enzymes or enzymatic complexes that the host cell contributes to the retroviral life cycle or by identifying the one enzyme or enzymatic complex that the host cell does NOT contribute to the retroviral life cycle. Reviewing each step of the retroviral life cycle may be helpful when answering this question.

Key: C

The retroviral reverse transcriptase that generates the DNA version of the RNA retroviral genome has an RNA-dependent DNA polymerase activity that allows it to synthesize a DNA strand that is complementary to an RNA template. This answer is correct because it describes a polymerase that is contributed by the virus, instead of by the host, to the retroviral life cycle.

Distractors

A   As is true of the mRNAs of other viruses, retroviral mRNAs are translated by host cell ribosomes.

B   The genes of the provirus are transcribed by the host cell DNA-dependent RNA polymerase.

D   Because the provirus is integrated into the host cells' chromosomes, the proviral sequence is replicated by the host cell DNA-dependent DNA polymerase.

Difficulty Level: Medium (45%)

34. Which of the following would NOT change within a sarcomere during skeletal muscle contraction?

    A. The length of the thick filaments
    B. The overlap between the thick and the thin filaments
    C. The position of troponin–tropomyosin complexes on the thin filaments
    D. The positions at which the globular heads of the thick filaments bind to the thin filaments

Content Classification: Specialized Eukaryotic Cells and Tissues/Muscle Cell (Contractile)

Cognitive Classification: Hypothesis Testing

This question requires you to predict a result on the basis of background knowledge. You need to know the structural components of a sarcomere and how these components are affected by muscle contraction. Sarcomeres are the basic contractile units of skeletal muscle and contain thin filaments of actin that overlap with thick filaments of myosin. The thin filaments also contain the regulatory proteins tropomyosin and troponin. The thin filaments

 Try identifying the three features of a sarcomere that _do_ change during muscle contraction and then confirm that the remaining feature does not change.

are bound to the thick filaments through the globular heads of the thick filaments. Tropomyosin and troponin influence the ability of these globular heads to bind to the thin filaments. An increase in the cytosolic Ca^{2+} concentration in a muscle cell causes the position of the troponin–tropomyosin complex on the thin filaments to shift, exposing myosin head binding sites on the thin filaments. The globular myosin heads bind to these newly exposed sites on the thin filaments and pull the thin filaments inward over the thick filaments, causing the muscle to contract.

Key: A

This answer is correct because the length of the thick filaments (as well as the length of the thin filaments) _does not_ change during skeletal muscle contraction.

Distractors

B   This is an incorrect answer because the extent of the overlap between the thick and the thin filaments _does_ change during muscle contraction.

C   This is an incorrect answer because the position of troponin–tropomyosin complexes on the thin filaments _does_ change during muscle contraction.

D   This is an incorrect answer because the positions at which the globular heads of the thick filaments bind to the thin filaments _does_ change during muscle contraction.

Difficulty Level: Medium (70%)

35. During the respiratory cycle, contraction of the diaphragm causes:

   A. exhalation.
   B. elevation of the ribs.
   C. the intrapleural pressure to increase.
   D. the intra-alveolar pressure to decrease.

Content Classification: Respiration System/Respiratory System

Cognitive Classification: Seeking Clarification

This question requires you to use relevant background information to identify one of the consequences of an event, the contraction of the diaphragm. Contraction of the respiratory diaphragm causes the diaphragm to move downward, thus increasing the volume of the thoracic cavity. This increase in volume causes a decrease in the intrapleural pressure, the pressure in the closed space between the outside of the lungs and the inside of the thoracic wall. Expansion of the thoracic cavity causes the lungs to expand. Expansion of the lungs causes the intra-alveolar pressure, the pressure in the alveoli, to decrease below atmospheric pressure and draws air into the lungs through the trachea.

 A common error would be to assume that contraction of the diaphragm directly causes the ribs to elevate because contraction of the diaphragm causes inhalation, which also involves elevation of the ribs.

Key: D

Contraction of the diaphragm causes the lungs to expand, which results in a decrease in the intra-alveolar pressure.

Distractors

A   Contraction of the diaphragm causes air to enter the lungs, which is inspiration, not exhalation.

B   The ribs are elevated during inspiration, but this elevation is not a direct consequence of contracting the diaphragm. During inspiration, the ribs are moved up and out by the external intercostal muscles, not by the diaphragm.

C   Contraction of the diaphragm increases the volume of the thoracic cavity, causing the intrapleural pressure to decrease, not increase.

Difficulty Level: Hard (30%)

36. The layer of adipose tissue that insulates and cushions the human body is located directly between the:

    A. skin sublayer of keratinized dead cells and the rest of the epidermis.
    B. skin sublayer of keratinized dead cells and the rest of the dermis.
    C. dermis and underlying muscle or bone.
    D. epidermis and the dermis.

Content Classification: Skin System/Skin System

Cognitive Classification: Identification of Components of a Situation and Relationships Among Them

This question requires you to test basic relationships among variables, those variables being the layers and the sublayers of the skin. To answer this question, you need to know the general structure of the skin. The top layer of the skin is the epidermis, the outermost layer of which is a sublayer of keratinized dead cells. The dermis lies directly beneath the epidermis, and a layer of adipose tissue, or the *hypodermis*, lies directly beneath the dermis. The hypodermis anchors the skin to the underlying muscle or bone.

Key: C

The hypodermis lies directly beneath the dermis. Muscle and bone are under the hypodermis.

Distractors

A   This answer is incorrect because adipose tissue is not a sublayer of the epidermis.

B   This answer is incorrect because neither adipose tissue nor keratinized dead cells make up sublayers of the dermis.

D   This answer is incorrect because the hypodermis lies beneath, and not between, the epidermis and the dermis.

Difficulty level: Medium (70%)

37. Constriction of the afferent arteriole that supplies blood directly to the glomerulus of a nephron would *most immediately* affect the volume of renal filtrate in which of the following tubular components of that nephron?

   A. Loop of Henle
   B. Proximal tubule
   C. Collecting tubule
   D. Bowman's capsule

Content Classification: Digestive and Excretory Systems/Excretory System

Cognitive Classification: Flexibility and Adaptability in Scientific Reasoning

This question requires you to use your background knowledge and the given information to solve a problem. Specifically, you need to know the general structure of a nephron. The blood entering a nephron through the afferent arteriole is filtered through the endothelial walls of the glomerulus (a tuft of highly porous blood vessels) into the tubular components of the nephron.

Key: D

Constriction of the afferent arteriole would decrease the glomerular filtration rate and consequently the volume of the renal filtrate. The glomerulus is within Bowman's capsule. Because blood is filtered from the glomerulus into Bowman's capsule, the effect of constricting the afferent arteriole on the renal filtrate volume would first be observed in Bowman's capsule.

Distractors

A   The loop of Henle is a nephron tubular component that is downstream of Bowman's capsule. Therefore, the effect of reducing the glomerular filtration rate on renal filtrate volume would be observed in the loop of Henle after it is observed in Bowman's capsule.

B   The proximal tubule is a nephron tubular component that is downstream of Bowman's capsule. Therefore, the effect of reducing the glomerular filtration rate on renal filtrate volume would be observed in the proximal tubule after it is observed in Bowman's capsule.

C   The collecting tubule is a nephron tubular component that is downstream of Bowman's capsule. Therefore, the effect of reducing the glomerular filtration rate on renal filtrate volume would be observed in the collecting tubule after it is observed in Bowman's capsule.

Difficulty Level: Medium (65%)

38. Assume that a certain trait is determined by a single gene that has only two alleles and that the phenotype produced by the dominant allele is completely dominant. Given that 9% of a particular population in Hardy–Weinberg equilibrium displays the recessive phenotype, what percentage of this population would both display the dominant phenotype and be capable of producing a child who displays the recessive phenotype? (Note: Assume no new mutations in the gene occur.)

    A. 21%

    B. 42%

    C. 49%

    D. 91%

Content Classification: Genetics/Analytical Methods

Cognitive Classification: Reasoning Using Quantitative Data

This question requires you to use the presented data to calculate the percentage of a population that meets specific requirements outlined in the question. You are told that the population is in Hardy–Weinberg equilibrium and that the trait under consideration is caused by a single gene with two alleles, one of which is completely dominant over the other. In this case, the standard Hardy–Weinberg equation, $p^2 + 2pq + q^2$, applies. In this equation, p equals the frequency of the dominant allele, p^2 equals the frequency of the homozygous dominant genotype, q equals the frequency of the recessive allele, q^2 equals the frequency of the homozygous recessive genotype, and $2pq$ equals the frequency of the heterozygous genotype. You are asked to calculate the percentage of this population that would both display the dominant phenotype and be capable of producing a child who displays the recessive phenotype. Individuals who have either the homozygous dominant or the heterozygous genotype will display the dominant phenotype. However, to produce a child who displays the recessive phenotype, both parents must possess at least one recessive allele. Of the individuals who display the dominant phenotype, only those who are heterozygous possess a recessive allele that can be passed on to their child. Therefore, you should calculate the percentage of the population that is heterozygous, or $100 \times 2pq$.

 This question has several steps, none of which is particularly difficult, but all of which are needed to determine the correct answer. Breaking the question down into the individual steps and using scratch paper to keep track of what you figure out will make this question less overwhelming.

Key: B

You are told that 9% of the population displays the recessive phenotype. The only genotype that produces the recessive phenotype is q^2; thus, $q^2 = 0.09$. Taking the square root of 0.09, q is calculated to be 0.3. The value of p is found by using the equation $p = 1 - q$, or $p = 1 - 0.3 = 0.7$. The percentage of the population that is heterozygous is equal to $100 \times 2pq$, or $[100 \times 2(0.7)(0.3)] = 42\%$.

Distractors

A   This choice fails to multiply pq by a factor of 2 and therefore accounts for only half the number of heterozygotes in the population.

C   This choice is equal to $100p^2$, or the percentage of individuals in the population who are homozygous dominant. This answer could be reached by failing to recognize both that heterozygotes will display the dominant phenotype and that the individuals who are homozygous dominant are incapable of producing a child who displays the recessive phenotype, given that no new mutations in the gene occur.

D   This choice is equal to $100[p^2 + 2pq]$, or the total percentage of individuals in the population who display the dominant phenotype. This answer could be reached by failing to recognize that of those individuals who display the dominant phenotype, only heterozygotes can produce a child who displays the recessive phenotype.

Difficulty Level: Medium (50%)

MCAT® is a program of the
Association of American Medical Colleges

39. Of postpubescent human male and female reproductive organs, in which, if either, do the germ cells regularly undergo *mitosis* to produce daughter cells that go on to become gametes?

A. In male reproductive organs only
B. In female reproductive organs only
C. In both male and female reproductive organs
D. In neither male nor female reproductive organs

Content Classification: Reproductive System and Development/Reproductive System

Cognitive Classification: Seeking Clarification

This question requires you to identify relevant background information about gametogenesis in the human reproductive system, specifically whether germ cells undergo mitosis in the reproductive organs of postpubescent males and females. The testes and ovaries contain a limited number of spermatogonia and oogonia, the male and female germ cells, respectively. These germ cells divide by mitosis: one daughter cell remains a germ cell and the other begins to differentiate into a gamete. In males, spermatogenesis begins at puberty and continues throughout the rest of the person's life. The spermatogonia divide by *mitosis*, providing cells for gametogenesis while also maintaining the germ cell population. The cells that are destined to become spermatozoa divide twice more by mitosis before undergoing meiosis and packaging to become mature spermatozoa. In females, oogenesis begins before birth. The oogonia divide mitotically, producing oogonia and cells that differentiate into primary oocytes. These cells begin meiosis, which arrests midway through meiosis I prior to birth, forming a female's entire lifetime complement of primary oocytes. These cells remain primary oocytes until puberty when they recommence the maturation process and begin to be released from the ovary at a rate of approximately one secondary oocyte per month. Secondary oocytes are arrested in metaphase of meiosis II. Meiosis is completed when and if the oocyte is fertilized by a spermatozoan.

 There is such a strong association between gametogenesis and meiosis that it is easy to overlook that germ cells must first divide by mitosis in order to replenish the germ cell population while simultaneously providing cells that can differentiate into gametes.

Key: A

This choice correctly identifies that germ cells in postpubescent human males, but not those in postpubescent human females, undergo mitosis to produce daughter cells that eventually become gametes.

Distractors

B   This choice incorrectly identifies that germ cells in postpubescent human females, but not those in postpubescent human males, undergo mitosis to produce daughter cells that eventually become gametes.

C   This choice incorrectly identifies that germ cells in postpubescent human males and those in postpubescent human females undergo mitosis to produce daughter cells that eventually become gametes.

D   This choice incorrectly identifies that neither germ cells in postpubescent human males nor those in postpubescent human females undergo mitosis to produce daughter cells that eventually become gametes.

Difficulty Level: Medium (45%)

40. Osteoblasts and osteoclasts were noted to be extensively remodeling a certain tissue in a patient's arm. To which tissue type does this remodeled tissue most likely belong, and from which of the primary germ layers was the tissue most likely derived?

A. Epithelial tissue derived from the ectoderm
B. Connective tissue derived from the endoderm
C. Endothelial tissue derived from the mesoderm
D. Connective tissue derived from the mesoderm

Content Classifications: Muscle and Skeletal Systems/Skeletal System; Specialized Eukaryotic Cells and Tissues/Other Specialized Cell Types; Reproductive System and Development/Embryogenesis

Cognitive Classification: Identification of Components of a Situation and Relationships Among Them

This question requires you to identify relationships among different variables presented in the question. Osteoblasts and osteoclasts are two types of bone cells. Osteoblasts build new bone, whereas osteoclasts break down bone tissue. Once you have identified the tissue in the question as bone, you can determine the tissue type and the primary germ layer from which it was derived. Bone is a type of connective tissue, tissue that is characterized by relatively few cells dispersed throughout an extensive extracellular matrix. In addition to bone, connective tissues include blood, adipose tissue, and cartilage. Along with these other connective tissues, most bone—except for bones of the skull—is derived from the mesoderm. The mesoderm also gives rise to the heart, kidneys, and muscles.

 Even if you are unsure of what osteoblasts and osteoclasts do, the prefix *osteo-* can help you determine that the tissue in question is most likely bone. This question is one in which knowing only part of the answer can help you to eliminate several answer choices. Just by knowing that the tissue is a type of connective tissue, you can immediately eliminate choices A and C without having to consider the primary germ layer from which the tissue was derived. If you know only that the tissue was derived from the mesoderm, you can immediately eliminate choices A and B without having to consider the tissue type.

Key: D

This choice correctly identifies that the tissue being described in the question is a type of connective tissue that was derived from the mesoderm. This conclusion can be reached after first determining that the tissue being remodeled is most likely bone.

Distractors

A   This choice incorrectly identifies the tissue as a type of epithelial tissue, tissue that is characterized by sheets of cells bound together by cellular junctions. Epithelia cover body surfaces and line body cavities. The primary germ layer is also incorrectly identified as the ectoderm. The ectoderm gives rise to the epidermis, nervous system, and bones of the skull, but not the bones of the arm.

B   This choice correctly identifies the tissue as connective tissue, but incorrectly identifies the primary germ layer as the endoderm. The endoderm gives rise to the lungs, liver, pancreas, and organs of the gastrointestinal tract, but not bone.

C   Even though the primary germ layer is correctly identified as the mesoderm, this choice incorrectly identifies the tissue type as endothelial, a type of simple squamous epithelial tissue that lines the entire circulatory system.

Difficulty Level: Medium (70%)

MCAT® is a program of the
Association of American Medical Colleges

41. The affinity that hemoglobin has for oxygen is affected by many factors, including the partial pressure of oxygen in the blood (P_{O_2}), the partial pressure of carbon dioxide in the blood (P_{CO_2}), and temperature. Which of the following best describes what happens to these parameters in the blood as blood flows through highly metabolically active tissue and how hemoglobin's affinity for oxygen would most likely be affected under these conditions?

    A. P_{O_2}, P_{CO_2}, and temperature would all increase, causing hemoglobin's affinity for oxygen to decrease.
    B. P_{O_2} would decrease, and P_{CO_2} and temperature would increase, causing hemoglobin's affinity for oxygen to increase.
    C. P_{O_2} would decrease, and P_{CO_2} and temperature would increase, causing hemoglobin's affinity for oxygen to decrease.
    D. P_{O_2} would increase, and P_{CO_2} and temperature would decrease, causing hemoglobin's affinity for oxygen to increase.

Content Classifications: Circulatory, Lymphatic, and Immune Systems/Circulatory System; Enzyme Structure and Function/Basic Metabolism

Cognitive Classification: Hypothesis Testing

This question requires you to predict a result by applying your background knowledge of basic metabolism and the characteristics of hemoglobin. Metabolically active tissue requires large amounts of ATP, much of which is generated through cellular respiration. Cellular respiration consumes oxygen and releases carbon dioxide. Oxygen enters metabolically active tissue from the blood, whereas carbon dioxide moves in the opposite direction. This causes blood P_{O_2} to decrease and blood P_{CO_2} to increase. As the metabolically active cells hydrolyze ATP to do work, heat is released, causing the temperature in the tissue and surrounding blood vessels to increase. Factors that affect hemoglobin's affinity for oxygen tend to facilitate the release of oxygen where it is most needed. Because metabolically active tissues require large amounts of oxygen, the conditions in these tissues would tend to decrease hemoglobin's affinity for oxygen, causing the oxygen to be released and subsequently available for consumption by the tissue.

 Although this question may appear to require specialized knowledge of the hemoglobin–O_2 binding curve, the answer can be reasoned out using only fundamental knowledge of metabolism and the function of hemoglobin. Starting with a basic requirement of metabolically active tissues, specifically, a supply of ATP, you can deduce the P_{CO_2}, P_{CO_2}, and temperature conditions in these tissues. Combining these conditions with hemoglobin's function of facilitating oxygen delivery to body cells, you can determine that hemoglobin's affinity for oxygen is likely to decrease.

Key: C

This choice correctly indicates that P_{O_2} would decrease and P_{CO_2} and temperature would increase, causing hemoglobin to release oxygen by decreasing hemoglobin's affinity for oxygen.

Distractors

A   This choice incorrectly indicates that P_{O_2} would increase, which is the opposite of what would occur in metabolically active tissues.

B   This choice incorrectly indicates that hemoglobin's affinity for oxygen would increase, which is the opposite of what would occur under these conditions.

D   Although the conditions of increased P_{O_2} with decreased P_{CO_2} and decreased temperature will increase hemoglobin's affinity for oxygen, these conditions are the opposite of what occurs in metabolically active tissues.

Difficulty Level: Easy (75%)

Organic Chemistry
Passage Set I

Organic Chemistry

Passage I: Questions 1–4

(Passage Format: Problem Solving)

Amines play important roles in many biochemical processes. Many methods of preparing amines have been explored. Alkylation of primary amines with haloalkanes is a well-established procedure in synthesizing secondary amines. Unfortunately, this method is limited by the risk of further alkylation to tertiary amines and subsequently to quaternary ammonium compounds. A selective synthesis, shown in Scheme I, in which ethanolamine reacts with carbonyl compounds via an imine intermediate that equilibrates with an oxazolidine ring (Compound 1), does not experience the same problem.

Scheme I

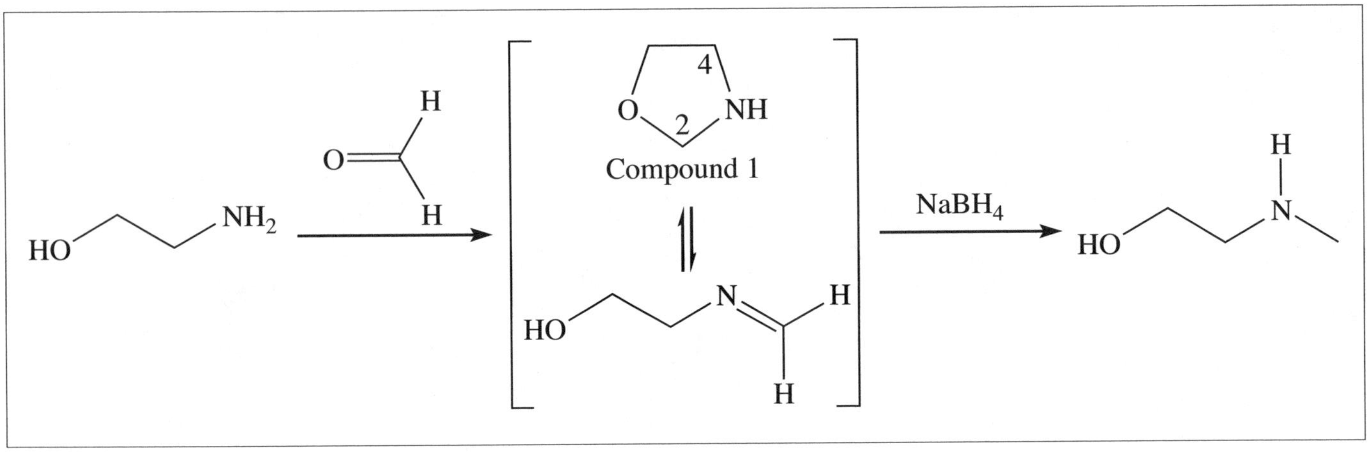

Scheme II

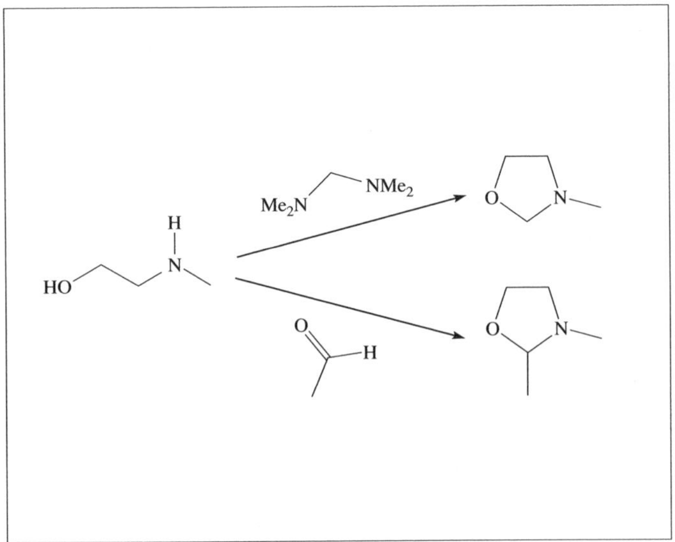

The secondary amine generated upon reduction can react with different compounds to produce stable oxazolidine rings, shown in Scheme II, with different topicity on the *N*,*O*-acetal carbon atom and, more important, with a tertiary amine functional group.

Adapted from S. Saba et al., "Synthesis and NMR Spectral Analysis of Amine Heterocycles: The Effect of Asymmetry on the ^{1}H and ^{13}C Spectra of N,O-Acetals." ©2007 by the Division of Chemical Education, Inc., American Chemical Society, and references cited therein.

MCAT® is a program of the Association of American Medical Colleges

1. Based on the passage, when ethanamine reacts with 2-bromopropane, which of the following compounds will NOT be produced?
   A. *N*-Ethyl-2-propanamine
   B. *N*-Ethyl-*N*-propyl-2-propanamine
   C. *N*-Ethyl-*N*-isopropyl-2-propanamine
   D. Ethyltriisopropylammonium bromide

2. Which of the following compounds will NOT react with ethanolamine and form a secondary amine upon reduction?
   A. Benzaldehyde
   B. Butanal
   C. Cyclohexanone
   D. Cyclopentanol

3. After the reaction with acetaldehyde in Scheme II, the identity check of (±)-2,3-dimethyloxazolidine is performed by thin-layer chromatography, with the secondary amine together on the same silica gel plate. If a 9:1 hexanes:ethyl acetate mixture is used as the eluent, which of the following is most likely to be observed in terms of the retention factor (R_f)?
   A. (±)-2,3-Dimethyloxazolidine has an R_f identical to that of the secondary amine.
   B. (±)-2,3-Dimethyloxazolidine has a larger R_f than does the secondary amine.
   C. (±)-2,3-Dimethyloxazolidine has a smaller R_f than does the secondary amine.
   D. There is insufficient information to predict the outcome.

4. *N,O*-Acetal in the oxazolidine ring is similar to the common acetal except that one of the alkoxy groups is replaced by an alkyl amino group. Given this, which of the following compounds does NOT contain any type of acetal?

A.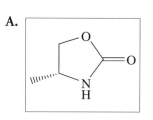

B.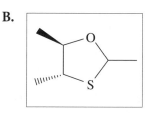

C.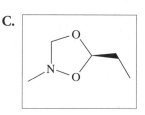

D.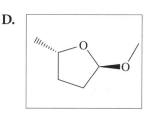

Solutions for this passage begin on next page.

1. Based on the passage, when ethanamine reacts with 2-bromopropane, which of the following compounds will NOT be produced?

    A. *N*-Ethyl-2-propanamine
    B. *N*-Ethyl-*N*-propyl-2-propanamine
    C. *N*-Ethyl-*N*-isopropyl-2-propanamine
    D. Ethyltriisopropylammonium bromide

Content Classification: Amines/Major Reactions

Cognitive Classification: Flexibility and Adaptability in Scientific Reasoning

This question requires using given information to determine which compound is LEAST likely to be produced. According to the passage, alkylation of a primary amine produces mainly a secondary amine; the reaction can further result in a tertiary amine and then a quaternary ammonium salt.

Ethanamine, $CH_3CH_2NH_2$, is a primary amine. The nucleophilic substitution takes place at C-2 of 2-bromopropane, $CH_3CHBrCH_3$. Once the reaction occurs, the $CH_3CH_2NH_3$ would displace the bromide of 2-bromopropane. The main product, a secondary amine, would have the longest straight alkyl chain of three carbon atoms with an amine functional group at C-2. Thus, the ethyl group inherited from ethanamine becomes a substituent on the nitrogen atom.

Even if further alkylation of this secondary amine occurs, the longest straight alkyl chain in the tertiary amine product will remain three carbon atoms. Hence, 2-bromopropane, also commonly known as *isopropyl* bromide, would be the source of *isopropyl* substituents thereafter. When there are four groups on the nitrogen atom, all alkyl groups are named as substituents of the ammonium cation.

Key: B

The propyl group, $CH_3CH_2CH_2-$, is a straight alkyl chain with three carbon atoms. However, the substituent or functional group is attached at C-1. This particular compound is the main nucleophilic substitution product of 1-bromopropane, also commonly known as *propyl* bromide, rather than the product of 2-bromopropane.

Distractors

A   This is the main product of the reaction between ethanamine and 2-bromopropane.

C   This is the tertiary amine product of the reaction in the question.

D   This is the quaternary ammonium product of the reaction in the question.

Difficulty Level: Hard (30%)

2. Which of the following compounds will NOT react with ethanolamine and form a secondary amine upon reduction?

    A. Benzaldehyde
    B. Butanal
    C. Cyclohexanone
    D. Cyclopentanol

Content Classification: Oxygen-Containing Compounds/Aldehydes and Ketones

Cognitive Classification: Seeking Clarification

This question requires you to translate presented information into a more understandable or useful form. According to the passage, ethanolamine reacts with carbonyl compounds. It is essential to recognize the carbonyl-containing functional groups by using the common and the IUPAC nomenclature. The suffix -*al* indicates that the main functional group in the compound is an aldehyde; the suffix -*one* indicates that the main functional group in the compound is a ketone; and the suffix -*ol* indicates that the main functional group is an alcohol.

Key: D

Cyclopentan*ol* contains an –OH (alcohol) group as the primary functional group.

Distractors

A   Benzaldehyde contains one carbonyl group. It is unmistakable that the compound is an aldehyde.

B   Butan*al* contains an aldehyde functional group. The carbonyl group is located at the terminal carbon atom of a four-carbon chain.

C   Cyclohexan*one* is a cyclic compound that contains a ketone functional group. The carbonyl carbon is automatically assigned as C-1 of a six-membered ring.

Difficulty Level: Medium (65%)

3. After the reaction with acetaldehyde in Scheme II, the identity check of (±)-2,3-dimethyloxazolidine is performed by thin-layer chromatography, with the secondary amine together on the same silica gel plate. If a 9:1 hexanes:ethyl acetate mixture is used as the eluent, which of the following is most likely to be observed in terms of the retention factor (R_f)?

    A. (±)-2,3-dimethyloxazolidine has an R_f identical to that of the secondary amine.
    B. (±)-2,3-dimethyloxazolidine has a larger R_f than does the secondary amine.
    C. (±)-2,3-dimethyloxazolidine has a smaller R_f than does the secondary amine.
    D. There is insufficient information to predict the outcome.

Content Classification: Separations and Purifications/Chromatography

Cognitive Classification: Hypothesis Testing

This question requires you to predict a result on the basis of background knowledge. Understanding the solvent effect is important in separations. (±)-2,3-dimethyloxazolidine is less polar than the secondary amine in which the –OH and –NH– groups exist. *Like dissolves like.* If a 9:1 hexanes:ethyl acetate mixture, a fairly nonpolar solvent, is used, (±)-2,3-dimethyloxazolidine is expected to migrate more efficiently than the secondary amine.

Key: B

The more efficient migration of (±)-2,3-dimethyloxazolidine indicates that this compound is likely to have a larger R_f than the secondary amine.

Distractors

A   The dipole moment of (±)-2,3-dimethyloxazolidine is different from that of the secondary amine, so it is unlikely for both compounds to have the same R_f.

C   (±)-2,3-dimethyloxazolidine is less polar than the secondary amine. Therefore, the secondary amine is likely to have a smaller R_f than (±)-2,3-dimethyloxazolidine.

D   Like dissolves like. Based on the dipole moments of the compounds and the given eluent, the outcome can be predicted.

Difficulty Level: Medium (50%)

4. *N,O*-Acetal in the oxazolidine ring is similar to the common acetal except that one of the alkoxy groups is replaced by an alkyl amino group. Given this, which of the following compounds does NOT contain any type of acetal?

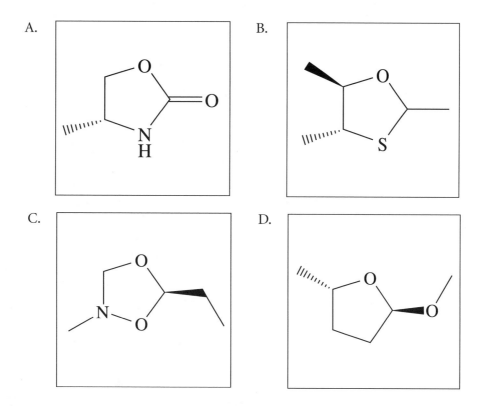

A.

B.

C.

D.

Content Classification: Oxygen-Containing Compounds/Aldehydes and Ketones

Cognitive Classification: Evaluation Processes

This question requires you to judge on the basis of specific criteria whether a compound contains a structure that is acceptable as any type of acetal. A common (*O,O*-)acetal is derived from an aldehyde functional group. The four groups bonded to a carbon atom are a hydrogen atom, an alkyl group (or another hydrogen atom), and two alkoxy groups. An *X,O*-acetal, where *X* is commonly N or S, is similar to an acetal except that one of the alkoxy groups is replaced by an alkyl amino group or an alkyl sulfide. In oxazolidine (Compound 1), the *N,O*-acetal carbon atom is located at C-2.

Key: A

This structure has no carbon atom that fits the description of any kind of acetal.

Distractors

B An *S,O* acetal is located at the carbon atom between S and O.

C Two types of acetals are found in this molecule: a common (*O,O*)acetal is located at the carbon atom between two O atoms, and an *N,O* acetal is located at the carbon atom between N and O.

D A common acetal is located at the carbon atom between two O atoms.

Difficulty Level: Hard (35%)

Organic Chemistry
Passage Set II

Organic Chemistry

(S)-Monosodium glutamate (MSG) is an additive to enhance the flavor of foods. The monosodium salt of glutamic acid has a strong synergistic effect with otherwise almost tasteless disodium guanylate, the disodium salt of guanosine monophosphate, which is found in meats and vegetables. All methods for the industrial production of MSG are by neutralization of L-glutamic acid (hydrochloride) with sodium hydroxide.

The isolation of glutamic acid from protein hydrolysates of wheat gluten was the predominant method until fermentation became important in the mid-1960s. The advantage of fermentation using bacteria is the reliability of producing only the desired enantiomer according to the following equation:

$$C_{12}H_{22}O_{11} + 3O_2 + 2NH_3 \rightarrow 2C_5H_9O_4N + 2CO_2 + 5H_2O$$

There was no chemical synthesis of glutamic acid to compete with extraction methods until the discovery of the oxo reaction. Its application to acrylonitrile, $NCCH=CH_2$, made possible the synthesis of β-cyanopropionaldehyde (Equation 1). The previously established Strecker process was known to convert an aldehyde to an amino analog of a cyanohydrin (Equation 2), a Strecker intermediate, which could subsequently be hydrolyzed to glutamic acid (Equation 3).

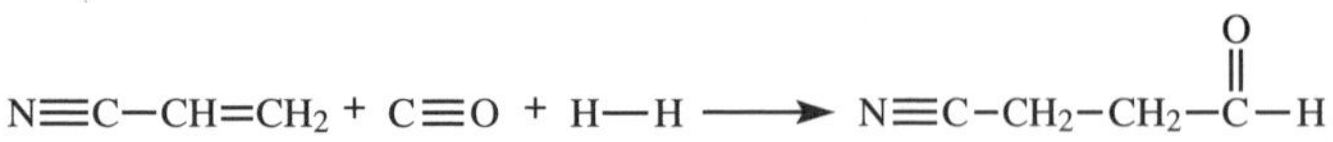

Equation 1

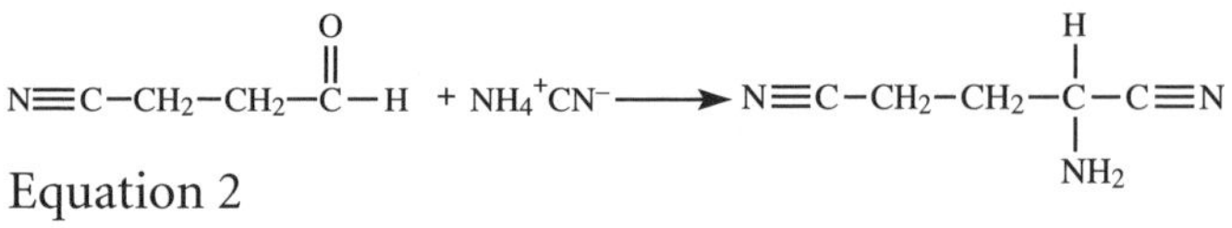

Equation 2

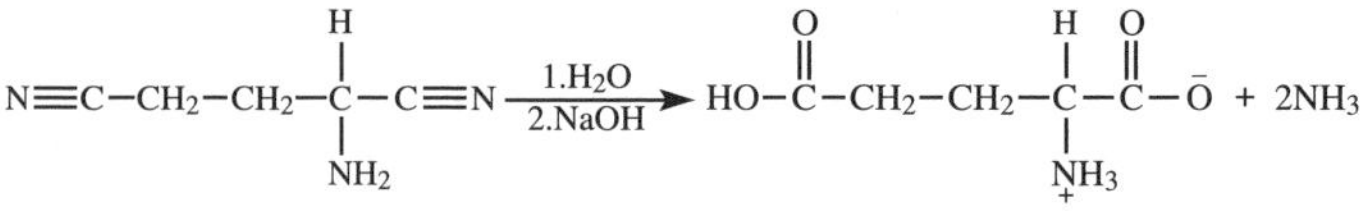

Equation 3

The chemical synthesis of glutamic acid, as well as many other amino acids, can be carried out on a very large scale; however, the disadvantage is that the product is racemic. For this reason, microbial fermentation is often the preferred method of amino acid production.

Adapted from A. Ault, The Monosodium Glutamate story: The commercial production of MSG and other amino acids, *Journal of Chemical Education*. © 2004 by American Chemical Society.

5. Which of the following is NOT a component of guanylate?

    A. Glucose
    B. Guanine
    C. Phosphate
    D. Ribofuranose

6. Beet and cane molasses are sources of fermentation. Which of the following types of biological compounds are most plentiful in these sources?

    A. Carbohydrates
    B. Lipids
    C. Nucleic acids
    D. Proteins

7. A total of how many π bonds exist in acrylonitrile?
    A. 2
    B. 3
    C. 5
    D. 6

8. After hydrolyzing the Strecker intermediate, which of the following changes are most likely to be observed in the IR spectrum of glutamic acid?

    A. New signals appear at 2000 cm^{-1}, and the signals at 2250 cm^{-1} disappear.
    B. New signals appear at 1715 cm^{-1}, and the signals at 2250 cm^{-1} disappear.
    C. New signals appear at 2000 cm^{-1}, and the signals at 2950 cm^{-1} disappear.
    D. New signals appear at 1715 cm^{-1}, and the signals at 2950 cm^{-1} disappear.

9. Based on the passage, industries would most likely prefer chemical synthesis over fermentation to produce which of the following amino acids?

    A. Glutamic acid
    B. Glycine
    C. Lysine
    D. Tyrosine

Solutions for this passage begin on next page.

5. Which of the following is NOT a component of guanylate?

   A. Glucose
   B. Guanine
   C. Phosphate
   D. Ribofuranose

Content Classification: Molecular Biology: DNA and Protein Synthesis/DNA Structure and Function

Cognitive Classification: Seeking Clarification

This question requires you to translate presented information into a more understandable or useful form. According to the passage, disodium guanylate is the disodium salt of guanosine monophosphate, the disodium salt of a nucleoside monophosphate. A nucleoside monophosphate consists of three components, the sugar ribose, a phosphate, and one of the heterocyclic bases: A, T, U, G, or C.

Key: A

Glucose is not a component of a nucleoside or nucleotide.

Distractors

B *Guan*ine is the heterocyclic base in guanylate.

C Disodium guanylate is the disodium salt of a nucleotide *monophosphate*. Thus, it contains a phosphate group.

D *Ribo*furanose is the cyclic form of sugar ribose.

Difficulty Level: Medium (45%)

MCAT® is a program of the
Association of American Medical Colleges

6. Beet and cane molasses are sources of fermentation. Which of the following types of biological compounds are most plentiful in these sources?

    A. Carbohydrates
    B. Lipids
    C. Nucleic acids
    D. Proteins

Content Classification: Biological Molecules/Carbohydrates

Cognitive Classification: Identification of Main Ideas

This question requires you to identify a major point explicitly made in the passage. Microbial fermentation uses carbohydrates, specifically sucrose, as the source to produce (S)-glutamic acid. The dry weight of beet molasses is about 50% carbohydrates. Among the biological molecules in the given choices, only carbohydrates or lipids have a formula that contains only C, H, and O.

Key: A

$C_{12}H_{22}O_{11}$ is a general formula of disaccharides among carbohydrates. Monosaccharides have a general formula of $C_6H_{12}O_6$. A disaccharide molecule is formed by the condensation of two monosaccharide molecules ($C_6H_{12}O_6 + C_6H_{12}O_6 \rightarrow C_{12}H_{22}O_{11} + H_2O$).

Distractors

B   Lipids, which have no general formula, include steroids, triglycerides, and phospholipids. Long-chain fatty acids and steroids contain considerably more carbon atoms than oxygen atoms.

C   Nucleic acids do not have a general formula. Although phosphate and (deoxy)ribofuranose are the fixed components, nucleic acids have five different bases: A, G, T, U, and C.

D   Proteins have no general formula. Each α–amino acid residue in a protein has three main parts bonded to the carbon atom: an amino group, a carboxyl group, and a hydrogen atom. The differences between amino acid residues are in the side-chain structure.

Difficulty Level: Easy (85%)

These four classes of biological molecules all contain C, H, and O. Among carbohydrates, monosaccharides and disaccharides have general formulas of $C_6H_{12}O_6$ and $C_{12}H_{22}O_{11}$, respectively. The number of hydrogen atoms is twice the number of oxygen atoms. Nucleic acids and proteins contain nitrogen as well. Phosphorus exists in nucleic acid, and sulfur exists in protein.

7.   A total of how many π bonds exist in acrylonitrile?

    A. 2
    B. 3
    C. 5
    D. 6

Content Classification: The Covalent Bond/Sigma and Pi Bonds

Cognitive Classification: Reasoning Using Quantitative Data

This question requires you to identify the number of π bonds in acrylonitrile, $NCCH=CH_2$. A π bond exists only in a double bond or triple bond. The first molecule in Scheme I contains a double bond and a triple bond. A double bond has one σ bond and one π bond. A triple bond has one σ bond and two π bonds.

Key: B

Two π bonds exist in the C≡N bond, and one π bond exists in the C=C bond.

Distractors

A   A common mistake is to consider π "regions."

C   A common mistake is to consider all bonds in a double or triple bond as π bonds. The first bond is *always* a σ bond.

D   A common mistake is to confuse σ bonds with π bonds. Acrylonitrile has six bonds: one in the C≡N bond, one in the C=C bond, one C–C bond, and three C–H bonds.

Difficulty Level: Easy (80%)

MCAT® is a program of the
Association of American Medical Colleges

8. After hydrolyzing the Strecker intermediate, which of the following changes are most likely to be observed in the IR spectrum of glutamic acid?

   A. New signals appear at 2000 cm^{-1}, and the signals at 2250 cm^{-1} disappear.
   B. New signals appear at 1715 cm^{-1}, and the signals at 2250 cm^{-1} disappear.
   C. New signals appear at 2000 cm^{-1}, and the signals at 2950 cm^{-1} disappear.
   D. New signals appear at 1715 cm^{-1}, and the signals at 2950 cm^{-1} disappear.

Content Classification: Molecular Structure and Spectra/Absorption Spectroscopy

Cognitive Classification: Hypothesis Testing

This question requires you to predict a result on the basis of background knowledge. After the Strecker intermediate is hydrolyzed, the C≡N bonds become carboxyl groups. A C≡N bond has a stretching frequency at about 2250 cm^{-1}. A carboxyl group has a few stretching frequencies: a C–O bond at about 1000–1300 cm^{-1}, a C=O bond at about 1700–1850 cm^{-1}, and an O–H bond at about 3200–3500 cm^{-1}.

Key: B

New signals at 1715 cm^{-1} are the stretching bands of the C=O bonds. The signals for the C≡N bonds at 2250 cm^{-1} disappear. Both changes indicate the formation of carboxyl groups.

Distractors

A   A signal at 2000 cm^{-1} is quite unusual. This region is almost exclusively for the diagnosis of some metal–carbonyl complexes; this part of the answer is incorrect. Nonetheless, the signals for the C≡N bonds at 2250 cm^{-1} disappear; this part of the answer is correct.

C   A signal at 2000 cm^{-1} is quite unusual. The signals at 2950 cm^{-1} are the stretching bands of the C–H bonds. Slight changes may occur in the region, but the signals do not disappear. Neither part of the answer is correct.

D   New signals at 1715 cm^{-1} are the stretching bands of the C=O bonds; this part of the answer is correct. The signals at 2950 cm^{-1} are the stretching bands of C–H bonds. Slight changes may occur in this region, but the signals do not disappear; this part of the answer is incorrect.

Difficulty Level: Medium (55%)

9. Based on the passage, industries would most likely prefer chemical synthesis over fermentation to produce which of the following amino acids?

   A. Glutamic acid
   B. Glycine
   C. Lysine
   D. Tyrosine

Content Classification: Biological Molecules/Amino Acids and Proteins

Cognitive Classification: Identification of Components of a Situation and Relationships Among Them

This question requires you to identify the relevant issues in the passage. A disadvantage of chemical synthesis is that a racemic mixture is obtained. If an amino acid contains a chiral center, the chemical synthesis will produce a racemic mixture. This is not a concern in the case of glycine.

Key: B

Glycine has no chiral center.

Distractors

A   Glutamic acid has two stereoisomers. Fermentation is used to produce this compound.

C   Lysine has two stereoisomers. To produce (*S*)-lysine, an industry would use a mutant of the bacteria that produce (*S*)-glutamic acid.

D   Tyrosine has two stereoisomers. Extraction is the most economical process for the production of (*S*)-tyrosine.

Difficulty Level: Medium (55%)

Organic Chemistry
Passage Set III

Organic Chemistry

Persistent organic pollutants (POPs), which include certain synthetic pesticides and unintended byproducts of industrial processes, are resistant to environmental degradation. Once these pollutants are absorbed through respiration or food consumption by animals and plants, they tend to accumulate in fat stores of these organisms. Subsequent consumption of these meats and vegetables by a higher consumer allows the pollutants to be bioaccumulated up the food chain. The initial list of 12 POPs, including mirex (Compound 1) and DDT (Compound 2), are all polychlorinated hydrocarbons.

These hazardous compounds are usually hydrophobic and slowly metabolized. DDT is perhaps the most well-known POP because of its insecticidal properties. It can be synthesized by reacting trichloroacetaldehyde with chlorobenzene, a weak nucleophile, in the presence of sulfuric acid. Mirex can be made by dimerization of hexachlorocyclopentadiene, C_5Cl_6 (MW = 272.77), in the presence of aluminum chloride. DDT is considered a probable carcinogen, and mirex has been clearly demonstrated to be carcinogenic in fish and small animals. All of these POPs are now banned in the United States, but some are still being used in many developing countries.

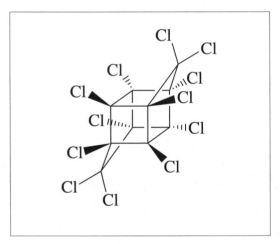

Compound **1**

Compound **2**

10. Which of the following best describes the solubility of a POP in water and lipids?

  A. Low in both water and lipids
  B. High in both water and lipids
  C. Low in water and high in lipids
  D. High in water and low in lipids

11. Given that only one of the initial 12 POPs is a polychlorinated saturated hydrocarbon, which of the following compounds was NOT on the initial list?

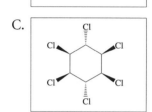

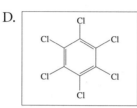

C.

D.

12. The total number of stereogenic centers found in Compound 1 is:

  A. 10.
  B. 8.
  C. 4.
  D. 0.

13. What is the total number of sp^3 hybridized carbon atoms that can be found in DDT?

  A. 12
  B. 2
  C. 1
  D. 0

14. How does sulfuric acid catalyze the synthesis of DDT?

  A. It protonates the carbonyl oxygen atom in trichloroacetaldehyde; the elimination of a water molecule creates a carbanion that subsequently attacks the weak nucleophile.
  B. It provides a platform upon which trichloroacetaldehyde and the weak nucleophile interact.
  C. It protonates the carbonyl oxygen atom in trichloroacetaldehyde; the carbonyl carbon becomes more susceptible to nucleophilic attack by the weak nucleophile.
  D. It deprotonates the weak nucleophile to increase its nucleophilicity for attacking the electrophilic carbon atom of the carbonyl group in trichloroacetaldehyde.

Solutions for this passage begin on next page.

10. Which of the following best describes the solubility of a POP in water and lipids?

   A. Low in both water and lipids
   B. High in both water and lipids
   C. Low in water and high in lipids
   D. High in water and low in lipids

Content Classification: Hydrocarbons/Alkanes

Cognitive Classification: Identification of Main Ideas

This question requires you to translate presented information into a more understandable or useful form. In the passage, information related to the solubility behavior of POPs was given in two places: (1) POPs are hydrophobic, and (2) they tend to accumulate in fat stores. Therefore, POPs generally have low solubility in water but high solubility in lipids.

Key: C

POPs are hydrophobic and lipophilic.

Distractors

A   Low solubility in both water and lipids is incorrect. POPs tend to be hydrophobic but not lipophobic.

B   High solubility in both water and lipids is incorrect. POPs are not hydrophilic but tend to be lipophilic.

D   High solubility in water is incorrect. Low solubility in lipids is also incorrect. POPs tend to be neither hydrophilic nor lipophobic.

Difficulty Level: Easy (90%)

MCAT® is a program of the
Association of American Medical Colleges

11. Given that only one of the initial 12 POPs is a polychlorinated saturated hydrocarbon, which of the following compounds was NOT on the initial list?

A.
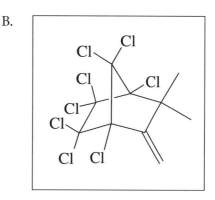

B.
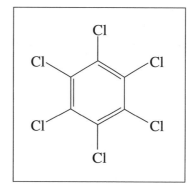

C.

D.

Content Classification: Hydrocarbons/Alkanes

Cognitive Classification: Reasoning Using Quantitative Data

This question requires you to demonstrate your understanding of bond-line structure and use given information to solve a problem. The initial 12 POPs are polychlorinated hydrocarbons. Among them, only mirex is *saturated*. No other polychlorinated *saturated* hydrocarbon was on the initial list.

Key: C

This is the structure of lindane, also known as γ-hexachlorocyclohexane, or γ-HCH. The structure does not contain any double or triple bonds. It was not on the initial list.

(Note: The most updated list of POPs contains more than 12 compounds; lindane was a later addition to this list.)

Distractors

A   This is the structure of aldrin, which is derived from a tetracyclic aliphatic hydrocarbon. The structure contains two double bonds. Thus, it is unsaturated.

B   This is the structure of toxaphene, which is derived from a bicyclic aliphatic hydrocarbon. The structure contains one double bond. Thus, it is unsaturated.

D   This is the structure of hexachlorobenzene, which is derived from a non-aliphatic hydrocarbon. Thus, this compound is not saturated.

Difficulty Level: Medium (65%)

12.   The total number of stereogenic centers found in Compound 1 is:

   A. 10.
   B. 8.
   C. 4.
   D. 0.

Content Classification: The Covalent Bond/Stereochemistry of Covalently Bonded Molecules

Cognitive Classification: Flexibility and Adaptability in Scientific Reasoning

This question requires you to interpret a figure and demonstrate your knowledge of chirality. For a carbon atom to be chiral, it must bond to four different groups. There are 10 carbon atoms in the molecule. It would be very time-consuming to consider them individually. However, grouping the carbon atoms by using internal symmetry elements could simplify the process greatly. Since only two types of bonds exist in mirex, namely, C–Cl and C–C bonds, considering only the connectivity of C–C bonds is sufficient to categorize the carbon atoms. After removing the chlorine atoms, it is clear that internal mirror planes exist in this compound.

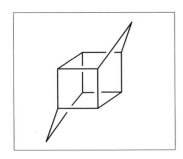
rotates about
45° clockwise
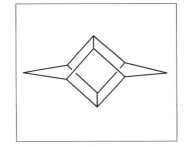
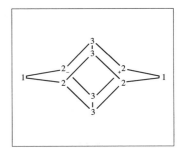

As shown at right in the numbered structure above, the symmetry results in three groups of equivalent carbon atoms: (1) the two bridgehead carbon atoms, (2) the four carbon atoms that are directly connected to the bridgehead carbon atoms, and (3) the remaining four carbon atoms in the middle. A group 1 carbon atom is not chiral because it is bonded to two chlorine atoms. A group 2 carbon atom is not chiral because there is a horizontal plane of symmetry that dissects all group 1 and group 2 carbon atoms. The upper part of the plane is the reflection of the lower part. Group 3 carbon atoms also are not chiral because a vertical plane of symmetry dissects them. The left side of the plane is the reflection of the right side.

Key: D

When a mirror plane dissects a carbon atom, that particular carbon atom is not a chiral center.

Determining the chirality of a carbon atom can be complicated. Symmetry is a very helpful tool in simplifying the task.

Distractors

A   The compound has a total of 10 carbon atoms. Since at least one of them is not chiral, this answer choice cannot be correct.

B   This answer results from the process of elimination when using an incorrect assumption that the carbon atoms in a relatively complex molecule are usually chiral. Subtracting the two bridgehead carbon atoms known to be achiral from the total of 10 carbon atoms leaves eight that are assumed to be chiral.

C   This answer results from noticing the existence of one mirror plane but neglecting to see the others.

Difficulty Level: Hard (40%)

13. What is the total number of sp^3-hybridized carbon atoms that can be found in DDT?
    A. 12
    B. 2
    C. 1
    D. 0

Content Classification: The Covalent Bond/Sigma and Pi Bonds

Cognitive Classification: Reasoning Using Quantitative Data

This question requires you to interpret a figure and understand the basic principles of covalent bonds and geometry. The sp^3-hybridized carbon atoms are those with four *single* bonds.

Key: B

The trichloroethyl group in the middle contains two sp^3-hybridized carbon atoms.

Distractors

A   Mistakenly considering the 12 carbon atoms in the rings leads to this answer. These are actually sp^2-hybridized carbon atoms.

C   Neglecting the existence of the methine hydrogen atom at the center leads to this answer.

D   This answer results from reversing the concepts of sp- and sp^3-hybridization. DDT has no sp-hybridized carbon atom.

The combinations of bonds and bond angles for hybridizations are as follows:

- ***sp*-hybridization** explains the linear geometry in which a carbon atom forms either two double bonds or one single bond and one triple bond with a bond angle of 180°
- ***sp²*-hybridization** explains the trigonal planar geometry in which a carbon atom forms two single bonds and a double bond with a bond angle of approximately 120°
- ***sp³*-hybridization** explains the tetrahedral geometry in which a carbon atom forms four single bonds with a bond angle of 109.5°

Difficulty Level: Easy (80%)

14. How does sulfuric acid catalyze the synthesis of DDT?

   A. It protonates the carbonyl oxygen atom in trichloroacetaldehyde; the elimination of a water molecule creates a carbanion that subsequently attacks the weak nucleophile.
   B. It provides a platform upon which trichloroacetaldehyde and the weak nucleophile interact.
   C. It protonates the carbonyl oxygen atom in trichloroacetaldehyde; the carbonyl carbon becomes more susceptible to nucleophilic attack by the weak nucleophile.
   D. It deprotonates the weak nucleophile to increase its nucleophilicity for attacking the electrophilic carbon atom of the carbonyl group in trichloroacetaldehyde.

Content Classification: Oxygen-Containing Compounds/Aldehydes and Ketones

Cognitive Classification: Seeking Clarification

This question requires you to translate presented information into a more understandable form. To answer this question, you must understand the reaction mechanism. Sulfuric acid is a source of protons. The first step is presumably a protonation reaction. Thus, it creates a positive charge on the carbonyl oxygen, and the carbonyl carbon becomes more electrophilic. Even if the nucleophile is rather weak, the reaction will proceed.

Key: C

Protonation of the oxygen atom in trichloroacetaldehyde makes the carbonyl carbon atom more electrophilic. Even if the nucleophile is weak, the reaction will be more likely to proceed.

Distractors

A   The protonation of the oxygen atom in trichloroacetaldehyde makes the carbonyl carbon atom more electrophilic. The nucleophilic attack results in an alcohol functional group. The second protonation of the oxygen atom promotes the elimination of a water molecule. The intermediate is a carbocation rather than a carbanion.

B   Catalytic sulfuric acid does not interact with both compounds at the same time.

D   Sulfuric acid does not deprotonate the nucleophile.

Difficulty Level: Medium (70%)

MCAT® is a program of the
Association of American Medical Colleges

Organic Chemistry
Discrete Questions

Organic Chemistry

Discrete Questions 15–19

15. Which of the following compounds will NOT be a product of the given reaction?

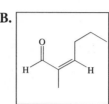

+ NaOH(aq) →

A.

B.

C.

D.

16. Cyclopentanol has a higher boiling point (139°C) than does *n*-hexane (69°C) because cyclopentanol:

    A. has a higher molecular weight.
    B. contains a cyclic alkane.
    C. contains an alcohol functional group.
    D. contains fewer carbon atoms.

17. Upon heating, 2-oxocyclohexanecarboxylic acid would most likely be converted to:

    A. cyclohexanone ($C_6H_{10}O$).
    B. cyclohexanol ($C_6H_{12}O$).
    C. cyclohexane (C_6H_{12}).
    D. cyclohexene (C_6H_{10}).

18. Which of the following carboxylic acids will have the lowest pK_a?

    A. 2 Methylbutyric acid
    B. 3-Chlorobutyric acid
    C. 2-Ethylbutyric acid
    D. 3-Bromobutyric acid

19. Why do the two methylene protons of the dimethylaminomethyl group of the compound shown give separate, coupled signals in the ^1H NMR spectrum?

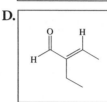

    A. Because they are anisotropic
    B. Because they are diastereotopic
    C. Because they are equivalent
    D. Because every proton in a compound gives a separate signal by high-field NMR

Solutions for this passage begin on next page.

15. Which of the following compounds will NOT be a product of the given reaction?

A.

B.

C.

D.

Content Classification: Oxygen Containing Compounds/Aldehydes and Ketones

Cognitive Classification: Hypothesis Testing

This question requires you to predict a result on the basis of background knowledge. The given reaction is an aldol condensation reaction. Sodium hydroxide removes one of the α–hydrogen atoms from an aldehyde molecule to create an enolate ion, which attacks the carbonyl group of another molecule of the same aldehyde or of a different aldehyde. The subsequent dehydration of the aldol (upon heating) produces an α,β-unsaturated aldehyde. The reaction between propanal and butanal can produce up to four pairs of geometrical isomers. The general scheme of this reaction is shown as follows:

An aldehyde can undergo a self-aldol condensation if an α-hydrogen atom is present.

MCAT® is a program of the
Association of American Medical Colleges

Key: D

This compound is one of the products for the reaction between propanal and ethanal, not the reaction between propanal and butanal.

Distractors

A   Propanal can undergo a self-aldol condensation reaction to produce this compound.

B   The aldehyde part of this compound is derived from propanal; the other part is derived from butanal.

C   The aldehyde part of this compound is derived from butanal; the other part is derived from propanal.

Difficulty Level: Hard (40%)

16. Cyclopentanol has a higher boiling point (139°C) than does *n*-hexane (69°C) because cyclopentanol:

   A. has a higher molecular weight.
   B. contains a cyclic alkane.
   C. contains an alcohol functional group.
   D. contains fewer carbon atoms.

Content Classification: Oxygen-Containing Compounds/Alcohols

Cognitive Classification: Hypothesis Testing

This question requires you to determine the likely cause of a particular event or result. The boiling point of a compound is attributed primarily to intermolecular forces. A more polar compound of similar molecular weight generally exhibits a higher boiling point. When two compounds are comparable in polarity, the one with stronger London dispersion forces usually has a higher boiling point.

Key: C

Cyclopentanol is a polar compound; its alcohol functional group forms intermolecular hydrogen bonds.

Distractors

A   The molecular weight of cyclopentanol (MW = 84) is very similar to the molecular weight of *n*-hexane (MW = 82). Higher molecular weight generally implies stronger London dispersion forces among the molecules. Nonetheless, the slight difference in molecular weight is not sufficient to cause the increase in the boiling point of 70°C.

B   A cyclic alkane has a higher boiling point than does the *n*-alkane of similar molecular weight. However, cyclopentane (bp = 49°C) contains one carbon atom less than *n*-hexane (bp = 69°C). Thus, the London dispersion forces are weaker in cyclopentane than in *n*-hexane.

D   A molecule with fewer carbon atoms usually exhibits a lower boiling point because of weaker London dispersion forces.

Difficulty Level: Easy (80%)

17. Upon heating, 2-oxocyclohexanecarboxylic acid would most likely be converted to:

    A. cyclohexanone ($C_6H_{10}O$).
    B. cyclohexanol ($C_6H_{12}O$).
    C. cyclohexane (C_6H_{12}).
    D. cyclohexene (C_6H_{10}).

Content Classification: Oxygen-Containing Compounds/Keto Acids and Esters

Cognitive Classification: Seeking Clarification

This question requires you to identify appropriate clarifying information. When a single compound is heated, either no reaction or one of two scenarios will likely occur: self-addition or decomposition. Since the two functional groups, ketone and carboxylic acid, do not usually react with each other, decomposition is more likely to occur. Upon heating, a β–keto acid decomposes and releases carbon dioxide.

Key: A

The rearrangement tautomerizes an enol to a ketone.

Distractors

B   This answer results from omitting the double bond in the process of pushing electrons.

C   This answer results from omitting all functional groups in the process of pushing electrons.

D   This answer results from omitting the alcohol functional group in the process of pushing electrons.

Difficulty Level: Medium (45%)

18. Which of the following carboxylic acids will have the lowest pK_a?

    A. 2-Methylbutyric acid
    B. 3-Chlorobutyric acid
    C. 2-Ethylbutyric acid
    D. 3-Bromobutyric acid

Content Classification: Oxygen-Containing Compounds/Acid Derivatives

Cognitive Classification: Hypothesis Testing

This question requires you to predict a result on the basis of background knowledge and specific facts about a situation. A substituent has an inductive effect on the acidity of the carboxyl group. An electron-withdrawing substituent reduces the electron density of the carboxyl group and increases the acidity. A more electron-withdrawing substituent reduces the electron density of the carboxyl group further; thus, the hydrogen becomes even more acidic. The closer the substituent is to the carboxyl group, the stronger is the inductive effect.

Key: B

A chlorine atom is the most electron-withdrawing substituent among the substituents in the choices. The pK_a of this compound is 4.05.

Distractors

A   A methyl group is considered electron donating. The pK_a of this compound is 4.48.

C   An ethyl group is considered electron donating. The pK_a of this compound is 4.41.

D   A bromine atom is electron withdrawing but is less electronegative than a chlorine atom.

Difficulty Level: Medium (55%)

19. Why do the two methylene protons of the dimethylaminomethyl group of the compound shown give separate, coupled signals in the ¹H NMR spectrum?

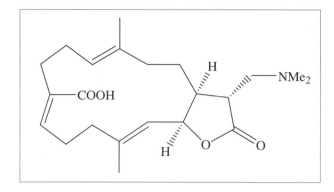

A. Because they are anisotropic
B. Because they are diastereotopic
C. Because they are equivalent
D. Because every proton in a compound gives a separate signal by high-field NMR

Content Classification: Molecular Structure and Spectra/NMR Spectroscopy

Cognitive Classification: Reasoning Using Quantitative Data

This question requires you to identify the component given in the structure and to employ an informative structural presentation to help distinguish nonequivalent hydrogen atoms in a *chiral* molecule. The geminal hydrogen atoms of a methylene group in a chiral molecule are quite often nonequivalent when the methylene group is directly attached to a rigid ring system. As shown, the two methylene protons of the dimethylaminomethyl group (–CH₂NMe₂) always experience different environments.

The conjugate base of carboxylic acid is an anion. Anions are rendered less basic by additional electronegative groups such as halogens.

R = Ring

Another example of diastereotopic geminal hydrogen atoms can be found in the (±)-2,3-dimethyloxazolidine from Scheme II of Passage VI in this guide. The ¹H NMR spectrum for the racemic mixture is the same for individual enantiomers. The structure of (S)-2,3-dimethyloxazolidine is shown in a Fischer projection.

The two methylene groups (–CH$_2$–) within the ring are nonequivalent because of the heteroatoms (O and N). The *geminal* hydrogen atoms on each methylene group are nonequivalent as well: the hydrogen atom above the ring is across from the methine proton; the one below the ring is across from a methyl group. Therefore, a total of seven types of protons would most likely be detected by high-resolution ^{1}H NMR at room temperature: four for the methylene protons, two for the methyl groups, and one for the methine proton.

Even when both of the hydrogen atoms on C-5 are changed to methyl groups, the total number of types of protons remains seven. If the methine proton is changed to a methyl group, the molecule is no longer chiral. The total number of types of protons becomes four: two for two CH$_2$ groups, one for the CH$_3$ groups at C-2, and one for the CH$_3$ group on the N atom.

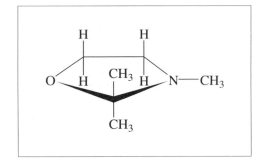

Key: B

Understanding that the hydrogen atoms in this methylene group are nonequivalent will lead you to the correct answer.

Distractors

A   The orientations do not affect the equivalency of these methylene protons because the dimethylaminomethyl group is freely rotating.

C   The geminal protons do not experience the same environment. Thus, they cannot be equivalent.

D   The three protons in a methyl group give the same signal.

Difficulty Level: Medium (45%)

MCAT® is a program of the
Association of American Medical Colleges

Chapter 10:
Verbal Reasoning (VR)

As we move beyond the two sciences sections and on to Verbal Reasoning, it's obvious we're dealing with very different substance. That's because, unlike the sciences, this part of the exam does not require mastery of any particular subject matter and instead is solely a test of one's reasoning skills. Everything you'll need to answer VR questions can be found within the passages themselves.

In other words, there's no real content to study.

That's not to say, though, that there's no real way to get ready. Just as with the PS and BS sections, you'll gain by knowing what to expect in terms of content, understanding the skills we're assessing, and preparing with real MCAT passages and questions. Here again, we provide you with those very tools.

VR Section Recap

- Seven passages with five to seven questions each, for a total of 40 questions

- 60 minutes

I. Overall Section Format

The Verbal Reasoning section is composed of 40 passage-based, multiple-choice questions that test your ability to read attentively and make reasonable inferences based on the information provided to you. These passages are selected and adapted from a variety of publications intended for well-educated readers—material similar to those a college junior would be assigned.

It's important to realize that you are not expected to have any background knowledge about these subjects or any previous expertise in them. Rather, the correct answer for each question can either be found directly in the passage itself or by applying the information within the passage to any new information contained within the question.

How General Reading Can Help You Prepare

Remember the first Shakespeare play you read? Although you initially may have been thrown by the 16th (and early 17th) century English, you probably had a much easier time of it with the next play, and easier still with the one after that. You became accustomed to the language.

The same holds true for reading passages that address a topic within humanities, social sciences, or natural sciences—especially for science majors whose coursework did not involve as much of this type of reading as, say, humanities majors.* You'll become more proficient with it, and these passages will seem less "foreign."

*In fact, some might conjecture that humanities majors score higher in VR than biology majors because the former are more accustomed to this very type of reading!

II. Content Areas

With that, let's move on to a description of the three broad content areas from which the VR passages are drawn.

1. Humanities

Passages in the humanities area are drawn from excerpts in *architecture, art, literature, music, philosophy, popular culture, religion,* and *theater*. Often focusing on relationships between ideas, humanities passages are more likely to be written in a conversational or opinionated style than the passages in the social sciences and the natural sciences and technology areas. You may therefore be required to glean information from the author's tone and word choice in addition to the passage assertions themselves.

> **Tips to Keep in Mind**
>
> Some tips to help you with the VR section....
>
> - Pay attention to any qualifying language. Notice, for example, whether the question asks if something is least or most likely or whether a fact is always, never, or sometimes true about all, a few, or most of something.
>
> - Make sure you answer the questions based solely on the information provided by the author and not on your background knowledge of a subject.
>
> - With seven passages and 60 minutes, you have an average of eight minutes per passage. Pace yourself!

2. Social Sciences

Passages in the social sciences focus on *anthropology, archaeology, economics, education, history, linguistics, political science, psychology,* and *sociology*. These excerpts frequently center on the interpretation, implications, or applications of research in the social sciences, and often are based on studies about people in general or particular social groups. Frequently these passages are structured around a central claim that is either being supported or undermined by the information provided by the author. Sometimes the information in these passages can be very "rough" because the passage deals with complex issues and events in an artificially simplified manner.

3. Natural Sciences and Technology

With the focus on *astronomy, botany, computer science, ecology, ethology, geology, meteorology, technology,* and *zoology*, passages in the natural sciences and technology area emphasize the significance of scientific and technological issues and advances. Natural sciences passages, which center on factual knowledge and its implications or applications, are often straightforward in their presentation since the claims they support tend to be well defined and clearly circumscribed.

The Verbal Reasoning section of the MCAT is designed to test your ability to **comprehend** information presented in a passage, **evaluate** the relationships between passage information, **apply** passage information to situations outside of the immediate scope of the passage, and **incorporate** additional information into your analysis of passage information. In this section, we describe these four different question types, give examples of each, and provide you with some suggestions or caveats to help you arrive at the best answer.

A. Comprehension

Comprehension questions are designed to test your ability to recognize the meaning of passage assertions. Some of these questions may ask you to identify information that is explicitly stated in the passage, some questions may ask you to draw valid inferences from passage information, and others may ask you to compare distinct ideas that are presented in the passage. In all cases, however, the emphasis is on your comprehension of the information provided in the passage.

A common comprehension question asks you to identify the central argument, concern, or thesis of the passage. To do so, read the entire passage carefully, paying close attention to how the author has chosen to structure the passage. There is no simple formula you can use to identify the main idea, but it can be helpful to ask yourself the following questions:

- Is there a central argument presented early in the passage that the author supports with subsequent information?

- Does the author conclude the passage with a claim that incorporates earlier passage information?

- Does the body of the passage provide several examples that all support a common claim?

While these questions may not lead you directly to the passage's main idea, they can provide you some insight into what the author may have been thinking when writing the passage.

Of course, there are always caveats. Some sentences that look like summaries of main ideas—for example, sentences late in the passage that begin with words such as *therefore, thus, in conclusion* —often will address only a minor or tangential point in the passage and should not be mistaken for the broader "main idea."

On the other hand, some comprehension questions will have a narrower focus and will ask you to identify the relationship between two concepts, such as how certain passage information supports other passage information. With questions of this type, the relationship between the items in the question is often explicitly spelled out. This does not mean that the material doing the supporting and the idea being supported are necessarily mentioned near each other in the passage, but the relationships are mentioned in the passage. Comprehension questions of this type are testing your ability to recognize this.

Other common types of comprehension questions will ask you to do one of the following:

- determine, from context, the meaning of significant terminology or vocabulary used in the passage

- recognize a theory that is implicit in the passage

- identify an unstated assumption made by the passage author

- determine an appropriate paraphrase of complex passage information

- recognize a comparative relationship among ideas or pieces of information in the passage sample

A somewhat different sort of comprehension question asks you to identify appropriate questions of clarification. To put it another way, these questions ask you to identify gaps in the passage author's explanation or argument and to recognize what information is needed to fill those gaps.

B. Evaluation

Evaluation questions—which focus primarily on your ability to identify the relationships between concepts in the passage (such as consistent, relevant, or supporting relationships) and your ability to assess the accuracy, reliability, or credibility of a claim or a source of information—differ from comprehension questions in that the information you are asked to provide is not explicitly mentioned in the passage. You need to read carefully and assess the information provided in the passage with rational analysis. For example, these questions will often direct your attention to an argument or step of reasoning in the passage and then ask you to assess the plausibility of that argument or logic of that step of reasoning.

When approaching these questions, it is important to remember that you are not being asked to provide your opinion. In other words, you may in fact disagree with a conclusion that the author reaches in the passage, even if that conclusion is a reasonable inference from the other passage information. Keep in mind that you are not to base your answers on anything other than the information provided in the passage and the information provided in the questions themselves. You may know of some reason outside of the scope of the passage that makes one of the author's conclusions unreasonable or implausible, but you need to make sure that your answers to evaluation questions—as with all Verbal Reasoning questions—are not based on any information outside of the passage or the question. Other evaluation questions will ask you to judge the credibility of a source of information in the passage.

Because all of the information needed to answer Verbal Reasoning questions is found either in the passage or in the question itself, you need to look for clues in the passage that will give you an objective basis for making assessments of credibility. A credible source is usually someone who has specific expertise in the area about which he or she is speaking. This may be indicated in the passage by the person's title, level of education, or specific research that he or she has conducted. A less credible source may not have any stated background that would equip him or her to address the topic knowledgably. Or if the passage indicates that the source has a vested interest in the situation—that is, if that person has some bias about the subject—you may think that the source is less credible.

Many evaluation questions ask you to assess the logic of an argument used by the passage author or other people in the passage. Sometimes this will take the form of asking you to identify possible alternative conclusions that can be drawn from passage information. At other times these questions will ask you to evaluate the strength of the evidence provided for a generalization, conclusion, or claim, or to judge the relevance of passage information to an argument or claim.

One of the most common evaluation questions may ask you to distinguish between passage claims that are supported by other information in the passage and those claims which are not so supported. These questions are asking you to identify logical relationships between concepts, independent of how close they appear to each other in the passage. For example, an assertion may be made in one part of the passage, but the author does not support it until much later.

A final common type of evaluation question asks you to infer an attitude, belief, or intention of the author on the basis of passage assertions or word choice. These questions can often be answered by evaluating the tone of the passage. If the passage author frequently refers to some person, idea, or subject in unflattering terms, then you can generally assume that the author disapproves of that person or those things. Usually, though, the author's opinion is derived from subtle, but consistent, treatment of some person, idea, or subject using either a positive or negative tone. These questions will often ask you outright what the author's likely opinion is, and sometimes they will ask what the author most likely meant by using a certain example or figure of speech.

C. Application

Application questions require you to apply your understanding of the passage information to situations, real or hypothetical, outside the immediate scope of the passage. In these questions, as in all Verbal Reasoning questions, it is important to select which option is the most likely based on the information provided. It is possible that the information presented in the question when combined with passage information will result in several probable outcomes. In these situations, first eliminate any options that lead to improbable outcomes. Then try to determine which of the remaining probable outcomes is the most likely when compared to the other answer options. This may, at times, seem as though you are selecting between subtle shades of difference, but be assured that each question has one answer option that is definitely more likely than the others.

Of the four categories of Verbal Reasoning questions, application questions probably have the most variability in their appearance. Because they present additional material, these questions can come in a countless number of different forms. They will sometimes give you some new information and ask you to determine what conclusion should be drawn from this additional information when combined with the passage. In other instances, these questions may ask you to identify which of the following answer options the passage author would most likely support or most likely agree with on the basis of passage information. Other application questions may provide you with a real or hypothetical scenario and ask you to determine, on the basis of passage information, the most likely cause of that scenario. Still others may ask you to apply a passage concept to real world situations or to determine the scope of a passage concept.

No matter the form an application question takes, all ask you in some way to apply your understanding of the passage to situations similar to—but beyond the scope of—the passage itself. It is important to remember to base your answers on the information given in the passage and in the question. You may come across situations in which you believe, on the basis of your own knowledge outside of the test, that the author would not agree with something, that a term is not appropriately applied to certain situations, or that a result may not be what the passage suggests. Remember that when you approach a Verbal Reasoning question, you are limited to the world of the passage and the question, whether you agree with it or not.

D. Incorporation of Information

Incorporation of information questions ask you to reevaluate passage assertions on the basis of new information, true or hypothetical, that is introduced in the question itself. Unlike application questions that ask you how the new information is affected by the information in the passage, incorporation of information questions ask you to determine what modifications might be necessary in the passage in light of this novel element.

These questions usually state some fact or hypothetical statement and ask you what relationship this new information has to other information in the passage. These questions often will ask whether the new information supports, fails to support, or is consistent with other information in the passage. Remember that in situations in which, for example, more than one of the options provides support for other passage information, you need to pick the option that provides the most support (or is the most consistent, or provides the least support, depending on the question type).

A common incorporation of information item asks you to identify which of the answer options would most challenge or would most weaken claims, hypotheses, arguments, or assertions made in the passage. Another type of incorporation of information question tests your understanding of the affect that additional information has on the passage in a different way. Rather than asking you whether the new information weakens, supports, or is consistent with the passage, these questions ask how the author's argument or how other information in the passage should be modified so that it could be made consistent with the new information. These questions can come in a variety of forms. They may ask whether a passage argument would need to be modified to be made consistent with the new information, but most often they ask which of the following modifications would be most appropriate.

When approaching these questions, it is important to identify the relevant detail that the question hinges upon. The information provided in an incorporation of information question usually will be consistent with some, or perhaps most, of the information in the passage. You need to be able to identify what specifically in the passage argument is least consistent with the new information, and identifying it will lead you to the part of the argument that most needs to be modified in light of the new information.

Incorporation of information questions may occasionally take a different approach and ask which of the answer options provided most resembles or is most analogous to a situation or argument that is presented in the passage. For these questions, it is important to identify the relevant detail of the analogy. Ask yourself whether some of the items are of a similar type or represent an action or an approach to a problem similar to one in the passage? Often it is helpful to first compare the provided answer options with each other, asking yourself how they resemble each other, and in what respects they are different. Analyzing how the answer options relate to one another may help you determine the relevant detail of the analogy.

A similar type of incorporation of information question will ask you to recognize a plausible alternative to a passage hypothesis or solution. These questions usually require you to determine whether some information that supports one theory in the passage may also work well as support for an alternate theory that is not considered in the passage.

IV. Introduction to Practice Sets for Verbal Reasoning

Although the cognitive classifications we test in VR differ from those in the two science sections and there is no real "content" to test, our approach to the practice sets that follow is the same. Please see page 86 if you'd like a refresher before you begin.

Verbal Reasoning

Passage Set I

Verbal Reasoning

Why, at the height of their dominance, did the dinosaurs suddenly disappear from the face of the Earth? In the aftermath of several recent discoveries, some scientists now believe they have the answer. They believe that the great reptiles perished because of a change in climate caused by a collision between Earth and a huge object from space.

The evidence that supports this catastrophic-extinction theory began coming to light in 1978, when Walter Alvarez, a geologist, made a startling discovery. While studying a 65-million-year-old layer of petrified sedimentary clay, Alvarez found that it contains dramatically elevated levels of the rare element iridium, even though the rock layers above and below the clay layer contain normal amounts of the element. Seeking to explain this anomaly, Alvarez hypothesized that the excess iridium must have arrived via an extraterrestrial source, probably a comet or asteroid, because iridium is abundant in many of these bodies. Because this same iridium "spike" appears in similarly aged rock layers gathered from a number of widely
scattered locations, Alvarez surmised that the collision, wherever it occurred, must have been powerful enough to spread iridium atoms over most of the globe.

Realizing that such a massive impact would have caused a variety of other effects, Alvarez wondered if it might also be responsible for the disappearance of the dinosaurs, an event that occurred during the same time period. Alvarez found his answer when his calculations revealed that a blast that powerful would have sent huge quantities of dust into the air, enough dust to prevent most sunlight from reaching Earth. This would have caused the surface of Earth to cool dramatically, and the climate would have changed rapidly from balmy to cold. The theory concludes that it was this climatic shift that sounded the death knell for the dinosaurs, not only because they were assumed to be cold-blooded animals, but also because the green plants that were the basis of their food chain could not have survived with the reduced sunlight.

Since the catastrophic-extinction theory was first proposed in 1980, corroborating evidence has continued to emerge. Several years ago, for example, other scientists independently discovered that the aforementioned sediment layer also showed evidence of certain physical changes that are produced only by an event involving enormous heat and pressure, such as a massive impact. Recently, another scientific team discovered that this same sediment layer also contains extremely high levels of soot, indicating that vast vegetation fires had burned during that time period. Such fires are consistent with the catastrophic-extinction theory because such a tremendous collision could have scattered white-hot fragments of rock for hundreds of miles around the impact site.

Agreement about the cause of the dinosaurs' demise remains far from universal. Some scientists adhere to other theories, and some of the currently available evidence does appear to conflict with the catastrophic-extinction theory. Despite these disagreements, however, the
catastrophic-extinction theory has become a widely accepted explanation of this phenomenon.

1. Which of the following passage assertions is the LEAST supported by evidence or explanation in the passage?

    A. The collision must have been powerful enough to spread iridium atoms over most of the globe.
    B. Some of the currently available evidence appears to conflict with the catastrophic-extinction theory.
    C. The climate shift was responsible for the disappearance of the dinosaurs.
    D. Since the catastrophic-extinction theory was first proposed, corroborating evidence has continued to emerge.

2. Which of the following findings would provide the LEAST support for the catastrophic-extinction theory, as described in the passage?

    A. Green plants cannot survive without normal amounts of sunlight.
    B. Dinosaurs could not adapt to cold climates.
    C. Dinosaurs died out very gradually, rather than suddenly.
    D. Smoke from large vegetation fires can significantly block sunlight.

3. Which of the following facts mentioned in the passage about the sediment layer is LEAST relevant to the catastrophic-extinction theory?

    A. The layer was composed of petrified sedimentary clay.
    B. The layer shows evidence of enormous heat and pressure.
    C. The layer contains high levels of soot.
    D. The layer was formed at the time the dinosaurs became extinct.

4. Which of the following *alternatives* to the catastrophic-extinction theory, if true, could also plausibly explain the extinction of the dinosaurs?

    I. Blue-green algae common in the seas that covered much of the globe during the reign of the dinosaurs could concentrate iridium and release it into the environment.
    II. Lightning storms common at the time of the dinosaurs' demise were capable of igniting vegetation fires large enough to block significant amounts of sunlight with the smoke and soot that they produce.
    III. Volcanoes active at the time of the dinosaurs' demise could produce great heat and pressure, release iridium into the atmosphere, and block sunlight with huge quantities of soot and smoke.

    A. I only
    B. II only
    C. I and III only
    D. II and III only

Solutions for this passage begin on next page.

1. Which of the following passage assertions is the LEAST supported by evidence or explanation in the passage?

   A. The collision must have been powerful enough to spread iridium atoms over most of the globe.

   B. Some of the currently available evidence appears to conflict with the catastrophic-extinction theory.

   C. The climate shift was responsible for the disappearance of the dinosaurs.

   D. Since the catastrophic-extinction theory was first proposed, corroborating evidence has continued to emerge.

Cognitive Classification: Evaluation

Key: B

This question asks you to determine the amount of support that passage assertions receive from other information provided in the passage. The claim that "some of the currently available evidence does appear to conflict with the catastrophic-extinction theory" is made in the final paragraph. Although this is asserted, the author provides no support for it: no explanation is given for this evidence or for why it appears to conflict with the catastrophic-extinction theory. Because this option is not supported by any evidence or explanation in the passage, **B** is the best option.

When answering questions that ask you which option receives the LEAST support, it is often helpful to begin by eliminating those options that receive significant support.

Distractors

A The assertion that "the collision . . . must have been powerful enough to spread iridium atoms over most of the globe" occurs at the end of the second paragraph. This paragraph states that Alvarez reached this conclusion because the "spike" of the rare element iridium, which Alvarez suspects came from an extraterrestrial source, "appears in similarly aged rock layers gathered from a number of widely scattered locations." The passage discussion about the source and distribution of iridium support the claim "The collision must have been powerful enough to spread iridium atoms over most of the globe." Therefore, **A** is not the best option.

C The claim that the climate shift was responsible for the disappearance of the dinosaurs is made at the end of the third paragraph. The author explains that the dinosaurs "were assumed to be cold-blooded animals" and that "the green plants that were the basis of their food chain could not have survived with the reduced sunlight." The claim "The climate shift was responsible for the disappearance of the dinosaurs" is supported by explanation in the passage. Therefore, **C** is not the best option.

D The claim that "since the catastrophic-extinction theory was first proposed in 1980, corroborating evidence has continued to emerge" is made in the beginning of the fourth paragraph. This paragraph continues by discussing the discovery of "evidence of certain physical changes that are produced only by an event involving enormous heat and pressure, such as a massive impact." This paragraph also discusses the discovery of "extremely high levels of soot" in the sediment layer that indicated that vast vegetation fires burned during that period and explains that "such fires are consistent with the catastrophic-extinction theory." Because the claim in **D** receives significant support from both evidence and explanations in the passage, it is not the best option.

Difficulty Level: Easy (90%)

MCAT® is a program of the
Association of American Medical Colleges

2. Which of the following findings would provide the LEAST support for the catastrophic-extinction theory, as described in the passage?

 A. Green plants cannot survive without normal amounts of sunlight.
 B. Dinosaurs could not adapt to cold climates.
 C. Dinosaurs died out very gradually, rather than suddenly.
 D. Smoke from large vegetation fires can significantly block sunlight.

Cognitive Classification: Incorporation of Information

Key: C

This question asks you to identify the amount of support that new information would provide for the catastrophic-extinction theory. The passage begins by stating that the catastrophic-extinction theory may best answer the question "Why, at the height of their dominance, did the dinosaurs suddenly disappear from the face of the Earth?" In the third paragraph, the author explains that a massive impact could "have sent huge quantities of dust into the air," which "would have caused the surface of Earth to cool dramatically, and the climate would have changed rapidly from balmy to cold." The catastrophic extinction-theory concludes that this rapid climate shift caused the dinosaurs to die suddenly. The finding that the dinosaurs died out very gradually would not be consistent with the catastrophic-extinction theory, and thus it would not provide any support for the theory. Therefore, **C** is the best option.

Distractors

A The third paragraph states that one of the reasons the climate shift resulting from a massive impact would have killed the dinosaurs was that "the green plants that were the basis of their food chain could not have survived with the reduced sunlight." Because option **A** provides support for the catastrophic-extinction theory, it is not the best option.

B The third paragraph states that the disappearance of the dinosaurs could have followed a massive impact that "sent huge quantities of dust into the air," thereby causing "the surface of Earth to cool dramatically" and sounding "the death knell for the dinosaurs." The inability of the dinosaurs to adapt to cold climates is central to the catastrophic-extinction theory, and the finding that this was true would provide strong support for the catastrophic-extinction theory. Therefore, **B** is not the best option.

D The fourth paragraph indicates that other scientists studying the sediment layer discovered evidence of vast vegetation fires that burned during the time of the impact. These fires are said to be "consistent with the catastrophic-extinction theory because such a tremendous collision could have scattered white-hot fragments of rocks for hundreds of miles around the impact site." The discovery that smoke from such fires can significantly block sunlight would support the catastrophic-extinction theory because the theory claims that reduced sunlight caused Earth's climate to cool. Therefore, **D** is not the best option.

Difficulty Level: Easy (90%)

3. Which of the following facts mentioned in the passage about the sediment layer is LEAST relevant to the catastrophic-extinction theory?

    A. The layer was composed of petrified sedimentary clay.
    B. The layer shows evidence of enormous heat and pressure.
    C. The layer contains high levels of soot.
    D. The layer was formed at the time the dinosaurs became extinct.

Cognitive Classification: Comprehension

Key: A

This question asks you to determine the relevance of the passage information about the sediment layer to the catastrophic-extinction theory. According to the passage, the catastrophic-extinction theory postulates that a massive impact caused a change in Earth's climate that killed the dinosaurs. The fact that scientists were studying a layer of sediment composed of petrified clay is not itself relevant to the theory. The evidence found within the layer and the time when the layer was formed are what provide the support for the theory. Therefore, **A** is the best option.

 The fact that the sediment layer is composed of clay is *consistent* with the catastrophic-extinction theory does not mean it is relevant to the theory. Pay close attention to the relationship you are being asked to identify.

Distractors

B   The catastrophic-extinction theory postulates that the dinosaurs were killed by a climate change resulting from "a collision between Earth and a huge object from space." The fourth paragraph states that a massive impact is "an event involving tremendous heat and pressure." The layer showing evidence of tremendous heat and pressure provides support for and is relevant to the catastrophic-extinction theory. Therefore, **B** is not the best option.

C   The fourth paragraph states that "a tremendous collision could have scattered white-hot fragments of rocks for hundreds of miles around the impact site," which could have sparked "vast vegetation fires" that would have produced high levels of soot. Because the high level of soot in the layer provides evidence for a large collision, the elevated soot levels are relevant to the catastrophic-extinction theory. Therefore, **C** is not the best option.

D   The sediment layer mentioned in the passage contains evidence of elevated iridium levels as well as physical changes that are produced only by an event involving enormous heat and pressure. The fact that the layer was formed when the dinosaurs became extinct ties the impact to their extinction, which makes this fact relevant to the theory. Therefore, **D** is not the best option.

Difficulty Level: Easy (90%)

4. Which of the following *alternatives* to the catastrophic-extinction theory, if true, could also plausibly explain the extinction of the dinosaurs?

    I. Blue-green algae common in the seas that covered much of the globe during the reign of the dinosaurs could concentrate iridium and release it into the environment.

    II. Lightning storms common at the time of the dinosaurs' demise were capable of igniting vegetation fires large enough to block significant amounts of sunlight with the smoke and soot that they produce.

    III. Volcanoes active at the time of the dinosaurs' demise could produce great heat and pressure, release iridium into the atmosphere, and block sunlight with huge quantities of soot and smoke.

A. I only
B. II only
C. I and III only
D. II and III only

Cognitive Classification: Incorporation of Information

Key: D

This question asks you to recognize a plausible alternative to the passage hypothesis about the extinction of the dinosaurs. When approaching these questions that present three options, it is easiest to begin by eliminating the options that contain explanations that are not plausible on the basis of passage information. In this question, Option I can be eliminated because the release of iridium is not mentioned in the passage as a possible cause of the extinction of the dinosaurs. The iridium is discussed in the passage as an indicator of an asteroid impact but not as a contributor to the demise of the dinosaurs. With Option I eliminated, you can eliminate

When answering a question that asks you to recognize a plausible alternative to passage information, remember that it needs to be plausible on the basis of the passage information. An explanation that is plausible in the real world but inconsistent with some information provided in the passage is NOT a plausible explanation for the purpose of this type of question.

choices **A** and **C**. This will leave you to decide between **B** and **D**. Because both of these options contain Option II, it is most expedient to simply skip the step of analyzing Option II and focus on the factor that differentiates choices **B** and **D** from each other, namely, whether Option III is a plausible explanation for the extinction of the dinosaurs. In this case, Option III is a plausible explanation because it describes a scenario that would result in significant amounts of sunlight being blocked, and the passage indicates that reduced sunlight would have caused Earth to cool and that "the green plants that were the basis of [the dinosaurs'] food chain could not have survived with the reduced sunlight." Similarly, Option II also describes a scenario that results in significant sunlight being blocked, and as such it too provides a plausible explanation of the extinction of the dinosaurs. Because both Option II and Option III provide plausible alternative explanations of the extinction of the dinosaurs, **D** is therefore the best option.

Distractors on next page.

Distractors

A   Because Option I does not provide a plausible explanation of the extinction of the dinosaurs (see **Key**), **A** is not the best option.

B   Although Option II is a plausible alternative explanation of the extinction of the dinosaurs because it focuses on blocked sunlight, so is Option III (see **Key**). Because this choice excludes one of the other plausible explanations, **B** is not the best option.

C   Because Option I does not provide a plausible explanation of the extinction of the dinosaurs (see **Key**), **C** is not the best option.

Difficulty Level: Easy (85%)

MCAT® is a program of the
Association of American Medical Colleges

Verbal Reasoning

Passage Set II

MCAT® is a program of the
Association of American Medical Colleges

Author of the famous five-part Leatherstocking series, twenty-seven other novels, and a box of historical and miscellaneous works, James Fenimore Cooper remains one of the most innovative yet most misunderstood figures in the history of U.S. culture. Almost single-handedly in the 1820s, Cooper invented the key forms of U.S. fiction—the Western, the sea tale, the Revolutionary romance—forms that set a suggestive agenda for subsequent writers, even for Hollywood and television. In producing and shrewdly marketing fully 10 percent of all U.S. novels in the 1820s, most of them best sellers, Cooper made it possible for other aspiring authors to earn a living by their writings. Cooper can be said to have invented not just an assortment of literary genres but the very career of the U.S. writer.

Despite Cooper's importance, he continues to be profoundly misunderstood, and this is partly his own fault. Although it was becoming common for writers in the early nineteenth century to indulge public curiosity about their lives, the usually chatty Cooper turned reticent when asked for biographical details. Whereas contemporaries, such as Sir Walter Scott and Washington Irving, made prior arrangements for authorized biographies, Cooper refused to follow suit. When nearing death in 1851, he insisted that his wife and children protect his life and his papers from outsiders. His private documents remained out of reach to most scholars until the 1990s.

The biographical problem is only one reason for Cooper's languishing reputation. Another reason is that he's always been the object of strong feelings, pro and con. Almost from the start of his career, Cooper was admired, imitated, recited, and memorized. In his day, he was reportedly the author most widely translated into German, and what has been called "Coopermania" hit France especially hard as early as the 1820s. Yet, from the outset, he was also subjected to various criticisms that, when combined with later politically motivated assaults, have hampered true appreciation of his work. Critics have at times faulted him for his occasional bad grammar, his leisurely pacing, and his general inability to eclipse his greatest contemporary, Sir Walter Scott.

The criticisms were not without merit. But the problems in Cooper's first books need to be understood in their proper context. At least some of Cooper's failings were owing to the very newness of what he was attempting. Robert E. Spiller summed up this point in 1931 by noting that Cooper "always suffered from the crudities of the experimenter."

Cooper was not just a pathbreaking figure in the history of writing in the U.S., or a potent visionary; he was a remarkably representative man. He was as much at home in the salons of New York City or the country houses of the rural Hudson Valley as in the raw frontier villages where his family's life had taken its root and rise. Knowing the country's most characteristic landscapes in ways that few of his contemporaries did, Cooper wrote of them with unexampled authority. He closely followed the War of 1812, partly because his friends fought in it, and partly because so much hinged on its outcome. Cooper thereafter joined in the effort of his most influential contemporaries to forge a new culture for the reaffirmed nation. One might say that Cooper's story is almost incidentally a literary story. It is first a story of how, in literature and a hundred other activities, Americans during this period sought to solidify their political and cultural and economic independence from Great Britain and, as the Revolutionary generation died, stipulate what the maturing Republic was to become.

Adapted from W. Franklin, In defense of Cooper. ©2007 by W. Franklin.

5. Which of the following best describes an assumption made by the passage author in the first paragraph?

   A. Ten percent of all U.S. novels produced in the 1820s were best sellers.
   B. The most innovative figures in U.S. culture are often the most misunderstood.
   C. Before the 1820s, U.S. writers were unable to earn a living by their writings.
   D. Cooper was the only U.S. author writing during the 1820s.

6. Which of the following statements about authors is most strongly implied by information in the second paragraph?

   A. The public is most curious about authors who are reticent when asked about their lives.
   B. Authors who authorize biographies of themselves are likely to be better understood than authors who do not.
   C. Authors did not share biographical details of their lives before the early nineteenth century.
   D. Most authors' papers are not protected from outsiders after the authors die.

7. Which of the following people would the passage author most likely consider to be *remarkably representative*, as this concept is used in the final paragraph?

   A. Someone who has written many stories set in various locations
   B. Someone who has an understanding of a variety of diverse locations
   C. Someone who is well liked by people from different backgrounds
   D. Someone who has written descriptions of many famous landscapes

8. Which of the following situations in the automotive industry is the most analogous to the one described in the fourth paragraph regarding Cooper's early writings?

   A. An automobile manufacturer introduces a new model that quickly becomes the best-selling vehicle in its class.
   B. An automobile manufacturer designs a vehicle that becomes popular with a group of people different from the group the manufacturer had anticipated.
   C. An automobile manufacturer has unexpected mechanical issues with an innovative new vehicle after its release.
   D. An automobile manufacturer offers an extended warranty on its vehicles in an attempt to shed its reputation for poor craftsmanship.

9. Information in the passage suggests that rather than misunderstanding Cooper, some people may have considered him to be too:

   A. sloppy in his writing.
   B. narrow in his literary focus.
   C. pretentious to relate well with most people.
   D. concerned about his popularity in other countries.

10. Which of the following passage assertions is the LEAST supported by examples or explanations in the passage?

   A. "Cooper can be said to have invented not just an assortment of literary genres but the very career of the U.S. writer."
   B. "[Cooper] continues to be profoundly misunderstood, and this is partly his own fault."
   C. "Cooper was not just a pathbreaking figure in the history of writing in the U.S. . . . ; he was a remarkably representative man."
   D. "[Cooper] closely followed the War of 1812, partly because his friends fought in it, and partly because so much hinged on its outcome."

Solutions for this passage begin on next page.

5. Which of the following best describes an assumption made by the passage author in the first paragraph?

   A. Ten percent of all U.S. novels produced in the 1820s were best sellers.
   B. The most innovative figures in U.S. culture are often the most misunderstood.
   C. Before the 1820s, U.S. writers were unable to earn a living by their writings.
   D. Cooper was the only U.S. author writing during the 1820s.

Cognitive Classification: Comprehension

Key: C

This question asks you to identify an assumption that the passage author makes in the first paragraph. This paragraph states, "In producing and shrewdly marketing fully 10 percent of all U.S. novels in the 1820s, most of them best sellers, Cooper made it possible for other aspiring authors to earn a living by their writings." The statement that Cooper "made it possible" implies that before Cooper's work in the 1820s, it was not possible for writers to earn a living by their writings. The final sentence in the first paragraph further strengthens this point by stating that "Cooper can be said to have invented . . . the very career of the U.S. writer." These statements indicate that the passage author most likely assumes that U.S. writers were unable to earn a living by their writings before Cooper's writings in the 1820s. Therefore, **C** is the best option.

Distractors

A   The first paragraph states that Cooper produced and marketed "fully 10 percent of all U.S. novels in the 1820s, most of them best sellers." This suggests that the majority of Cooper's writings were best sellers, but it does not suggest what percentage of novels produced in the 1820s were best sellers. Therefore, **A** is not the best option.

B   The first paragraph states that "Cooper remains one of the most innovative yet most misunderstood figures in the history of U.S. culture." This indicates that the passage author believes that Cooper was both innovative and misunderstood, but not that the most innovative people are often the most misunderstood. Therefore, **B** is not the best option.

D   The first paragraph states that Cooper produced "fully 10 percent of all U.S. novels in the 1820s," thus indicating that Cooper did not produce 90 percent of U.S. novels in the 1820s. The passage author clearly does not assume that Cooper was the only U.S. author writing in the 1820s. Therefore, **D** is not the best option.

Difficulty Level: Easy (85%)

6.	Which of the following statements about authors is most strongly implied by information in the second paragraph?

	A.	The public is most curious about authors who are reticent when asked about their lives.
	B.	Authors who authorize biographies of themselves are likely to be better understood than authors who do not.
	C.	Authors did not share biographical details of their lives before the early nineteenth century.
	D.	Most authors' papers are not protected from outsiders after the authors die.

Cognitive Classification: Comprehension

Key: B

This question asks you to identify a theory about authors that is implicit in the information provided in the second paragraph of the passage. The second paragraph begins by stating, "Despite Cooper's importance, he continues to be profoundly misunderstood, and this is partly his own fault." The passage states that this "fault" lies with his refusal "to follow suit" with his contemporaries and make arrangements for an authorized biography. In addition to failing to make arrangements for an authorized biography, Cooper "insisted that his wife and children protect his life and his papers from outsiders." This discussion implies that had Cooper been more willing to share biographical details about his life, he would have been less likely to be "profoundly misunderstood." From these statements, it is reasonable to conclude that authors who authorize biographies of themselves are likely to be better understood than authors who do not. Therefore, **B** is the best option.

Distractors

A	The second paragraph states that "it was becoming common for writers in the early nineteenth century to indulge public curiosity about their lives," but that Cooper "turned reticent when asked for biographical details." That Cooper was asked about biographical details implies that the public was curious about his life; however, the passage does not indicate whether the public was any more or less curious about Cooper's life because of this reticence. Therefore, **A** is not the best option.

C	The second paragraph states that "it was becoming common for writers in the early nineteenth century to indulge public curiosity about their lives," which does not imply that authors did not share such details before the early nineteenth century, only that it was less common. Therefore, **C** is not the best option.

D	The second paragraph states that when Cooper was nearing death, "he insisted that his wife and children protect his life and his papers from outsiders" and that "his private documents remained out of reach to most scholars until the 1990s." This provides an example of one author whose papers were protected, but it does not indicate whether this occurrence was common or rare. Therefore, **D** is not the best option.

Difficulty Level: Easy (85%)

7. Which of the following people would the passage author most likely consider to be *remarkably representative*, as this concept is used in the final paragraph?

    A. Someone who has written many stories set in various locations
    B. Someone who has an understanding of a variety of diverse locations
    C. Someone who is well liked by people from different backgrounds
    D. Someone who has written descriptions of many famous landscapes

Cognitive Classification: Application

Key: B

This question asks you to determine how the passage concept of being a *remarkably representative* person applies to a hypothetical situation outside of the passage. The final paragraph states that Cooper "was a remarkably representative man. He was as much at home in the salons of New York City or the country houses of the rural Hudson Valley as in the raw frontier villages where his family's life had taken its root and rise. Knowing the country's most characteristic landscapes in ways that few of his contemporaries did, Cooper wrote of them with unexampled authority." This implies that Cooper's writings showed his understanding of a variety of locations, thus making him remarkably representative. It is reasonable to conclude that the passage author would most likely consider someone who understands a variety of diverse locations to be remarkably representative. Therefore, **B** is the best option.

Distractors

A   The passage states that Cooper wrote many stories set in various locations, but this is not what the passage author claims makes Cooper remarkably representative. The final paragraph states that "Cooper was not just a pathbreaking figure in the history of writing in the U.S. . . . ; he was a remarkably representative man. . . . Knowing the country's most characteristic landscapes in ways that few of his contemporaries did, Cooper wrote of them with unexampled authority." This distinction implies that it was not Cooper's writing itself that made him representative, but rather his understanding of a variety of locations. Therefore, **A** is not the best option.

C   The final paragraph does not discuss whether Cooper was well liked by people from different backgrounds, and nothing in the passage indicates that the passage author considers being well liked as something contributing to Cooper being remarkably representative. Therefore, **C** is not the best option.

D   According to the final paragraph, Cooper knew "the country's most characteristic landscapes in ways that few of his contemporaries did," and he "wrote of them with unexampled authority." Cooper's descriptions of landscapes contribute to the passage author considering Cooper to be remarkably representative because these descriptions displayed greater understanding of those landscapes than did the writings of his contemporaries. Simply writing descriptions of the landscapes is insufficient to make someone remarkably representative, as the passage author uses this concept. Therefore, **D** is not the best option.

Difficulty Level: Easy (85%)

MCAT® is a program of the
Association of American Medical Colleges

8. Which of the following situations in the automotive industry is the most analogous to the one described in the fourth paragraph regarding Cooper's early writings?

A. An automobile manufacturer introduces a new model that quickly becomes the best-selling vehicle in its class.
B. An automobile manufacturer designs a vehicle that becomes popular with a group of people different from the group the manufacturer had anticipated.
C. An automobile manufacturer has unexpected mechanical issues with an innovative new vehicle after its release.
D. An automobile manufacturer offers an extended warranty on its vehicles in an attempt to shed its reputation for poor craftsmanship.

Cognitive Classification: Incorporation of Information

Key: C

This question asks you to determine which of the options provided represents a situation that is the most analogous to the one involving the problems in Cooper's early writings. The fourth paragraph states that the criticisms of Cooper's work "were not without merit," and "some of Cooper's failings were owing to the very newness of what he was attempting." The paragraph concludes with the quotation from Spiller who said that Cooper "always suffered from the crudities of the experimenter." Option **C** describes a situation in which an automobile manufacturer encounters problems relating to the newness of what it is attempting, and in this respect, the situation is the most analogous to the one described in the fourth paragraph. Therefore, **C** is the best option.

 When answering a question that asks which of the options is the most analogous to a situation described in the passage, it is helpful to determine in what respect the situations are analogous. Situations can be analogous because of similar objects or similar actions.

Distractors

A   The fourth paragraph states that Cooper's early works had "failings . . . owing to the very newness of what he was attempting." The fourth paragraph does not address Cooper's popularity or the number of books that he sold. Thus, an automobile manufacturer that releases a model that sells very well is not the most analogous situation. Therefore, **A** is not the best option.

B   The fourth paragraph discusses the "problems in Cooper's first books," not which audiences enjoyed them or which audiences Cooper expected would enjoy them. Thus, an automobile manufacturer that creates a vehicle that is popular with a different audience than had been anticipated is not the most analogous situation. Therefore, **B** is not the best option.

D   Although the fourth paragraph addresses some "problems in Cooper's first books," it does not suggest that Cooper was aware that his writing was perceived as having "failings" or that he attempted to change such perceptions. Because of this, an automobile manufacturer who offers an extended warranty in an attempt to change a bad reputation is not the most analogous situation. Therefore, **D** is not the best option.

Difficulty Level: Easy (90%)

9. Information in the passage suggests that rather than misunderstanding Cooper, some people may have considered him to be too:

A. sloppy in his writing.
B. narrow in his literary focus.
C. pretentious to relate well with most people.
D. concerned about his popularity in other countries.

Cognitive Classification: Evaluation

Key: A

This question asks you to determine which of the given reinterpretations of the information about Cooper presented in the passage is the most reasonable. The third paragraph states that critics faulted Cooper "for his occasional bad grammar [and] his leisurely pacing." The fourth paragraph adds that these "criticisms were not without merit" and concludes with the quotation by Spiller that Cooper "suffered from the crudities of the experimenter." It is reasonable to conclude from these assertions that rather than misunderstanding Cooper, some people may have objected to the craftsmanship of his writing. Therefore, **A** is the best option.

Distractors

B   The first paragraph states that Cooper wrote "the famous five-part Leatherstocking series, twenty-seven other novels, and a box of historical and miscellaneous works." The paragraph goes on to state that "almost single-handedly in the 1820s, Cooper invented the key forms of U.S. fiction—the Western, the sea tale, [and] the Revolutionary romance" and that it can be said that Cooper invented "an assortment of literary genres." Based on this discussion, it is not reasonable to conclude that Cooper had a narrow literary focus. Therefore, **B** is not the best option.

C   The final paragraph states that Cooper was "a remarkably representative man" who was "as much at home in the salons of New York City or the country houses of the rural Hudson Valley as in the raw frontier villages where his family's life had taken its root and rise." The claim that Cooper was "at home" in a variety of environments suggests that he likely did relate well to a variety of people. Furthermore, the passage does not suggest that Cooper was pretentious. Therefore, **C** is not the best option.

D   The third paragraph states that Cooper was "reportedly the author most widely translated into German, and what has been called 'Coopermania' hit France especially hard as early as the 1820s." This discussion indicates that Cooper was popular in other countries, but it does not suggest that Cooper was concerned about this popularity or that his popularity abroad was a source of criticism from people. Therefore, **D** is not the best option.

Difficulty Level: Easy (80%)

10. Which of the following passage assertions is the LEAST supported by examples or explanations in the passage?

    A. "Cooper can be said to have invented not just an assortment of literary genres but the very career of the U.S. writer."

    B. "[Cooper] continues to be profoundly misunderstood, and this is partly his own fault."

    C. "Cooper was not just a pathbreaking figure in the history of writing in the U.S. . . . ; he was a remarkably representative man."

    D. "[Cooper] closely followed the War of 1812, partly because his friends fought in it, and partly because so much hinged on its outcome."

Cognitive Classification: Evaluation

Key: D

This question asks you to determine the amount of support that passage assertions receive from other information provided in the passage. The claim that "[Cooper] closely followed the War of 1812, partly because his friends fought in it, and partly because so much hinged on its outcome" is made in the final paragraph of the passage, and no additional explanation or support is provided. Because this passage assertion receives no support from any examples or explanations in the passage, **D** is therefore the best option.

Distractors

A   The claim that "Cooper can be said to have invented not just an assortment of literary genres but the very career of the U.S. writer" is the concluding sentence of the first paragraph, and the entire first paragraph serves to support this claim. The first paragraph mentions that "Cooper invented the key forms of U.S. fiction" and that by "producing and shrewdly marketing fully 10 percent of all U.S. novels in the 1820s," he "made it possible for other aspiring authors to earn a living by their writings." Because this claim is supported by examples and explanations in the passage, **A** is not the best option.

B   The claim that "[Cooper] continues to be profoundly misunderstood, and this is partly his own fault" is made in the first sentence of the second paragraph. This paragraph goes on to explain that Cooper refused to make arrangements for an authorized biography and that "he insisted that his wife and children protect his life and papers from outsiders," which resulted in his private documents remaining "out of reach to most scholars until the 1990s." Because this claim is supported by explanations in the passage, **B** is not the best option.

C   The claim that "Cooper was not just a pathbreaking figure in the history of writing in the U.S. . . . ; he was a remarkably representative man" is made at the beginning of the final paragraph. The first part of this claim, that he was a pathbreaking figure, is supported throughout the passage, particularly in the first paragraph (see **A**) as well as in the discussion in the fourth paragraph where the passage mentions that what Cooper was doing was very new and that Cooper was an "experimenter." The second part of the claim, that Cooper was remarkably representative, is supported by the discussion in the final paragraph that describes Cooper as being comfortable in many different settings as well as being knowledgeable about different areas of the U.S. Because this claim is supported by examples and explanations in the passage, **C** is not the best option.

Difficulty Level: Medium (60%)

Verbal Reasoning

Passage Set III

Some people may say that a language is to be preserved not so much because it provides a social glue or warm communal bath for those who need to escape chilling selfhood, but because it is poetry—a unique and untranslatable way of seeing and knowing the universe. Maybe it is. Any threatened language should be given the benefit of the doubt—treated as though it might be an irreplaceable product of mind and emotion. Still, I am inclined to guard against excessive romanticism, for on the face of it, a nation of poets—a people whose speech is regularly punctuated by words of freshly minted significance—is unlikely. Ethnographic evidence and our own experience among speakers of an unfamiliar tongue hardly confirm linguistic creativity as a common state of affairs. A well-meaning outsider may think an unfamiliar tongue poetry because many figures of speech in it are new to her. But they are not new—they have probably become verbal tics—to native speakers. It is both humbling and healthy to remember that when people anywhere, including erudite academics, meet to talk socially, they are seldom poetic whatever language they use. They are more likely to say "Pass the salt" and "How are the kids?" than anything that stirs the emotions, elevates the mind and the spirit.

Speech binds human individuals and groups with their nonhuman environment. It does so most effortlessly and effectively by means of similes and metaphors, which are a universal feature of language. Apparently human beings can only know who they are through the use of animal and plant references: "I am a fox; he is a prickly cactus." In the process of learning who they are, people also become aware of their intimate ties to other living things; the two processes are inseparable, melded into one by the character of language. As for things in the mineral realm, anatomical metaphors, such as foothills and headlands, the spine of a ridge, the mouth of a river, the face of a cliff, make them all seem familiar and personal. Indeed, language tricks people into believing that rises and hollows, wind and rivers are all in some sense alive. And because human beings and human speech are coeval, there never was a time when speech did not generate this useful and reassuring illusion. Language animates; that and human bonding are two of its most primitive and potent effects. One problem of language is that ordinary speech lacks neutral ways of referring to that which is not alive. The inanimate is a sophisticated idea that depends on the prior conception of the animate.

We think we are losing the knack of figurative utterance. We speak prose, and pundits have offered the opinion that this prose is becoming more and more impersonal. There is, however, an important difference between impersonal prose and plain prose. Speaking or even writing plain logical prose with minimum metaphorical embellishment is a high and rare achievement. In any age, it lies well beyond most people's competence. On most occasions we modern people, no less than people in earlier times, are "poets." We speak poetry—just not good poetry; and although fresh metaphors are normally beyond our grasp, our daily speech is nonetheless peppered with metaphors, other tropes, and literary conceits. "Hi, honey," "angry sky," "bullish market," and suchlike are certainly not original, yet so long as such expressions are used, we maintain a personal link between nature and self. No wonder the idea of the world's indifference, other than under some dire circumstance, seems so oddly contrary to experience and common sense.

Adapted from Y. F. Tuan, *Escapism*. © 1998 by Johns Hopkins University Press.

11. Based on passage information, which of the following factors most likely contributes to people thinking that they are "losing the knack of figurative utterance"?

   A. People tend to speak or write in plain logical prose.
   B. People consider themselves to be poets who speak bad poetry.
   C. People overlook the metaphorical elements in their own language.
   D. People believe the similes and metaphors in their own language are not original.

12. Which of the following statements about similes and metaphors is most clearly implied by the information in the passage?

   A. Most people cannot avoid using similes and metaphors in daily speech.
   B. Similes and metaphors bind human individuals to each other.
   C. Some languages use more similes and metaphors than do others.
   D. The most developed languages use the most similes and metaphors.

13. Based on passage information, which of the following features must a particular language have to convince the author that the language is "poetry—a unique and untranslatable way of seeing and knowing the universe"?

   A. The language has more figures of speech that refer to animals and plants than do most other languages.
   B. The language describes the natural world in more personal terms than do most other languages.
   C. The language has more romantic expressions than do most other languages.
   D. The language enables speakers to regularly craft new metaphors in their everyday speech.

14. Suppose that a particular group of people uses metaphors that reference mechanical objects to describe living creatures. Based on the reasoning in the passage, these people would most likely believe that:

   A. mechanical objects are in some sense alive.
   B. living creatures are in some sense mechanical.
   C. mechanical metaphors are a neutral way of referring to living creatures.
   D. the idea of the mechanical depends on a conception of the animate.

15. Which of the following statements, if true, would most undermine the author's view about the role of metaphor, as presented in the second paragraph?

   A. To describe human features, people often use metaphors that refer to the mineral realm.
   B. Most people develop a sense of who they are before they become aware of other living things.
   C. Languages bind people to one another using other features of language in addition to similes and metaphors.
   D. Most people prefer to use neutral expressions for inanimate objects when such expressions are available.

Solutions for this passage begin on next page.

11. Based on passage information, which of the following factors most likely contributes to people thinking that they are "losing the knack of figurative utterance"?

    A. People tend to speak or write in plain logical prose.
    B. People consider themselves to be poets who speak bad poetry.
    C. People overlook the metaphorical elements in their own language.
    D. People believe the similes and metaphors in their own language are not original.

Cognitive Classification: Evaluation

Key: C

This question tests your ability to judge how the claim that people think they are "losing the knack of figurative utterance" is related to other ideas presented in the passage. The final paragraph states that speaking or writing "with minimum metaphorical embellishment . . . lies well beyond most people's competence," but their "speech is nonetheless peppered with metaphors, other tropes, and literary conceits." The first paragraph says that to people unfamiliar with a language, figures of speech seem like "poetry," but to native speakers, they are merely "verbal tics," suggesting that native speakers do not consider such expressions poetic or metaphorical but just an ordinary way of speaking. If most people cannot minimize their use of metaphorical embellishment, and if those embellishments are merely "verbal tics" to native speakers of a language, it is likely that people speak figuratively and do not notice that they are doing so. Therefore, **C** is the best option.

Distractors

A   The final paragraph states, "Speaking or . . . writing plain logical prose . . . is a high and rare achievement. In any age, it lies well beyond most people's competence." Thus, option **A** directly contradicts passage information, and so it is unreasonable to believe on the basis of passage information that this is a likely factor contributing to people thinking that they are "losing the knack of figurative utterance." Therefore, **A** is not the best option.

B   The final paragraph states that "we modern people . . . are 'poets.' We speak poetry—just not good poetry," but does not discuss whether people think this about themselves. The author expresses an opinion about people's speech without claiming that others share this opinion. Therefore, **B** is not the best option.

 Be careful to distinguish the source to whom an assertion, belief, or attitude is attributed. This distractor erroneously claims that the author's statement "we modern people . . . are 'poets.' We speak poetry—just not good poetry" is a view that is held by people in general.

D   The final paragraph states that "our daily speech is . . . peppered with metaphors, other tropes, and literary conceits," but that these figures of speech "are certainly not original." The author expresses an opinion without claiming that others share this opinion. Therefore, **D** is not the best option.

Difficulty Level: Medium (65%)

MCAT® is a program of the
Association of American Medical Colleges

12. Which of the following statements about similes and metaphors is most clearly implied by the information in the passage?

   A. Most people cannot avoid using similes and metaphors in daily speech.
   B. Similes and metaphors bind human individuals to each other.
   C. Some languages use more similes and metaphors than do others.
   D. The most developed languages use the most similes and metaphors.

Cognitive Classification: Comprehension

Key: A

This question tests your ability to recognize which of the options best represents a paraphrase of the information about similes and metaphors presented in the passage. The final paragraph states that usually people's "daily speech is ... peppered with metaphors, other tropes, and literary conceits," and that "it lies well beyond most people's competence" to speak or write in "plain logical prose with minimum metaphorical embellishment." Option **A**, "Most people cannot avoid using similes and metaphors in daily speech," is a reasonable paraphrase of the assertions that people's daily speech usually contains metaphors and other literary devices and that it is beyond most people's abilities to write or speak without using such literary devices. Therefore, **A** is the best option.

Distractors

B   The second paragraph states that "speech binds human individuals and groups with their nonhuman environment ... most effortlessly and effectively by means of similes and metaphors," but does not state that similes and metaphors bind people to each other. The second paragraph states that human bonding is one of the "most primitive and potent effects" of language but does not specify that this effect is achieved through similes and metaphors. Therefore, **B** is not the best option.

C   The second paragraph states that similes and metaphors "are a universal feature of language"; however, nothing in the passage gives any basis for determining how often one language uses them compared to another. The author focuses on the features of language that are "universal," not on comparative relationships among different languages. Therefore, **C** is not the best option.

D   The second paragraph states that similes and metaphors "are a universal feature of language," but the passage does not suggest that languages that use them the most often are the most developed. The author focuses on the features of language that are "universal," not on comparative relationships among different languages. Therefore, **D** is not the best option.

Difficulty Level: Easy (75%)

13. Based on passage information, which of the following features must a particular language have to convince the author that the language is "poetry—a unique and untranslatable way of seeing and knowing the universe"?

 A. The language has more figures of speech that refer to animals and plants than do most other languages.
 B. The language describes the natural world in more personal terms than do most other languages.
 C. The language has more romantic expressions than do most other languages.
 D. The language enables speakers to regularly craft new metaphors in their everyday speech.

Cognitive Classification: Application

Key: D

This question asks you to use the information in the passage about poetry to determine which of the available options represents a feature that a language would have to have for the author to consider that language "poetry." The first paragraph states that "some people may say that a language is to be preserved . . . because it is poetry," but the author is "inclined to guard against" this claim because "a nation of poets—a people whose speech is regularly punctuated by words of freshly minted significance—is unlikely." In the final paragraph, the author says that "our daily speech . . . is peppered with metaphors," even though "fresh metaphors are normally beyond our grasp." This suggests that for the author to consider the speech of a particular group of people to be "poetry," it would have to be "regularly punctuated by" newly created, significant metaphors. Therefore, **D** is the best option.

Distractors

A The second paragraph states that "apparently human beings can only know who they are through the use of animal and plant references," a statement that the author applies, without qualification, to languages in general. The author does not discuss the relative frequency of these types of references in different languages. Therefore, **A** is not the best option.

B The second paragraph states that "speech binds human individuals and groups with their nonhuman environment," in part through the use of "anatomical metaphors" that trick people into believing that inanimate things are "familiar and personal." The author does not discuss the relative frequency of these types of personal descriptions in different languages. Therefore, **B** is not the best option.

C In the first paragraph, the author states that "I am inclined to guard against excessive romanticism" regarding the idea that a language might be poetry. The passage does not discuss romantic expressions or the relative frequency of such expressions in different languages. Therefore, **C** is not the best option.

Some distractors use concepts from the passage to imply relationships beyond what the passage author probably intended. In this question, all these distractors describe comparative relationships among different languages, whereas the passage author focuses on "universal" features of all languages.

Difficulty Level: Medium (50%)

14. Suppose that a particular group of people uses metaphors that reference mechanical objects to describe living creatures. Based on the reasoning in the passage, these people would most likely believe that:

   A. mechanical objects are in some sense alive.
   B. living creatures are in some sense mechanical.
   C. mechanical metaphors are a neutral way of referring to living creatures.
   D. the idea of the mechanical depends on a conception of the animate.

Cognitive Classification: Application

Key: B

This question tests your ability to apply the passage argument about the effect that using metaphors has on people's beliefs to a situation in which people use mechanical metaphors to describe living creatures. The second paragraph states, "As for things in the mineral realm, anatomical metaphors, such as foothills and headlands, . . . make them all seem familiar and personal. Indeed, language tricks people into believing that . . . [inanimate things] are all in some sense alive." Thus, following this line of reasoning, if people were to refer to living creatures using mechanical metaphors, then they would most likely be tricked into believing that living creatures are in some sense mechanical. Therefore, **B** is the best option.

 When a question asks you to apply the passage reasoning to a new situation, it is sometimes helpful to insert the terms given in the question into the passage argument. This passage argues that "anatomical metaphors" make "things in the mineral realm" appear to be "in some sense alive." If you substitute *mechanical metaphors* for *anatomical metaphors* and *living creatures* for *things in the mineral realm*, it will help you to arrive at the parallel construction that mechanical metaphors make living creatures appear to be in some sense mechanical.

Distractors

A   The second paragraph states that "anatomical metaphors" trick "people into believing that . . . [inanimate things] are all in some sense alive." By applying this argument to the case of mechanical metaphors being used to describe living creatures, the most reasonable conclusion is that mechanical metaphors trick people into believing that living creatures are in some sense mechanical (see **Key**). Option **A** reverses this relationship and is therefore not the best option.

C   The second paragraph states that "anatomical metaphors" trick "people into believing that . . . [inanimate things] are all in some sense alive," and that "ordinary speech lacks neutral ways of referring to that which is not alive," suggesting that metaphors are not neutral ways of referring to living creatures. Therefore, **C** is not the best option.

D   In the second paragraph, the author's explanation of the role that metaphor plays in animating the inanimate prefaces the author's claim that "the inanimate is a sophisticated idea that depends on the prior conception of the animate." The parallel construction in this case would be that using mechanical metaphors to refer to living creatures suggests that the conception of the animate depends on the prior conception of the mechanical. Option **D** reverses this construction and is therefore not the best option.

Difficulty Level: Hard (40%)

15. Which of the following statements, if true, would most *undermine* the author's view about the role of metaphor, as presented in the second paragraph?

    A. To describe human features, people often use metaphors that refer to the mineral realm.

    B. Most people develop a sense of who they are before they become aware of other living things.

    C. Languages bind people to one another using other features of language in addition to similes and metaphors.

    D. Most people prefer to use neutral expressions for inanimate objects when such expressions are available.

Cognitive Classification: Incorporation of Information

Key: B

This question tests your ability to recognize which of the available options would pose the greatest challenge to the author's view of the role of metaphor. The second paragraph states, "Apparently human beings can only know who they are through the use of animal and plant references. . . . In the process of learning who they are, people also become aware of their intimate ties to other living things; the two processes are inseparable, melded into one by the character of language." Option **B** suggests that people learn about themselves before they are aware of other living things, which directly contradicts the passage author's claim that "the two processes are inseparable" from each other. Option **B** also implies that people do not need plant and animal references to know who they are. Therefore, **B** is the best option.

Distractors

A   The second paragraph states that "speech binds [people] with their nonhuman environment . . . by means of similes and metaphors," and that "anatomical metaphors . . . make [objects in the mineral realm] all seem familiar and personal." The fact that people use mineral metaphors to describe human features does not imply that these claims in the second paragraph are untrue. Therefore, **A** is not the best option.

C   The second paragraph states that "speech binds [people] with their nonhuman environment . . . most effortlessly and effectively by means of similes and metaphors," thus allowing for the possibility that other features of language can bind people to their environment. Furthermore, although the second paragraph does say that human bonding is an effect of language, the passage does not say that similes and metaphors are the mechanism by which bonding takes place. Therefore, **C** is not the best option.

D   The second paragraph states that "ordinary speech lacks neutral ways of referring to that which is not alive," but the passage does not discuss whether people are, or would be, inclined to use such expressions if they were available. Therefore, **D** is not the best option.

Difficulty Level: Medium (55%)

Verbal Reasoning
Passage Set IV

What is a plant? In the most basic and fundamental terms, what is it about a plant that makes it a plant and not an animal? I believe that the principal factor shaping the evolution of plants and animals is the fundamental difference in their nutritional modes. This has resulted in the differences we now observe between them.

In order to live and grow, all organisms require a source of carbon and a source of energy in addition to mineral elements and water. Plants are autotrophs or "self-feeders." They synthesize their own food, using carbon dioxide from the atmosphere as a source of carbon and sunlight as a source of energy. These two resources, along with minerals and often water, are present in the environment at very low concentrations. In order to collect these diffuse resources, plants produce a great deal of surface area in the form of stems, leaves, roots, and root hairs. The high ratio of surface area to volume found in plants is one of their most characteristic features. It is through this extensive surface area, literally spread out into the environment, that plants absorb the diffuse resources needed for growth. These resources are converted into organic molecules through photosynthesis and subsequent metabolism, and in that state represent concentrations of carbon, energy, and minerals. Plants therefore may be characterized as "collectors and concentrators."

Animals are heterotrophs or "other-feeders." They cannot make their own food and must rely on preformed, concentrated sources of carbon, energy, and minerals— that is, "food"—consisting of plants or organisms that have eaten plants. Animals are motile and much more compact than plants, having a much lower surface-area-to-volume ratio. Being compact and motile, animals are able to seek out concentrated sources of food and water in their environment. By "using" the food—that is, by respiration—the animal returns the carbon, energy, and minerals to the environment in an unconcentrated form: atmospheric carbon dioxide, heat energy, and mineral elements no longer incorporated in organic molecules. Animals therefore may be characterized as "scatterers."

The collector-concentrators (plants) and scatterers (animals) constitute a recycling system in the earth's ecosystem. It has been suggested that if multicellular life-forms are discovered on other planets, they will undoubtedly exhibit these two basic lifestyles.

There are, of course, a number of qualifications to be added to this simplistic view. One very important point is that everything in the ecosystem, except energy, is recycled. Energy reaches the earth as sunlight energy. A small fraction (1 percent or less) is captured in photosynthesis and transformed into chemical energy, which is released eventually and leaves the earth in the form of infrared radiation (heat energy). A second point is that bacteria and fungi are also very important in the scattering process. In fact, these heterotrophs are more crucial than animals to the completion of the decomposition process started by the animals. A third point is that oxygen is also important in this recycling system. Oxygen released by plants as a byproduct of photosynthesis is required by both heterotrophs and autotrophs for respiration.

Adapted from W. M. Darley, The essence of "Plantness.", *American Biology Teacher.* © 1990 by National Association of Biology Teachers.

16. The author asserts that oxygen, which is released by plants, is required for respiration by both autotrophs and heterotrophs. This assertion is most likely intended to support which of the following conclusions?

   A. Plants and animals constitute a recycling system in the earth's ecosystem.
   B. The view that plants and animals form a recycling system in the earth's ecosystem is too simplistic.
   C. Bacteria and fungi are more crucial than animals to the completion of the decomposition process.
   D. Plants may be characterized as "collectors and concentrators" of resources.

17. Based on the information in the passage, which of the following best explains why bacteria and fungi are more crucial than animals to the completion of the decomposition process?

   A. Bacteria and fungi are more compact than animals.
   B. Bacteria and fungi add more oxygen to decomposing material than do animals.
   C. Bacteria and fungi break down organic molecules better than do animals.
   D. Bacteria and fungi enable animals to initiate the decomposition process.

18. Assume that plants in the cactus family have maximized volume and minimized surface area to help them retain water in an arid environment. Given this, which of the following changes to the author's assertions is the most necessary?

   A. The difference between plants and animals is not fundamentally about modes of nutrition.
   B. Some autotrophs are able to collect diffuse resources with a low ratio of surface area to volume.
   C. Cactus plants constitute a third part of the recycling system in addition to collector-concentrators and scatterers.
   D. Plants that have a high ratio of surface area to volume require concentrated resources in the environment.

19. Based on passage information, two plants that have extremely different ratios of surface area to volume will most likely have *different*:

   A. rates of heat loss.
   B. access to resources.
   C. nutritional modes.
   D. sources of energy.

_____

Solutions for this passage begin on next page.

16. The author asserts that oxygen, which is released by plants, is required for respiration by both autotrophs and heterotrophs. This assertion is most likely intended to support which of the following conclusions?

    A. Plants and animals constitute a recycling system in the earth's ecosystem.
    B. The view that plants and animals form a recycling system in the earth's ecosystem is too simplistic.
    C. Bacteria and fungi are more crucial than animals to the completion of the decomposition process.
    D. Plants may be characterized as "collectors and concentrators" of resources.

Cognitive Classification: Comprehension

Key: B

This question asks you to identify which of the available options is most likely to be the conclusion the author intended to support with the assertion about oxygen being released by plants. The final paragraph states that "there are, of course, a number of qualifications to be added to this simplistic view" described in the fourth paragraph that plants and animals "constitute a recycling system in the earth's ecosystem." The claim regarding oxygen is listed as the "third point." Because this claim is listed as a qualification to the "simplistic view," it is likely intended to support the conclusion that the view that plants and animals form a recycling system is too simplistic. Therefore, **B** is the best option.

Distractors

A   The final paragraph states that "there are, of course, a number of qualifications to be added to this simplistic view" described in the fourth paragraph that plants and animals "constitute a recycling system in the earth's ecosystem." The claim about oxygen is listed as a qualification to the view described in **A**. Therefore, **A** is not the best option.

C   The final paragraph lists the claim that bacteria and fungi "are more crucial than animals to the completion of the decomposition process" as the second qualification "to this simplistic view" that plants and animals "constitute a recycling system in the earth's ecosystem." By enumerating the claims in the final paragraph (that is, by labeling them as "one . . . point," "a second point," and "a third point"), the author indicates that each of these assertions is relevant to a single conclusion that "there are, of course, a number of qualifications to be added to this simplistic view." Even though the claims in the question and in option **C** are used to support the same conclusion, they are not used to support each other. Therefore, **C** is not the best option.

 Statements that are enumerated (for example, *first, second, third*) usually support a single explicit or implicit conclusion. The conclusion in this case is implied by the following passage statements: "The collector-concentrators (plants) and scatterers (animals) constitute a recycling system in the earth's ecosystem," and "There are, of course, a number of qualifications to be added to this simplistic view."

D   The second paragraph states that "plants absorb . . . resources [that] are converted into organic molecules. . . . Plants therefore may be characterized as 'collectors and concentrators.'" The fact that oxygen is *released* by plants is unlikely to be used to support the view that plants are "collectors and concentrators" of resources. Therefore, **D** is not the best option.

Difficulty Level: Hard (35%)

17. Based on the information in the passage, which of the following best explains why bacteria and fungi are more crucial than animals to the completion of the decomposition process?

    A. Bacteria and fungi are more compact than animals.
    B. Bacteria and fungi add more oxygen to decomposing material than do animals.
    C. Bacteria and fungi break down organic molecules better than do animals.
    D. Bacteria and fungi enable animals to initiate the decomposition process.

Cognitive Classification: Application

Key: C

This question tests your ability to determine which of the potential explanations for why bacteria and fungi "are more crucial than animals to the completion of the decomposition process" is the most consistent with passage information. The second paragraph states that plants convert resources "into organic molecules," and the third paragraph states that animals use plants as food. Animals "may be characterized as 'scatterers'" because, by using food, they return resources "to the environment in an unconcentrated form . . . no longer incorporated in organic molecules." In the final paragraph, the author uses the phrases "scattering process" and "decomposition process" in a parallel manner, thereby suggesting that decomposition involves removing resources from organic molecules. If bacteria and fungi are "more crucial than animals to the completion of the decomposition process started by the animals," it is likely that bacteria and fungi are more crucial to the process of breaking down organic molecules into their component resources. Therefore, **C** is the best option.

Distractors

A The author uses the word *compact* in the third paragraph to describe how the ratio of surface area to volume of animals is lower than that of plants. Although bacteria and fungi are compact in the sense that they are small, the passage does not say bacteria and fungi have a low ratio of surface area to volume, nor does it discuss how compactness relates to "the completion of the decomposition process." Therefore, **A** is not the best option.

Option A takes advantage of an ambiguity in the word *compact*. In ordinary speech, it can mean "small," but in the context of this passage, it specifically means "having a low ratio of surface area to volume." Be careful to read words in the same way as they are used in the passage.

B The final sentence states that oxygen "is required by both heterotrophs and autotrophs for respiration" and that "oxygen [is] released by plants"; however, the passage does not say that animals, bacteria, and fungi can release oxygen or that they add it to the materials they decompose. Therefore, **B** is not the best option.

D The final paragraph states that bacteria and fungi are crucial "to the completion of the decomposition process started by the animals," whereas option **D** implies that bacteria and fungi enable animals to begin the process. Although it may be true that bacteria and fungi help animals to initiate the decomposition process, nothing in the passage suggests this is the case. Therefore, **D** is not the best option.

Difficulty Level: Easy (85%)

18.   Assume that plants in the cactus family have maximized volume and minimized surface area to help them re-
      tain water in an arid environment. Given this, which of the following changes to the author's assertions is the
      most necessary?

      A. The difference between plants and animals is not fundamentally about modes of nutrition.
      B. Some autotrophs are able to collect diffuse resources with a low ratio of surface area to volume.
      C. Cactus plants constitute a third part of the recycling system in addition to collector-concentrators and
          scatterers.
      D. Plants that have a high ratio of surface area to volume require concentrated resources in the environment.

Cognitive Classification: Incorporation of Information

Key: B

This question tests your ability to modify an assertion from the passage to make it consistent with the information
about cactus plants provided in the question. The second paragraph states that "plants are autotrophs" and that "in
order to collect . . . diffuse resources, plants produce a great deal of surface area." You can deduce that plants in the
cactus family are autotrophs that have a low ratio of surface area to volume, and the question states that they live in
arid environments where water is particularly "diffuse." Given this information about plants in the cactus family, the
statement that "in order to collect . . . diffuse resources, plants produce a great deal of surface area" would need to be
modified to allow for the possibility that a low ratio of surface area to volume is sufficient for a plant to collect the
necessary resources. Therefore, **B** is the best option.

Distractors

A   Regarding nutritional modes, the second and third paragraphs state that "plants are autotrophs" and "animals are
    heterotrophs." Nothing in the information provided in the question about cactus plants suggests they have a
    different "nutritional mode" from other plants. Therefore, **A** is not the best option.

C   The fourth paragraph states that "the collector-concentrators (plants) and scatterers (animals) constitute a recycling
    system in the earth's ecosystem." The information about cactus plants in the question does not suggest that they
    play a different role than other plants in the "recycling system." Therefore, **C** is not the best option.

D   That cactus plants are able to absorb resources with a low ratio of surface area to volume does not imply that
    plants with a high ratio of surface area to volume are unable to "absorb . . . diffuse resources." Therefore, **D** is not
    the best option.

Difficulty Level: Easy (90%)

MCAT® is a program of the
Association of American Medical Colleges

19. Based on passage information, two plants that have extremely different ratios of surface area to volume will most likely have *different*:

   A. rates of heat loss.
   B. access to resources.
   C. nutritional modes.
   D. sources of energy.

Cognitive Classification: Application

Key: B

This question asks you to use passage information to determine what would most likely cause two plants to have extremely different ratios of surface area to volume. The second paragraph states that "carbon and sunlight . . . , along with minerals and often water, are present in the environment at very low concentrations. In order to collect these diffuse resources, plants produce a great deal of surface area." If a plant's ratio of surface area to volume is a response to the level of resources available to it in the environment, then two plants that have each evolved in response to a different level of access to resources will most likely each have a different ratio of surface area to volume. The passage does not suggest any other reason for plants to have different ratios of surface area to volume. Therefore, **B** is the best option.

Distractors

A The final paragraph states that plants capture a small amount of sunlight energy "in photosynthesis and [transform it] into chemical energy, which is released eventually . . . in the form of infrared radiation (heat energy)." Although it is probably true that two plants with extremely different ratios of surface area to volume are likely to have different rates of heat loss, the relationship between surface area and heat loss is not discussed in the passage. Therefore, **A** is not the best option.

C The first paragraph states that "the principal factor shaping the evolution of plants and animals is the fundamental difference in their nutritional modes." Regarding nutritional modes, the passage states that "plants are autotrophs" and "animals are heterotrophs," but the possibility that different plants have different nutritional modes is not discussed in the passage. Therefore, **C** is not the best option.

D The second paragraph states that plants use "sunlight as a source of energy." The passage does not discuss alternative sources of energy. Therefore, **D** is not the best option.

Difficulty Level: Easy (85%)

Verbal Reasoning

Passage Set V

Young children will frequently seek out and enjoy physical challenges in their play, yet safety regulations can make it very difficult for teachers to provide children with experiences that feel satisfyingly "risky." Too often the concern to remove all hazards from a playground can inadvertently also lead to the removal of all opportunities for risk-taking. For those whose priority is "keeping children safe," this may seem a small cost, but for those who are concerned with the wider issues of children's learning, it is likely to have far more significance.

Because the consequences of physical hazard are so dire, they frequently overshadow the need to provide children with stimulating and challenging physical play outdoors. What are the implications of making playgrounds hazard free? Some implications are widely recognized. The most immediate is that, in making an area hazard free, inadvertently it will also be made challenge free. In an environment that is too "safe" and restrictive, children are likely to become bored; and this in turn may lead them to use equipment in unanticipated and truly dangerous ways in an effort to create challenges for themselves. In the longer term, children may grow up lacking confidence in their own physical ability through lack of opportunities to extend their skills and to meet appropriate physical challenges. Moreover, physical confidence and competence have repeatedly been linked with general feelings of competence.

In order to understand the strength of the resistance to children's physical risk-taking, it is useful to be aware of wider social discourses that may be underpinning the debate. The concern with children's physical safety sits within a discourse of risks that "threaten" children, and of consequent restrictions placed upon them to protect them. But, as some researchers suggest, those concerns in turn sit within an even wider framework of "risk anxiety" that is a pervasive feature of contemporary life. Their analysis highlights the extraordinary level of concern for safety that now focuses on children, as the increasing society-wide concern with risk is "superimposed" onto the already existing "'protective discourse' within which children are located as vulnerable innocents." Traditional play areas—even backyards sometimes—are often now seen as unsafe for children. The age at which children are allowed out on their own has risen. Children are driven or accompanied to school; they are warned not to speak to strangers. As a result of these increasing restrictions, children have less experience making decisions on their own, less opportunity to assess their own personal frontiers, and less opportunity to gain confidence and self-esteem through coping independently. Some researchers argue that being allowed to take risks is an essential part of the ongoing process of "becoming at home in the world." The discourses that surround us tend to focus us on the downside of risk—seeing the uncertainty, the possibility of failure, of injury. However, it is important that we ensure that the positive aspects of risk are also acknowledged—the possibility of discovering that one is adventurous, daring, brave, strong, confident, and successful.

My observations have convinced me that many children enjoy, and seek out, experiences for physical risk-taking; and the literature identifies being adventurous and taking risks as useful dispositions in thinking and problem solving. Conversations with teachers show that many are convinced that there is a connection between successful physical risk-taking and a willingness to undertake risks in other areas of learning. We need therefore to continue to reflect on the implications that increasingly rigorous safety standards in our playgrounds may be having for our children.

Adapted from A. Stephenson, Physical risk-taking: Dangerous or endangered?, *Early Years: Journal of International Research and Development*. © 2003 by Routledge.

20. Of the following statements, which one best describes the central thesis of the passage?

   A. The hazards that children face in their everyday lives are exaggerated partly because of the "risk anxiety" that pervades contemporary life.
   B. A child who successfully takes on physical risks will be more likely to undertake risks in other areas of learning.
   C. People need to consider the positive aspects of risk-taking behavior when they develop safety regulations for children's play areas.
   D. A result of increasing restrictions on children is that they lack opportunities to make their own decisions.

21. Information in the passage most strongly suggests that the author believes that people who are resistant to children's physical risk-taking:

   A. do not allow their children to play in their backyards because they consider it to be unsafe.
   B. insufficiently acknowledge the positive aspects that may result from children taking physical risks.
   C. have less opportunity to gain confidence and self-esteem through coping independently.
   D. are mistaken when they consider the consequences of physical hazard to be dire.

22. Which of the following is NOT mentioned in the passage as one of the potential benefits of children's physical risk-taking?

   A. A feeling of competence in their abilities
   B. A willingness to undertake other risks in learning
   C. An adventurous disposition that is useful for problem solving
   D. A tendency to use equipment in novel ways

23. Assume that the current safety regulations for playgrounds have substantially reduced the number of children injured on playground equipment each year. If true, is this assumption consistent with the author's primary argument?

   A. No; it shows that the author has not sufficiently appreciated the positive effects that safety regulations have had on children.
   B. No; it shows that the author incorrectly claims that the debate about children's safety is simply the result of societal anxiety.
   C. Yes; the author's argument allows for the possibility that playgrounds are becoming less physically hazardous.
   D. Yes; injuries are to be expected when children use playground equipment in unanticipated ways.

24. It is reasonable to infer from the language used in the passage that the author most likely considers which of the following benefits of children's risk-taking to be the most important?

   A. Greater physical abilities
   B. Increased self-confidence
   C. Experience making decisions
   D. Better problem-solving abilities

Solutions for this passage begin on next page.

20. Of the following statements, which one best describes the central thesis of the passage?

   A. The hazards that children face in their everyday lives are exaggerated partly because of the "risk anxiety" that pervades contemporary life.
   B. A child who successfully takes on physical risks will be more likely to undertake risks in other areas of learning.
   C. People need to consider the positive aspects of risk-taking behavior when they develop safety regulations for children's play areas.
   D. A result of increasing restrictions on children is that they lack opportunities to make their own decisions.

Cognitive Classification: Comprehension

Key: C

This question requires you to identify the main idea of the passage. The first paragraph discusses children's desire to seek out "experiences that feel satisfyingly 'risky,'" and how "the removal of all opportunities for risk-taking" is likely to have significance for "those who are concerned with the wider issues of children's learning." The second paragraph focuses on the implications of making playgrounds hazard free, such as children using the equipment in dangerous ways and growing up lacking confidence in their physical abilities. The third paragraph discusses the reasons behind "the resistance to children's physical risk-taking." The passage concludes by summarizing the importance of children's risk-taking and by explaining that it is important to "reflect on the implications that increasingly rigorous safety standards in our playgrounds may be having for our children." Given the overriding focus on the positive aspects of risk-taking behavior, coupled with the discussion about the effects that safety regulations are having on that behavior, **C** is therefore the best option.

 The central thesis can often be identified by examining the overall structure of the passage and particularly by paying close attention to the language the author uses to open and close the passage.

Distractors

A   The discussion about the "risk anxiety" that is pervasive in contemporary life appears only in the first half of the third paragraph, and it addresses only one aspect of the debate that underpins the discussion on children's safety. Furthermore, this option does not mention the positive role of risk-taking. This claim is too narrow in scope to reasonably be considered the central thesis. Therefore, **A** is not the best option.

B   This claim is mentioned in the final paragraph as one of the benefits of children's risk-taking behavior. However, it is only one of several benefits mentioned in the passage, and it does not address such issues as increased self-confidence and "the possibility of discovering that one is adventurous, daring, brave, strong, confident, and successful." This claim is too narrow in scope to reasonably be considered the central thesis. Therefore, **B** is not the best option.

D   This option mentions the safety regulations that are part of the main focus of the passage. However, it only mentions a single consequence of these regulations, whereas the passage focuses on several consequences. This claim is too specific to reasonably be considered the central thesis. Therefore, **D** is not the best option.

Difficulty Level: Medium (70%)

21. Information in the passage most strongly suggests that the author believes that people who are resistant to children's physical risk-taking:

   A. do not allow their children to play in their backyards because they consider it to be unsafe.
   B. insufficiently acknowledge the positive aspects that may result from children taking physical risks.
   C. have less opportunity to gain confidence and self-esteem through coping independently.
   D. are mistaken when they consider the consequences of physical hazard to be dire.

Cognitive Classification: Evaluation

Key: B

This question asks you to determine which of the options the author would most likely believe about people who are resistant to children's physical risk-taking. The first two paragraphs imply that the people "whose priority is 'keeping children safe'" are the same people who are concerned "to remove all hazards from a playground," and that the dire consequences of physical hazard "overshadow the need to provide children with . . . challenging physical play outdoors." The third paragraph states that the social discourses underpinning the debate on children's safety tend to focus "on the downside of risk" and that it is important that the "positive aspects of risk are also acknowledged." It can reasonably be inferred from this discussion that the author believes that the people who are resistant to children's physical risk-taking insufficiently acknowledge the positive aspects that may result from children taking physical risks. Therefore, **B** is the best option.

Distractors

A The author claims in the third paragraph that backyards "are often now seen as unsafe for children." However, this claim in the passage is not nearly as strong as the one in this option. The passage claim allows for the possibility that some people who are resistant to children's physical risk-taking may not agree that backyards are unsafe, or they may agree, yet still let their children play in their backyards. The claim in this option is too strong. Therefore, **A** is not the best option.

C This option conflates the people who are resistant to children's physical risk-taking with the children who are denied the opportunity to challenge themselves. The passage does not discuss whether people who are resistant to children's risk-taking have opportunities to cope independently, and it cannot reasonably be inferred that this is an opinion held by the author. Therefore, **C** is not the best option.

D The second paragraph states that the consequences of physical hazard are dire, so it is unlikely that the author believes that people who are resistant to children's physical risk-taking are mistaken to believe this. Therefore, **D** is not the best option.

Difficulty Level: Easy (90%)

22. Which of the following is NOT mentioned in the passage as one of the potential benefits of children's physical risk-taking?

    A. A feeling of competence in their abilities
    B. A willingness to undertake other risks in learning
    C. An adventurous disposition that is useful for problem solving
    D. A tendency to use equipment in novel ways

Cognitive Classification: Comprehension

Key: D

This question asks you to differentiate between claims made in the passage that are offered as examples of the benefits to children as a result of their physical risk-taking and claims that are not offered as examples of such benefits. Although the second paragraph discusses children's tendency to use equipment in novel ways, it is presented as a potential consequence resulting from "an environment that is too 'safe' and restrictive," not as a consequence of children taking physical risks. Moreover, this result is not considered to be a benefit, as the passage describes this tendency as one to "use equipment in unanticipated and truly dangerous ways." Because this tendency is a result of being in a challenge-free environment, and because it is not considered to be a benefit, **D** is the best option.

 Although the claim that children may use equipment in novel ways appears in the passage near other examples of the benefits of children's risk-taking, the claim is not offered as one of those benefits. Pay attention to what is specifically being either supported or weakened by passage assertions.

Distractors

A   The second paragraph states that one of the implications of making a playground hazard free is that "inadvertently it will also be made challenge free," which could cause children to "grow up lacking confidence in their own physical ability." The next sentence states that physical confidence has "repeatedly been linked with general feelings of competence." This discussion implies that children's feelings of competence are one of the benefits of their taking risks. Therefore, **A** is not the best option.

B   The final paragraph states that "conversations with teachers show that many are convinced that there is a connection between successful physical risk-taking and a willingness to undertake risks in other areas of learning." This claim is clearly stated as a potential benefit of children's physical risk-taking. Therefore, **B** is not the best option.

C   The final paragraph states that "the literature identifies being adventurous and taking risks as useful dispositions in . . . problem solving." This claim is clearly stated as a potential benefit of children's risk-taking. Therefore, **C** is not the best option.

Difficulty Level: Easy (90%)

MCAT® is a program of the
Association of American Medical Colleges

23. Assume that the current safety regulations for playgrounds have substantially reduced the number of children injured on playground equipment each year. If true, is this assumption consistent with the author's primary argument?

    A. No; it shows that the author has not sufficiently appreciated the positive effects that safety regulations have had on children.

    B. No; it shows that the author incorrectly claims that the debate about children's safety is simply the result of societal anxiety.

    C. Yes; the author's argument allows for the possibility that playgrounds are becoming less physically hazardous.

    D. Yes; injuries are to be expected when children use playground equipment in unanticipated ways.

Cognitive Classification: Incorporation of Information

Key: C

This question asks you to assess how information provided about the results of current safety regulations relates to the author's primary argument. The author's primary argument can best be summarized by the closing sentence in the passage: "We need therefore to continue to reflect on the implications that increasingly rigorous safety standards in our playgrounds may be having for our children." The implications are, according to the author, that "the concern to remove all hazards from a playground can inadvertently also lead to the removal of all opportunities for risk-taking." The fact that the current safety regulations do reduce the number of children injured is consistent with the author's views. Presumably, safety regulations exist because people believe that they make playgrounds safer for children. The author is concerned that playgrounds are being made "challenge free," not that they are being made "hazard free." The author's claim in the second paragraph is that children's environments can be made "too 'safe' and restrictive" and not that current safety regulations fail to make children safer. Therefore, **C** is the best option.

Distractors

A   The author acknowledges in the second paragraph that "the consequences of physical hazard are . . . dire," so it is reasonable to assume that the author might appreciate the positive effects that safety regulations can have for children. The author focuses on children's opportunities to challenge themselves, not on their exposure to actual physical hazard. However, even if it were true that the author did not sufficiently appreciate the positive effects of safety regulations, this is not relevant to the author's primary argument about the need to consider the implications of rigorous safety standards. Therefore, **A** is not the best option.

B   It may be true that the positive results of safety regulations would undermine a claim that the debate about children's safety is motivated simply by societal anxiety; however, the author does not make this claim. Instead, the author suggests in the third paragraph that "risk anxiety" is a pervasive feature of contemporary life and that it underpins the debate on children's safety; the author does not suggest the debate about children's safety is simply the result of societal anxiety. Moreover, even if the author had made this claim, this claim is not central to the author's primary argument. Therefore, **B** is not the best option.

D   The claim in the second paragraph that children may use equipment in unanticipated ways refers to a potential consequence of making a child's environment "too 'safe' and restrictive" through safety regulations. The claim that current safety regulations have actually reduced the total number of injuries may be consistent with the author's primary argument, but it would not be consistent because "injuries are to be expected when children use play-ground equipment in unanticipated ways." Therefore, **D** is not the best option.

Difficulty Level: Medium (60%)

24. It is reasonable to infer from the language used in the passage that the author most likely considers which of the following benefits of children's risk-taking to be the most important?

    A. Greater physical abilities
    B. Increased self-confidence
    C. Experience making decisions
    D. Better problem-solving abilities

Cognitive Classification: Evaluation

Key: B

This question asks you to infer what would be a likely opinion of the author based on the language used in the passage. The author considers all of the options in the question to be benefits of children taking risks, but does not explicitly describe them as being relatively more or less important than each other. However, one can reasonably infer that the author most likely considers children's increased self-confidence to be the most important of the benefits mentioned on the basis of its pervasiveness in the passage. The author ends the second paragraph by noting that children in a restrictive environment "may grow up lacking confidence in their own physical ability" and that "physical confidence" has "been linked with general feelings of competence." In the third paragraph, the author claims that restrictions on children have caused them to have "less opportunity to gain confidence and self-esteem through coping independently." The author concludes the third paragraph by noting that the discovery that one is confident is a positive aspect of risk. Because of the repeated mentions of self-confidence, and because self-confidence contributes to the benefits mentioned in options **A**, **C**, and **D**, it is reasonable to conclude that the author considers increased self-confidence to be the most important. Therefore, **B** is the best option.

Distractors

A   The author only briefly refers to children's greater physical abilities. In the second paragraph, the author mentions the "lack of opportunities to extend their skills and to meet appropriate physical challenges" as a long-term implication of an environment that is too restrictive. At the end of the third paragraph, the author mentions the possibility of discovering that one is "strong" as a positive aspect of risk-taking. It is reasonable to conclude from the infrequent and indirect references in the passage that the author does not consider this benefit to be the most important. Therefore, **A** is not the best option.

C   The author only refers to making decisions once in the third paragraph and only to point out how it contributes to children having "less opportunity to gain confidence." This single reference implies that the author does not consider experience making decisions to be the most important benefit. Therefore, **C** is not the best option.

D   Problem solving is only mentioned once in the final paragraph. This single reference implies that the author does not consider this to be the most important benefit. Therefore, **D** is not the best option.

Difficulty Level: Medium (65%)

MCAT® is a program of the
Association of American Medical Colleges

Verbal Reasoning

Passage Set VI

The most important developments in Western civilization in the last four centuries include not only the application of the scientific method but also the growth of historical consciousness. The importance of the former has been exaggerated; however, the implications of the latter are not yet sufficiently understood. Throughout the twentieth century, the growing importance of historical consciousness in the West was often overshadowed by critiques of "presentism," or of what some critics called the trend toward "post-historic" consciousness. Around 1930, the philosopher José Ortega y Gasset in his work *The Revolt of the Masses* depicted a type of democratic mass-citizen who lives only for the present, whose mind is wholly unhistorical, and who is no longer influenced by the past.

More relevant, however, is historian Johan Huizinga's proclamation, around the same time, that "historical thinking has entered our very blood." How does historical consciousness affect our thinking? Let me attempt to give a simple answer: *history, for us, has become a form of thought*. This means that historical thinking may be applied—indeed, that we often apply it, consciously or otherwise—to every kind of human experience. We can describe and consequently understand a person, a nation, any kind of human society, virtually any kind of human endeavor, not only through its physical or psychic characteristics but through its history. The character of a person will best emerge not from information about his or her physical or psychic properties but from what we know of the history of his or her life, the "case history." The same is true of the character of a nation. The history of a problem may reveal its evolving diagnosis; the history of a theory may reveal its limitations or explain its utility; the history of a discipline may reveal its biases and omissions. There is no field of human action that may not be approached and understood through its history.

Inevitably this brings us to the relationship between history and science. History as a form of thought is "larger" than science because human science is nothing more than the sum total of its history. Science is part of history and not the reverse. As a form of thought, therefore, history is "more" than science. But in a different sense, our knowledge of history is "less" than our knowledge of any single science. History is not a science in the modern sense of the word: historical information is often inaccurate and necessarily incomplete. Science and scientific knowledge are the same things; however, such a complete identity between the historical past and our knowledge of the past does not exist. But, then, the purpose of acquiring historical knowledge is not so much to accurately reconstruct facts; it is to acquire a certain kind of understanding.

Historical knowledge is human knowledge about other human beings, and this is different from the knowledge which human beings possess of their environment. Although there are sciences, such as anthropology, sociology, medicine, which involve the study of human beings, these too are unlike history because history cannot borrow its methods from the natural sciences. History is unpredictable, and historical causalities are different from the categories of scientific causality. While science (including the so-called social sciences) deals principally, though not exclusively, with what is typical and routine, history deals primarily (though not exclusively) with what is unique and exceptional. As a form of thought, history is a pragmatic but unsystematic body of knowledge acquired by one group of human beings about another.

Adapted from J. Lukacs, Historical thinking, *Historical Consciousness: Or the Remembered Past*. © 1968 by Harper & Row.

25. Which of the following statements is most likely to be true about "the character of a person," based on the passage author's use of the phrase?

    A. This character best emerges from what is unique in a person's life.

    B. This character cannot be described in physical or psychic terms.

    C. This character reveals a person's limitations and biases.

    D. This character determines a person's level of historical consciousness.

26. Knowing the answer to which of the following questions would best help one determine the truth of the passage author's claim in the first paragraph that the importance of the application of the scientific method has been exaggerated?

    A. Which is more important, the application of the scientific method or the growth of historical consciousness?

    B. Do the critics of "presentism" emphasize the importance of the application of the scientific method?

    C. How much influence has the application of the scientific method had on Western civilization?

    D. What other developments are important aside from the application of the scientific method and the growth of historical consciousness?

27. Based on the information presented in the passage, one can reasonably infer that the passage author is the most sympathetic to the views of:

    A. Ortega y Gasset.

    B. Huizinga.

    C. social scientists.

    D. the supporters of "presentism."

28. Which of the following statements, if true, would best support the passage author's view of the relationship between history and science, as presented in the final paragraph?

    A. History is the science of human societies.

    B. History uncovers the universal principles of human nature.

    C. Historical events can almost never be replicated in the present.

    D. People cannot escape either history or the desire to understand.

29. Assume that psychology is a part of science and not the reverse. Given this, and based on the reasoning in the third paragraph, which of the following statements is the most likely to be true?

    A. Our knowledge of psychology is "less" than our knowledge of science.

    B. The purpose of psychology is not to accurately reconstruct facts.

    C. Psychology is not a science in the modern sense of the word.

    D. As a form of thought, science is "more" than psychology.

30. Passage information most clearly implies that historical thinking and the scientific method are both:

    A. historical developments.

    B. intrinsic to human understanding.

    C. applicable to every kind of human experience.

    D. pragmatic and unsystematic.

Solutions for this passage begin on next page.

25.   Which of the following statements is most likely to be true about "the character of a person," based on the passage author's use of the phrase in the final paragrapgh?

A.   This character best emerges from what is unique in a person's life.
B.   This character cannot be described in physical or psychic terms.
C.   This character reveals a person's limitations and biases.
D.   This character determines a person's level of historical consciousness.

Cognitive Classification: Comprehension

Key: A

This question tests your ability to use the context provided in the passage to determine what the passage author most likely means by the phrase "the character of a person." The second paragraph states, "The character of a person will best emerge not from information about his or her physical or psychic properties but from what we know of the history of his or her life." The final paragraph states, "While science . . . deals principally, though not exclusively, with what is typical and routine, history deals primarily (though not exclusively) with what is unique and exceptional." Thus, the passage implies that gathering information that "deals primarily . . . with what is unique and exceptional" to a person will better help you understand the character of that person. Therefore, **A** is the best option.

Distractors

B   The second paragraph states, "The character of a person will best emerge not from information about his or her physical or psychic properties but from what we know of the history of his or her life." Although this clearly states that understanding a person's history is the best way to understand his or her character, this statement also allows for the possibility that understanding can emerge from information about the person's physical or psychic properties. Therefore, **B** is not the best option.

C   The second paragraph states, "The history of a problem may reveal its evolving diagnosis; the history of a theory may reveal its limitations or explain its utility; the history of a discipline may reveal its biases and omissions." However, the passage does not state that "the character of a person" reveals any of these. Therefore, **C** is not the best option.

D   The second paragraph answers the question of how historical consciousness affects our thinking by explaining that "*history, for us, has become a form of thought.*" This paragraph goes on to state that by applying this thinking to a person's life, "the character of a person will best emerge." The passage does not discuss whether a person's character influences his or her level of historical consciousness. Therefore, **D** is not the best option.

Difficulty Level: Medium (55%)

26. Knowing the answer to which of the following questions would best help one determine the truth of the passage author's claim in the first paragraph that the importance of the application of the scientific method has been exaggerated?

   A. Which is more important, the application of the scientific method or the growth of historical consciousness?
   B. Do the critics of "presentism" emphasize the importance of the application of the scientific method?
   C. How much influence has the application of the scientific method had on Western civilization?
   D. What other developments are important aside from the application of the scientific method and the growth of historical consciousness?

Cognitive Classification: Comprehension

Key: C

This question tests your ability to discern what information would be most helpful when trying to determine whether the passage author's claim that the importance of the application of the scientific method has been exaggerated is true. The first paragraph states, "The most important developments in Western civilization in the last four centuries include not only the application of the scientific method but also the growth of historical consciousness. The importance of the former has been exaggerated." The two pieces of information needed to determine if this claim is true are the importance of the application of the scientific method and its alleged importance. Of the options given, only **C** addresses either of these points and is therefore the best option.

Distractors

A   The only information needed to determine the truth of the passage author's claims has to do with the actual importance of the application of the scientific method and its alleged importance. The relative importance of the application of the scientific method with that of "the growth of historical consciousness" does not help clarify the pertinent information. The application of the scientific method could be more important than "historical consciousness," but people still might or might not exaggerate its importance. Therefore, **A** is not the best option.

B   The first paragraph states, "The most important developments in Western civilization . . . include not only the application of the scientific method but also the growth of historical consciousness," and "Throughout the twentieth century, the growing importance of historical consciousness in the West was often overshadowed by critiques of 'presentism.'" These statements do not suggest that critiques of "presentism" are responsible for the perceived importance of the application of the scientific method, nor do they suggest that emphasizing the scientific method's importance is equivalent to exaggerating its importance. Because option **B** addresses neither the importance of the scientific method nor its alleged importance, it is therefore not the best option.

D   Knowing what developments are important aside from the application of the scientific method is irrelevant to knowing whether the importance of the application of the scientific method has or has not been exaggerated. The importance of the application of the scientific method might or might not be exaggerated regardless of the existence of other important developments. Therefore, **D** is not the best option.

Difficulty Level: Medium (70%)

27. Based on the information presented in the passage, one can reasonably infer that the passage author is the most sympathetic to the views of:

    A. Ortega y Gasset.
    B. Huizinga.
    C. social scientists.
    D. the supporters of "presentism."

Cognitive Classification: Evaluation

Key: B

This question asks you to infer the passage author's most likely opinion on the basis of information presented in the passage. The second paragraph quotes Huizinga as saying that "historical thinking has entered our very blood," which the passage author explains by stating that *"history, for us, has become a form of thought."* The remainder of the second paragraph describes how people "can describe and consequently understand . . . virtually any kind of human endeavor . . . through its history." Not only are the passage author's comments prefaced by the quotation from Huizinga, but the quote itself is labeled "more relevant" than the information preceding it about Ortega y Gasset. Given this characterization of Huizinga's views, as well as the similarity between Huizinga's quotation and the passage author's discussion of history that follows, **B** is the best option.

Distractors

A   The first paragraph states, "The philosopher José Ortega y Gasset in his work *The Revolt of the Masses* depicted a type of democratic mass-citizen who lives only for the present, whose mind is wholly unhistorical, and who is no longer influenced by the past." The second paragraph begins by saying that Huizinga's view that "historical thinking has entered our very blood" is, however, "more relevant." The passage author explicitly accepts Huizinga's viewpoint as "more relevant" than Ortega y Gasset's. Therefore, **A** is not the best option.

C   The only mention in the passage of the social sciences is in the final paragraph: "While science (including the so-called social sciences) deals principally, though not exclusively, with what is typical and routine, history deals primarily (though not exclusively) with what is unique and exceptional." Given that the passage explains how the application of historical thinking helps people to arrive at a certain kind of understanding that science does not, it is unlikely that the passage author is particularly sympathetic to the views of social scientists. Therefore, **C** is not the best option.

D   The passage author does not appear to agree with the views of Ortega y Gasset, who is a critic "of 'presentism,' or of what some critics called the trend toward 'post-historic' consciousness." However, given the emphasis in the passage on the understanding people can gain by using historical thinking, it is unlikely that the passage author would be sympathetic to people living "only for the present," having minds that are "wholly unhistorical," and who are not being "influenced by the past." Therefore, **D** is not the best option.

Difficulty Level: Easy (90%)

MCAT® is a program of the
Association of American Medical Colleges

28. Which of the following statements, if true, would best support the passage author's view of the relationship between history and science, as presented in the final paragraph?

A. History is the science of human societies.
B. History uncovers the universal principles of human nature.
C. Historical events can almost never be replicated in the present.
D. People cannot escape either history or the desire to understand.

Cognitive Classification: Incorporation of Information

Key: C

This question tests your ability to judge which of the available options provides the strongest evidence for the passage author's view of the relationship between history and science as discussed in the final paragraph. The final paragraph states, "History is unpredictable. . . . While science (including the so-called social sciences) deals principally, though not exclusively, with what is typical and routine, history deals primarily (though not exclusively) with what is unique and exceptional." Option **C** suggests that historical events usually cannot be repeated and are thus unique. Therefore, **C** is the best option.

Distractors

A   The final paragraph states, "Although there are sciences, . . . which involve the study of human beings, these [sciences] are unlike history because history cannot borrow its methods from the natural sciences. History is unpredictable, and historical causalities are different from the categories of scientific causality. While science (including the so-called social sciences) deals principally, though not exclusively, with what is typical and routine, history deals primarily (though not exclusively) with what is unique and exceptional." Given that the passage describes history as a discipline distinct from science, it is unlikely that a statement labeling history as a science would lend support to the passage author's point of view. Therefore, **A** is not the best option.

B   The final paragraph states that "history is unpredictable" and that it "deals primarily (though not exclusively) with what is unique and exceptional." Option **B** suggests that history deals with what is common or universal to all people instead of what is unique, and it is therefore not the best option.

D   The second paragraph states that "*history, for us, has become a form of thought,*" and that "historical thinking may be applied—indeed, that we often apply it, consciously or otherwise—to every kind of human experience," thereby claiming that people *often* think historically. The third paragraph states that this form of thought can bring people to a "certain kind of understanding," but the passage author does not claim that history or the desire to understand is *inescapable*. Therefore, **D** is not the best option.

Difficulty Level: Hard (30%)

29. Assume that psychology is a part of science and not the reverse. Given this, and based on the reasoning in the third paragraph, which of the following statements is the most likely to be true?

A. Our knowledge of psychology is "less" than our knowledge of science.
B. The purpose of psychology is not to accurately reconstruct facts.
C. Psychology is not a science in the modern sense of the word.
D. As a form of thought, science is "more" than psychology.

Cognitive Classification: Application

Key: D

This question tests your ability to use the reasoning in the third paragraph to make a prediction, given the assumption that "psychology is a part of science and not the reverse." The third paragraph states, "Science is part of history and not the reverse. As a form of thought, therefore, history is 'more' than science." This states explicitly that a consequence of science being "a part of history" is that "as a form of thought, therefore, history is 'more' than science." Applying the same reasoning to the statement that "psychology is a part of science and not the reverse" leads to this conclusion: As a form of thought, science is "more" than psychology. Therefore, **D** is the best option.

Distractors

A   The third paragraph states, "Science is part of history and not the reverse. As a form of thought, therefore, history is 'more' than science. But in a different sense, our knowledge of history is 'less' than our knowledge of any single science." Based on the reasoning in the third paragraph, if you are to "assume that psychology is a part of science and not the reverse," then it would be more reasonable to conclude that our knowledge of science is "less" than our knowledge of psychology than it would be to conclude that our knowledge of psychology is "less" than our knowledge of science. Therefore, **A** is not the best option.

B   The third paragraph contains two arguments. The first begins with the premise that "science is part of history and not the reverse" and concludes by stating that "as a form of thought, therefore, history is 'more' than science. But in a different sense, our knowledge of history is 'less' than our knowledge of any single science." The second argues that "history is not a science in the modern sense of the word," and the remainder of the third paragraph gives several reasons why history cannot be considered a science, including the statement that "the purpose of acquiring historical knowledge is not so much to accurately reconstruct facts." If the statement that historical knowledge is not about gathering facts actually followed from the premise that "science is a part of history and not the reverse," then option **B** would be a reasonable inference from the information provided in the question; however, there is no clear sense in which the information in the second argument follows from the first argument. Therefore, **B** is not the best option.

Some passages have a literary style that can make it difficult to determine exactly what the author means by some of the terms. In this passage, the author uses several phrases that are somewhat vague, such as *historical thinking and history as a form of thought.* To help make sense of the author's use of otherwise nebulous concepts, look for words that express explicit logical relationships with other information in the passage, such as *therefore, because, since, in light of, thus.* Also, pay close attention to qualifying language. Words such as *wholly, total, complete,* and *always* indicate categorical claims that do not allow for exceptions; words such as *often, some, virtually,* and *not only* indicate contingent claims that do allow for exceptions.

MCAT® is a program of the
Association of American Medical Colleges

C The third paragraph contains two arguments (see B). The statement in the question is written to resemble the statement in the first argument that "science is a part of history and not the reverse," whereas option **C** is written to resemble the statement in the second argument that "history is not a science in the modern sense of the word." There is no clear sense in which the information in the first argument implies the information in the second argument. Therefore, **C** is not the best option.

Difficulty Level: Medium (65%)

30. Passage information most clearly implies that historical thinking and the scientific method are both:

    A. historical developments.
    B. intrinsic to human understanding.
    C. applicable to every kind of human experience.
    D. pragmatic and unsystematic.

Cognitive Classification: Comprehension

Key: A

This question tests your ability to recognize which of the available options represents the most accurate paraphrase of passage claims about historical thinking and the scientific method. The end of the second paragraph states, "There is no field of human action that may not be approached and understood through its history." Therefore, the passage implies that everything that humans do or endeavor to do is within the realm of history. Earlier in the second paragraph, the passage author states that "historical thinking may be applied—indeed, that we often apply it, consciously or otherwise—to every kind of human experience," which indicates that historical thinking is a human action. The third paragraph states explicitly that "science is a part of history and not the reverse," which suggests that the development of science, and thereby its method, is a part of history. Because both historical thinking and the scientific method are human endeavors and thus part of history, a reasonable paraphrase of the information presented in the passage is that both historical thinking and the scientific method are historical developments. Therefore, **A** is the best option.

Distractors

B   The second paragraph states that *"history, for us, has become a form of thought"* and that "historical thinking may be applied—indeed, that we often apply it . . . to every kind of human experience." This implies that historical thinking is commonly a part of human understanding, but this does not imply that it is intrinsic. To be considered intrinsic, historical thinking would need to be a required component of human understanding, which the passage does not support. Furthermore, there is no discussion that the scientific method is indispensable to human understanding. Therefore, **B** is not the best option.

C   Although the second paragraph states that "historical thinking may be applied . . . to every kind of human experience," there is no comparable mention of the scientific method being applicable in this way. Therefore, **C** is not the best option.

D   Although the final sentence states, "As a form of thought, history is a pragmatic but unsystematic body of knowledge," there is no comparable statement regarding the scientific method. On the contrary, the author makes several distinctions in the final paragraph between the methods and modes of causality of history and science, stating that "while science . . . deals principally . . . with what is typical and routine, history deals primarily . . . with what is unique and exceptional." This contrast suggests that although the author does think that history is "unsystematic," the same cannot be said of science. Therefore, **D** is not the best option.

Difficulty Level: Medium (45%)

Chapter 11:
Writing Sample (WS)

We can almost hear you moaning from over here....*why does the MCAT exam test writing skills at all?!!*

It's not without reason. Beginning decades ago, the public emphasized the need for physicians to communicate with patients as active participants in their own health care. Medical deans and faculty, aware that communication and writing skills often were deficient among medical students, joined in the discussion and asked that an assessment of these skills be added to information available about applicants. As a result, the AAMC added the Writing Sample to the MCAT as a way to provide medical school admission committees with evidence of their applicants' ability to develop and present ideas in a cohesive manner.

WS Section Recap

- Two 30-minute essays written in response to writing "prompts"

I. Overall Format and the Writing Prompts

The Writing Sample consists of two 30-minute essays, which you will write in response to "prompts." These prompts are statements that express an opinion, discuss a philosophy, or describe a policy—and are selected from areas of general interest such as business, politics, history, art, education, or ethics. Following are some examples of WS prompts:

What Topics WON'T I Find?

Topics do not pertain to biology, chemistry, or physics; to the medical school applications process (or reasons you have chosen medicine as a career), to social and cultural issues not in the general experience of college students; or to religious or other emotionally charged issues.

- To obey an unjust law is to approve of it.
- There are times when an individual's private acts should become a public concern.
- Freedom of speech is an absolute right that must never be limited.
- A good movie usually teaches a moral lesson.
- Technology solves many problems, but in the process often creates new problems.
- Government regulation of business is necessary in a democracy.

If you are looking for more examples, the AAMC has released a list of MCAT Writing Sample prompts (with instructions) for your information and use in preparing for this section of the test. Topics selected for use in MCAT exams will be similar or identical to those listed. Go to www.aamc.org/mcatguide to view the list.

II. The Three Writing Tasks

Following each prompt will be three writing tasks (or instructions). All three, regardless of the specific prompt, generally have the same basic blueprint: For most prompts you will be asked to explain or interpret the statement. Generally, you then will be required to provide a specific example in which the statement might be contradicted. And third, you typically will be expected to discuss ways in which the conflict between the initial statement and its opposition (the second task) might be resolved. In this way, you will be required to write in both an "expository" style, in which you provide information to the reader, as well as an "argumentative" style, in which you persuade the reader to adopt a particular viewpoint. One describes…the other influences.

> **What is Meant by "Unified Essay"?**
>
> Don't let the word "unified" that appears in the WS instructions throw you. All we mean is that the essay should be organized, coherent, and that you draw connections (either explicit or implicit) among the parts.

Keeping in mind the expository and argumentative styles you will be asked to demonstrate, let's look at a few of the sample prompts just provided and see how your "task assignment" might look:

To obey an unjust law is to approve of it.

- Explain what you think the above statement means.
- Describe a specific situation in which obeying an unjust law might not require approving of it.
- Discuss what you think determines whether or not obeying an unjust law requires approving of it.

There are times when an individual's private acts should become a public concern.

- Explain what you think the above statement means.
- Describe a specific situation in which an individual's private acts should not become a public concern.
- Discuss what you think determines whether or not the acts of an individual should become a public concern.

Freedom of speech is an absolute right that must never be limited.

- Explain what you think the above statement means.
- Describe a specific situation in which freedom of speech might justifiably be limited.
- Discuss what you think determines when freedom of speech should be limited.

III. How Your Essay Is Scored

Each essay is rated in terms of its overall effectiveness, determined for the most part by its depth, cohesiveness, and the clarity with which the writing tasks are addressed, the extent to which ideas are developed, and proper use of language. Essays are scored in the following way:

- Scores are not influenced by length (although an essay must be long enough so that its ideas are developed).

- Minor errors in grammar, spelling, sentence structure, or punctuation do not reduce scores, since it is understood that some mistakes will be made as a result of the time constraints in which the Writing Sample is completed.

- Essays are scored using the six-point score described below. The final score for each essay is the total of both scores. (If an essay receives scores that are more than one point apart— such as a 2 and a 4—a supervisory third reader determines the final score.)

IV. Score Point Descriptions

Following are typical characteristics of essays receiving each score:

> We analyze various essays and their associated scores in more detail beginning on page 373.

Score	Typical Characteristics of Essays
6	These essays show clarity, depth, and complexity of thought. The treatment of the writing assignment is focused and coherent. Major ideas are substantially developed. A facility with language is evident.
5	These essays show clarity of thought, with some depth or complexity. The treatment of the rhetorical assignment is generally focused and coherent. Major ideas are well developed. A strong control of language is evident.
4	These essays show clarity of thought and may show evidence of depth or complexity. The treatment of the writing assignment is coherent, with some focus. Major ideas are adequately developed. An adequate control of the language is evident.
3	These essays show some clarity of thought but may lack complexity. The treatment of the writing assignment is coherent but may not be focused. Major ideas are somewhat developed. While there may be some mechanical errors, some control of language is evident.
2	These essays may show some problems with clarity or complexity of thought. The treatment of the writing assignment may show problems with integration or coherence. Major ideas may be underdeveloped. There may be numerous errors in mechanics, usage, or sentence structure.
1	These essays may demonstrate a lack of understanding of the writing assignment. There may be serious problems with organization. Ideas may not be developed. There may be so many errors in mechanics, usage, or sentence structure that the writer's ideas are difficult to follow.

Your total point score—the four scores resulting from both essays—is converted to an alphabetic scale ranging from J (the lowest) to T (the highest). The same alphabetic score can result from different combinations of individual scores; for example, a candidate whose individual scores are 4 and 5 on the first topic and 4 and 4 on the second—for a total of 17—would receive the same alphabetic score as a candidate who scored 3 and 3 on the first topic and 5 and 6 on the second. Only the alphabetic score (and not the point total) appears on your MCAT score report.

V. Sample Essays and Score Explanations

At this point, we thought it would be helpful to illustrate the distinctions we've just discussed with some examples. Who better to walk you through them than actual Writing Sample raters—the very people who score genuine MCAT essays (or who have scored them in the past)?

In the pages that follow, we've asked our raters to select six sample essays that represent each of the six score points. In addition, we've asked them to explain why each particular essay was scored as it was so you could more fully see what our raters look for when distinguishing between excellent, average, and poor writing.

We use four different WS prompts for this exercise: The first and third prompt are followed by essays that illustrate a 6, a 4, and a 2 (with scoring explanations); the second and fourth have essays that illustrate a 5, a 3, and a 1 (also with explanations).

Consider this statement:
No matter how oppressive a government, violent revolution is never justified.

Write a unified essay in which you perform the following tasks. Explain what you think the above statement means. Describe a specific situation in which violent revolution might be justified. Discuss what you think determines whether or not violent revolution is justified.

Essay Sample #1
6 Points

The familiar idiom, "He who lives by the sword shall die by the sword," is echoed in any statement that condemns violence. It is a very simple principle based on a very logical argument. Violence invites more of the same. If government is overthrown by violent means, then a precedent has been set and there is nothing stopping others from doing the same again. Therefore, revolutionary governments topple almost a quickly as they rise or else they become as oppressive as that which they fought to replace. These cycles make no sense to large number of people and thus, there are many who prescribe to a similar line of thought. Often, these people dream of changing the world around them only by example and quiet protest.

However, time and again, this seemingly laudable course of action is forgone in favour of the quick, simpler, more violent situations to problems. It cannot be argued that Vladmir Lenin was not a thinking man, and yet it was he who invited the masses to take part in what he correctly forsaw as a "bloody revolution." His reasons were complex, and not without regret. Basically, Lenin saw no hope of change, not only in the near future of the Russian proletariat, but **ever**. The ruling minority was too firmly entrenched and counting on the fear instilled in the people to help maintain rule. Worse than this, at the time Lenin could find no other way to appeal to the government via quiet protest, as this would fall upon deaf ears. Furthermore, Lenin needed a device to spur the masses to action. Faced with the long-term suffering and perhaps extinction of so many, he essentially forced a confrontation through violence. Although there are differing opinions as to the success of the Russian Revolution, there is no doubt in the minds of many oppressed peoples that quiet revolution can go only so far. Essentially, then, violence justifies itself **in the minds of the masses** when they become overburdened with layer upon layer of mistreatment.

Many have theorized that the confrontation between royalty and subjects brought about Lenin would have happened eventually in any case. It is also argued that it could have happened in a more peaceful manner; faced with the possibility of massive genocide, could **any** ruling faction resist to the people's demand? The ideal, of course, is when rulers are quick to realize that oppression denies fundamental humanity to many. In practice, this is often not the case. If the rulers are human themselves, they are subject to greed and corruption. Thus, violent revolutions do occur. Whether or not they are justified (in terms of democratic thinking) depends on whether some form of oppression is lifted from the masses as a net result. Whether or not violent revolutions will be successful or not depends more on the quality of the new government installed. However, in terms of absolute right and wrong, one is forced to return to the initial premise and state that it only sets the stage for a renewal of violence.

This paper received 6 points. It is clear and well-focused, presenting a thorough analysis of the central idea, expressed by the writer as "violence invites more of the same." The paper moves logically from one paragraph to the next, sustained by an effective organization and fluent prose. The writer offers both concrete details (the Russian Revolution) and an abstract discussion of the nature of violence in political struggles. Though there are minor lapses in language control (for example, "prescribe to" instead of "subscribe to"), the argument is cohesive and the writer generally uses appropriate words and phrases to convey ideas. Given the time limitations for the Writing Sample, the paper is impressive.

In addition to stating a concise thesis, the writer explains the topic statement and begins to explore its implications in the opening paragraph. The writer suggests that the use of violence to force change sets a precedent, noting that "revolutionary governments topple almost as quickly as they rise." People who view "these cycles" as senseless are those who support change "only by example and quiet protest." Thus, the writer explains the logic behind the topic statement.

The first sentence of the second paragraph serves as a lucid and effective transition to a description of a specific situation in which violent revolution might have been justified. The writer then provides extensive detail and analysis of Lenin's thinking and role in the Russian Revolution. This section of the paper provides a deliberate and reasoned reflection on the "bloody revolution." The writer states that "violence justifies itself in the minds of the masses when they become overburdened with layer upon layer of mistreatment." Throughout this paragraph, the writer uses words and phrases ("laudable," "entrenched," "extinction of so many," "overburdened,") effectively. The choices are deliberate (such as the repetition of the phrase "quiet revolution" in the middle of this paragraph to contrast with the similar phrase in the first paragraph) and indicate a strong control of language.

The last paragraph is a discussion of the terms by which the success of a violent revolution may be judged. The paragraph completes a process of reasoning that began with the opening sentences of the paper. The sentences vary in structure and progress logically throughout the paragraph. The final sentence, "…one is forced to return to the initial premise and state that it only sets the stage for renewal of violence," brings the paper to a conclusion and reinforces the central idea.

The paper demonstrates a high degree of proficiency in organizing and communicating ideas. The major ideas are substantially developed and their implications fully explored. The writer's control of language contributes significantly to this well-integrated response.

Essay Sample #2
4 Points

"No matter how oppressive a government, violent revolution is never justified." This statement can be argued when the term government is understood to mean a legislative and judicial body which is concerned with carrying out the daily business of running a society. Oppression is a subjective term. What one member of society might describe as oppressive may be beneficial to another member of the same society. In imposing stricter taxes for foreign goods, the government is attempting to protect the industries and jobs of its citizens. One man wishing to buy foreign goods may view the situation as oppressive while a factory worker within the society finds the policy fair. Violent overthrow of the government due to its oppressive policies is not always clear-cut. This is certainly evident in the previous example. Therefore, to insure continued success in its day to day business of government, the governing body should never succumb to coup d'éttas for reform.

History has given numerous examples of justifiable and violent reform movements. The coup in Haiti in 1986 was considered justifiable. The ruling family of Duvaliers no longer cared about the governing of its society members. Every reasonable attempt at reform was snuffed out by secret police. When attempts to change government policies and societal conditions are no longer permitted by the entrenched few within the government, society members have the unalienable right to demand a return of government's powers into their hands.

When determining what guidelines should be used to decide when violent revolution is justifiable, one must be careful to delineate between governmental policies which do not agree with the individual and policies which do not agree with the whole body of the governed. Attempts at reform must always work from within the governing body. When the government fails to listen to its constituents, the people must resort to the right to reestablish a "people's" government.

Score Explanation for Essay Sample #2

This paper received 4 points. It shows clarity of thought, presents a central idea (the perception of whether or not a government is oppressive depends on the perspective of individual citizens), and adequately supports this central idea with specific and relevant examples. The writer recognizes some complexity in the issue and responds appropriately to each of the three writing tasks. Despite some lapses in word choice and sentence structure, the writing displays a command of the language.

In the first paragraph, the writer makes an attempt to define one of the key critical terms by stating that "government is understood to mean a legislative and judicial body which is concerned with carrying out the daily business of running a society." An attempt also is made to define the term "oppression." The writer provides a hypothetical example (the notion of an import tax) to illustrate that what is oppressive to one member of society (a consumer wishing to purchase foreign goods) is "fair" to another citizen (the factory worker whose job is protected). In this manner, the writer accomplishes the first writing task. In addition, the writer handles the complexity of the issue by noting that the need for a "violent overthrow...is not always clear-cut." The conclusion provides some analysis of the issue and summarizes the ideas presented.

The second paragraph presents a contrasting scenario, a specific situation in which "violent reform" is justifiable. Instead of using a hypothetical example, the writer chooses to describe the background of an actual event, the 1986 Haitian coup. The writer explains that the nation's rulers, the Duvaliers, "no longer cared about governing and had resisted" every reasonable attempt at reform." The last sentence of the paragraph indicates the conditions within a society that must exist before violent reform is justified. Although the paragraph is brief, each sentence expresses a new idea and moves the writer's argument forward.

In the final paragraph, the writer expands somewhat on the criteria established in the previous paragraph, noting that one must distinguish between policies "which do not agree with the individual and policies which do not agree with the whole body of the governed." There is not much additional development in this paragraph, but the ideas presented are consistent with the ideas and examples presented earlier. The paper's focus remains constant.

In a few instances, imprecise word choice or awkward sentence construction makes the argument hard to follow. For example, the word "delineate" is used when the writer should use "differentiate." This lack of precision also can be seen in some of the sentences, such as "Violent overthrow of the government due to its oppressive policies is not always clear-cut."

To receive a higher score, the paper would have to include additional support and analysis of the central idea and exhibit a stronger command of the language. The treatment of the rhetorical assignment is coherent, however, and demonstrates a degree of proficiency at expressing the writer's ideas about the topic.

Essay Sample #3
2 Points

Violent revolution is just that—violent. Even under oppressive government it is not justified. Oppression is no excuse to cause countless deaths and injuries. If government is oppressive and revolution is necessary then other means besides violence should be employed. The end does not justify the means.

However, if a government becomes so oppressive that it tries to silence those against it by violence than a violent revolution may be justified. If, for example, the government is committing mass murders, such as what seems to be happening right now in Iraq against the Kurds, then the only way to stop that violence is violence. If its government is causing deaths to occur among the people then violent revolution might be called for.

Violent revolution, in my opinion, can only be justified under extreme oppressive conditions. It is justified if its government causes people's death either by murder or by such things as starvation. Under these types of conditions, when the government has absolutely no regard for the well being of its people, violent revolution may be the only option the people have for freeing themselves.

This paper received 2 points. Though clearly written, it leaves the major ideas underdeveloped. A single specific example appears in the second paragraph, and general references are presented elsewhere ("countless deaths," "murder," "starvation"), but there is little elaboration of the central ideas of the paper. Although the essay addresses each of the required writing tasks in a separate paragraph, there is little integration or connection between the paragraphs.

The first paragraph explains the topic statement by declaring that "even under oppressive government" violent revolution "is not justified." The writer declares that "oppression is no excuse to cause countless deaths" because "other means" are available. The last sentence of the paragraph, though a cliché, effectively sums up the ideas expressed to this point.

The writer shifts focus and argues in the next two paragraphs that under certain circumstances ("extreme oppressive conditions") violent revolution is justified. The idea that a murderous government invites overthrow is briefly illustrated in the example of the Kurds being murdered in Iraq. This ideas, however, is simply repeated without much further development. For example, the following phrases in the second and third paragraphs restate the same idea: "If the government . . . is committing mass murders…"; "If the government is causing deaths to occur…"; and "…if its government causes people's death either by murder or by such things as starvation." These phrases help to define some criteria determining whether or not violent revolution is justified (the third writing task), but no new information is offered. The writer does not deal with the complexity of the topic.

The writer moves smoothly from one sentence to another, in paragraph, often using transitional words or phrases to link the sentences ("however," "for example." under these types of conditions"). The reader has no trouble following the writer's ideas, except when the focus abruptly changes after the first paragraph.

The paper could be improved by a more thorough and complete examination of the issue. While the writer offers brief definitions of the critical terms ("Violent revolution is just that—violent."), more explanation and discussion of the important concepts (violent revolution, oppressive government, justified actions) would have been helpful. In short, for this paper to receive a higher score, additional elaboration of ideas would be necessary.

> Consider this statement:
>
> **In a free society, individuals must be allowed to do as they choose.**
>
> Write a unified essay in which you perform the following tasks. Explain what you think the above statement means. Describe a specific situation in which individuals in a free society should not be allowed to do as they choose. Discuss what you think determines when a free society is justified in restricting an individual's actions.

Essay Sample #4
5 Points

The social and political ideals that have shaped society since the founding of the country make it almost inevitable that in a democratic society, a "free" society, and formation of personal identify would hinge upon the individual's right to self-determination. In America, for example, the "self-made" person receives the highest praise, and the romantic notion still exists that anyone in American can become anything—that not even the Presidency is out of reach for the humblest and least well-off of us.

The lessons of history—slavery, economic hardship, and tendency for power to concentrate within select groups blessed by accidents of birth to occupy positions of political leadership or financial control—teach us that the ideal of an equal society blind to social station is often more a dream than a reality. But even so, there is something undeniably sacred about the individual's right to do as he or she choses, an idea that shares the same root as "all people are created equal." although in much more personal context. We are a country might not be able to offer the worse off of us the guarantee of a better life, but we cannot deny them the freedom to try for themselves.

Hence the essential trust of the statement, "In a free society, individuals must be allowed to do as they choose," To live in a society that often (benignly?) neglects its citizens is chilling enough. But for a government to deny this most basic of rights—in a sense, taking away the individual's freedom to dream of self-sufficiency, or to work toward that dram—would be essentially to practice a form of totalitarianism.

There are, however, situations in which the freedom to do as one choses must be restricted: for example, "hate crimes", i.e., the oppression of one person or group of people based on prejudical notions about the person or group. Hate crimes cover a broad spectrum of offenses: everything from sexual harassment in the work place to the brutal murders of blacks by whites. People who inflict such hate upon others are certainly "dong as they choose"; no one is forcing them to exercise such violent "rights" and just as certain, these people should not be permitted to exercise "such" freedom.

I believe the question that must always be asked about the exercise of individual rights is: does such exercise endanger or in fact harm others? Do one person's demands for self-determination involve limiting others' rights to the same freedom? If the answer is yes, then I believe society, even a "free society" is justified in restricting that individual's actions. There are certain acts that must not be tolerated, for to do so is to award greater personal freedom to those who least deserve it, and at the cost of a nation's soul.

Score Explanation for Essay Sample #4

The paper received 5 points. As a whole it focuses clearly on the topic defined by the statement and fully addresses each of the three writing tasks in the rhetorical assignment. Paragraphs one, two, and three respond to the first task ("Explain what you think the statement means"), paragraph four responds to the second task ("Describe a specific situation in which individuals in a free society should not be allowed to do as the choose"), and paragraph five responds to the third task ("Discuss what you think determines when a free society is justified in restricting an individual's actions").

The paper presents a thoughtful analysis of both the statement and the implications of the statement. The explanation of the statement begins in the first two sentences with an examination of the importance of the ideal of self-determination to a democratic society and a discussion in the following two sentences of how this ideal often conflicts with reality. This introduction clearly focuses the paper on the statement's central idea and provides a foundation for the second and third writing tasks. Paragraph four brings the statement into conflict with an example that would seem to contradict it, and paragraph five resolves, or synthesizes, these opposing ideas with a discussion of the basis upon which one should decide when to limit the exercise of individual rights.

The paper conveys its ideas in a unified, logically connected manner. The paragraphs are clearly and appropriately organized around a particular topic and are related to one another. There is cohesiveness to the paper, with appropriate transitions used both within and between paragraphs (i.e., "Hence the essential trust of the statement" in paragraph three or "There are, however, situations in which freedom to do as one choses must be restricted" in paragraph four). Generalizations are explained with varying levels of specificity as needed (as in paragraph four).

The writing is clear and precise overall. For example, there is variety in sentence structure (compare complex sentences, such as sentence three to the shorter, more direct sentence 12 or to the use of questions in paragraph five) and precision in word choice ("the ideal of an equal society blind to social station is often more a dream than a reality" or "the oppression of one person or group of people based on prejudicial notions about that person or group", for example). Although the paper contains some minor errors (such as the misspelling of "totalitarianism" and "prejudicial" and the incomplete nature of sentence six), they do not detract from its overall effectiveness.

Essay Sample #5
3 Points

Our country was created on the basis of a haven for freedom. Since landing of the Piligrims people have often come to American because they were being oppressed by a foreign government that tried to restrict their action. The first settlers of this country wished to allow themselves the freedom their own country denied them. One of the main rights our forefathers developed was the idea that people should be allowed to live, work and worship as they chose to. Also that they would have the freedom to say and think what they believe. This idea has stayed true throughout America's history. What I think the statement "In a free society individuals must be allowed to do as they choose" means is just that. If we cannot do what we want then there is no freedom and the idea of America is a lie.

Under some circumstances it is not right to allow people to do whatever they want to do. Take draft dodging. If the nation needs you in a time of war, it is not right of you to avoid the responsibility of fighting for your country that allows you to live so freely. The nation has laws that must be obeyed if everyone is to enjoy their democratic rights. Dodging the draft is breaking a law plus avoiding responsibility. It is true that war is dangerous. Many people lost their lives in battle, but the country also make heros from its soldiers. Look at Dwight "Ike" Eisenhower, General McArthur, or further back in the Civil War people like U.S. Grant and Sherman. In Civil War days there were African Americans who had to struggle for the right to even sign up for battle. They were trained in separate camps and most of them had to do menial work like cleaning the latrine. But most of the also got to fight and they were brave. They helped to keep the country together in one piece and free of slavery.

What I think determines when a free society is justified in restricting an individual's actions is this—if their actions break a law. Whether it is destructive criminal behavior such as robbery or a more important issue like draft dodging. It doesn't matter. What is important is to not break the law because by doing something illegal you are threatening the well being of your fellow citizens. If you steal something you are hurting the person you took it from. If you run away from the draft you are avoiding the duty of serving the country in a time of war and that hurts all of us. By obeying the law you are protecting from committing a crime against others. This is how we keep the country running. If you cannot stick to the rules you are only causing trouble for those around you.

Score Explanation for Essay Sample #5

The paper received 3 points. It addresses each of the three writing tasks in the rhetorical assignment. Paragraph one responds to the first task, paragraph two responds to the second task, and paragraph three responds to the third task. However, the paper as a whole is only generally focused on explaining the statement and its implications.

The paper conveys its ideas at great length but with little depth. The paragraphs are ordered around particular topics, but the logical connections between sentences are not always apparent, and the ideas discussed in each paragraph are not entirely linked to one another with examples. For example, it is not clear how "draft dodging" is related to soldiers becoming heroes.

Other examples in the essay tend to drift from a focused exploration of the statement. In particular, the discussion of war in paragraph two quickly digresses from the subject of justifiable restriction on an individual's actions, and the discussion of lawbreaking in paragraph three suffers from repetition.

The ideas are expressed with some clarity, but problems are evident. For example, note that in the opening sentence the prepositional phrase "on the basis of a haven for freedom" should read "on the basis of freedom" or "as a haven for freedom." There is some variety in sentence structure (compare sentence four to sentence ten, for example) but little variety in word choice (the repeated reliance throughout the paper on words "country," "freedom," "right," and "law").

The most dramatic improvements to be made in this paper are in the areas of focus and organization. Rather than digress or repeat itself, the paper would benefit from a more focused analysis of the statement and its implications. Logical transitions between sentences would sharpen the connection between the ideas discussed in the paper. Finally, some practice of the sort offered in an introductory writing course may help the writer in composing more varied sentences and unified paragraphs.

Essay Sample #6
1 Point

In a country like in the United States, we all as citizens have freedom-of-choice. There are for example free to choose; where to live, what type of work to do, how to spend their money. This ability to choose for myself makes the difference between a nation like ours and those with the communist rule. If everybody could'nt choose, would be just like living back in communist country all over again. Who wants that?

For me, stay with the freedom to choose and leave all the other nonsense where it belongs, with the dictator country and the communist ruled country. To each his own…

Then, however, an individual should NOT be able to choose for himself. Take murder. You cant go around killing whoever you choose to without conseqences! This isn't even up for discussion by most of us.

I would say individuals should not be allowed to do as they chooe in a free society when murder is being talked about, even steal, assault others, and so forth, are other good examples. That would just be too much, even in the the good old U.S. of A.

Score Explanation for Essay Sample #6

This paper received 1 point. It addresses freedom of choice and even specifies a few of the freedoms that comprise a free society (choice of occupation, living arrangements, a capitalist economy), but the writer fails to address any of the three tasks clearly. Other than listing a few of the freedoms in American society and drawing a brief, hazy distinction between American society and "communist rule," the writer fails to explain the meaning of the prompt statement. This superficial contrast remains undeveloped and certainly fails to explore any of the nuances in the topic statement or to address the range of behaviors that must be accounted for as allowable in a free society.

The second paragraph is simply a personal endorsement of the vague distinction that was previously asserted twice in the previous paragraph—that "communist rule countr[ies]" are somehow less than ideal, presumably because they limit freedom. But the paper never develops this point or explains the reasons why (from this writer's perspective) communist countries are less free than America.

Ideas are expressed without being clarified or connected to other ideas, and the presentation of ideas is neither clear nor logical. The third paragraph gives us an abrupt shift in positions, with the assertion that "an individual should NOT be able to choose for himself." While we recognize this as an attempt to bring in the opposing perspective with an example for the second task, this awkward shift in logic undermines what has been asserted in the first task. Furthermore, the example is not developed beyond a mere assertion that "most of us" would agree that murder is immoral.

Again, an inability to extend or develop ideas keeps the paper from successfully achieving clarity of ideas, as we get no clear articulation of how murder violates the earlier assertion arguing in favor of freedom of choice. Perhaps some discussion of how murder and other violent crimes start to impinge on the rights of others and their freedom would have clarified its usefulness as a counter-example, but this is not provided.

Indeed, no resolution is given for the apparent contradiction presented by the writer, and this failure to address the third task shows us that the writer does not understand the rhetorical assignment. Even the final paragraph is a simple restatement of the second task's example, and fails to describe any broader determining principles for when a free society is justified in restricting an individual's actions.

Finally, the language in this response shows serious and frequent problems. Ideas are difficult to follow, word choice is overly informal and colloquial throughout, and syntax problems exist in almost every sentence. The writer has very poor control of punctuation and grammar. This inconsistency in language control confirms the score of 1.

Writing Sample Prompt #3

Consider this statement:
Environmental concerns should take priority over economic concerns.

Write a unified essay in which you perform the following tasks. Explain what you think the above statement means. Describe a specific situation in which environmental concerns should not take priority over economic concerns. Discuss what you think determines whether or not environmental concerns should take priority over economic concerns.

MCAT® is a program of the
Association of American Medical Colleges

Essay Sample #7
6 Points

Persuasive arguments for prioritizing environmental over economic concerns began to take shape in the 1960s, when a budding ecology movement brought to public light the environmental damage created by the bi-products and excesses of the modern industrial economy. Technological and economic success after WWII was coming at a high price. Pesticides and radioactive substances were infiltrating ecosystems, poisoning water and air, plants and animals, and ultimately threatening human health on a massive scale. To many observers, the global ecosystem itself looked to be in peril. What if whole populations and species were exterminated because of environmental collapse? What if over-population, increasing pollution, and chemical poisoning pressed the intricate web of earthly systems past the breaking point? The solution, many argued, was to pull back, stop the reckless economic and technological exploitation of the planet, realize that perpetual economic growth was not sustainable, and try to find a way to live on the planet so as not to ruin it and our own chances for survival. In other words, to place environmental concerns above economic concerns.

While these arguments were valid to an extent, the predicament did not turn out to be as dire as many had thought. In the sixties, writers such as Rachel Carson and Paul Ehrlich were predicting the utter collapse of the planet and a living hell for everyone on it within twenty years. But the worst fears of environmentalists did not, thankfully, come true. This was due in part to the intervention of environmental laws and regulations, industrial efforts to curb pollution, etc. But mostly the environmental hell on earth did not occur because the fears were overstated to begin with. Maybe necessarily so, because nothing short of the prospect of planet-wide catastrophe was likely to move the political and industrial powers to change in even the slightest way on their own. But because these fears and doomsday scenarios were overstated in the sixties, it is now, 50 years later, more difficult to persuade people in the U.S. at least, that environmental concerns are real and pressing and potentially catastrophic. Thus, the endless wrangling about global warming, the very existence of which some politicians and business leaders feel confident in disputing despite the consensus of the environmental science community. Why so confident? Because they can point to the first wave of post-war environmentalism as full of alarmism, shoddy science, and political motivation. Today's global warming fear-mongers, they say, are simply the latest generation of environmentalist doomsdayers and naysayers bent on savaging the economy for their own selfish political ends.

So how does one know how to respond? Who to believe? Clearly, industry can generate truly damaging environmental catastrophes. DDT, oil spills, cancer alleys, extinctions, the shrinking Amazon, the collapse of ocean fisheries, etc. Yet, clearly, after 50 years of hand-wringing over everything from the ozone layer to the spotted owl, Nature is still out there, holding itself (and us) together, apparently weathering even the very worst we throw at it. Despite all speculation to the contrary, natural systems and economic growth have continued to coexist and may well continue to do so, even when the ice caps melt and Miami and New York disappear like Atlantis. In part, this is because responses to environmental problems are themselves often engines for economic activity. Hybrid cars, solar panels, no-doubt soon-to-be new technologies for drilling in deep water or de-oiling turtles, etc. – all of these create new economic activity while mitigating some of the worst environmental effects of other kinds of economic activity.

So if we can't totally believe industry when it says global warming is a ruse then neither can we completely trust environmentalists, who would have us think that the end times are upon us perpetually. Maybe the best we can do is to trudge on as always, trusting that things will work out okay, as they have, more or less, since the question first arose back in the sixties. Try to get a little better gas mileage, slather the kids in sun screen, recycle our beer cans, perhaps, but keep going to work every day, and get a little shopping in, too. And turn off the News.

Score Explanation for Essay Sample #7

Clear, effective prose and sustained critical analysis contribute to the score of 6 here. The writer explains the prompt statement by describing the rise and rationales of the environmental movement of the 1960s. This broadening and contextualization of the prompt topic is a hallmark of many high-scoring essays—by grounding us in the history of this debate, the writer is able to shed light on the tensions that underlie the debate in more recent times. This history ultimately provides a basis for the writer's reconciliation of the two perspectives at the essay's close, as she is able to characterize our society's current ambivalence as at least partially a byproduct of the exaggerated origins of the environmentalist movement.

Instead of generating a rote counter-example in Task 2, she points out the ways in which time has countered the most dire predictions of these early environmentalists, and examines the present-day consequences of their over-stated claims. This analysis leads directly to a central problem invoked by the writing prompt: who to trust? The writer's observation that environmental problems generate their own brand of economic activity is an insightful piece of analysis, showing the kind of complexity of thought and critical analysis that can lead to a more meaningful resolution of the prompt's tensions. Her resolution to the overarching dilemma, however, is not particularly satisfying; she leaves us muddling through, hoping for the best, and burying our heads. The point of the writing exercise, however, is not to solve the large and intractable problems plaguing society. It is rather to demonstrate writing competence and an ability to organize and develop a persuasive essay with effective critical reasoning.

In this regard, the writer succeeds in superior fashion, producing a unified, clearly-written response that recognizes the complexity of the topic and explores it in depth. It's worth noting that some instances of misspellings and unnecessarily overburdened syntax, along with a few sentence fragments, do not interfere with a clear communication of the writer's meaning. Indeed, the overall outstanding diction and fluent, varied writing style lend additional authority to the writer's insightful claims.

Essay Sample #8
4 Points

The environmental catastrophe currently unfolding in the Gulf of Mexico clearly shows that we need to measure the environmental impact of our economic choices before we end up destroying nature just to make a buck. Most Americans would agree that the price we pay for cheap gasoline and disposable products is too much when we see our important marshland covered in crude oil and watch dead sea turtles wash up on our beaches. Big businesses like this should be held responsible for these disasters, but even more importantly, every economic decision that has the potential to damage the environment should be overseen by a governing body to make sure that whatever impact a business has is minimized. There needs to be a shift away from profits as the be-all-end-all drive in the world toward ideas that are more environmentally friendly, because if we don't take care of the earth, then profit will be the last thing on our minds as we try to survive on a polluted planet.

On the other hand, it's easy to say that we should all be environmentally conscious. But when we look at developing countries, we see that even though these countries contribute much of the global pollution, there must be some room for developing economies to grow at the cost of environmental concerns. Much of the developed world —the United States, Germany, England—has benefited from the use of environmentally damaging technologies since the Industrial Revolution, so it would be unreasonable to expect China, India, and Brazil to harm their countries' progress by stopping the use of damaging coal and oil based technologies. When these countries look at the American way of life, they see an easy existence, and they seek to try to be like us by using the same blueprint for a modern society—the cornerstone of which is heavy fossil fuel use.

Technology is a double edged sword most of the time. It allows us to do amazing things, but as we see with the Deepwater Horizon disaster, the potential harm is devastating. What determines when environmental concerns take priority over economic ones is whether or not the nation in question is developed enouth to allow that nation to use alternative fuel sources. The United States has an economy and a level of technology that allows it to easily convert from fossil fuels to things like wind, solar, and biofuels. Developing countries don't have that ability, but shouldn't be forced to not use the cheaper more polluting technologies, because we ourselves have benefited from those same technologies. Hopefully the sacrifices of developed countries will offset the pollution of the undeveloped while they achieve the same level of living conditions as the US. Once this happens, then they will be better able to ween themselves off of fossil fuels as we have done. Hopefully we have the time for this to happen without doing irreversible harm.

Score Explanation for Essay Sample #8

Good language control, full development of ideas, and a well-reasoned argument mark this essay as adequate. Its general claims are made clear through the use of specific examples–notably, the BP oil disaster and the emerging economies of China, India and Brazil. Rooting the essay's ideas in these real-world examples lends credence to the writer's claims and establishes the authenticity of the essay's analysis. On the other hand, the first paragraph indulges a bit in unsupported, prescriptive assertions: for example, "Big businesses like this should be held responsible for these disasters, but even more importantly, every economic decision that has the potential to damage the environment should be overseen by a governing body to make sure that whatever impact a business has is minimized." But such a minor misstep is quickly corrected by a return to examples and analysis. For the most part, the essay's points are made persuasive through logical discussion.

The writer's "determining factor"—a nation's level of development—follows from the discussion that preceded it, giving the essay unity and focus. This essay relies on a simple idea and expresses it clearly. It does not need to explore the complexities of the prompt topic in order to earn a score of 4.

Fluid, varied sentence structure and reasonably precise diction help the writer to express the intended meaning clearly, and the presence of transitions and topic sentences in these unified paragraphs help to keep the response's ideas clear and focused. A solid foundation in writing skills helps to support the clear structure of the essay's well-reasoned argument.

Essay Sample #9
2 Points

Environmental concerns should take priority over economic concerns. What the statement is pointing to is the constant and ever ongoing battle between the making of profits for manufactured goods at the expense of the natural world via extracting of resources in the forefront, and damage to the environment by pollution (air, water, land, etc.) from farming, factories and transportation on the backside. In America money usually wins.

In the northwest the rainforests are being felled at the rate of fifty acres per day. The people who work in the lumber industry have to feed their families too, and America is hungry for wood for housing, paper and other things. The famous spotted owl debate illustrates this. We export timber from publicly owned lands to other countries (namely Japan) for furniture and housing. This garners income to americans.

The environment is important to humans and all living things; it's our home; it's what feeds us, clothes us, shelters us, but money is important too. We need it to live on. We have to balance these out. How much industry is enough without being too much strain on the environment? It's a struggle ever since the Industrial Revolution.

Score Explanation for Essay Sample #9

This response demonstrates a partial understanding of the prompt, but its ideas are underdeveloped and lack the explanation and coherence that are typically found in more successful responses. The essay sets up a conflict between the need for a healthy natural environment and the need for resource-depleting, sometimes pollution-generating economic activity. This is a move that suggests the beginnings of a cogent response and helps lift the essay above the 1 score point. But references to the forests of the Northwest, to the timber economy, and to the spotted owl are merely gestures toward explaining and examining this conflict of needs. The debate over the spotted owl, for example, is not self-evident and needs explication if it is to play a meaningful role in the discussion. Likewise, the essay invokes the Industrial Revolution, but does not explain its significance to the question at hand.

Furthermore, the response neglects the "determining factor" portion of the writing assignment. No attempt is made to discuss factors that might determine whether or not environmental concerns should precede economic concerns. Language use, while mostly comprehensible, is vague and awkward throughout. Several sentences exhibit poor usage and poorly constructed syntax, which hinder a clear expression of the writer's intended meaning.

MCAT® is a program of the
Association of American Medical Colleges

> Consider this statement:
>
> **When there is a choice between obeying the law and following one's own beliefs, it is best to follow one's beliefs.**
>
> Write a unified essay in which you perform the following tasks. Explain what you think the above statement means. Describe a specific situation in which one should obey the law at the expense of following one's beliefs. Discuss what you think determines whether or not one should follow the law or one's beliefs.

Essay Sample #10
5 Points

The notion that a person should follow her beliefs rather than obey existing laws appears to be rooted in the idea that the laws are wrong somehow. Perhaps the law goes against a person's individual value system, such as in the case when an individual believes that she should not have to pay taxes because she does not support big government. That's one example and rationale. Another, more compelling one is the law might be systemically and fundamentally flawed and impinge on entire groups of peoples' rights, as in the case when segregation was literally the law in the United States. Interestingly, it seems that when laws truly are flawed—that is, when they negatively affect some of its citizenry in fundamental ways, e.g. their civil or human rights— most often those laws eventually are changed because people follow their personal beliefs not to merely rebel against the system, but in an attempt to actually change the law. By contrast, the person who merely does what she wants because she doesn't like a law, or even feels a law goes against her core principles, that person is unlikely to change the law simply by ignoring it.

While it is true that the State or governing bodies (this could also be local governments) may not always keep the best interests of its citizens in mind, or may err by maintaining laws that currently reflect popular beliefs rather than be guided by ethical principles, usually the State tries to keep its citizenry's best interests as a first priority. After all, theoretically speaking, governments represent the people and must therefore protect its citizenry by instating certain restrictions to protect the harmony and well-functioning of society. In this regard, Rousseau's Social Contract serves as a rallying cry and self-referential shorthand explanation for the best reasons people obey laws rather than their own personal beliefs. (And, for the most part, laws tend not to be at odds with citizens' beliefs, as we all share core humanity and values and our laws are meant to bolster the best community possible). In a contract, parties enter into agreement with one another in order to ensure certain benefits for both sides. If the non-tax payer must visit the emergency room without having insurance to boot, chances are good that some kind of federal healthcare funding is aiding in the payment of charges incurred. Therefore, the iconoclast who does not wish to pay taxes to the State is not living up to her part of the Social Contract even while she is reaping the benefits from it.

In discussing the idea of rejecting existing laws in favor of following one's own beliefs, the issue becomes more complex as we regard the many ways that an individual might understand a law to be "wrong." There seems to be a distinction between laws that are displeasing on principle (such as not wishing to contribute to a system you deeply disagree with like the disgruntled [non] taxpayer) and ones that do actual harm to a citizen's rights as they have been defined within the charters or tenets of that government or system. To wit: at present there is a slow surge in the legalization of gay marriage and the repeal of "don't ask, don't tell," two bedrock instances of discrimination against gay men and women according to some. These individuals have not been able to follow their own beliefs and do what they want (get married, be 'out' in the military) without grave consequences. However, they have been able to follow their beliefs insofar as they (and other people who also believe this group's civil rights are being violated) have been working to change the laws that affect them adversely. As citizens they have earned this right to follow their beliefs just as surely as they have upheld their part of the 'contract' by contributing to society as defenders of the country, as taxpayers, as law-abiding citizens whose laws ironically exclude them.

Score Explanation for Essay Sample #10

This essay represents a disorderly but thoughtful response to the writing assignment. Like many essays that achieve a score of 5 or 6, this one employs a conceptual framework that is useful in uncovering and exploring the complexities of the prompt. In this case, the writer frames the question in terms of the idea of the "social contract" in order to explore some of the complexity of the issue. The essay also makes a valuable distinction in the third paragraph between laws that displease and laws that harm, leading to a satisfactory reconciliation of the two competing perspectives outlined in the first two tasks of the rhetorical assignment. This distinction is combined effectively with the social contract idea in the ending discussion of gay rights, lending unity and force to the overall argument.

Like most essays earning scores of 5 or 6, this one keeps pushing and extending its analysis clear through to the end, taking advantage of multiple opportunities along the way to include insightful ideas and support them with detailed, nuanced discussion. Subtle points are conveyed through the writer's careful word choice, although sentences do frequently seem to trip over themselves, causing the essay to lose precision and fluidity. Cleaner writing, plus more attention to organization and transitions, would have made the complex thinking here clearer, and thus even more persuasive.

Grammatical errors, a somewhat wavering focus and coherence at a sentence-to-sentence level, and some imprecision in phrasing hamper the communication of the writer's sophisticated analysis and prevent the writer from sustaining the kind of focused critical analysis that would be more typical of an essay earning a score of 6.

Essay Sample #11
3 Points

Everyday it seems like we're faced with having to choose to break laws in order to follow our personal beliefs of right and wrong. Take, for example, the medical marijuana in California. Even though federal law prohibits its use, there are plenty of people with diseases like glaucoma, multiple sclerosis, and Alzheimer's that believe that medical marijuana can cure or alleviate pain. These people are right to ignore the federal law and shouldn't be forced to endure migraines, depression, and nausea.

But sometimes one's own beliefs should be ignored when it comes to personal safety. This is case when operating a motor vehicle. Even though you may personally believe that stop signs and traffic lights shouldn't apply to you, you must obey the laws to keep yourself and those around you safe. Instead of following one's beliefs about traffic laws and driving right through an intersection and potentially injuring pedestrians, a cost/benefit analysis seems to point out the relatively low personal cost (stepping down on the break pedal) while providing a substantial benefit (not killing innocent people).

One should always follow one's beliefs—they are what this country was founded on, after all. The only exception to this rule would be when one's beliefs put others in danger. The old saying, "You have the freedom to swing your fist, but that freedom ends at the other person's nose." The same is true in this case. Since a terminal cancer patient isn't hurting anybody when using marijuana, they should be able to follow their beliefs, but traffic laws should be followed despite contrarianist personal beliefs, because the potential for injury is great.

Score Explanation for Essay Sample #11

This writer attends to the three tasks of the rhetorical assignment, explaining the prompt statement, offering a counter example, and resolving the conflict with a determining factor—in this case, the simple criteria of "safety." It is not an adequate response overall, however, because its claims are only somewhat developed. The medical marijuana example is potentially productive, but the assertion that suffering people are right to ignore the law is not self-evident and begs for a rationale, which the writer does not sufficiently supply. The counter example—believing that stop signs don't apply to you—is contrived and trivial rather than illustrative.

From this discussion, the essay arrives at the general principle that safety considerations trump following one's beliefs. However, because it does not examine this conclusion in more depth, the essay raises more questions than it answers. For example, is the author suggesting that people are wrong to fight for their belief in justice or freedom if it means someone may get hurt? Or conversely, are we each privately justified in breaking the law so long as no one else is injured? Language control and organization are reasonably good here, despite some rough edges in word choice and usage, but more thoughtful discussion is needed to reach a score higher than 3.

Essay Sample #12
1 Point

Obeying the law means doing what your government tells us to do. Beliefs means what you think are true, probably Gods laws or your parents rules you internalized. The statment means to say that when you have the choice between obeying the law or doing what you believe in, its best if you don't do what the government says, but what your higher power says.

Its better if you follow the government because disobeying the law would put you in jail, or cost you a high fine. Putting aside your beliefs for the law would make more sense. It is better to hold onto your beliefs because the goverment may not know what that is anyway. They don't know that your going against your beliefs.

It depends on what you believe and how much it will cost to obey or not obey god or your parents or the government. You can pay the fines (or go to jail) if you can afford it. But you will always have your beliefs and no body can take that away from you.

Score Explanation for Essay Sample #12

The ideas in this brief response are virtually undeveloped, leaving us with very little to evaluate in determining the writer's understanding of the rhetorical assignment. This response lacks clarity because of this absence of development and because of poor language skills. Most sentences are garbled, while any potentially meaningful statement goes unexplained. The writer makes a few assertions, but there is no attempt to justify or develop them. For example, see the statement that "It is better to hold onto your beliefs because the goverment may not know what that is anyway. They don't know that your going against your beliefs." The writer does not appear to be capable of further clarifying explanation of this largely impenetrable claim, and the point is lost.

The essay has only the most elementary organization and fails to provide clear transitions from one idea to the next. Ultimately, the writer does not demonstrate a sufficient understanding of the prompt statement or the rhetorical assignment.

With this, we complete the chapters that review the exam segments in depth, analyze cognitive classifications, and provide real MCAT passages and questions. Our next stop? It's the third area we touched upon as part of preparing for the exam—effective practice—which we discuss in the following chapter.

Chapter 12:
Practice Effectively

Before astronauts launch into the stratosphere, they do many run-throughs in a simulated spacecraft. Before couples get married, they have a dress rehearsal. And before medical students attempt to attach an I.V. to a live patient for the first time, they do a dry-run on themselves, their classmates, or, in an increasingly large percentage of medical schools, with the aid of technical simulation.

In other words, they practice. That way, when the big moment arrives, they have eliminated (at least some) of the anxiety inherent in stressful situations and increased their likelihood of a smooth operation.

The same holds true for the MCAT exam. You'll want to create your own mock testing environment—one which allows for a quiet and uninterrupted session and allows you to adhere to time allocations and breaks—so that you mimic the operational exam. You'd also want an easy way to focus much of your effort on your weak spots (or even help identify them!) so that you'll arrive at the test center with as much confidence as possible.

We have a resource that can help.

I. Emulating the Operational Exam

There's simply no better way to experience the "look and feel" of an operational exam than with an official AAMC Practice Test (PT). And because we want to ensure that no one skips this vital step, **we provide a PT to anyone who requests one—free-of-charge.***

---

*The AAMC provides free access to one online practice test—PT3. (If you'd like more than one PT, you can purchase additional ones directly from our Web site for $35 each.) Go to www.aamc.org/mcatguide for more information.

For starters, the passages and questions that appear on the PT have all been retired from previous MCAT examinations, so that you're practicing with real MCAT items—and not the "MCAT-like" items that may be found in practice tests developed by anyone other than the AAMC. Next, the AAMC Practice Tests replicate the format, features, and functionality found in the operational MCAT exam. Just as in the actual exam, for example, you can highlight text, strike out answer choices, and right-mouse click only. (Because this is a practice test, we also include options that are not available on the real test, such as the opportunity to view solutions, turn the timing feature off, and search text.)

II. Identifying Your Weaknesses

The astronaut in the simulator and the engaged couple in the midst of their dress rehearsal are doing more, though, than simply practicing for an upcoming event. They are on the lookout for areas that do not go well in order to correct mistakes and strengthen weak spots. (A little flub in a wedding ceremony can be funny—years later, anyway—but an error in a spaceship can be fatal.)

Similarly, you will want to identify those areas you have found the most challenging and focus your study efforts there. And because you have, in a sense, been preparing for this exam through your undergraduate coursework, you probably already have an inkling as to where you are weak. All A's in biology and chemistry, for example, but a C in physics? Great in all sciences, but could never get better than a B in your English classes? Your academic record alone is a strong indicator of where you are strong and weak.

Don't fall prey to the very human tendency to concentrate on that with which you are comfortable and avoid those areas that make you feel insecure.

Beyond that, what about your studies specific to this exam—be they on your own, through a review of your textbooks and notes, or through a commercial prep course? It is likely that some signs of strength and weakness have become apparent through that process, as well.

III. Using AAMC Practice Tests for Diagnostic Purposes

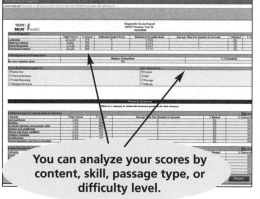

You can analyze your scores by content, skill, passage type, or difficulty level.

Finally, there are the practice tests themselves. They provide a general snapshot of your strengths and weaknesses in the multiple-choice sections (PS, BS, and VR), and, as such, can help you determine where to allocate your study efforts. Have you taken a couple of practice tests, for example, and found that you scored higher in General Chemistry and lower in Physics—both times? Clearly, a pattern has emerged.

The AAMC Practice Tests make such patterns easy to discern. Upon completion of the entire test (or after individual sections, if you prefer), you'll have access to a score report that will break down your test responses by percentage correct as well as time taken to complete. The score report, pictured at left, shows you how your PT scores will be reported to you.

In addition to results by section scores, the score reports also include feedback at a much finer level of detail within the sections—right down to specific topic areas. That said, you need to use this information very cautiously, for two reasons. First, there are more potential topic areas on a given PT than there are questions. Each PT includes a sampling of items from among the extensive list of potential topics listed in this book. Some topics will appear on some exams and not others. And second, the number of items included at this level of detail is very small—sometimes only a few questions—and therefore your performance on a single practice test may not represent either mastery or deficiency in that precise area.

IV. Customizing Your Practice Test

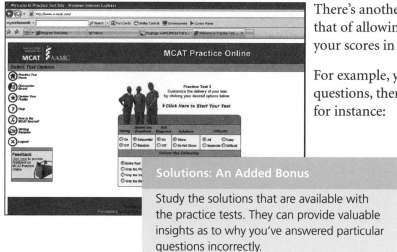

Solutions: An Added Bonus

Study the solutions that are available with the practice tests. They can provide valuable insights as to why you've answered particular questions incorrectly.

There's another big advantage to an AAMC Practice Test, beyond that of allowing you to emulate the exam environment and analyze your scores in detail: You can customize it.

For example, you can order your PT to target specific types of questions, thereby focusing your efforts in particular areas. You can, for instance:

- Receive questions from only one of the sections (PS, BS, VR, or WS)

- Receive questions that fall into a specified difficulty level (easy, medium, difficult)

- Receive content that focuses in a specific topic area, such as electrochemistry, genetics, or humanities

- Receive questions that measure a specific cognitive classification

- Receive questions of a specific passage type

In addition, you can select certain delivery features. You can turn the timing on or off, have questions delivered in random or sequential order, view a self-diagnosis to help you determine the probable cause(s) for each of your incorrect answers, and view solutions.

Practice Test Tips:

- Take a timed test to develop proper pacing and speed.

- Remember, there's no penalty for guessing.

- Practice writing your essays on the computer, since this will be the mode of testing.

V. A Word About the Writing Sample

The WS portion of the practice test provides you with the opportunity not only to time yourself (remember…30 minutes for each essay) but also to experiment with different approaches. How do you plan to respond to the prompts? Is it helpful to outline your key points first? How much time will you allocate for planning your response versus the actual writing of it? What about review and revisions—how much time should you allow for that? These questions, and others like them, are ones to explore during your practice sessions.

As you might recall from an earlier chapter, we post on our website a very large pool of WS prompts from which your two actual prompts may be drawn. It's not realistic, however, to expect yourself to draft a response to each and every one of them; instead, practice with several—perhaps including a few with which you are less comfortable—in an effort to demonstrate the characteristics evident in a high-scoring essay. (These characteristics, along with essay samples that contain them, were described in the preceding chapter.) Then, ask an experienced writer or professor to read and critique your work, requesting that he or she point out the essay's positive attributes as well as its shortcomings (specifically as it relates to the scoring method described previously). In such a way, you can identify your strengths and weaknesses, and focus your practice more effectively.

This wraps up the review of the three-pronged approach—(1) master the content, (2) know the test, and (3) practice effectively—that we first introduced at the start of Part II. Together, these three will help you prepare for the MCAT exam and move you one step closer to the day someone first addresses you as "Doctor."

On behalf of the MCAT team, the entire AAMC wishes you the best of success as you gear up for this challenging—and exciting—step of your journey.

"Some succeed because they are
destined to.
But most succeed because they are
determined to."

—Unknown.

Addendum

Periodic Table of the Elements

1 H 1.0																		2 He 4.0
3 Li 6.9	4 Be 9.0											5 B 10.8	6 C 12.0	7 N 14.0	8 O 16.0	9 F 19.0	10 Ne 20.2
11 Na 23.0	12 Mg 24.3											13 Al 27.0	14 Si 28.1	15 P 31.0	16 S 32.1	17 Cl 35.5	18 Ar 39.9
19 K 39.1	20 Ca 40.1	21 Sc 45.0	22 Ti 47.9	23 V 50.9	24 Cr 52.0	25 Mn 54.9	26 Fe 55.8	27 Co 58.9	28 Ni 58.7	29 Cu 63.5	30 Zn 65.4	31 Ga 69.7	32 Ge 72.6	33 As 74.9	34 Se 79.0	35 Br 79.9	36 Kr 83.8
37 Rb 85.5	38 Sr 87.6	39 Y 88.9	40 Zr 91.2	41 Nb 92.9	42 Mo 95.9	43 Tc (98)	44 Ru 101.1	45 Rh 102.9	46 Pd 106.4	47 Ag 107.9	48 Cd 112.4	49 In 114.8	50 Sn 118.7	51 Sb 121.8	52 Te 127.6	53 I 126.9	54 Xe 131.3
55 Cs 132.9	56 Ba 137.3	57 La* 138.9	72 Hf 178.5	73 Ta 180.9	74 W 183.9	75 Re 186.2	76 Os 190.2	77 Ir 192.2	78 Pt 195.1	79 Au 197.0	80 Hg 200.6	81 Tl 204.4	82 Pb 207.2	83 Bi 209.0	84 Po (209)	85 At (210)	86 Rn (222)
87 Fr (223)	88 Ra (226)	89 Ac† (227)	104 Rf (261)	105 Db (262)	106 Sg (266)	107 Bh (264)	108 Hs (277)	109 Mt (268)	110 Ds (281)	111 Uuu (272)	112 Uub (285)		114 Uuq (289)		116 Uuh (289)		

*	58 Ce 140.1	59 Pr 140.9	60 Nd 144.2	61 Pm (145)	62 Sm 150.4	63 Eu 152.0	64 Gd 157.3	65 Tb 158.9	66 Dy 162.5	67 Ho 164.9	68 Er 167.3	69 Tm 168.9	70 Yb 173.0	71 Lu 175.0
†	90 Th 232.0	91 Pa (231)	92 U 238.0	93 Np (237)	94 Pu (244)	95 Am (243)	96 Cm (247)	97 Bk (247)	98 Cf (251)	99 Es (252)	100 Fm (257)	101 Md (258)	102 No (259)	103 Lr (260)

The periodic table of elements will be available during the actual MCAT exam. It is provided here as a reference for use while completing the practice items.

MCAT® is a program of the
Association of American Medical Colleges

As you explore the resources available to you, consider the ways in which your health professions advisor can be of service. He or she can direct you to courses that will help you prepare for the MCAT exam, point you to other pre-med students (with whom you might want to create a study group), assist you in developing a timeline for applying, and, in general, support you through the medical school admissions process. The following is reprinted with permission from the National Association of Advisors for the Health Professions (NAAHP) to provide you with additional information.

About Your Health Professions Advisor

Who are health professions advisors?

Students exploring or planning a career in medicine should seek out the health professions advisor on their campus to assist them. Most U.S. colleges and universities designate an individual as the school's health professions advisor. That person may be a faculty member, often in the sciences, who advises health professions students as well as teaches them, and perhaps even performs scientific research. The health professions advisor may be a member of the academic dean's office who oversees all academic advising at the institution. Another possibility is that the advisor is housed in the school's career center, specializing in advice regarding health careers. The common denominator is that health professions advisors are knowledgeable, supportive individuals whose role is to provide information and guidance as you prepare for your chosen profession.

How can a health professions advisor help you?

Your advisor can help you determine which courses satisfy premedical requirements, how to best sequence them, and how to find tutoring or other academic support if you are having difficulty. An advisor can guide you in incorporating study abroad, a double major, or a senior honors thesis into your course of study and still prepare well for medical school. Your advisor will encourage you to seek experience in the health care field as a way of informing yourself about the profession as well as strengthening your application to medical school. Your advisor will encourage and support you as you try to determine the right career path for yourself, by assessing your own strengths and weaknesses, values, and life's goals. Although it may be possible to choose the proper courses, find meaningful health-related experience, explore your own personal strengths and weaknesses, and negotiate the complexities of the medical school admissions process independently, seeking the advice of your health professions advisor will greatly ease your burden.

Reprinted with permission from the National Association of Advisors for the Health Professions (NAAHP)

Who can be aided by a health professions advisor?

All health professions advisors meet with students individually at their campuses to offer the assistance described above. But while many students applying to medical school are college-age, some are not. Increasingly, advisors work with older or "nontraditional" students who have graduated from their institution or who have come to the school to pursue postbaccalaureate coursework. All students, regardless of age or status, should seek out the health professions advisor where they are currently studying or at their alma mater. Policies differ from school to school, but some students with access to health professions advising are unaware of this valuable resource.

How can your health professions advisor help you decide which medical schools you should consider?

Your health professions advisor is knowledgeable about many aspects of the various medical schools. Each American medical school has a stated mission for its school, and the missions are not all the same. Some schools have a very high commitment to global health. Others are committed to training clinical and laboratory researchers who will be academic faculty at American medical schools. Others have a higher commitment to primary care, and even that commitment may be focused at a given school specifically on rural primary care or inner-city primary care. Therefore, in counseling you about where you might apply to medical school, your health professions advisor will review with you not only your academic record and coursework but also your background and ultimate career goals in helping you select which medical school or medical schools best suit your individual strengths and aspirations.

> **If your institution does not have a health professions advisor, please visit www.naahp.org/ default.aspx?tabid=3238. There you will find a list of health professions advisors (and NAAHP members) who have volunteered to be available to those who have no other access to guidance.**

Resources from the Association of American Medical Colleges

The AAMC offers numerous resources to assist you on your path to medical school, many of which have been referenced in this guide. Please visit www.aamc.org/mcatguide to link directly to the sites listed below.

Exploring Medicine as a Career

- **Considering a Medical Career**
  From deciding whether a career in medicine is right for you to getting into medical school, this section of the AAMC Web site provides an overview of the entire process.

- **AspiringDocs Web Site**
  Here you'll find tools, information, and support you need to explore whether a career in medicine is right for you and to help you prepare an application to medical school that presents you at your best.

- **Medical Career Fairs**
  Visit this Web site for information about the AAMC Student Medical Career Awareness Workshops and Recruitment Fair as well as other events nationwide.

Programs for Pre-Medical Students

- **Summer Medical and Dental Education Program**
  The **SMDEP** is a **FREE** (full tuition, housing, and meals) six-week summer academic enrichment program that offers eligible freshman and sophomore college students intensive and personalized medical and dental school preparation. Read here to learn about eligibility requirements and to search for available program sites.

- **Summer Enrichment Programs**
  Search this free database resource to help locate enrichment programs on medical school campuses according to institution, region, area of focus, and/or length of program.

- **Postbaccalaureate Premedical Programs**
  A number of schools offer postbaccalaureate premedical programs to assist individuals to pursue a medical career after they have already received a bachelor's degree. This searchable database enables you to search according to program type and other program characteristics.

Application and Admissions Resources

- **AAMC Recommendations for Medical School Applicants**
  These are recommendations to help ensure that applicants are afforded timely notification of the outcome of their medical school applications and timely access to available first-year positions.

- **AMCAS (American Medical College Application Service)**
  Here you will learn about AMCAS, a nonprofit, centralized application processing service operated by the AAMC for applicants to the first-year entering classes at participating U.S. medical schools.

- **MSAR (Medical School Admission Requirements)**
  The MSAR is the #1 source for application procedures and deadlines, and GPA data, medical school class profiles, and costs and financial aid packages. This trusted source is available as a printed guide book as well as a searchable Web site.

- **Medical School Admissions Offices**
  This site lists the admissions offices for medical schools and programs. Also included is the application service the school participates in, if appropriate, as well as whether the school is public or private.

- **National Association of Advisors for the Health Professions**
  This national association is a resource for advisors. If you do not have access to an advisor, visit the Resources section on "Finding an Advisor" to learn what options are available.

- **MCAT Essentials**
  This is required reading for all MCAT exam registrants and provides information about registration, preparation, and administration.

- **MCAT Exam Schedule**
  View the current exam schedule, including dates and times.

- **MCAT Registration Deadline and Score Release Schedule**
  Here you'll find the complete registration schedule, with dates for opening and closing registration, along with tentative dates for score release.

- **Accommodated Testing**
  The AAMC is committed to providing all individuals with opportunities to demonstrate their proficiency on the MCAT exam, and that includes ensuring access to those with disabilities in accordance with relevant law. Find out how and when to apply for accommodated testing.

- **Registration Tips**
  From e-mail settings to credit card charges, this web page provides helpful hints surrounding the registration process.

- **Test Locations**
  Here you can find a listing of all test locations throughout the United States, Canada, and the rest of the world.

- **Registration**
  After you have read MCAT Essentials, you may register for the exam through the online registration system. (You may make changes to or cancel your registration through this system, as well.)

- **Test Day Tips**
  Follow these test day tips to help make your MCAT experience as smooth as possible.

- **Online Writing Sample Prompts**
  The AAMC has released a listing of MCAT Writing Sample items (topic statements and instructions) for your information and use in preparing for that section of the test. Topics selected for use in MCAT exams will be similar or identical to those in this list.

- **MCAT Practice Tests Online**
  The best way to prepare for the operational MCAT is to practice with tests that provide a live test experience. Our new practice tests provide the same look and feel as the real MCAT exam. Get a free practice test and purchase additional ones here.

- **Medical Minority Applicant (Med-MAR) Release**
  Med-MAR was created to enhance admission opportunities for groups currently underrepresented in medicine or who are economically disadvantaged.

- **THx (Testing History) Score Report**
  Sign in here to check your MCAT scores, print your own official MCAT score report, send scores to schools that do not participate in the AMCAS system, and more.

Research and Data

- **Validity of the Medical College Admission Test for Predicting Medical School Performance**
  This report is a comprehensive summary of the relationships between MCAT scores and (1) medical school grades, (2) United States Medical Licensing Examination (USMLE) Step scores, and (3) academic distinction or difficulty.

- **Additional MCAT Research and Articles**
  Here you will find a bibliography of MCAT Research. Among the areas explored are test validity, reliability and equating issues, medical school selection procedures, and issues related to acceptance to medical school.

- **FACTS: Applicant and Matriculant Data**
  This site includes dozens of tables that provide the most comprehensive and objective information regarding medical school applicants, matriculants, enrollment, and graduates available to the public free of charge.

- **Fee Assistance Program**
  The AAMC Fee Assistance Program (FAP) assists MCAT® examinees and AMCAS applicants who, without financial assistance, would be unable to take the MCAT or apply to medical schools that use the AMCAS application. This site provides eligibility and application information.

- **Financing Your Medical Education**
  Here you'll find financial planning guidance for pre-medical students, information on the types of financial aid available, a searchable database where you can research the financial aid form policies of specific medical schools, the Layman's Guide to Educational Debt Management, and more.

- **Financial Information, Resources, Services and Tools (FIRST) for Medical Education**
  The FIRST is designed to help medical school borrowers expand their financial literacy, make smart decisions about student loans, and manage their student debt wisely.

Timeline for Application/Admission

This should be considered a general guide for applicants. It is important that an applicant considering medical school consult with his or her prehealth advisor to devise a schedule that works for him or her.

COLLEGE YEAR 1	• **Fall semester**
	  o Meet prehealth advisor and investigate prehealth advisory program
	  o As applicable, ensure that prehealth advisor receives course directors' evaluations
	  o Successfully complete first-semester required premedical coursework and other degree requirements
	• **Spring semester**
	  o Visit "Considering a Career in Medicine" Web site at *www.aamc.org/students*
	  o Identify summer employment/volunteer medically related opportunities
	  o Successfully complete second-semester required premedical coursework and other degree requirements
	  o Ensure that prehealth advisor receives course directors' evaluations

SUMMER 1	• Complete summer employment/volunteer medically related experience • Attend summer school, if desired or necessary

COLLEGE YEAR 2	• **Fall semester**
	  o Check in with prehealth advisor and participate in prehealth activities
	  o Investigate available volunteer/paid medically related clinical or research activities
	  o Successfully complete first-semester required premedical coursework and other degree requirements
	  o Ensure that prehealth advisor receives course directors' evaluations
	• **Spring semester**
	  o Check in with prehealth advisor and participate in prehealth activities
	  o Participate in volunteer/paid medically related clinical or research activities
	  o Identify summer employment/volunteer medically related opportunities
	  o Successfully complete second-semester required premedical coursework and other degree requirements
	  o Ensure that prehealth advisor receives course directors' evaluations

SUMMER 2	• Complete summer employment/volunteer medically related experience • Participate in a summer health careers program, if available • Attend summer school, if desired or necessary

COLLEGE YEAR 3	• **Fall semester**
	  o Check in with prehealth advisor and participate in prehealth activities
	  o Continue participation in volunteer/paid medically related activities
	  o Investigate:
	    • Medical education options in MSAR and *www.aamc.org/members/listings/msalphaae.htm*
	    • Medical College Admission Test (MCAT®) Web site *www.aamc.org/mcat*
	    • Information about the Medical College Admission Test (MCAT®) and American Medical College Application Service (AMCAS) fee assistance on the AAMC Fee Assistance Program Web site *www.aamc.org/fap*, as appropriate
	    • AAMC's "Applying to Medical School" Web site *www.aamc.org/students/applying/start.htm*
	    • As applicable, information for students from groups underrepresented in medicine on the AAMC Minorities in Medicine Web site *www.aamc.org/students/minorities/start.htm*
	  o Begin preparation and register for desired MCAT® administration; visit MCAT® web site *www.aamc.org/mcat* for available test date options
	  o Successfully complete first-semester required premedical coursework and other degree requirements
	  o Ensure that prehealth advisor receives course directors' evaluations
	• **Spring semester**
	  o Consult regularly with prehealth advisor regarding:
	    • Schedule for completion of school-specific requirements for advisor/committee evaluation
	    • Advice about medical education options
	  o Continue participation in volunteer/paid medically related activities
	  o Prepare for and take desired MCAT® administration; visit MCAT® web site *www.aamc.org/mcat* for available test date options

continued...

COLLEGE YEAR 3	o Continue review of medical education options
	o Take desired MCAT® administration. Registration opens for summer MCAT® administrations
	o Investigate information about medical school application services:
	   • the American Medical College Application Service (AMCAS) on the AMCAS Web site *www.aamc.org/amcas*
	   • the Texas Medical and Dental Schools Application Service (TMDSAS) on the TMDSAS Web site *www.utsystem.edu/tmdsas/*
	   • the Ontario Medical School Application Service (OMSAS) on the OMSAS Web site *www.ouac.on.ca/*
	   • the American Association of Colleges of Osteopathic Medicine Application Service (AACOMAS) on the AACOMAS Web site *https://aacomas.aacom.org/*
	o Investigate as applicable, the AAMC Curriculum Directory Web site *http://services.aamc.org/currdir* for information about medical school curricula and joint, dual, and combined-degree programs
	o Successfully complete second-semester required premedical coursework and other degree requirements
	o Ensure that prehealth advisor receives course directors' evaluations

SUMMER 3	• Participate in a summer health careers program, if available
	• Complete AMCAS application
	• Take desired MCAT® administration
	• Attend summer school, if desired or necessary
	• Become familiar with:
	   o AAMC Recommendations for Medical School Applicants document *www.aamc.org/students/applying/policies*
	   o AAMC Recommendations for Medical School Admission Officers document *www.aamc.org/students/applying/policies*

COLLEGE YEAR 4	• **Fall semester**
	   o Complete supplementary application materials for schools applied to
	   o Consult regularly with prehealth advisor regarding:
	      • Completion of school-specific requirements for advisor/committee evaluation
	      • Status of application/admission process at medical schools applied to
	   o Continue participation in volunteer/paid medically related activities
	   o Interview at medical schools
	   o Continue review of medical education options
	   o Investigate:
	      n Financial aid planning process process
	      n Financial aid forms required by school of interest with the AAMC *Financial Aid Forms Required by Medical Schools* searchable database *http://services.aamc.org/msar_reports/*
	   o Successfully complete first-semester elective science and non-science coursework and other degree requirements
	   o Ensure that prehealth advisor receives course directors' evaluations
	• **Spring semester**
	   o Make interim and final decisions about medical school choice
	   o Immediately notify medical schools which you will not be attending
	   o Ensure that all IRS forms are submitted as early as possible for financial aid consideration
	   o Successfully complete second-semester elective science and non-science coursework and other degree requirements
	   o Graduate

SUMMER 4	o Prepare for medical school enrollment: purchase books and equipment and make appropriate living arrangements o Relax and prepare for medical school o Attend orientation programs and matriculate at medical school

You can change the face of medicine.

From left: Romeu Azevedo, M.D., Candelaria Martin, M.D., Kahlil Johnson, M.D., Claudine Morcos, M.D.

If you really want to make a difference in people's lives, consider a career in medicine. Too many African Americans, Latinos/as, and Native Americans don't get the care they need. Help us change this reality. Log on to **AspiringDocs.org™**, a new resource from the Association of American Medical Colleges, to learn more.

AAMC
Tomorrow's Doctors, Tomorrow's Cures®

© 2006 AAMC

MCAT | AAMC
Medical College
Admission Test

Official MCAT® Preparation

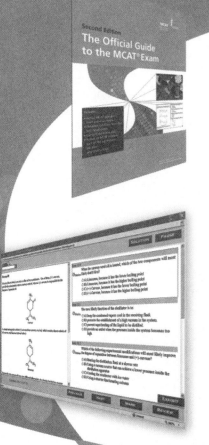

Step 1: Learn the basics

The Official Guide to the MCAT® Exam
Full of tips and data to help you plan,
along with 138 unique test items with solutions.
www.aamc.org/officialmcatguide

Step 2: Get a baseline score

Free MCAT Practice Test 3
Take a timed test to learn how you might perform
on the actual exam.
www.e-mcat.com

Step 3: Study & track progress

Seven additional practice tests
Take more timed tests to track improvements
and to study with real test items.
www.e-mcat.com

MCAT® is a program of the
Association of American Medical Colleges

MSAR®
Medical School Admission Requirements

MSAR® is the preeminent and most reliable resource on medical schools. MSAR's printed guidebook includes abridged profiles of each medical school, while comprehensive listings of U.S. and Canadian medical schools and baccalaureate/M.D. programs appear online. It's the #1 source for applicants and the only resource fully authorized by medical schools.

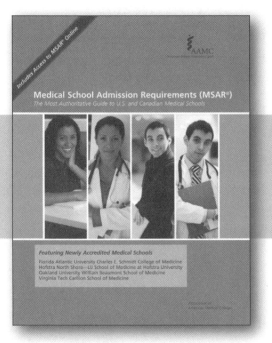

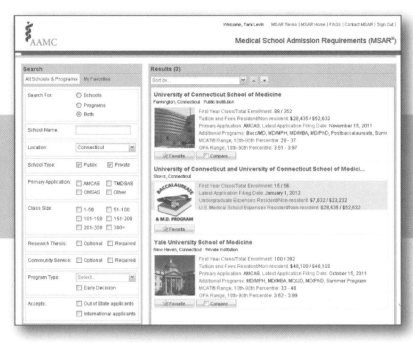

MSAR Guidebook $25
(Price includes 1 year of access to MSAR Online)

MSAR Online $15
(1 year of access)

Preview the guidebook and web site today
www.aamc.org/msar

An AAMC publication

Medloans® Organizer and Calculator
presented by FIRST *for Medical Education*

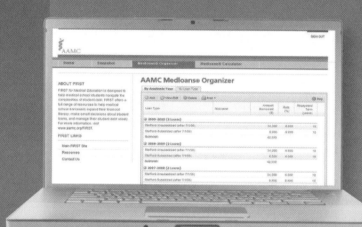

- Organize and keep track of your student loans

- Develop repayment strategies using the calculator

- Use the only calculator designed specifically for medical students

Access the Organizer and Calculator
www.aamc.org/FIRST

What is FIRST?

Financial Information, Resources, Services and Tools (FIRST) *for Medical Education* is designed to help medical school students navigate the complexities of student debt. FIRST offers a full range of resources to help medical school borrowers expand their financial literacy, make smart decisions about student loans, and manage their student debt wisely.

Association of
American Medical Colleges

If you are serious about a career in Medicine or Dentistry, consider attending the Summer Medical and Dental Education Program.

SMDEP is a FREE six-week summer academic enrichment program administered at one of 12 program sites across the country.

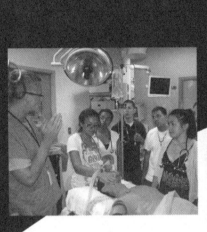
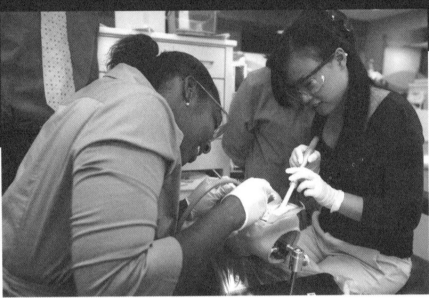

Application Open: November 1st

Application Deadline: March 1st

www.smdep.org

For more information, call the National Program Office at 1.866.58.SMDEP (587-6337)

The Participating SMDEP Institutions include:

Case Western Reserve University Schools of Medicine and Dental Medicine

Columbia University College of Physicians and Surgeons and College of Dental Medicine

David Geffen School of Medicine at UCLA and UCLA School of Dentistry

Duke University School of Medicine

Howard University Colleges of Art & Sciences, Dentistry, and Medicine

The University of Texas Dental Branch and Medical School at Houston

UMDNJ New Jersey Medical and New Jersey Dental Schools

University of Louisville Schools of Medicine and Dentistry

University of Nebraska Medical Center, Colleges of Medicine and Dentistry

University of Virginia School of Medicine

University of Washington Schools of Medicine and Dentistry

Yale University School of Medicine

Robert Wood Johnson Foundation

SMDEP is a national program funded by the Robert Wood Johnson Foundation with direction and technical assistance provided by the Association of American Medical Colleges and the American Dental Education Association.